For Nicholas, Angie, Jessica, Lyla, Jeremy, Kirk, Phoenix, and Summit; "may they find faith in the earth!"

Recent Titles in
Contemporary Psychology

Resilience for Today: Gaining Strength from Adversity
Edith Henderson Grotberg, editor

THE DESTRUCTIVE POWER OF RELIGION

Violence in Judaism, Christianity, and Islam

Volume 3
Models and Cases of Violence in Religion

J. Harold Ellens, Editor

Foreword by Martin E. Marty
Ad Testimonium by Archbishop Desmond Tutu

Contemporary Psychology
Chris E. Stout, Series Editor

Westport, Connecticut
London

Library of Congress Cataloging-in-Publication Data

The destructive power of religion : violence in Judaism, Christianity, and Islam / edited by J. Harold Ellens; foreword by Martin E. Marty.
    p. cm.—(Contemporary psychology, ISSN 1546–668X)
  Includes bibliographical references and index.
  ISBN 0–275–97958–X (alk. paper)
    1. Violence—Religious aspects. I. Ellens, J. Harold, 1932– II. Contemporary psychology (Praeger Publishers)
BL65.V55D47 2004
291.1'78—dc21   2003051061

British Library Cataloguing in Publication Data is available.

Library of Congress Catalog Card Number: 2003051061
ISBN: 0–275–97958–X (set)
         0–275–97972–5 (vol. I)
         0–275–97973–3 (vol. II)
         0–275–97974–1 (vol. III)
         0–275–98146–0 (vol. IV)
ISSN: 1546–668X

First published in 2004

Praeger Publishers, 88 Post Road West, Westport, CT 06881
An imprint of Greenwood Publishing Group, Inc.
www.praeger.com

Printed in the United States of America

The paper used in this book complies with the Permanent Paper Standard issued by the National Information Standards Organization (Z39.48–1984).

10 9 8 7 6 5 4 3 2

CONTENTS

Foreword

"Too bad this set of books is so relevant." That phrase is not a dismissal of, but an advertisement for, this work that will inform and provide perspective for people anywhere who are trying to make sense of the outburst of religiously based violence around the world.

That phrase also echoes the title and theme of the talk, "Too bad we're still relevant!" that I gave at the annual meeting of the American Academy of Arts and Sciences (AARS) in 1996, while closing the books on a six-year, twelve-conference, hundred(s)-scholar, five-volume work, *The Fundamentalism Project*, that the AARS had sponsored between 1988 and 1994.

For more than six years, my associate R. Scott Appleby and I labored with that anxiety, "What if we are irrelevant by the time this is finished?" while we directed the project. My talk included a reminder to the academy that in 1988 they could have chartered all kinds of relevant studies (e.g., U.S.-Soviet Relations in the Twenty-First Century, or Exporting Apartheid from South Africa) that would have been irrelevant by 1996. Since he and I had not asked for the work but had been chosen by the academy, we armed ourselves with yellow highlighters and daily marked the newspaper references that dealt with our subject. We went through many yellow markers, and found the number of references to such hard-line religion increasing.

That report foresaw frustrations and rages of religion-rooted conflict in the new millennium and mentioned that even terrorism would be an instrument of the religiously violent. Still, there were some reasons to hope for a measure of decreased religious conflict, even if it was only to be replaced by other kinds, such as territorial or ethnic conflict, as in Kurdish areas of Turkey or in Rwanda or the former Yugoslavia. Yet all of these conflicts are eclipsed by religious furies and violence.

It is in that context that I help J. Harold Ellens turn this subject over to you who, in libraries, at desks, in classrooms, or at home, are working your way through bafflement over the explosion of violence that grows out of the dark side of religion. "Too bad it's relevant."

Twenty years ago I was blithely teaching American religious history, remarking on the relative tolerance to which we citizens had worn each other down in values and practice. On days off from history, as a former pastor and a theologian-at-the-margins I also found many ways to affirm the healing side of religion. As peers in my generation face the debilitation and death that come with our advanced years, we find ourselves consoling each other with stories about the promises of God the healer. At the same time, many of us have joined forces, professionally, to measure and encourage efforts at employing spiritual means to address issues of health and healing.

We see religion represented through churches, synagogues, and mosques, located cozily next to each other in the alphabets of the Yellow Pages. There are few dead bodies in America as a result of religious conflict. Of course, there were always tensions, bloodless schisms, arguments, and contentions, but the violence related to each has been reasonably held in check.

Then *The Fundamentalism Project* forced me and people with whom I worked to "go global," where we got a very different perspective. Domestically, as we listened to the voice of people who had been victimized or oppressed in the name of religion, we noted how many other words ending in *–press* matched "oppress": repressed, suppressed, and so on, suggesting the negative and destructive roles of religion. We had begun to explore an underside of the presence and power of this force in life and history.

Two days after 9/11 I was scheduled to lecture at the University of Illinois on a theme chosen a year before: "Religion: The Healer that Kills; the Killer that Heals." When the terrorists struck in the name of God in New York, they ensured good crowds for talks like that and gave new impetus for scholars to explore the themes gathered so conveniently in these four books on *The Destructive Power of Religion, Violence in Judaism, Christianity, and Islam.*

I am no newcomer to this field, and I know that most of the authors in these volumes, from biblical scholars to psychoanalysts, have long been at their inquiries. Many of them include just enough autobiography for us to learn that they themselves were often among those who experienced the destructive side of religion. They tell us how they countered it, and some testify to its lasting effects. As I read those chapters, however, I noticed also how often they "kept the faith," pursued the spirit, or stayed with religion, however one wishes to put it, even as they wanted to rein in the destructive forces that issue from it. Professor Ellens himself slips in a word that he thinks characterizes the dimensions of religion that one can affirm: *grace.*

How does one square the study of destruction and the affirmation of construction in this one area of life, religion, as many of the authors undertake to do on these pages? Rousseau once said that readers could expect his thoughts to be consistent with each other, but they could not expect him to express them all at the same time. So here, too, one pictures that when assigned another topic, when placed in the role of the therapist, healer, or pastor, these authors could write essays of note about the constructive side.

But if there is anything consistent in these essays, or, rather, because there is much that is consistent in these essays, it is this coherence that the authors bring to their theme, namely, "it is futile to experience grace or healing so long as":

- People think that all would be peaceful if the whole world turned godless, secular, free of religion.
- Humans live with delusion or illusion about the really destructive aspects of faith and faiths.
- We believe that the dark side of religion is all in the mind, heart, and company of "the other," those people who have the wrong God, the wrong books, the wrong nation in which to live.
- People fail to explore their own scriptures, traditions, and experiences, as they have inherited them from ancestors (e.g., when Christians see *jihad* as the main mark of Islam or when Muslims think *crusades* against infidels are what Christians are all about).
- Humans do not engage in psychological probing of themselves and others, to unearth the tangle of themes and motifs that are destructive when faith or God enters the scene.

The authors of these books are helpful to all who want to effect change in the destructive power of religion. For example, the biblical scholars among them bring to light many destructive stories in scriptures that adherents want to overlook. More and more we learn from these volumes the complex, nether-side of the animating stories of the strangers' faiths. We are compelled here to look at their traditions and sacred scriptures: Qur'an, Torah, New Testament, and more. Too often we read them only in ways that portray an ugliness associated with the other person or company.

Since most writers of these volumes stand in biblical traditions, they take on the stories most would like to overlook: Abraham and Isaac, Jephthah and his daughter, some aspects of God the Father and Jesus the Son relations. They see no way around such texts, and do not offer trivializing pap to give them easy interpretations; but they give us instead tools for interpreting those narratives. These can make us aware and can be liberating.

Psychology plays a very big role in these volumes, in keeping with their auspices and intentions. During the six years of *The Fundamentalism Project*, Dr. Appleby and I, with our board of advisers, jokingly said that we would not let the psychologists in until the third or fourth year. Then we did, and they were very helpful. What we were trying to show the academy and readers around the globe was the fact that there were some irreducibly religious elements in Fundamentalisms.

Of course, religious Fundamentalists think they are *purely* religious; but many scholars in the social sciences "reduced" them: their hard-line views were considered by such scholars to be "nothing but" a reflection of their social class (Marx), or of their relations to their fathers (Freud), or a reflection of their descent from particularly vicious simian strands (Darwin).

In our project we were not able to disprove all that the reducers claimed, and had no motive to do so. *The Fundamentalism Project*, like this one, was to issue new understanding, not new evasion or new apologetic sleights of hand. We simply wanted readers of those books to see, as readers of *The Destructive Power of Religion* should see, the psychological dynamics that are present at the center of all human faith commitments and explanations. One sees much of such connection and illumination in these essays. The introduction of insights from the humanities balances those of social scientists. The religiously committed authors, and those who, at least in their essays, are noncommittal, together with numerous other aspects of these important volumes, help produce a balanced depiction.

What I took away from the chapters, especially, is a sense of the pervasiveness of violence across the spectrum of religions. Not many years ago, celebrated students of myth, or romantic advocates of anything-but-our historic religious traditions, won large enthusiastic audiences for their romantic pictures. *If only* we could get away from Abraham's God, Jesus' Father, and Mother Church's Mary; if only we could move far from Puritan Protestantism with its angry God; if only we left behind Judaism with its Warrior God; if only. . . .

There was great confidence in and propaganda for the notion that we could find refuge in any number of alternatives: gentle, syncretic Hinduism; goddess-rule; mysticism; transcendentalism; animism; Native American thought. However, closer scrutiny showed that only relative distance and the intriguing exoticism of nonconformist alternatives made these other models seem tolerant and gentle. The closer and informed view found violent stories of Hindu-Muslim warfare, tyrannies by what were proposed as the "gentle" human sacrifice, and tribal warfare everywhere. All this is not designed to violate what we are not supposed to violate after reading *The Destructive Power of Religion*, namely, the principle that we are to be self-critical and not irrationally attacking the "other" with finger-pointing. Of course, the "others" *are* in some degree also victims and often perpetrators of the violent and destructive sides of faith.

What goes on, however, as these chapters show, is that there is a dark underside, a nether, shadowed side to every enduring and profound system of symbols and myths, hence to every religion. That may result from deep psychic forces discerned by many of the scholars authoring these volumes. It may result from the realization that the grand myths and stories deal with the wildest and deepest ranges of human aspiration and degradation.

Most of these authors are anything but fatalistic. While there are no utopians here, no idealists who think all will always be well, most of them have a constructive purpose that becomes manifest along the way.

We historians learned from some nineteenth-century giants that we overcome history with history. That is, there is no escape from the world of events and stories and constructions; but we are not doomed to be confined among only violent actions. So with these essays, they make it plain that we are to overcome analysis with analysis, analysis of destruction, which gives insight that can lead to construction. These essays are not preachy: the authors set forth their cases and let readers determine what to do with whatever emerges. I picture a good deal of self-discovery following the discovery of this important work. One hopes that here will be found some glint of discernment that is an expression of—yes, grace!

Martin E. Marty

Fairfax M. Cone Distinguished Service Professor Emeritus
University of Chicago Divinity School

Lent 2003

Ad Testimonium

The Destructive Power of Religion is a work of profound research and engaging writing. It is a groundbreaking work with tremendous insight, a set of books that will inform and give perspective to people anywhere trying to make sense of religiously based violence. Professor Ellens has assembled a brilliant stable of insightful and concerned authors to produce four volumes of readable, thoughtful analysis of our present world situation. This contribution will have permanent value for all future research on the crucial matter of religion's destructive power, which has been exercised throughout history, and continues today to give rise to violence in shocking and potentially genocidal dimensions. Future work on this matter will need to begin with this publication. This will become a classic.

Professor Ellens and his team have not produced this important work merely out of theoretical reflection or as viewed from a distant ivory tower. I first met Professor Ellens while he was heavily engaged in psycho-social research in the Republic of South Africa in the 1970s and 1980s, when my country was struggling with some of the worst oppression wreaked upon much of its citizenry by the religiously driven, destructive policies of Apartheid. His comparative studies of educational, health care, and psycho-spiritual resources provided for the black South Africans and the black citizens of the United States were important contributions at a critical time. His orientation is always from the operational perspective, down on the ground where real people live and move and have their being.

In consequence, this massive work is a challenge to those in the professional worlds of psychology, sociology, religion, anthropology, pastoral care, philosophy, biblical studies, and theology. At the same time, it is so highly readable that it will be accessible and downright informative to the layperson or general reader who finds these volumes at the local library. These books are helpful to all who want to effect change in the destructive process in our world, a process too often created or fostered by religious fervor.

It must be noted with equal enthusiasm that the four volumes of *The Destructive Power of Religion* are as urgent in their emphasis upon the positive power—religion's power for healing and redemption of personal and worldwide suffering and perplexity—as they are in boldly setting forth the destructive side. Particularly, the numerous chapters by Professor Ellens, as well as those by Professors Capps, Aden, Wink, Sloat, and others, constantly move us toward the healing perceptions of grace and forgiveness.

Professor Ellens has repeatedly, here and in other works on his long list of publications, called attention to the role redemptive religious power played in the formulation and operation of the Truth and Reconciliation Commission in my country at a time of extreme crisis, thus making possible a thoroughgoing sociopolitical revolution with virtually no bloodshed. He claims, quite correctly, I think, that if it had not been for the pervasive presence of biblical concern and religious fervor in the black, white, and colored populations of our republic at that time, there would have been no way through that sociopolitical thicket without a much greater denigration of the quality of life in our society, and an enormous loss of life itself. I am grateful to him for his insight and his articulation of it for the larger world community. That is typical of the practical approach evident in his work and that of his entire team, which has provided us with this very wise work, *The Destructive Power of Religion*. I commend them unreservedly. I am honored that I have been asked to provide this testimony to the profound importance of these volumes for the worldwide community of those who care.

Archbishop Desmond Tutu
Pentecost 2003

PREFACE

While deeply occupied with the preparation of these volumes, during the Christmas season of 2002, I fell rather inadvertently into a conversation with a young and thoughtful woman, Mollie, who has, consequently, become a genuine friend. Pain prompted our connection; hers, which was more than anyone so young and vital should have to bear, reawakening mine, long, old, deep, soaked in my earliest memories from when I was less than five. Mollie was injured at a tender age and in a manner that made her feel betrayed by God and humankind. My particular personal perplexity started with my mother's frequent illness and absence in my infancy, and was fixed forever in my character and consciousness by the death of my dearest friend on August 3, 1937. Her name was Esther Van Houten, we were both five years old, and we were madly in love. We talked all that summer of starting school together in the fall. We were infinitely joyful. We were gracefully oblivious of the Great Depression in which both our families were caught, and of the lowering clouds of war which would soon take away my older brother and five of hers.

August 3 of that year was a brilliantly sunny day on our remote farmstead southwest of McBain, Michigan. I was standing by the well outside the kitchen window of our farmhouse, vaguely conscious of my mother's image in the window as she prepared my father's mid-morning "lunch." I was thinking of Esther and expected any moment to run across the country road and up the driveway to her yard to while away the morning with her. I heard the screen door of her home slam shut.

My heart leaped, and I looked up anticipating seeing her with her long blond hair and bright blue eyes—like my mother's eyes. There she stood, at the top of the driveway, completely on fire, and she burned to death right there. I helplessly called for my mother, but there was nothing one could do out in that remote place on August 3, in 1937. A sheet of darkness came down on me and did not begin to rise again until I was seven. During those two years, my brother Gordon died, my sister, my dear grandfather, and two neighbor children. Death seemed everywhere. The darkness has never completely gone away.

What connected me with Mollie is our common "case regarding God." It is our common case in that we discovered that we hold it in common and that is how we found each other; but it is also a common case because the longer I live and the more I learn the clearer it is that this is the case every thinking and feeling person has regarding God. It is common among humans to live with this perplexity. The ancient Israelites who gave us their Bible, and with it the heritage Jews, Christians, and Muslims hold in common, formulated the perplexity in the question, "How is God in history, particularly our usually troubled and often wretched history of wickedness, destruction, and death?" How can God promise so much prosperity and security through the prophets and deliver so little safety for faithful, vulnerable, hopeful humans? How can God entice a fourteen-year-old girl into the quest for faith and in that very context fail to protect her from injury and betrayal? God seems perfectly capable of engineering a majestic creation and strategizing its evolution through eons of productive time, but he cannot keep a five-year-old girl from death by fire? I spent my entire life, from age seven on, devoted to a single course toward, into, and in the ministry of theology and psychology, confidently trying to recover the trust that God, in a prosperous providence, would embrace my children and carefully shepherd them into health, wisdom, safety, and success; in the faith, in fruitful marriages, in joyful parenting, and in the fulfillments of love. I entrusted my children to God's care while I was busy "doing the work of God's Kingdom." I did my side of the "bargain" very well. God did not do as well on his side of the equation.

All this has caused me to work very hard to rethink my entire notion of God, and especially my theology of sacred scriptures. I do not see how any honest and honorable person can get through an entire lifetime without being forced to do this very same thing, forced by what has always been the ordinary horror and daily trauma of life, personal and universal. Unless one is able to see the unsacred in sacred scriptures, what can the sacred mean? Unless one has a comprehensive way to come to terms with the horror of life, how can celebration of the gracious be anything but psycho-spiritual denial? There can be no question that the God of the Hebrew Bible, and the God who is reported to have killed Jesus because, after getting ticked off at the human race, he could not get his head screwed on right again unless he killed us or somebody else, is abusive in the extreme. To salvage a God of grace out of that requires some reworking of the traditional Judaic, Christian, and Muslim theologies of sacred scripture. The difficulty that prevents us from writing God off completely and permanently is the fact that both the Old Testament and the New Testament, as well as the Qur'an, have woven through the center of their literary stream a more central message as well. The notion, unique in all human religions, that Abraham seems to have discovered, which is so redemptive in these sacred scriptures, is the claim that the real God is a God of unconditional grace—the only thing that works in life, for God or for humans. The human heartache is universal. The perplexity pervades everything in life. The question is, "Is there any warrant that the claims for grace do too?"

I do not feel like the Lone Ranger in this matter. Of course, there is Mollie's case, but everyone who has been around for a while knows a long list of the Mollies in this world. I have sat in my psychotherapist and pastoral counselor chairs for 40 years and have noticed that this is the "case regarding God" that perplexes most thoughtful and informed people; and most have been afraid to say it aloud, or have had no good opportunity to do so. Mollie said it aloud to me and immediately I recognized the sound of it. It is our common human story. It has ever been so, since reflective humans first opened wondering eyes upon this planet. Many years ago Barbara Mertz wrote a telling book about ancient Egypt. She called it, *Red Land, Black Land.*[1] She noted that we cannot speak of those mysterious days and people of so long ago without being awed by their way of dying and their funerals. They recorded them grandly in their even grander tombs. It is a simple story, the same as ours; a story in Mertz's sensitive words, "of our common human terror and our common hope."

The Destructive Power of Religion, Violence in Judaism, Christianity, and Islam, is a work in four volumes about our common human terror and our common hope. I hope you will find it stirring, disturbing, and hopeful.

J. Harold Ellens
Epiphany 2003

Note

1. New York: Dell Publishing, 1966, 367.

ACKNOWLEDGMENTS

Dr. Chris Stout invited me to write a chapter in his earlier, remarkably important four-volume set, *The Psychology of Terrorism.* I was pleased to do so, and we published my chapter there under the title "Psychological Legitimization of Violence by Religious Archetypes." Debbie Carvalko, acquisitions editor at Greenwood Press, found the chapter valuable and asked me to expand it by editing a work, which I have titled *The Destructive Power of Religion.* Thus, these four volumes were thoughtfully conceived and wisely midwifed. The birth is timely, since it seems everywhere evident that the world needs these reflections just now, more than ever. I wish, therefore, to acknowledge with honor and gratitude, Debbie's kind proficiency and Chris' professional esteem. I wish, as well, to thank the 30 authors who joined me in creating this work. I wish to express my gratitude to Beverley Adams for her meticulous work in reading the proofs of these volumes, while I was too ill to do so.

CHAPTER 1

Introduction: Toxic Texts

J. Harold Ellens

Sacred scriptures motivate ordinary people to amazing achievements in spirituality, religion, and cultural creativity. I am continually surprised by how remarkably constructive that inspiration can be. Think of Handel's *Messiah*. A simple list of sacred texts inspired ethereal paeans of music. Its transcendent crescendos of baroque composition, hundreds of years later, still transport the listener to worlds of imagination and spiritual ecstasy that are normally beyond our personal possibilities. Think of the grand European cathedrals of towering Gothic reach—for heaven and for God. They were created literally out of thin air—and they ascend delicately into thin air—by the power that moved in people who read the Bible. Remember, as well, the ornate basilicas of Eastern Christianity. The stunningly beautiful mosques, temples, and synagogues that dot the face of history and its creative cultures are of equal grandeur and inspiration. The Dome of the Rock in Jerusalem, the renovated Santa Sophia of Istanbul, and the Ba'hai Temples in numerous places around the world are stunning in their spiritual beauty and leave one almost gasping in awe. The marvelous meditative masses of Mozart, Bach, Beethoven, and Bernstein will last forever in their capacity to stir the human soul to heights of hope. They came simply and directly from the phrases of the Hebrew Bible and from simple scenes of sacred Christian scriptures.

Christ Heals the Blind-Born Man, by Eustache Lesueur. Erich Lessing/Art Resource, New York.

However, the inspiration of sacred scriptures can also be devastatingly destructive, spiritually, psychologicaly, and culturally. Indeed, they often are and frequently have been throughout the history of religions. This work in four volumes is about *The Destructive Power of Religion*. This volume presents *Models and Cases of Violence in Religion*. I wish here, by way of simple introduction, to stimulate a dialogue about a sacred text which is generally prized by Bible scholars and religious devotees but which has a dangerous subtext or underside that has been ignored. This subtext can have a destructive effect on persons, communities, and cultures by the negative archetypes that it may generate at the unconscious psychological level. The narrative which will be addressed here is a familiar one, relatively simple to reconstruct for our purposes and easy to expound upon. Everybody knows this story. It is the story from John 9 about the healing of the blind man. One might present a similar analysis of the story about the cure of the men possessed by demons (Matt. 8:28–34, Mark 5:1–20, Luke 8:26–39) and the narrative of David and Goliath (1 Sam. 17:19–58). However, space permits only an address to the man born blind.

Exposition

In Jerusalem, one Sabbath day around the time of the Jewish Feast of the Passover, Jesus healed a man who had been born blind. Jesus' medical practice, even in that day, may have been somewhat questionable. What recommended it, according to John's report, is that it worked. Everyone who ever reads this story comes away from it with a great sense of relief and satisfaction. It is a story of human suffering, a story of human care for the needy, a story about a number of types of human triumph, and a story with quite a surprising mix of good humor. No one wants to hear, therefore, that there might be a pathogenic underside to this Johannine report. But let us look at the story as it stands.

At the outset, one is given the impression that Jesus' encounter with this blind man was rather inadvertent. That should already alert us to the fact that there is more going on here than meets the eye. There is nothing inadvertent about the way the story unfolds. It is really quite likely that Jesus had often seen this blind fellow sitting there begging on the street. The man was a fixture at that place on the sidewalk and had been there for decades. You could go down that busy street many times every day and ignore him, pay no attention to him, not even notice how you skillfully avoided stumbling over him when the crowd pressed you. However, like the bright red fire hydrant at the corner that you never notice, though you always see it and walk carefully around it, he was one of those fixtures which simply make up the landscape of that place. If he died and the next morning you came by and he was gone, you would suddenly *see* him, suddenly notice his presence by his absence. Jesus knew this guy, like you know your fire hydrant, your brass door knocker that you have not knocked for decades, and the cushion on the seat of your car. It is with you every day. You always sit on it. You never think of it. Unless, of course, it is stolen.

So we know from the outset that something unseen is to be seen here. The clues come quickly. The disciples ask Jesus the question. Not just a question, *the* question. What question? The one always stuck in the back of your mind, my mind, every human's mind, since time immemorial. The question about pain, human pain, animal pain, pain everywhere, the "whole creation groaning and travailing in pain until now," as St. Paul says in Romans 8:18–22. This story is a setup to pose the big question of the problem of evil and suffering. The disciples ask Jesus, "Rabbi, who sinned, this man or his parents, that he was born blind?" They no longer wonder whether the evil of suffering is a result of the evil of sinning. They already are sure they know the answer to that. Of course, suffering is the result of sin, otherwise how can you get God off the hook? Their simple worldview is that of a theodicy; that is, they want to explain the perplexing things in life in a way that at least justifies God, even if it is at the expense of unfortunate humankind—and at the expense of truth.

Jesus is not given the option or freedom, in terms of the constraints of their question, to deny that it must be *his* sin or his *parents'* that inflicted this fellow with blindness. The equation must be preserved: sin always produces suffering, suffering always comes from sin. As long as that equation holds, our world is coherent and rational. Do not disturb the equation. And there is another reason not to disturb it. Many of us are not suffering right now. That is our best assurance of our self-justification. That was the persistent argument, remember, of Job's three friends; *there* was a *real* case of self-justification at the expense of a pathetic suffering human.

Jesus does not seem to care about the disciples' theological comfort or discomfort. He wades right into the center of their equation and blows it up. "It was not that this man sinned or his parents, that he was born blind." That sounds good. Jesus is obviously a regular twenty-first-century liberal theologian. He certainly is no legalistic Fundamentalist Evangelical with a compulsive need for some kind of quid pro quo theology: you mess up—you catch hell; you do well—you catch heaven or the earthly equivalent, namely, no suffering, maybe even riches. However, Jesus does not stop there with his answer, unfortunately. Obviously he does not care about our theological comfort either. "It is not that this man sinned, or his parents, that he was born blind, but that the works of God might be made manifest in him."

Now this is disturbing! Is Jesus implying that God made this poor fellow blind from birth, caused him to wait around for 40 years begging and blind on the crappy streets of Jerusalem, degraded and neglected by the unloving crowd, so that God could send Jesus along eventually, "in the fullness of time" perhaps, and then make a big deal out of spectacularly healing him, so that we would forever remember what a great and graciously healing person God is? A lot of Christians think so! Most Christians throughout the past 2,000 years have thought so.

Personally, I hope that is not what Jesus meant. That would be monstrously manipulative and abusive of a vulnerable and sensitive human being. The blind man, if asked, might very well have wanted to make God look as good as possible in history, but he ought at least to get to vote on the decision. Moreover, how about God trying to look good, instead, by taking good care of this man from birth so that he has the full healthy use of all his five senses, his whole body, mind, and spirit, and is able to be a roaring success as a wealthy, godly gentleman who really looks after the needy blind beggars and undereducated children running around the streets of his city? Who *is* this arbitrary, negative-minded, and abusive God in this story?

Well, perhaps what Jesus meant was that this poor guy was just a victim of the accidents of life and history. No one's sin made him blind. Sin is not the cause of evil and suffering in the world. Stuff happens! This world is finite and far from perfect since it is an evolutionary experiment, and a generally delightful one, in spite of its limitations. But one of the prices we pay for the freedom to grow and evolve is that accidents happen. A microbe overcomes a child's immunity. The microbe succeeds in *its* God-given business, but the child suffers blindness all his life. Maybe this poor guy was premature, he barely survived, he was bitten by a fly on his first day of life. The infection resulting from that caused a chronic running infection in both eyes, and he could not see. Now in this amazingly serendipitous moment of transcendental providence, it just happens to be Jesus who comes ambling down the street and runs into this needy human. Absolutely existential inadvertency, but a great chance God can take advantage of for his own self-aggrandizement. God can heal the fellow through the medical intervention of Jesus, and God comes off "real good." Now everybody knows that God is a grace-filled healer of hopeless people.

That suits me. I am in favor of as much divine intervention as possible in the lives of all the hopeless, needy, and anguished people of this world, whom I have seen everywhere all over the face of this planet. Moreover, I am willing that God employ all our efforts to the utmost to make that happen; and, frankly, he can have all the glory for it, as far as I am concerned, if that is what he wants and needs. I say, "Let's just get the job done! I don't care who gets the credit. It is amazing what you can accomplish with that outlook."

Well, that is just what Jesus did; that is, he got the job done. He picked up a handful of clay, spit on it a few times until it was moist, and applied it as a salve on the eyes of the blind man. Then he sent him for a swim in the pool of Siloam. When the guy came up for air, he could see. I wonder if we could find some of that clay over there in Jerusalem? It must have some amazing chemical qualities or something. Do not be too surprised by that. There is a type of soil that William Smith discovered in England that is now called Fuller's Earth. The Scots use it as a kind of cleaning fluid for washing the lanolin out of sheep's wool. That is how it got its name. There are lots of natural substances in this world that have miraculous powers to heal, if you can just find them and know how to use them.

I have a friend, Grant Taylor, who is a professor of chemistry at the University of Louisville, who tells me that all healing medications we have come ultimately from some natural plant or soil or other substance that is just waiting out there in God's wonderful world. That is how primitive people managed to find herbs and such things to use as healing agents, and it is often from the clues received from them that chemical companies undertook the research which has produced our fine medicines of the twenty-first century. Jesus knew something the people around him did not know, and he used it wisely to heal a suffering human soul. He tended to do that sort of thing wherever he went.

Now, people had passed along that street numerous times each day and had noticed the blind beggar as you would notice a fire hydrant in the landscape. That day, however, he had moved. Blind beggars are not supposed to move much. Indeed, he was walking along the street as one of *them*. God help us! The landscape has been disturbed. I mean, the theological landscape. Do not tell me that sin does not produce suffering or that suffering does not come from sin. What can this blind beggar have done to get out of that equation? It cannot be so. Somebody actually dared to say it out loud: "Is not this the man who used to sit and beg?" A rather unconventional fellow who seldom darkened the door of the synagogue and whom you could never catch discussing theology sensibly—probably the local drunk—carelessly betrayed his religious unconcern by quickly answering, "Yes! It's the same guy."

Now the danger with a quick answer like that is that it is liable to commit the unpardonable sin of telling the truth. Not to worry! A more proper citizen immediately solved the problem by pointing out, "No, it is not him, but someone who looks like him." It reminds me of the wag who said that the plays of Shakespeare were not written by William Shakespeare but by another man of the same name. In any case, the blind beggar cleared it all up by saying, "I am the man." If you have not already noticed, this is the place in the story where the fun starts. The crowd asks the man what happened. He tells them what Jesus did. They ask where Jesus is. The man wisely demurs. He claims he does not know.

It is obvious at this point that, having given the crowd Jesus' name, the healed man discerns something sinister in their question about Jesus' whereabouts, and from that point to the end of the story, he will tell no one where to find Jesus. Maybe he really did not know. Frequently, in such stories in the gospels, we are told that Jesus surreptitiously withdrew himself from public view. In any case, whatever sinister intent he may have discerned proved to be real. The crowd hustled the healed man off to the authorities to be held accountable in some way. One of the interesting aspects of the formal composition of this narrative is the fact that the description of Jesus' medical procedure for healing the man is described in great detail three times over. First, it is reported as it happens, then it is recounted for the crowd, and now the man repeats it again for the authorities. In the end the Pharisees ask him to tell it a couple more times, because of which he plays a joke on them.

The religious authorities immediately respond, "This man is not from God, for he does not keep the Sabbath." With whom they were arguing cannot be imagined. No one has claimed so far in the story that Jesus is from God. Why are they making that the issue? Who knows? However, this response to the healed man's report is necessary for the story because, remember, this whole thing is a setup to make a point. So the Pharisees' question had to be injected here in order to invite the response in verse 16. "Others [Pharisees] said, 'How can a man who is a sinner do such signs?' " Moreover, the Pharisees' disclaimer that Jesus cannot be from God implies the inherent falsification of their own claim. Why would anyone need to say that this miraculous healer is not from God if all the evidence had not already established the fact that he must be, for no one of lesser stature could possibly accomplish this miracle? The humor is building in the story. The authorities are split over the central theological issue in Israel: "How is God in history, and how does this relate to the problem of evil and suffering?" Moreover, the division has been caused by a fire hydrant, that is, by an object off the street, a piece of social refuse out of the gutter. The key theological issue has been raised by a blind beggar in such a way as to completely mystify all the authorities. It is crucial to see this, or we will miss the punch line of this grand joke, which arrives in verses 32 to 33.

Since the appearance of the former blind man off the street has blown up the theological faculty of the university, they lunge back at him in hopes of saving themselves. They ask him again about it. This time they just want to take simple testimony. They have obviously said to each other, "Let's just get the facts, man, just the facts." So their question is, "What do you say about this guy, since he has opened your eyes?" The man responded not with the facts but with an editorial: "He is one of God's prophets!" By now you can see the crowd hiding their heads under their arms and turning away, hardly able to contain their laughter.

The authorities were in deep trouble. They could see that the fellow could see. They had his report about how he got that way. They solved their problem by denying the reality to which the crowed gave multiple personal witness. They claimed that he had never been blind. Unfortunately, some troublesome character stuck the blind man's parents under the Pharisees' noses. So the fun continued. The authorities ask the parents if their son had been blind from birth, and the parents affirm it, explaining that they do not know how he was healed. "This is our son. He was always blind. Now he sees. We do not know who did it to him. Ask him. He is over 21. He can speak for himself." The crowd sticks their heads further under their arms. You can hear the guffaws.

The parents wanted to say no more because they knew that what was at stake here was the condemnation of Jesus for disobeying the law of Moses, the sacred Torah, by doing an act of healing on the Sabbath. This judgment could also fall upon anyone who endorsed such breach of the sacred scriptures, and if your son has been miraculously healed of lifelong blindness, how can you conceal it, how can you not affirm that? You cannot hide it. It must be celebrated, shouted from the housetops. You could get thrown out of the synagogue for that. Indeed, you could be excluded from the people of God altogether. The crowd knew it and therefore had brought the healed man to the authorities. The authorities had it in mind and therefore were interrogating everybody they could pick up as witnesses. The parents knew it and wanted to keep their mouths shut. Their son must have been well aware of the danger he was in as well. What is one to do?

The blind man saw readily what to do. When they hauled him before the authorities again, asking him to give his report a third and a fourth time, they told him to praise God for his healing but admit his healer was a sinner. The blind man's clear vision and hilarious humor was ready. This fire hydrant suddenly spewed forth a stream of refreshing profundity that always brings tears to my eyes and provokes me to laughter at the same time. He said quietly, profoundly, and with no apology, "Whether my healer is a sinner, I do not know. This one thing I do know, once I was blind, now I can see. That is a simple equation for me. Why do you keep asking me to repeat the story? Do you want to become his disciples?"

So the authorities beat the man up psychologically and declared, "We hold to Moses' law. That is why we are the religious authorities here, and we want you to know that we have no idea where this Jesus fellow comes from, or where he gets off breaking the Torah and healing on the Sabbath." They set themselves up for the hilarious punch line. The blind man, seeing better than anyone else there, says, "What a marvel! I see that this is a genuinely profound, complex, and transcendental theological enigma to all of you theological professors and sophisticated logicians, who see the inside and the outside, the top side and the bottom side, the heavenly side and the earthly side, the temporal and the eternal side of all these incredibly serious questions. So you are nonplussed to explain Jesus, especially because he opened my eyes."

"I am, of course, a simpleton. I could not study theology because I was perched like a fire hydrant, brooding on the street, a gutter fowl, a bottom feeder. Yet for me the matter is quite a simple equation. (1) God does not hire sinners. (2) He hires those who worship him, listen to him. (3) Never has a human cured blindness. (4) If Jesus were not God's man, he could not. (5) I was blind, now I see. So complicated for logicians and theologians! So plain for an ignorant blind man to see through!"

Well, that did it. They cursed him some more. They degraded him with the calumny that he was "born in utter sin; and had no business presuming to teach them." That, of course, kept *their* original equation intact. Sin causes suffering. Suffering comes from sin. So they made him suffer as much as *they* could. They threw him out of the synagogue and cut him off from the "people of God."

The Problem

This is a wonderful story. It is full of pathos, impasses, and resolutions. It is full of hurt and hilarious humor. It is the classic joke in which the mighty are chastened and the simple exalted. The strength fails, the weakness accidentally succeeds. Well, not quite! For this to be a fully satisfactory classic joke, the tragic must stand plainly before us as thoroughly inevitable and hopelessly unavoidable. Then at the last moment, by a hair's breadth, the tragedy must be enigmatically avoided and everyone get clean away. Pat and Mike were on the seventy-sixth floor of the Empire State Building. Pat needed a men's room; he opens a door with some difficulty, steps in. There is a long whoosh and a thud. It was the elevator. Mike is terrified but then hears Pat's voice, "Watch out for that first step!" Utter tragedy. Everyone gets clean away. Classic humor.

In the blind man's story, only Jesus gets clean away—and that at the blind man's great expense. That is the destructive subtext of this narrative, which we must face lest it seed in our personal and collective unconscious a kind of abusive conditionalism and manipulation in our treatment of others that is unacceptable. To tell the story in terms of its subtext, it goes like this. Jesus needed an opportunity to provoke a confrontation with the religious authorities because he wanted to take them on again about the rigid regulations of the Sabbath which they were destructively imposing upon the Israelite people. He had already confronted them about this issue sometime earlier when they asked why his disciples were harvesting grain on the Sabbath (Matt. 12:1 ff., Mark 2:23 ff., Luke 6:1 ff.).

Jesus had his eye on the blind man for some time, as a possible fall guy for an attention-getting demonstration. One Sabbath, either because he thought his time was running out to make this point in a colossal way or because a particularly opportune moment seemed to be developing with a lot of the authorities available in one place, he made his move. Sauntering up to the blind man, he set up the situation for doing whatever it was he did for him, making sure that a good crowd of restless witnesses was available to take in the drama. He treated the man and sent him for a swim. Jesus disappeared. The crowd took up the cause as Jesus knew it would. He may even have instigated it. The thing had to come to the authorities to do any good.

As a result of Jesus' action, the man was put through an excruciating process of interrogation, heresy trial, abuse, degradation, and condemnation. His sentence was "to be cast out of the community." I suppose that for a moment the thought flew through his head as to whether it is better to be a blind man in the community or a man of vision alienated and alone. Admittedly he handled himself with grace, humor, and aplomb throughout the ordeal. We cannot really imagine what is the ultimate weight and texture of the sentence "They cast him out!" I think I know what that would have meant in Bergen Belsen and Auschwitz. I know something of what that would mean for a Jew cast out of Israel today. I know firsthand and personally what it means to be tried for heresy. I can imagine to some degree what it would mean to be cast out of my family. I do not think I can really get to the depths of what it meant to be used by Jesus and then thrown away—by the community.

All the while, Jesus stayed hidden. Jesus let the poor victim of his manipulation and abuse suffer alone. He did not support him, empathize with him, counsel him, pray with him, meet him secretly in the dark of night, guide him, or guard him. Jesus hung the man out to dry, as we say! Moreover, all this was a setup for Jesus to make a point with the Pharisees. Of course, we can argue as Christians always do at this point, that the guy was greatly advantaged. His blindness was cured. Oh, Yeah! I remember. That was a benefit of some considerable size! No question! What I am concerned about, however, is the underlying principle of the thing. Psychologically it is utterly unacceptable to use another person for our own arbitrary self-aggrandizement, at that person's expense. It turns that person into an object, a chessman on a chessboard. God is against that. He was against it when Jesus abused the blind man despite healing his blind-ness! If he were not against it, God would be a monster.

If we still cannot see that this was a manipulative setup in which the blind man is a mere tool of Jesus' ulterior ambitions, we need only look again at where the story comes out. Jesus finally showed up. He confronted the blind man, who seemed glad to see him and believe in him as the Son of Man, a messianic figure from that mystical and rather neurotic hysteric religion called Apocalyptic Judaism. While talking with the former blind man, the Pharisees overheard Jesus say, "I came into this world to judge it, that those who do not see may get the vision, and that those who see may be blinded." The Pharisees asked him if he meant to imply that since the blind man sees, does he think that they who disagree with the blind man are blind. Jesus responded with another enigmatic joke: "If you were blind, you would have the true vision [you would be guilty of nothing], but since you claim you see, you are blind [guilty of having a false vision]."

Every reader enjoys the poignancy and ironic humor of the roman-tic story of the healing of the man born blind. However, the uncon-scious effects of the story cannot be ignored. There are four psychological units in the narrative: the reaction of Jesus, of the blind man, of the Pharisees, and of the man's parents. Jesus met a needy man and healed him. That seems admirable. However, while he could have done this on Monday or Thursday, he consciously chose to do it on the Sabbath, a lethal breach of the Torah. He was intentionally making maximum difficulty for the blind man and causing him to be thrown out of the synagogue and the community, cut off from his family and the support and nurture of friends. Obviously, Jesus was exploiting this unfortunate person to advance Jesus' own project of accosting the authorities who prized the prescriptions of the Torah. His objective was to set himself up as "greater than Moses and superior to the Torah." In his previous encounter with the authorities regarding the law of the Sabbath, he had already declared that he, the Son of Man, was Lord of the Sabbath. This is the claim that lies behind and is implied in Jesus' handling of this entire episode. He used the disturbance he caused with the blind man to get the attention of an audience.

It was abusive for Jesus to abandon the healed man to the assaults of the Pharisees, whose psychology was, in TA terms, taking the role of the scolding parents and putting the healed man down into the role of the naughty child. Of course, he had enough seasoning from decades of sitting blindly in his public suffering, fruitlessly praying, hopelessly trying to get healed, and noticing the superficiality or arrogance of authorities that he gamely outflanked the Pharisees' strategy and ridiculed their simplistic logic and legalism. He did so adroitly by setting it in contrast with his simple reality. The gamesmanship of the healed man does not obviate the fact that Jesus abused him, exploited him for his own purposes, abandoned him to significant persecution, and only thereafter, when all the damage was done, embraced him in a redemptive way. What kind of people care is that? It would get you fired today as a hospital chaplain or as a professor of pastoral care. You would be discreetly dismissed from a mental health clinic.

If Jesus had really been interested in this unfortunate man's blindness and healing, he would have healed him quietly and pastorally on Tuesday. Then the entire community, including, undoubtedly, the Pharisees, would have had enormous appreciation of Jesus. Of course, this text operates on a number of levels of meaning, including as a metaphoric statement about the Christians being cast out of the synagogues, an issue writ large across the face of John's entire gospel and apparently the Johannine Community from which the gospel came. In any case, the destructive pathogenics of this passage are usually missed by reason of the central poetic pathos of the pericope appealing so powerfully to our sentimentality. I doubt that there has ever been a single accurate hermeneutical treatment of the violent and abusive aspect of this narrative in 2,000 years or of the potentially destructive unconscious model it sets for Christian problem solving or relationship management.

Conclusion

Nobody likes to spoil this nice sentimental story about the blind man healed. No one can take away the redemptive poignancy of the blind man's simple reality: "Once I was blind and now I see." That is not just his story, it is the story of us all, or it must become our story if life is to have meaning and be worthwhile. The danger lurking here is not in the obvious story. It is in the understory, the shadow side of the way the narrative is cast. It legitimates using people for our narcissistic advantage. It trivializes the exploitation of others, the treating of people from ulterior motives rather than forthrightly, and the handling of people in ways that are clandestine. In these ways it offers a model of abuse, certifying exactly those kinds of abuses that are most rampant in human society everywhere. It seems to justify husbands taking their wives for granted in order to achieve some objective that "is good for the family." It approves wives using their husbands to fill their womb hunger, satisfy their sexual urges, and provide a steady paycheck and never feeling any need to love, respect, or cherish their man. It justifies relationships with others designed to gratify some need in us and then dispose of the other so they do not clutter up our lives or get in our way. It affords subtle psychological certification of nations using and abusing other nations to acquire political, economic, or cultural advantage by infecting our collective unconscious with Jesus' pathogenic model of objectifying the other human community. Unless we can root out these destructive metaphoric religious artifacts from our inner world, how can we expect to create any sustained decency in our outer world? Everyone surely sees the absurdity implied! Unless we can change our core story, how can we change the sad, sick story of human inhumanity to humans?

Eleven brilliant authors have joined me in pursuing the answer to that question in *Models and Cases of Violence in Religion*, this third volume of *The Destructive Power of Religion*. I have opened our dialogue with a case that lies at the root of who we are in the Western world today. The scholars who share this volume represent a wide range of perspectives and emphases. I welcome you to our dialogue and am sure you will find this book to be of great interest and value.

CHAPTER 2

THE VIOLENT JESUS

J. Harold Ellens

On Tuesday of Holy Week, Jesus cleansed the temple.[1] No, he did not go after spider webs, flies, and dust balls under the couches. Nor did he set himself to running all the candlesticks and lavers through the dishwasher. We have no indication that Jesus did windows. He cleansed the temple. My mother considered it a good Monday, as a homemaker on the farm in the 1930s, when she washed, baked, churned, and ironed all in one day. We do not have a very clear idea what Jesus did on Monday. On Sunday he made his spectacular trip on a small jackass from Bethany to Jerusalem, accompanied by a noisy crowd and the local choir. They were hailing him as the Jerusalem idea of a messiah, a human son of David who would bring back the golden age of David's kingdom and get rid of the Romans once and for all. They sang the Psalms about that Messiah written a thousand years earlier, in David's time, as they hurried Jesus to what they hoped would be the great revolution and the restoration of Israel as a nation.

Monday was a different matter. On Mondays my mother typically washed all the clothes for a family of nine, baked 12 loaves of bread for the week, churned five pounds of butter from the cream of our Holstein cows, and ironed our Sunday clothes for the next Christian Sabbath. However, we do not know much about what Jesus did. We only know that he went directly to the temple on Sunday and disappointed the crowd by not marching instead to the Roman

A Rembrandt Harmenszoon van Rijn etching of Christ driving the money changers from the temple, 1635. Library of Congress.

Praetorium; challenging Pilate, the local authority; and inciting the Israelites to a proper revolution. Then, on Monday, he got going fairly early, apparently without breakfast, and, in a petty fit of low blood sugar or something like that, cursed a fig tree because it would not feed him. Then late in the day, he returned to the temple, cased the joint, and left for Bethany.

It was the next morning that things began to happen. He cleansed the temple. For about 2,000 years, Christians have been hailing this event as a great, wise, and divine moment in Jesus' ministry. It is claimed that he purged the most sacred of all places in the world, the Jerusalem temple, of a kind of dead and deadening Judaism that had been turned into a corrupt, commercialized, formalistic, and meaningless religion. Nothing could be further from the truth.

The truth is that Jesus had one of his fits of violence. These happened more frequently than Christian tradition is willing to acknowledge.[2] We do not know much about the setting that would incite such a provocation. We know only that it was an event, psychologically speaking, which would be diagnosed today as situation-inappropriate behavior, maybe even borderline personality disorder. There has been much speculation about the nature and meaning of this event, particularly in recent psychological analyses of biblical narrative in general and of Jesus' life and ministry in particular. What we know is that this is the event that killed him. There is a straight-line cause-and-effect sequence of actions that led from the cleansing of the temple to his death on the cross. Moreover, there seems to be some clear evidence in the texts that Jesus knew very well that this was going to be the upshot of his violent act (John 2:1–22). He threw down the gauntlet, and the authorities did not mind picking it up and following through on the consequence.

Exposition

Judaism in Jesus' Day

Judaism was not dead, effete, corrupt, or meaningless in Jesus' day. In fact, Judaism as we know it today did not exist. Rabbinic Judaism, from which derive the four or five vigorous forms of twenty-first-century Judaism, arose during the development of the Babylonian and Jerusalem Talmuds, from 300 to 600 C.E. During Jesus' day, there was a very great variety of religious movements and forms of theological tradition among the ancient Israelites. Jews of that time lived throughout the Roman Empire, concentrated mainly in all the major cities, as well as in the land of Palestine and the city of Jerusalem. Indeed, we now find evidence of Jews having dispersed to urban centers and trading caravansaries beyond the boundaries of the empire, beyond where the Pax Romana reigned.

There were at least two major types of Jewish religion in the first century of the common era (C.E.): the religion of the Pharisees, Sadducees, and Scribes and the religion of Apocalyptic Judaism. The former was a relatively rational religious program oriented toward Israelite history and focused on the constructive and practical development of Israelite society and religious practices. It tended to be centered in the temple liturgies. It took numerous forms but in Jesus' day seems to have been associated largely with the three distinct but similar emphases of the Pharisees, Sadducees, and Scribes. Apocalyptic Judaism took many forms, including that of the cloistered Essenes of Qumran, who were the Dead Sea Scrolls people, and their cousins, the Urban Essenes, who, as our name for them indicates, lived throughout Palestine in their own quarters or ghettos of many of the Palestinian cities and towns.

Apocalypticism seems to have been a religious perspective derived from some notions that the Jews of the exile, who had lived in Babylon from approximately 586 to 500 B.C.E., had picked up from Zoroastrianism. That religious tradition of ancient Persia (Iraq and Iran) held that history and the present world were caught up in a cosmic conflict between God and the Devil, good and evil, light and darkness, the kingdom of righteousness and the kingdom of unrighteousness. This conflict was seen as a divine warfare carried out on the battlegrounds of history and the human heart. When the Israelites were carried off into exile in Babylon by the troops of Nebuchadnezzar, the large question that arose in their minds was, "How is God in history, particularly in view of the tragedy and pain of his own people, Israel?" Most particularly, therefore, "How is God in our history, as his special people?" Israelites had always been interested in this question. That is why they kept a scriptural record of the major events of their national experience and constantly tried to interpret that recorded tradition in terms of this main question. While in Babylon, they thought they had discovered in the insights of Zoroastrianism, the religion of the god Ahura Mazda, the answer to their question. People are either on the side of the good God, the God of Israel, or on the side of the evil god, the Devil—on the side of righteousness and light or on the side of unrighteousness and darkness.

Because Israel had been sinful before the exile, they determined, God had sent the Babylonians to carry them off into captivity. Had not their own prophets said that they were so wicked, avaricious, and socially irresponsible that they would sell the poor for a pair of shoes, because of which the smoke of their religious sacrifices was a stench of the nostrils of the Almighty? This gave a rationale to history even if it was distasteful medicine to swallow. The blessing in this cursed state of affairs, as they began to see it while languishing in Babylonian exile, lay in the fact that if they now lived perfect lives, God would see that they were in the company of the righteous, on the side of light and godliness. God would, therefore, bless them. Of course, they knew that the fundamental truths of life were somewhat more complicated than all this, but the picture had a lot to offer, and the Essenes worked the plan with vigor. They did not just talk the talk, they walked the walk. They separated themselves from the evil world, lived in their own conclaves, and spent their lives on contributing very constructively to their own pious communities and to the society at large. For the most part they were admired by almost everyone for their austere, communal, altruistic, and righteous lives.

It is of great interest to me that this notion of the cosmic conflict, depicting evil as a cosmic force virtually equal to the good God, still reigns as the primary metaphor in all the worldviews in Western thought. It may also be the case in Eastern thought, but it is much more identifiable in the heritage that comes originally from ancient Israelite religion reported in the Hebrew Bible and that took specific form in the traditions of Judaism, Christianity, and Islam. However, the remarkable thing about this is that even secular Western thought is shot through with this same model. I was reading a *Star Wars* dictionary to a young lad whom I love, and I was struck by the fact that the entire story of *Star Wars* is straight out of the Hebrew Bible, the story about a cosmic conflict between the Force, the equivalent of the Hebrew God, and the counter-Force, which is simply a part of the Force that has gone bad or wild or has been distorted by ill-will.

The Apocalypticists of Zoroastrianism and of Enochic Judaism during the Second Temple period would have felt right at home in the *Star Wars* story. They would have sensed immediately that it was their story, not something conjured up in the twentieth century. Even the implication that both good and evil come from the Force, God, is not only implicit but also openly explicit in this story. That would have raised a great debate in Second Temple Judaism between the supralapsarians and the infralapsarians. Those are wonderful terms that virtually no one knows anymore. When I was in college and graduate school in the 1950s, we thought those terms were part of our daily bread, so to speak. They mean something very important. Supralapsarianism means that God decided before creation who were elected to be the righteous and receive eternal salvation and who were to be damned for time and eternity as the unrighteous. This is sometimes referred to as double predestination, which has a rather bad name these days, and almost everybody is against it, even though almost nobody knows what it really means. Infralapsarianism means that God decided before creation to provide for the salvation of those who live righteous lives and to guarantee hell for those who did not, knowing in advance, of course, who belonged to the camp of the righteous and who to the crowd of unrighteous. *Star Wars* is sort of infralapsarian, with some overtones of the Force being the source of both good and evil. It is really the old story, the old model. Can we not get this erroneous thing out of our heads and hearts, even though it does not reflect objective reality in any sense? There is no evidence that there is such a thing as cosmic evil. The only evil we see is what humans do to each other. Moreover, there is no indication that there are really two camps of humans in history, the righteous and the unrighteous. "There is so much good in the worst of us and so much bad in the best of us that it hardly behooves any of us to talk about the rest of us!" as Bobby Burns perceived long ago. Jesus said it slightly differently: "Before you try to remove the splinter from your brother's eye, take the log out of your own." Jesus most likely got that from one of the rabbis, as he did most of his wise aphorisms.

In any case, this cosmic conflict model and its notion of the two camps of humans is amazingly pervasive. Henry Holt and Company has published an engaging book written by that incredibly prolific author Martin Gilbert. Gilbert has written more than 60 superior volumes (many of them about Churchill), one on the Holocaust, and this new volume from Henry Holt titled *The Righteous: The Unsung Heroes of the Holocaust.* The righteous in this book are those incredibly heroic non-Jews who put their lives on the line to save numerous Jewish people from the Holocaust. This is a good book that everyone should read and that most of us will find profoundly valuable. What strikes me about it, however, is that once again we encounter here the old model of the two camps of people, the righteous who are on the side of good and are glorified, and the unrighteous who are on the side of evil and are vilified. Behind this model stands the assumption of the ancient Israelite notion that the ontological cosmic conflict is real. The old metaphor is reified, given concrete existence, despite the fact that there is no such thing as an ontological or cosmic evil force. This thing is everywhere in our mind-set in the Western world, in spite of the fact that it does not exist.

It is easy, of course, to make the illogical leap that the horrors are so terrible in Hitler's final solution, in Stalin's lethal oppressions, and in the holocausts that nearly every community of people have suffered at some time in history that it must be the case that some suprahuman force infects us and this world. That is exactly what the ancient Apocalypticists believed, and they assigned the responsibility to God or some transcendental counterforce. We tend to do the same today. It is the easier solution to claim that there is such a thing as a cosmic evil force which contests the dominion of the good in history. That gets humans off the hook and transfers the ultimate blame to God. The trouble with such illogic is not just the fact that it assumes the existence of cosmic evil, which does not, in fact, exist; more important, that model terribly underestimates the size of the problem of human dysfunction. Let us finally face what the ancient Israelites and the Hebrews of the Second Temple Literature could not face (Charlesworth, 1983), namely, that human beings really are capable quite on their own, without any demonic assistance, to inflict the horrors of holocaust upon each other and have been doing it since time immemorial.

The ancient Israelites, according to their own records, did it to the Canaanites; the Romans did it to the Picts and others; the Greeks did it to the Trojans; the Turks did it to the Armenians; Genghis Khan did it to the Chinese, as did Mao Tse-tung, whose rise to power killed not six million Jews but eight million Chinese; Stalin did it to the Ukrainian farmers (five million) and to his officer corps (30,000); and we killed three million Native Americans. The story goes on ad infinitum. Hitler had no mortgage on holocaust, and the Jews are not unique in suffering attempts at genocide. Humans create evil, and it can be monstrous—it usually is when given half a chance. The problem of human evil is infinitely beyond what we are willing to imagine, but it is not an ontological cosmic force, a kind of evil god. "We have met the enemy, and it is us," said Pogo.

There was a vigorous debate among the Essenes, both in the city ghettos and at Qumran, about where the evil forces in the world came from. These forces were seen as nearly equivalent to God, and it often seemed to be a real question who would win out in the end: God and the people of the holy ones of the Most High, as Daniel calls them in chapters 7 to 9, or the Devil and his minions. Some Essenes thought that evil had come from heaven and corrupted the whole world hopelessly. God had made a decision before creating the world that a certain group of people would be saved because he would make them the righteous ones. All others would be unable to endure the rigors of being the righteous ones because God had chosen them from before creation to be damned to the destiny of evil. No one knew in advance for which camp he or she was destined, but trying to live the life of the righteous and being able to succeed in doing so indicated that one was elected from before time to be one of the righteous and to be saved eternally.

Other Essenes believed that there were, indeed, these two camps, righteous and unrighteous, but that one could affect one's own destiny by choosing to be righteous or not. You could choose to allow evil to have its way with you or choose to resist that. God had not preset one's destiny before creation but had given us life in this material world as the setting for our desire and moral ability to choose the good. Sin was not an incurable disease that infected all of creation with no possible remedy.

John the Baptist was probably an Essene, most likely not from Qumran but from one of the Urban Essene communities, or an independent, individual loner and desert hermit, as the gospels seem to describe him. John had developed a variation on the ancient Essene theme. He preached that even if you had not had the good sense to choose the life of a righteous one, there was still some hope even at the last minute because God had given us all both time and an alternative means for getting into the company of the holy ones of the Most High. What you had to do was to repent immediately of all your iniquity since the reign of God was then and there breaking in upon humanity. You then had to be baptized and bring your conduct and character into conformity with your creed and confession. You could not just talk the talk. You had to walk the walk. That brought you into the company of the committed, the fellowship of the faithful, even if it was at the last moment of your life or opportunity (Matt. 3:1–10).

Jesus' message took this entire matter of how one becomes one of God's people a step further. He said that all you had to do was to believe on the Son of Man (Luke 12:8–9, John 1:12, 3:16–18, 9:35). Initially, Jesus was one of those who had joined John the Baptist's crowd, but he parted from John rather soon. John was almost certainly an Essene, and Jesus, or at least the Jesus Movement, was heavily influenced by the theology and worldview of the Essenes. The Jesus Movement came out of Apocalyptic Judaism and not out of the movement of the Pharisees, Sadducees, or Scribes, which I am calling rational Judaism. So early Christianity was heavily influenced by the model of the world and of history that was taken from Zoroastrianism and shaped by the apocalyptic concept of a cosmic conflict between God and the Devil.

Throughout the period when apocalyptic forms of Judaism were taking shape, namely, from the exile in Babylon in the sixth century B.C.E. until the time of Jesus in the first century C.E., there was a great deal of conflict between the various types of the religions of the Jews. The cloistered Essenes of Qumran disagreed vigorously with the Urban Essenes on many points and tended to declare their cousins as people outside the kingdom of God, members of the Devil's band. Both kinds of Essenes looked at all other types of Jewish religion as badly flawed or false religions. Pharisees disagreed with Sadducees, particularly on whether there was a resurrection from the dead. The

entire company of what we might call the Jews of rational religion—
Pharisees, Sadducees, Elders, and Scribes—were vigorously opposed
by most of the rather neurotic hysteric Apocalyptic Jews, who imagined all sorts of supernatural things happening or about to happen in
life and history.

Most of the Apocalyptic Jews expected history to end rather soon
with a catastrophic final battle in the cosmic conflict. Then God
would send the Son of Man on the clouds of heaven with all the holy
angels to wrap up history like a scroll, gather the righteous together
into an eternal place of blessedness with God, and exterminate all the
unrighteous. Michael Knibb declares that in the worldview of this
religion, "We are in a situation where the exile is understood as a
state that is to be ended only by the intervention of God and the
inauguration of the eschatological era."[3] It is clear from the gospels
that the disciples' memory of Jesus depicted him as holding to this
same apocalyptic Essene view. He believed that the end of history
would come in the generation to which he had preached and that it
would come in the form of an apocalyptic eschatological event in
which he would descend from God, as the Son of Man, on the clouds
of heaven, in the glory of the Father, with all the holy angels, to be
the final judge as to who belonged in the company of the holy ones
of the Most High and who belonged with the people of darkness and
unrighteousness (Matt. 16:28, Mark 14:62). Jesus and the Jesus
Movement picked up this kind of ideation from Daniel 7:13, 1 Enoch
37–71, and other literature from what we call today Second Temple
Judaism (300 B.C.E.–300 C.E.).

One of the pervasive characteristics of a great deal of the Enochic
literature of Second Temple Judaism was about the ongoing guerrilla
warfare or the undercurrents of the running battle between the
Apocalyptic Jews on the one hand and the various parties of the
rational forms of Judaism on the other. The latter were the religious
authorities in Jerusalem. These authorities, particularly the
Sadducees, controlled the temple rituals and ancillary programs.
Thus, Second Temple Judaism is an era characterized by a rather continuing expression of hostility toward the temple on the part of the
Apocalyptic Jews, who felt that the priesthood which was in authority there was an impure and false priesthood.[4]

Knibb calls our attention to the fact that 1 Enoch 89:72–73 speaks
negatively of the rebuilding of the temple and the restoration of the
temple ritual in declaring that "they began again to place a table
before the tower, but all the (consecrated) bread on it (was) unclean

and was not pure." It was the claim of the Apocalyptic Jews in general and especially of the cloistered Essene Community at Qumran that the priesthood, the temple, and the holy city of Jerusalem had been rendered impure by the Babylonians and then again by Antiochus Epiphanes. This was the result of the conquest of the land, the entry into the city and the temple by foreigners, the destruction of the city and the temple, and the subsequent establishment of a shrine of himself in the temple by Antiochus Epiphanes. Moreover, the Jerusalem religious authorities and priesthood were seen by the Apocalyptic Jews to be political appointees of the foreign authorities and thus not in conformity with the prescribed temple rituals and rites of ordination for priests and rulers in Israel. This general state of hostility toward the temple and its rituals was widespread in Israelite religions of the Second Temple period.[5]

Jesus as Apocalyptic Jew

It cannot be accidental that when Jesus caught his stride, consolidated the focus of his ministry, and went on the offensive, so to speak, it was for some of the causes of Apocalyptic Judaism that he marched. He seemed to carry on a running conflict with the Pharisees particularly and with the Sadducees, Elders, and Scribes as well. In fact, he regularly went out of his way to pick fights with them when it was completely unnecessary to do so and could easily have been totally avoided.[6] Usually his fights with them were about their strict constructionist legalism in interpreting the Torah, Jewish law, and biblical narrative and about what he and Apocalyptic Jews in general saw as the authorities' arrogant presumption of power over Israelite religion and society. It is not surprising, therefore, that his most focused attack upon the nonapocalyptic forms of Judaism took the shape of an assault on the temple. He violently "cleansed it."

What in the world did Jesus think he was doing? Apparently he entered the temple that Tuesday and went over to the area in the outer court where the merchants were who sold birds and animals for the sacrifices pilgrims wished to make and exchanged money for those from distant places. There Jesus took a weapon and abused the merchants and the creatures they had there, overturned the tables, and poured the merchants' money out of their coffers onto the pavement. Then he accused the merchants of turning the temple from a house of prayer into a den of thieves. Finally, Jesus justified the whole event with the claim that he was consumed by a zeal for God's house and quoted an ancient prophet to that effect (Ps. 69:9).

The gospel of John tells us, probably on the basis of a later attempt to rationalize this ridiculous scene, that Jesus was setting up a case for how he would die and that he would be raised from the dead (John 2:14–22, Mark 11:15–19). That is a phenomenally lame rationalization, particularly when we consider that John's gospel was written three quarters of a century after Jesus' death. Moreover, the presence of the merchants and their chattel in the outer court was provided for in the temple regulations and was designed as a great convenience, a real grace, to the pilgrims who came from long distances, such as from Galilee, to worship and make the annual sacrifices required by the Torah. Those pilgrims did not need to drive their cattle or carry their turtledoves all that long way. They could carry money in their purses and buy the sacrificial animals or doves right at the temple. It was well regulated and incredibly helpful, violated no regulation, and had nothing impious about it. It was simply a part of what Gordon Allport would call extrinsic spirituality, while the reference to Jesus' zeal suggests he would fit into Allport's category of those who prefer intrinsic spirituality.

Allport's notion, based largely on the work of William James, suggested that some people derive great spiritual meaning from the formal and programmatic aspects of religion. This would include enactment of the rituals of worship liturgies and of the projects of ethical and social applications of religious imperatives to daily life. These folk get their meaning out of their relationship with God through such extrinsic functions. Others, according to James and Allport, get all their spiritual meaning out of the intrinsic experience of the inner life of the spirit: meditation, reflection, private prayer, and what the great Roman Catholic tradition of spirituality calls "the practice of the presence of God." The merchants in the temple undoubtedly received a great sense of religious meaningfulness out of their role in providing pilgrims with support for their spiritual services. The pilgrims must have felt an enormous sense of gratitude to the merchants for the convenience, comfort, and relief from burden that the merchants afforded the pilgrims.

Jesus' intrinsic need to disrupt all of this violently, abusively, and sacrilegiously must have been driven by some ulterior motive. Jesus does not seem generally, as portrayed in the gospel, to have been either stupid or crazy, so one must conclude that he understood the picture of the temple situation and practices as painted here. What could have been his ulterior motive? John's gospel indicates that it was a setup to emphasize his death and resurrection. The other gospels, written long before John's, give no hint of this far-fetched notion. Obviously, Jesus considered something about the entire practice of the temple program, however legitimate and in keeping with Torah and subsequent regulations, to be impious, out of keeping with an authentic zeal for God and his house of worship, and formalistically a self-serving enterprise of the "priests and their sycophantic minions" whose spirituality lacked much in purity, authenticity, and integrity.

There seems to be the clue to this scene. Jesus came to the temple with his Essene-like hostility toward the temple, grounded in the conviction that the priesthood currently in charge at the temple was inauthentic, and so the entire enterprise of the temple program and its liturgies was impure, ground and trunk, root and branch. Had he actually marched into the middle of the priestly ministrations and disrupted the actual liturgy, he would have moved the crowd against him immediately; moreover, he would have violated the Torah and the Levitical provisions for the liturgies. The one point at which the temple program was most vulnerable with the least likelihood of turning the crowd against him was in the outer court, far from the sacralized events of the Holy Place and the Holy of Holies. The obvious place to raise some considerable hob without directly violating the priests and the priestly offices was among the merchants and cattle. There he attacked. Mark's gospel (11:18) says the crowd liked this drama, and they also liked his point about intrinsic spirituality being more important than extrinsic spirituality.

Apocalyptic Jews were always talking about the spiritual experiences that were interior, mystical, and transcendent. They were quite sure they knew everything about what was in God's mind, what decisions he had made before creation, what he was up to in creation, and how he continued to be present in the world, fighting evil. They would have thought they knew the degree to which God would have the good sense to be against cows and pigeons in the temple, leaving behind the foul dirt and smells that animals and fowl leave. It is not hard to figure out, incidentally, how this story came to be called the *cleansing* of the temple. However, the narrative seems to say that Jesus just created a mess and then left town, leaving the cleansing to others. This is quite different from the legend of Hercules, who is set upon the labor of cleaning the stables and does a heroic and divinely effective job of it!

The poor animals, in the meantime of course, were chased away from their hay mangers, their watering troughs, and their straw beds out into the wilderness or the Valley of Gehenna, which was the city dump, just outside the wall, right at that corner where the temple stood; and the poor things would then have had to fend for themselves in a rather arid place. Nonetheless, Apocalyptic Jews would have been quite sure that God was interested in inner personal spirituality rather than the outer trappings of religion. We have those kinds of Jews, Christians, and Muslims with us even in our day. They are usually quite sure that the rest of us are just not quite as spiritually authentic as they are. This seems to have been Jesus' attitude that day and also the inclination in the crowd to which he appealed.

Psychological Assessment of Jesus

Donald Capps thinks he has discovered the reason why this is what Jesus was up to. In his very important book *Jesus: A Psychological Biography*, Capps developed a series of insights about Jesus' development as a person that he thinks led to the event of the cleansing of the temple.[7] Capps takes seriously, in terms of psychoanalytic assessments of childhood development, the data in the gospels that would lead us to conclude that Jesus grew up as a fatherless child. His understanding is that Jesus' failure to marry and his failure to establish himself in a profession, matters that a father would take care of for him in a Jewish family, as well as his obvious alienation from his mother and siblings, indicate that he did not find an established place and role within the family of Mary and Joseph. It is clear from the gospels that when Jesus, very late for that day and age, finally found his mission in life at about age 30, his family was sure that he was quite disturbed (John 7:2–5) and came to get him and take him home to protect him from himself in view of the fact that he was proclaiming himself to be the Messiah. Jesus' surprisingly frequent references to the need of true disciples to reject (even hate, Luke 14:26) father and mother in order to devote oneself authentically to God's cause, as well as Jesus' abuse and trivialization of his mother and brothers in the gospels whenever they came to see him (Matt. 12:46–50, Mark 3:31–35, Luke 8:19–21), strengthens Capps' case.

Capps is quite certain that Jesus was born out of wedlock, was seen by his community as a bastard son of an unknown father, was therefore the cause of his mother carrying a defiled reputation, and was not adopted by Joseph. By marrying the girl, Joseph legitimated Mary but not Jesus. Capps describes Jesus as, consequently, of a melancholic disposition, longing for a more perfect world and father affirmation, lacking self-esteem, but possessing surprising charismatic qualities and healing abilities. Having no father of his own,

Jesus projected all ideal parental qualities upon his heavenly father (Abba) and set about to spend and expend his life to do his father's will. This vision was for him both contagious and cathartic, according to Capps, and thus as an adult he came to project an idealized world that he could achieve for God.

This world, in my view, was shaped by the apocalyptic heritage of the Second Temple Judaism which was Jesus' spiritual context in Galilee. He could not have identified himself with and as the Son of Man if he had not ensconced himself solidly in that tradition. The Son of Man was the supreme redemptive figure in that apocalyptic religious worldview. The cleansing of the temple was an attack upon the impurities and inauthenticity that he and all Enochic or Essene Apocalypticists ascribed to the religious authorities and temple functionaries in Jerusalem. It was also, metaphorically, a cleansing of his father's house, restoring it to the integrity it deserved and required. This was a grand symbolic act in which psychotherapeutically and spiritually he was cleansing his mother's reputation; asserting his own legitimacy before the face of God, his father; and achieving rebirth as God's true son.

Cleansing the temple was a cathartic and redemptive act by an Apocalyptic Jew, attacking the religious system toward which his tradition had held three to five centuries of open hostility. In this attack upon the system, which had made him and many others outsiders, which had relegated his mother to an impaired reputation, and which had plagued his entire life with the melancholic need to rectify his world, Jesus, once and for all, established the integrity and legitimacy of his life as an authentic son of his true and heavenly father.

John W. Miller has a different take on this. In his book *Jesus at Thirty: A Psychological and Historical Portrait,* Miller asserts that the genealogies in Matthew 1:1–17 and Luke 3:23–38, Paul's ignorance of any virgin birth, and the testimony of early witnesses outside the Bible prove that Jesus was, in fact, Joseph's son and that the virgin-birth story is a late fabrication.[8] Jesus is presented by Miller as a balanced personality who, as he matured, was increasingly challenged by a transcendent vision of divine calling to preach the onset of God's kingdom, the reign of God's love and grace, in the world, which usually saw God as a threat and life's purpose as that of keeping to a rather oppressive legalistic code rather than a life of freedom in God's forgiveness.

As in Capps' view, Miller's explanation of Jesus' cleansing the temple arises out of an assessment of Jesus' personal development, for which the evidence is, admittedly, scarce. In a critique of Capps' work, Miller observes as follows:

> Perhaps Capps' various psychological explanations are less compelling for me because we hold differing perspectives on the importance of the role human fathers play in the internalization of social and religious images and values, especially during the oedipal years, from three to six. Capps makes much of Jesus' troublesome primal relation to his mother but has little to say about the negative emotional impact of his father(s). Indeed, he states that Jesus' lack of experiences with paternal love made it easier for him to project "all good parental qualities onto "Abba" (Capps, 2000, 182). Capps' portrait of Jesus is thus one of a deeply troubled man with a diffused identity, bereft of any caring human fathers, struggling to create, *ex nihilo*, an internalized spiritual father he never had, yet for whom he longed.[9]

Miller's view is that Jesus must have had a relatively healthful development rather than a disturbed and pathogenic one in order to "become the strong and compelling center of a movement whose distinguishing feature was a luminous faith in God as caring, gracious father."[10] What was Jesus up to, then, in his violence in the temple? Miller believes the story is to be taken in a straightforward way and understood as Jesus' expressed wish that the temple would become a center of pilgrimage for believers, proselytes to Judaism, from all nations of the world. He sees this way of presenting the story as reinforcing Jesus' notion of the divine kingdom coming in which people from the East and West, North and South, shall come and sit down with Abraham, Isaac, and Jacob, as Jesus envisioned in Matthew 8:11 and Luke 13:29. The difficulty with Miller's interpretation is that it does not explain Jesus' need to chase cattle, release birds, overturn money tables, annoy legitimate assistants to the temple program, and attack the temple itself. Why the violence? Why not a forthright call to faith and universal salvation, delivered in his apparently normal engaging rhetoric and attractive teaching style? There is more here than a great vision of a grand future in God's coming kingdom (Miller, 1997, 89–90).

Let us return briefly to Knibb's article, which is of some considerable help in explaining further for us the cultural backdrop of the long-standing hostility to the temple and toward the Jerusalem priesthood, pervasive in the literature of that religious heritage out of which came the Jesus Movement and evident in Jesus' behavior as well.

Knibb's article makes it quite clear to me that Jesus was identifying heavily with the historic and long-standing antipathy of Apocalyptic Jews to what I have called the rational forms of the Judaism of that era. Knibb points out that in the worldview of Apocalyptic Judaism, particularly that evident in the Enoch literature, the period from the beginning of the exile in 586 B.C.E. to the time of Antiochus Epiphanes, indeed to the divine intervention that would establish God's kingdom on earth, was a period characterized by sin (Knibb, 1976, 255, 257).

This perspective arose from the conviction that the exile had been a result of Israel's perversity. The foreign violation of the holy city and temple, its destruction, and the reestablishment of the temple, its ritual, and its priesthood under the wrong people rendered the sacral system defiled. Thus the priesthood was impure and the liturgies of the temple inauthentic. The Apocalyptic Jews believed that the eyes of the sheep (Israelites) were blinded, as well as those of their shepherds (the Jerusalem priests). Only divine intervention, inaugurating the era of the end time of history, could redeem this tragic state of affairs in Israel. A great deal of the religious literature which would have shaped the developing life of Jesus, as a child and young man in Galilee, would have repeatedly hammered home to him this antipathy to the priests and temple in Judea.[11]

The Testament of the Twelve Patriarchs, 1 Enoch, Jeremiah 24 and 29, numerous passages in Ezekiel, references in Daniel, the Damascus Document (Charlesworth, 1983), and especially the literature of the people of the Dead Sea Scrolls express antitemple sentiment. Jesus certainly would have been familiar with some of these documents. He seems to have been familiar with the biblical prophets such as Jeremiah, Ezekiel, and Daniel. From his acquaintance with John the Baptist, his cousin, he would have had an inside knowledge of the Essenes, maybe even of the people of Qumran. These people of the Dead Sea Scrolls were violently opposed to the priests and temple ritual of Jerusalem and had cloistered themselves in the desert, away from Jerusalem, for this specific reason.[12]

The Violent Jesus

Thus, we are forced to conclude that Jesus' violence in the temple was simply an expression of the worldview he had developed over his life time of identification with the various forms of Apocalyptic Judaism, all part of the theological strata of Galilee in his time. Surely, it was this worldview that prompted his initial identification with the movement of John the Baptist and his eventual move beyond John into a remarkable identification with the Son of Man, a metaphoric figure dominating much of the literature of Apocalyptic Judaism. Jesus seems initially to have seen himself as carrying out the work of the Son of Man by preaching the kingdom of God on earth. Eventually, he came to identify himself increasingly as the Son of Man, a messianic figure. By the end of his life, according the narrative of the gospels, he had coalesced the Jewish notion of God's suffering servant with the figure of the Son of Man, whom God would exalt to heaven and send back at the end of time as the eschatological judge of all the earth. This same coalescence had been achieved, interestingly, by the messianic figure at Qumran. This is another indication of Jesus' possible association with or at least awareness of the Essene perspective and even that especially conservative one among the people of the Dead Sea Scrolls.

It seems clear that by the time Jesus stood trial before the Sanhedrin and before Pilate, at the end of his life, he had so thoroughly identified himself with and as the Son of Man that he had actually moved out of the reality of his daily life on earth and had moved into the literary role of Son of Man in the cosmic drama, having lost all poetic distance between his real earthly person and the transcendental role in the literary drama. Thus, he could say to Pilate and to the Sanhedrin that he would soon return, to their great surprise, as the Son of Man on the clouds of heaven, in the glory of God, with a host of holy angels.

It is in this context that we must see the meaning of Jesus' violence in the temple. He had lost all patience with and orientation on the processes of Israel's religious life on this earth as in any legitimate way representative of God's coming kingdom. His mission effort in sending out the disciples two by two had failed. The 70 sent out returned to report failure. The Galileans were interested in him only because he did miracles and not because of his kingdom vision. When he disagreed with their notion of the Messiah, they tried to kill him (John 8:48). The crowds had deserted him to the extent that he wondered if the 12 disciples would as well (Mark 8). The Palm Sunday crowd had completely missed the point of his mission. The disciples still did not understand what he was up to (John 14:1–11). In short, his earthly enterprise was a total failure.

Thus, the model of Jesus' peculiar reality comes clear. He had lived a lifetime in the apocalyptic undercurrent of hostility toward the temple, the priesthood, and the religious authorities in Jerusalem. He had

endeavored for three years of ministry to insinuate a renewed spiritual vitality into the bloodstream of the Judaisms of his time. He had
worked hard to create a vision of God's reign in the world that
embodied grace, mercy, and peace for Jews, Greeks, Romans,
Samaritans, Syrophoenicians, and every other kind of folk. He had
cared about and declared God's forgiveness and embrace of the righteous and the unrighteous equally. He had been a radical friend of the
despised and the sinful. The entire enterprise had failed, and he saw
himself on a lethal course of hopeless conflict with the still-
prospering religious and political authorities.

He walked into the temple for the third time in three days, trying
to find a place of tranquillity in which to pray and an audience with
whom he could discuss the coming kingdom of God. All he could see
was the hated priests in their formalistic rituals. All he could hear was
the bawling of the cattle. All he could smell was the odors of the stable. All he could think was how everything was going to hell. He
cracked. He picked up a riding crop or bullwhip and started to abuse
those most available, expending his long-anguished anger, his weari-
ness with the spiritual mediocrity of human life, and his obsessive
need to feel the power of his delusional vision of the triumphal Son of
Man realized in the here and now.

It was a straight line from that Tuesday to Good Friday and Black
Saturday. The net result was that Judas dissociated himself from
Jesus, betrayed him, and committed suicide; the Sanhedrin and the
Romans colluded to crucify him. Joseph of Aramathea lent his tomb.
The 11 remaining disciples hid in an upper room "for fear of the Jews"
(John 20:19). Two friends on the way to Emmaus despaired that this
was a great tragedy because they "thought it was he who was to
redeem Israel" (Luke 24:21). Well, that was not the end. There were
a lot of reports that he was seen again thereafter. It took about a half
century for those reports to settle down into a coherent story, of
course, but in the end those reports made all the difference in the
world.

Jesus' Violent Church

What is overlooked in all this, however, is the underside of the
effect of the cleansing of the temple on Christians in the later centuries. This story was glorified quite early, as is indicated by the
report of it in Mark's gospel, the first to be written, appearing on the
scene about 40 years after Jesus' death. The story of the violence in
the temple, setting in motion the events leading to an impasse with

the religious authorities which caused his death, became the heart of the memory for at least the first half century of the Jesus Movement and the early life of the church. The Jesus of this story came very quickly to be celebrated as the sacrificial Christ. Strong emphasis was placed on his promise that no one would take his life from him, but he would lay it down himself (John 10:18). Thus, the heroic qualities of Jesus were celebrated for a variety of reasons in a variety of ways. One of the aspects of their memory of him that was glorified was the implicit suicide in his role as suffering servant, later to be interpreted as the sacrifice that redeems the world (Heb. 10).

As the church ran into sieges of persecution under Nero, Diocletian, and other Roman emperors, the sequence of events from Jesus' cleansing of the temple to his death on the cross, as intentional laying down of his life, was emulated in the martyrdom of countless Christians. But there were two sides to that memory. While the church was in a position of extreme vulnerability (most of the first three centuries), the suicidal model of martyrdom seems to have held prominence. However, when the church achieved the role of a powerful institution, particularly when it was baptized as the Queen of the Empire by Constantine in the second decade of the fourth century C.E., its memory of this last stage of Jesus' life shifted 180 degrees. Its memory became dominated by the model of the violence in the temple. So the church undertook to cleanse the world, God's temple of creation and culture, of all unbelief, non-Christian belief, unorthodox belief, and heresy.

One need only observe how Bishop Ambrose of Milan used his power to intimidate the emperor into submission to the bishop's insistence on violently exterminating all places of non-Christian worship in his region of Italy. One can note, further, how Cyril of Alexandria made Ambrose's fratricide look like kindergarten stuff as he proceeded to assail the Gnostics, Neoplatonists, and the constituencies of his fellow bishops who disagreed with him on fine points of theology or church politics. He had the famed Hypatia murdered viciously on the streets of Alexandria and dragged into the sanctuary of the church where the monks sliced her flesh from her bones while life was still quivering in it and set fire to her remains. When Cyril died, a fellow bishop, Theodoret, wrote of him, "His death made those who survived him joyful, but it grieved most probably the dead; and there is cause to fear lest, finding him too troublesome, they should send him back to us."[13]

Cleansing the temple became a Christian way of life from about the middle of the third century until well into the decrepitude of the Middle Ages. At first it was enormous violence to cleanse the world of pagans, then it was to cleanse the world of Christians who had a different idea than those in power, then it was cleansing the world of Jews. In every case the cleansing tended to be on a scale that approached genocide. The Christian Emperor Heraclius would certainly have exterminated the entire Egyptian (Coptic) Christian Church in the seventh century if the Muslims had not invaded Egypt and saved the Coptic Christians and their church from extermination by their Christian "brothers."

By the eleventh century it became the crusade of the European Christians to the Holy Lands "to deliver the holy places from the infidel Turks." However, before the crusaders got well on their way to the Holy Land, they attempted to cleanse Europe of the Jews one more time.[14] On the way to the Holy Land, they undertook to cleanse the world of Eastern Orthodox Christians who just happened to be politically and theologically at odds with the crusading Roman Catholics. In the sack of Constantinople, as everyone knows, the crusaders killed mostly fellow Christians. Apparently the temple must be cleansed at all costs in Christian tradition! Was that not Christ's way? Obsessive fits of incongruous violence!

Conclusion

In our attempts to understand the nature of religious dynamics in human life, too little attention has been given to the manner in which the narratives of our sacred scriptures and the metaphors they generate shape our unconscious motives and goals. Many memorable passages from sacred texts of all religions have been celebrated for centuries as depicting heroic or redemptive actions of God or God's prophets in history. At the same time, on the unconscious level at which psychological archetypes are formed, these very texts sow seeds causing and justifying the worst kinds of evil. Religious motives and values, conscious and unconscious, shape the psychological, social, and spiritual forces of personal formation and culture building in human society. Even in secularized societies, those ancient memories of religious metaphors still determine who we are by reigning undisturbed in our collective unconscious.

One of those metaphors which continues to do more harm than good is that of Jesus' cleansing of the temple. We should start to demystify it by calling it by its right name: Jesus' violence in the temple. Called by their right names, even the worst things can be managed more reasonably and responsibly. Religious enthusiasts of all three Western religions that derive from ancient Israelite biblical narrative—Judaism, Christianity, and Islam—have been busy for at least a millennium and a half cleansing God's temple. That is what the terrorists attempted on September 11, 2001. By their own testimony and the creed of al Qaeda, they wished to enact a devastating blow against the evil of secularized and non-Muslim America. They were cleansing this world, God's temple.

However, taking the long view, Christians have been far more devastating at this kind of mayhem than anyone else. In the present Islam-inflicted danger and pain in the Western world, decency and rationality will probably be better maintained if the dominant Christian and secularized "Christian" societies remind ourselves that the terrorists of the present moment have no mortgage on these terrible things. Moreover, the worst of it for us is that we have at the center of our unconscious and of our worldview this idealized picture of our nasty addiction to cleansing the temple. What makes us think that God wants his temple so sanitized? If we look at creation, it looks like God gets on rather well with randomness and profligate generosity. Is it possible that he is hung a lot looser than we are? His remarkable notion of grace at the center would suggest that he is.

This third volume of *The Destructive Power of Religion* treats models and cases. I have opened our dialogue with a crucial model and case that lies at the root of who we are in the Western world today. Eleven brilliant authors have joined me in developing our address to a variety of other models and cases. They represent a wide range of perspectives and emphases. I am sure you will find this volume to be of great interest and value.

Notes

1. Mark 11:15–19, Matthew 21:12–13, Luke 19:45–46, and John 2:13–17. Though Matthew and Luke are quite clearly copying Mark's gospel in this story and John's gospel has a different presentation, none of the four gospels agree on exactly what the days and the sequence of Holy Week events were, namely, Jesus' triumphal entry into Jerusalem, the healing of the blind son of Timaeus (Mark 10: 46–52, Luke 18:35–43) or of the two blind men (Matt. 20:29–34), the cursing of the fig tree, the various visits to the temple, and

the cleansing of the temple. The scenario created here is mainly for narrative effect and to present the best guesses regarding what the sequence might have been of the events and days in Holy Week when they took place. The point I wish to make in the presentation in this chapter is that the history of Christian interpretation of this event, which negativizes Judaism to glorify Jesus, is wide of the mark. Those who care about truth rather than religious propaganda should take note.

2. See also Jesus' fits of inappropriate response to people in John 2:3–4, Mark 8:27–33, John 9:1–34, and Mark 3:33.

3. Michael Knibb, "The Exile in the Literature of the Intertestamental Period," *The Heythrop Journal* 17, no. 3 (1976): 255.

4. See David W. Suter, "Fallen Angel, Fallen Priest: The Problem of Family Purity in I Enoch 6–16," *HUCA* 50 (1979): 115–135. See also Gabriele Boccaccini, ed., *The Origins of Enochic Judaism: The Proceedings of the First Enoch Seminar, Henoch*, vol. 24, no. 1–2 (Turin: Silvio Zamorani editore, 2002).

5. See Suter, "Revisiting 'Fallen Angel, Fallen Priest,' " in Boccaccini, *The Origins of Enochic Judaism*, 137–142.

6. John 9 is the story of a blind man healed by Jesus on the Sabbath, a thing forbidden by the Torah, as interpreted by the Pharisees. Jesus could have healed the man on Tuesday if he cared primarily about the man. Obviously, Jesus cared less about the man, who gets significantly abused by this entire sequence of events, though he is, of course, healed of his blindness. Jesus cared more about pitching a fight with the Pharisees at the blind man's expense. The poor fellow is thrown out of the community and out of Judaism as a consequence of Jesus' self-aggrandizing actions.

7. Donald Capps, *Jesus: A Psychological Biography* (St. Louis: Chalice Press, 2000). See also J. Harold Ellens, ed., *Pastoral Psychology* 50, no. 6 (July 2002), particularly Ellens' chapter, 401–407.

8. John W. Miller, *Jesus at Thirty: A Psychological and Historical Portrait* (Minneapolis: Fortress, 1997).

9. John W. Miller, "Review of Jesus," in Ellens, *Pastoral Psychology*, p. 413.

10. Ibid.

11. See James H. Charlesworth, ed., *The Old Testament Pseudepigrapha*, vols. 1 and 2 (New York: Doubleday, 1983).

12. See Gabriele Boccaccini, *Beyond the Essene Hypothesis: The Parting of the Ways between Qumran and Enochic Judaism* (Grand Rapids: Eerdmans, 1998), and *Roots of Rabbinic Judaism: An Intellectual History, from Ezekiel to Daniel* (Grand Rapids: Eerdmans, 2002).

13. Charles Kingsley, *The Works of Charles Kingsley*, 2 vols. (New York: Cooperative Publishing Society, 1899).

14. See Alfred J. Eppens, "The Crusade Pogroms," in *The Destructive Power of Religion*, J. Harold Ellens, ed., vol. 4 (Westport: Praeger, 2004), chap. 2.

References

Boccaccini, G. (1998). *Beyond the Essene hypothesis: The parting of the ways between Qumran and Enochic Judaism.* Grand Rapids: Eerdmans.

Boccaccini, G. (2002a). *Roots of Rabbinic Judaism: An intellectual history, from Ezekiel to Daniel.* Grand Rapids: Eerdmans.

Boccaccini, G. (2002b). (Ed.). *The origins of Enochic Judaism: The proceedings of the First Enoch Seminar. Henoch, 24* (1–2). Turin: Silvio Zamorani editore.

Capps, D. (2000). *Jesus: A psychological biography.* St. Louis: Chalice Press.

Charlesworth, J. H. (Ed.). *The Old Testament Pseudepigrapha.* Vols. 1 and 2. New York: Doubleday, 1983.

Ellens, J. H. (Ed.). (2002). *Pastoral Psychology, 50* (6).

Eppens, A. (2004). The Crusade pogroms. In J. H. Ellens (Ed.), *The destructive power of religion:* Vol. 4. Westport: Praeger, 2004.

Kingsley, C. (1899). *The works of Charles Kingsley (Vols. 1–2).* New York: Cooperative Publishing Society.

Knibb, M. A. (1976). The exile in the literature of the Intertestamental Period. *The Heythrop Journal 17* (3), 253–272.

Miller, J. W. (1997). *Jesus at thirty: A psychological and historical portrait.* Minneapolis: Fortress.

Miller, J. W. (2002). Review of Jesus. *Pastoral Psychology 50* (6), 409–414.

Suter, D. W. (1979). Fallen angel, fallen priest: The problem of family purity in I Enoch 6–16. *HUCA,* 50, 115–135.

Suter, D. W. (2002). Revisiting "Fallen angel, fallen priest." In G. Boccaccini (Ed.), *The origins of Enochic Judaism: The proceedings of the First Enoch Seminar. Henoch, 24* (1–2). Turin: Silvio Zamorani editore.

CHAPTER 3

JIHAD IN THE QUR'AN, THEN AND NOW

J. Harold Ellens

The Islamic concept of jihad is popularly assumed to mean "holy war." That is a very rough and inadequate understanding of the term. It is neither restricted to military operations nor particularly sacred. It may be political, economic, or cultural pressure applied toward Islamic domination of any sphere of influence, or it may be resistance to any non-Islamic forces that are contesting that power or hegemony. It may be social, psychological, or spiritual striving to a desired ideal end. It may refer as much to intellectual pursuits as to armed campaigns. Jihad is as much the struggle of the inner person against undesirable personality traits within as an outer struggle for legitimate or illegitimate achievement. Jihad may range widely from an intrinsic spiritual quest for personal sanctification to an extrinsic material quest for successful aggression on a battlefield. Jihad is both mysterious and highly complex.

When Osama bin Laden and his four radical Islamic colleagues issued their *fatwa* against the Western world, particularly against the United States of America, in February 1998, he was commanding the Muslim world and every individual in it to rise to the mandate of jihad specified in the Qur'an, the sacred scriptures of Islam. However, he and his colleagues insisted upon interpreting jihad as violent militant aggression. The *fatwa* was spelled out as a clear and unequivocal public policy statement for the forces of Islam. It declared,

Osama bin Laden seen in this April 1998
picture in Afghanistan. AP/Wide World
Photos.

In compliance with God's order, we issue the following fatwa to all
Muslims: the ruling to kill the Americans and their allies—civilians
and military—is an individual duty for every Muslim who can do it in
any country in which it is possible to do it, in order to liberate the al-
Aqsa Mosque (Jerusalem) and the holy mosque (Mecca) from their grip,
and in order for their armies to move out of the lands of Islam . . . , this
is in accordance with the words of Almighty God, "and fight the
pagans all together as they fight you all together," and "fight them
until there is no more tumult or oppression, and there prevail justice
and faith in God. (Johnson, 2002, 12)

Osama bin Laden renewed his call to terrorist war upon Americans
on February 10, 2003, calling Saddam Hussein and his Ba'ath Party
"a nest of infidels" but declaring common cause with them "against
the Crusaders" (the United States and Israel). It must be clear for all
humanity to see that these men of mean and meager minds mean
business. They really believe that their dogmatic view of God and

God's world is the only true way of looking at things and that all those who fail to hold to their view are not merely of a different opinion in an interesting theological dialogue. They believe that all those of other outlooks and other religions are a serious threat to, and alien from, God and his holy ways for humanity. Therefore, all persons who disagree with bin Laden's Muslim Fundamentalist view of things must be exterminated, together with their philosophies and faiths and the cultures they create.

In this case, then, jihad stands for a broadside assault upon every facet of the world of Western people, cultures, and sociopolitical systems. Those five men and their radical Islamic groups clearly intend that it is necessary and desirable to resort to armed aggression against the United States. Is it possible that this really is what the Qur'an, that Muslim holy book, really means for them to do? Are they bad theologians, or is that a bad book?

Exposition

Jihad

In the introduction to his very instructive volume *The Sword of the Prophet*, Serge Trifkovic (2002) crisply states, "The tragedy of September 11, 2001, and its aftermath have shown, yet again, that *beliefs have consequences:* the centrality of Islam to the attacks is impossible to deny" (7). His subtitle explains his book more fully. It invites us to expect *Islam History, Theology, Impact on the World,* and he contends that cultural leaders of the West still deny that the Trade Center tragedy is the kind of thing that is inherent to Islam, not merely the aberrant behavior of a band of terrorists. He sees this Western fuzzy thinking as dangerously erroneous. It invites greater vulnerability and greater violence.

To what extent may Trifkovic be correct? Is Islam inherently violent? Does the Qur'an teach primarily a violent and military or at least physically militant form of jihad? During the golden age of Muslim political hegemony in the Mediterranean and the Near East, from the Atlantic Ocean to the borders of India, Islam was mainly a powerful influence for the development of a relatively congenial culture. Its treatment of other religious communities was surprisingly ecumenical. The Jews did better under that Muslim rule than they have most any other time in history, certainly better than they ever did under Christianity. Of course, this was a time when Islam held undisputed power and could afford to be gracious and nondefensive.

Most of the populations it had rather ruthlessly conquered converted to Islam.

One might argue that there were really two golden ages of Muslim rule in the Mediterranean basin and eastward. The first witnessed the spread of Islam soon after the death of the prophet Muhammad. Within two generations Islam had conquered its world and imposed a Muslim peace that made for remarkable development in scholarship. Universities and libraries sprang up. Science, literary studies, and medicine flourished. The literature and science of the ancient Greeks, Romans, and Persians were preserved, analyzed, and richly interpreted. The critique and analysis of the Qur'an became a discipline in its own right. Theological studies burgeoned in this rich culture. Throughout its domain, particularly in Spain, Mesopotamia (Iraq and Iran), and Asia Minor (Turkey), Islam produced a more magnificent fruiting of wisdom and beauty in philosophy, science, aesthetics, the arts, and law than any other culture in the world at that time, except perhaps China. The second golden age was during the Ottoman Empire when something of this same cultural vigor manifest itself again.

So what is the real Islam? Is it the vicious violence of Osama bin Laden's jihad, or is it the culture-building vigor of the golden ages of Muslim power? It is usually true, of course, that when a culture or religious community perceives itself inadequate, unempowered, or under siege, it tends to be more vicious. When it is empowered, it can afford to be more gentle and gracious. The ancient Israelites were, apparently, a wandering band of Bedouin wilderness dwellers when they launched their biblically celebrated attack upon the Canaanite civilizations that inhabited Palestine. It is not surprising, therefore, that the Israelites perceived their power to achieve their arbitrarily acquisitive destiny to be somewhat questionable. They set themselves to steal the land that belonged to the Canaanites, with no better excuse than that they had a thousand-year-old legend that the land had been promised by God to their mistily remembered ancestor, Abraham. Since they were not sure of their birthright or their power, inexperienced as they were in military campaigning, they resorted rather quickly to a policy of vicious violence and genocide. This is as typical of the defensive aggressive behavior of threatened persons and groups as the evil method of Osama bin Laden today. There is no difference.

When Christianity came to power in the empire of Constantine, it proceeded almost immediately to viciously repress all non-Christians and all Christians who did not line up with official Orthodox ideology, policy, and practices. Thus, it consolidated its power and could afford to be somewhat more gracious for a few centuries. When it again felt jeopardized by the pressures of advancing Islam, in the late Middle Ages, it resorted to the violence of the mindless crusades against Muslims, Christians who did not adhere to the Western Roman Rite, and Jews in Europe and the Mediterranean basin.

Now we see a relatively unempowered but militant Fundamentalist Islam rising everywhere against Western Culture because of a belief that Islam is the only pure word and will of God and that it is in lethal spiritual jeopardy from the cultural dominance of the American presence in all spheres of life. Because of its sense of inferiority in power and its sense of arrogant superiority in spiritual and religious quality, this militant form of Islam feels thoroughly justified in resorting to the most vicious forms of violent assault on its identified enemy. America is the perceived source and center of its problems.

Moreover, because of the avaricious undercurrents of long-standing jealous antipathy toward the United States in France and Germany, the Islamic terrorists were aided and abetted in their cause. That European anti-Americanism clearly assured the terrorists that they could build their cells of horror in, and launch their assault upon, the United States from northern Europe, particularly Germany. The terrorists had every assurance from the cultural attitudes in France and Germany that when they launched their assault, they could count on European and perhaps world opinion to support them against the Americans. They may have slightly miscalculated there, but not by much. Each day makes it clearer how fickle French policy continues to be and how worthless is the word or commitment of either France or Germany on this matter of discerning the seriousness of the intentions and methods of Fundamentalist Islam.

Jihad in the Qur'an

The concept of jihad and its implications for fighting and for striving are present in approximately 150 major passages in the Qur'an. In most of these passages, jihad means human striving to do God's will. The phrase "striving in the way of God" appears so frequently throughout the Qur'an as to have the character of a slogan or proverbial expression. That constructive phrase appears numerous times in virtually every Surah (chapter). The notion of love appears only 10 notable times in the Qur'an, six regarding God's love and just four regarding human behavior. However, the notion of hospitality to strangers, care of the impaired or needy, and forgiveness of those who turn to God's ways may be noted almost everywhere in the Qur'an. In the Christian scriptures and the Hebrew Bible, the picture is somewhat different. References to charity for the poor and needy, the stranger, and those who are suffering is, of course, everywhere in the Bible. However, the word *love* appears in each testament about 300 times, a total of 600 instances. *Striving* is referred to in the Bible about 40 times, 26 in the Hebrew Bible, and 13 in the New Testament. Of course, the specific concept of jihad is not emphasized in the Bible, though the notion of fighting for Yahweh is a concept that appears in the Hebrew Bible about 14 times.

Of course, scholars of all sacred scriptures have long ago set aside word counts as a significant basis for critical analysis of texts. Just because a word or concept appear with a certain frequency does not inherently have any significance; that is, it does not tell us anything about the meaning or function of that word or concept in shaping the message, import, or impact of the sacred scriptures as a whole. Nor does it say anything about the way in which that word or concept functioned in the culture from which the sacred scripture came. I present this comparison only as an interesting formal way of entering into a more penetrating analysis of jihad in the Qur'an. What does the Qur'an intend us to understand by this term, which proves rather crucial in the history and present operation of Muslim culture?

The Qur'an gives the following instructions regarding jihad. These are passages in which the word itself appears in the Arabic language of the original book.[1] Surah 2:218 enjoins us with words that might have come from Judaism or Christianity as well. "Certainly believers who . . . labor with great vigor and diligence in God's way hope for God's mercy, and God is forgiving and merciful." Similarly, Surah 3:142 and 146, as well as 5:54, promise that God knows and remembers the diligent (striving) and patient ones who follow his way, and amply gives his grace to them. In Surah 25:52, Muhammad counsels, "Do not go along with unbelievers. Strive against them with great vigor." In Surah 28:15, Muhammad relates the story from Exodus 2:11–14 in which Moses finds an Egyptian and an Israelite fighting (striving against each other), and he kills the Egyptian. Surah 29:69 promises, "Those who strive vigorously for God and his prophet, we will surely direct along our path, for God is certainly present in those who behave properly." Surah 60:1 continues this thought, as does that entire Surah. It is a series of commandments about respecting those who do not make war upon you for your religion and striving against

Indonesian Muslim protesters shouting "Jihad" (Holy War) and "Allahu Akbar" (God is great). AP/Wide World Photos.

and refusing negotiation with those who make war against you because of your religion. In the first verse we read, "O you believers! Do not take my enemy and yours as a friend. Would you love them while they deny the truth given to you, driving you out as well as the Apostle, because of your faith in God, your Lord? If you strive vigorously in my way, desiring what I desire, is it possible for you to befriend them? I know what you are hiding and what you admit to. Those among you who do this have certainly departed from the proper road."

It is easy to see that in these places in the Qur'an where the word *jihad* itself specifically appears, the general meaning is that of working urgently for a certain godly objective, generally a positive one. It may be working to do the will of God or working to prevent evil from happening to you or others. In Surah 61:11 the same theme continues to sound: "Believe in God and his prophet, and strive vigorously in God's way, both with regard to your lives and your possessions. Surely you know that this is the best advantage for you."

It seems clear to me that when one focuses specifically upon the word itself, *jihad* intends to convey a message from God, through the prophet Muhammad, that calls people to expend a great deal of energy in trying to establish an order and economy upon the earth and in the communities of humankind that reflect the will of God. Surely, 90 percent of the references to *jihad* as "striving" refer to this constructive work to build the reign of God's will in the world. It can easily be seen why this was interpreted in the times and places of congenial Islamic graciousness as a call from God to work diligently against the evil impulses in ourselves and, by extension, to do the same in human society. This differs very little or not at all from the biblical injunctions to create a society of godliness and love, a world in which the reign of God's grace and acceptance is the overriding force. It is surely a reflection of the same sense we find in the New Testament, of God's ambition to establish the "kingdom of God" in this world through the devoted efforts of those who believe in the central importance of God's will and way for humanity.

The influence of this interpretation of these concepts in the Qur'an inspired powerful forces for intellectual and aesthetic culture building, enhancing and expressing the finest aspects of the life of the material, mental, and spiritual nature of humanness. It is impossible to savor the flavor of the eras of high Islamic culture without being sure of the power of this underlying and inner force of spiritual vision, driving the creativity of the spirit which was fulminating, flourishing, and burgeoning everywhere in the domain of Islam in those grace-filled times. It is a stunning disappointment and apparently horrendous tragedy, then, to find the wretched interpretations imposed on the concept of jihad by the fanatics of our day. Where do they get this insanity? Why do they believe so strongly that their interpretation of jihad is correct? Are they imposing a foreign and spiritually alien content upon this constructive and creative idea? How can jihad mean, for one Muslim or Islamic age, the inner personal quest for spiritual sanctification and, for another, the twenty-first-century Osama bin Laden and his al Qaeda, a crusade of terror to exterminate Americans wherever they can be found?

Unfortunately, the answer to these questions can also be found in the Qur'an, and that is undoubtedly where Osama bin Laden found it. Surah 66:9 is more aggressive against a specific human enemy than the previously cited passages. It declares, "O prophet! Strive vigorously against the infidels and those who are inauthentic in their faith, and be very aggressive against them. Hell is where they are at home, and their strategies are evil." This Surah may be interpreted in the light of other, more extensive passages, distributed rather profusely throughout the Qur'an, that call for militant and lethal action against those who believe differently than a literalist and Fundamentalist Muslim.

We need only turn to the beginning of the Qur'an, to Surah 2:190–193 and 244. The potential motives and horrors of terrorism are spelled out in detail:

> Fight against your adversaries with God's methods and strategies. Do not be excessive. God certainly does not love those who are abusive. Nonetheless, kill them wherever they can be found, take from them whatever territory they have taken from you. Torture is worse than extermination (take no prisoners). Do not fight them near the Holy Mosque unless they fight you inside it. If they do that, kill them all. They are infidels and they have it coming to them. If they stop fighting, God is forgiving and merciful. So fight them until the persecution is finished. Only the true religion of God should exist, but if the infidels quit fighting, there should be no more hostility, except to those who may continue the oppression.

Later in the same Surah, 216–217, a similar aggressive call in the name of Islam is articulated. It says that believers may not like fighting and bloodshed but that it is their duty anyway. Sometimes what we do not like is good for us. The infidels will try to turn believers from the faith, but infidels and backsliders alike deserve the fires of hell. Surah 9 is the prophet's call of Muslims to the jihad of war with those who revile Islam or promote contrary values, emphasizing that treaties and oaths between them and Muslims should be broken with impunity for the specific reason that such infidels are inferior beings. The Surah draws toward its close with the injunction of verse 123: "Believers, fight the unbelievers to whom you have access, be hard on them, knowing that God supports those who thwart evil."

Surah 48:16 seems particularly applicable to the present moment in history and is probably one of the sacred scriptures which has directly inspired Osama bin Laden and his al Qaeda minions. It declares, "Shortly you will have the opportunity to make war against an immensely powerful nation. You will continue the war until they give up. God will bless you greatly. If you relent or fail to follow through, as you failed in the past, God will inflict intense suffering upon you."

The obverse of this same coin, of course, is the reward that the Qur'an promises those who perform jihad, either inner spiritual struggle against the evil within or outer militant violence against the evil of the infidels "out there." Surah 4:74 states, "May the faithful fight for God's cause. If they forfeit their lives for the life to come, if they have fought the good fight in God's cause, God will give them an amazing reward." In 4:94c, "God shall bless those who strive a level of blessing far beyond that of those who hesitate."

Jihad Today

It is of great import for the contemporary understanding of jihad in Muslim communities that Muhammad called for a jihad, as war, very soon after he established his religious community. Initially his movement was rejected in Mecca. Efforts were made to exterminate his community altogether. His call to war raised a host of horsemen who counterattacked the forces of the established authorities and gained the victory, establishing Islamic hegemony throughout the immediate area in Arabia and within half a century throughout the Near East. This jihad that Muhammad himself incited proved to be a vicious and violent war, no quarter given or taken, and resulted in enormous slaughter. Muhammad exalted this endeavor as an act of God and promised all who were to die in this war a direct ascent to a heaven of the most delightful blessedness.

This historical precedent is of great import for today because it set the model, from the outset, for how jihad would be interpreted from that point on throughout Islamic history. Whereas in the Qur'an, jihad as warfare is the rare exception, in Muhammad's own practice and in Islamic images and strategies for jihad ever since, that model is never very far from the surface of consciousness. The prophet's precedent prevails over his preachments, as is usually the case in human society. Behavior speaks so loudly that verbal messages can hardly be heard!

Surely, al Qaeda's application of Surah 48:16 to the contemporary world situation is the result of their seeing its call for jihad through the lens of Muhammad's early model. Instead of jihad as warfare being the exception to the rule, as it is in the Qur'an, it tends today to function as the rule itself, appealing to the inherent human instincts for survival—instincts which move quickly to violence whenever psychological paranoia or material extremity create the impression of great danger. In the case of Osama bin Laden and his terrorist henchmen, it seems clear that the problem is *both* their psychopathological paranoia and their real perception that their power is limited by the other forces in their world, the governments or royal families of the Arab nations, and the formidable presence of the United States.

Trifkovic (2002) observes that "Islam is . . . a detailed legal and political set of teachings and beliefs. . . . To whatever political entity a Muslim believer may belong—to the Arab world of North Africa and the Middle East, to the nation-states of Iran or Central Asia, to the hybrid entities of Pakistan and Indonesia, to the international protectorates of Bosnia and Kosovo, or to the liberal democracies of the West—he is first and foremost the citizen of Islam, and belongs morally, spiritually, and intellectually, and in principle totally, to the world of belief of which Muhammad is the Prophet, and Mecca is the capital" (7). This would be all the more true of the Fundamentalist Muslims who seem to be the operatives of the al Qaeda network everywhere that it appears.

This unfortunate state of affairs has made for immense difficulty in dealing with the modern interpretation of jihad. It implies that the allegiance of every Muslim to any nation-state is in question every day. When it was possible to think of Islam as characterized mainly by its magnificent religious ecumenism and international congeniality, in the golden ages of its history, it was possible to assume the trustworthiness of every Muslim unless he contradicted that trust by his personal behavior. Now the world has been cast, by the repeated exercise of lethal violence perpetrated by al Qaeda, into the perplexity of being unable to trust any Muslim unless he has proven himself trustworthy. Even then, the general state of mind now prevailing suggests that the Muslim may change any minute, for religious reasons, and become a supporter of international terrorism.

It is clear that those who have the greatest investment in quelling the hellish enterprises of al Qaeda are all the Muslims in the world everywhere. They are the ones whose well-being is most at stake here. They are the people who are the most likely to benefit immediately and directly from the success of the war on terrorism. They are the ones who will pay the largest price in loss of credibility by any prolongation or failures in this war. They are the ones who will suffer most if al Qaeda launches another major attack upon any nation, but particularly on the United States.

Therefore, it is astonishing that the Islamic communities, both in the Arab countries of the Near East and in the major Islamic communities in Europe and the United States, are doing so little to support the neutralization of the terrorist Fundamentalists of their faith. There can be only two explanations for that. Either they are terrified that if they oppose the Fundamentalists, they—royal families, government officials, or expatriate communities—will themselves be exterminated in the dark of night by their terrorist "friends and brothers." Or they fit into the category that Trifkovic set forth. Their allegiance to an acquisitive Islam and a violent jihad is their real commitment in their heart of hearts.

The world must and almost certainly will soon know the answer to this question. The fact that Germany and France continue to play this equation so acquisitively for themselves, maneuvering to acquire as much power and advantage vis-à-vis the United States as they can exploit from this present dangerous international situation, aids and abets the Islamic nations and communities in continuing, themselves, to equivocate on the matter of repression of terrorism. It seems clear that both Germany and France would welcome another major terrorist assault on the United States directly if that would further trouble the American economy and morale, thus creating more of a vacuum into which the European Economic Community, dominated by the German bankers, can move.

In any case, the traditions of Islam, known as the Hadith, have reinforced the emphasis on jihad as warfare against infidels. Ram Swarup, in *Understanding the Hadith: The Sacred Traditions of Islam* (2002), clarified how deeply entrenched in Muslim cultural history is this violent type of interpretation of Jihad. He declares,

> *Jihad* is central to Islam and *mujahids* are its Army of Liberation. Without *jihad*, there is no Islam. *Jihad* is a religious duty of a Muslim state. All lands not belonging to the territory of Islam (*dar al-islam*) must be conquered by the Muslims, and are therefore called the "territory of war" (*dar al-harb*). But it is left to the discretion of the *imam* to decide when the attack should begin. According to some *fiqh* schools, one campaign at least must be undertaken against the unbelievers every year, but since this is not always practical, it is enough if he keeps his army in preparedness and trains it for *jihad*. . . . The spiritual merits that accrue to the believer for participating in *jihad* are equal to the merits he can obtain by performing all the other religious duties required by Islam, such as fasting, praying, and going on pilgrimage. "One who goes out for *jihad* is like a person who keeps fasts, stands in prayer constantly and obeys Allah's verses in the Quran" (Hadith 4636). (130, 131)

Conclusion

Jihad came into Islamic practice at the beginning as a concept of sanctification. Almost immediately Muhammad changed its operational character into militant aggression against the foes of Islam by his attack upon Mecca, subduing it and making it his capital. This progressive dominance of the central Arab landscape by the Prophet's movement took place during the decade of 622–632 C.E. The rationale for this change in the policy of jihad was the theological argument that jihad as military action was a kind of sanctification of the earth or world by means of the extermination or conversion of the infidels. As the concept originally had the intent, in the Qur'an, of promoting an inner struggle against evil within a person and the purification of the self and social relationships, it came to mean militant violence for the purification of the culture. Jihad is the struggle for righteousness within and without. In the ages of classical Islamic development of theology and jurisprudence, jihad was interpreted mainly as the rule of law for establishing a holy state and society. It had enormous constructive influence under the agency of that concept.

Today jihad has been stolen, as it were, by Fundamentalist Muslims who have turned it into the most vicious kinds of militant violence as a justification and promotion of terrorism. The beginning of this modern-day shift seems to have been in the decade from 1955 to 1965, when jihad was used to justify terrorism against Israel as a mechanism for countering the advance of Israeli society and the occupation of Palestine after the 1948 war. This radical form of jihad assumes that Islamic control of geographical regions inhabited by Muslims, as well as the Islamic conquest of adjoining territories to the extent possible, is the mandate of God for his Islamic people. This is an extreme view of the principle of jihad and includes the notion recently verbalized more boldly by the Israelis, namely, the concept of preemptive defense. This radical ideology of jihad legitimates, indeed makes imperative, "the use of violent means, indiscriminately and without principled limits, a binding obligation for all Muslims" (Johnson, 2002, 14).

To return to the *fatwa* of Osama bin Laden and his four colleagues, with which we began, we can see that this non-Qur'anic interpretation of the principle of jihad is currently invoked as justification for any kind of mayhem the Fundamentalists deem to be to their advantage. They have stolen an originally redemptive theological principle of Islam, the call to strive for sanctification in "the ways of God," and have bastardized it to serve their own power strategies and manipulative purposes with no regard to the deep historic strains of true Islam, shared with the best strains of Judaism and Christianity, namely, the perception of God as a God of grace, mercy, and peace.

The terrorists have hatched a dangerous heresy, denying and invalidating the best of their own religion and discrediting the long history of Islamic faith, communities, history, and nations. They have, in the process, created an intolerably dangerous world.

Note

1. All quotations from the Qur'an in this chapter are the author's translation directly from the original Arabic.

References

Esposito, J. L. (2002). *Unholy war: Terror in the name of Islam.* New York: Oxford University Press.

Johnson, J. T. (2002 June/July). Opinion, jihad and just war. *First Things,* 12–14.

McAuliffe, J. D. (2002). Is there a connection between the Bible and the Qur'an? *Theology Digest, 49,* (4), 303–317.

Shakir, M. H. (Trans.). (1999). *The Qur'an.* Elmhurst: Tahrike Tarsile Qur'an.

Swarup, R. (2002). *Understanding the Hadith: The sacred traditions of Islam.* Amherst: Prometheus Books.

Trifkovic, S. (2002). *The sword of the prophet: Islam history, theology, impact on the world.* Boston: Regina Orthodox Press.

CHAPTER 4

The Rape(s) of Dinah (Gen. 34): False Religion and Excess in Revenge

Ilona N. Rashkow

Genesis 34 is about the rape of a virgin, Dinah, and its consequences. Despite its prominence in the so-called Jacob cycle, it is a largely unknown story. Until recently, the story has received little attention in the history of interpretation, probably because Genesis 34 is a complicated and disturbing narrative. First, we are forced to deal with the rape of Dinah, Jacob's only daughter, by Shechem, son of the prince of the Shechemites, a neighboring tribe. Next, however, we must confront the actions of Simeon and Levi, Dinah's two brothers, who make a false pact with the Shechemites and then murder all the men, plunder their belongings, and "take" their women and children—all committed in the name of religion.

Perhaps what is most disturbing is that the actions of the patriarch's sons receive no words of reproof from Jacob, the biblical narrator, or the deity. Indeed, Jacob's response is self-serving rather than reproachful. Rather than condemning his sons' actions because of moral issues, he is concerned that "*I* shall be destroyed, *I* and my house" (Gen. 34:30). As Ron Clark (2001: 81) discusses it, a surface view of the text leaves a reader with questions, judgments, and/or accusations concerning the characters and the dilemma of right and wrong. Yet a deeper study of the text addresses issues of leadership, social justice, and violence within the community of YHWH. The story is provoking in part because of the silence of Jacob, the narra-

The Rape of Dinah, a painting left unfinished by Fra Bartolomeo and completed by Giuliano Bugiardini in 1531. Erich Lessing/Art Resource, New York.

tor, and God; the power struggle between Hamor, Shechem and Jacob's sons; and the blood revenge of Simeon and Levi.

The story line is simple: Dinah goes out alone one day from her father's house and is promptly raped by the local prince, Shechem. Shechem's lust, however, turns to love, and his desire for her is so great that he and his father go to Jacob, request Dinah as Shechem's wife, offer a covenant of mutual exchange of wives between the groups, and even agree to the request of Simeon and Levi that all the Shechemite men will have themselves circumcised in order to comply with Israelite laws. But Dinah's brothers, Simeon and Levi, are obsessed suddenly with a sense of outraged personal honor and religious fervor.[1] After deceptively agreeing to the pact, they wait until the third day after the circumcision (when the Shechemite men are incapacitated), seize Dinah from Shechem's house, pillage the town, kill all the males, carry off all the wives and children, and depart with their spoils.

The cast of characters is relatively small: Shechem, the son of Hamor; Hamor, the Hivite; Jacob, the patriarch; Simeon and Levi, his two sons and full brothers of Dinah; Dinah; and the entire tribe of Shechemites—men, women, and children—who are narratively relegated to a very small part despite their total annihilation.

My concerns are threefold. First, of course, I am disturbed by the physical rape of Dinah and her lack of voice in the narrative. As I discuss in this chapter, despite the fact that this narrative is usually referred to as "The Rape of Dinah," Dinah is actually a minor character. Second, I am troubled by Jacob's lack of reaction to his daughter's rape. While Shechem may have raped Dinah physically, Jacob's silence is, in effect, a psychological rape. Indeed, Simeon's and Levi's question at the end of the story ("Should one deal with our sister as with a harlot?") could apply equally to Jacob and Shechem. My third concern is the actions of Simeon and Levi. The brothers insist that intermarriage with the "uncircumcised" cannot be tolerated: "We cannot do this thing, to give our sister to a man who is uncircumcised, for that is a disgrace among us" (Gen. 34: 14). And yet, as Danna Nolan Fewell (1997) writes, "we are told (*a blurting out of the truth in the midst of a family quarrel?*) that, in their revenge against Shechem's rape of their sister, the sons of Jacob think nothing of capturing the women and children of Shechem as their booty" (138–139). While it is troublesome to me that Jacob's sons treated these captives exactly as Shechem had treated their sister, what is more distressing is that they did so under the guise of religiosity. They "took" the Shechemite women, as Shechem had asked to "take" Dinah.

To begin with, I would like to focus on the two major acts of violence within this text, rape and vengeance, within the context of the Hebrew Bible and related texts.

Rape

Cuneiform sources treat two main aspects of rape: the status of the victim and her lack of consent. The laws distinguish between a woman who is unattached, inchoately married (bride money has already been paid for her by another man), and married. According to Middle Assyrian Laws A 55, where an unattached girl is raped, her father has two options: he may demand that the rapist marry her without right of divorce and with payment of a set bride money, or he may demand the bride money without the marriage. If the rapist is married, his wife is to be assigned to the father for sexual abuse.

In the case of an inchoately married woman (a woman for whom bride money has already been paid by another man), her status aggravates the offense, thus making it punishable by death (Code of Hammurabi, cited by Driver & Miles 1952–55, 130). Presumably, the purpose of this rule is to equate this case with that of a fully married woman, where the rapist's penalty is likewise death (Middle Assyrian Laws A 12, 23; Hittite Laws, quoted in Pritchard 1969, 188–197). Middle Assyrian Laws A 12 relies for "lack of consent" on the fact that the woman was in the street on legitimate business and on testimony to her resistance to the rapist's attentions. Hittite Laws 197 (Pritchard 1969, 188–197) proposes a mechanical test: if the act took place in the city, consent is presumed; if in the country, it is not, and the offense is rape.

In the Hebrew Bible, only Deuteronomy discusses the laws pertaining to rape, and it preserves a fragment of the cuneiform sources. Rape of an inchoately married girl is punishable with death (Deut. 22:25), relying on the same context for consent as Hittite Laws (Pritchard 1969, 188–197): city or country. However, Deuteronomy provides a rationale, namely, that in the city the girl's cries for help will be heard, and consent is therefore presumed if she does not cry out (Deut. 22:24–27). Rape of an unattached girl leads, as in Middle Assyrian Laws A 55, to forcible marriage with no divorce and payment of a set bride money (Deut. 22:28–29). One major problem in Genesis 34 is that the rape of Dinah is regarded by the *offender's* family as deserving the penalties consistent with Deuteronomy 22: 28–29, that is, payment of a bride-price, in this case the circumcision of all the adult Shechemite males, and these penalties are agreed to by the *victim's* family. However, Simeon's and Levi's subsequent actions nullify any sense of honor and respect for the law since their revenge is beyond any normal biblical legal limits (see my discussion of vengeance later in this chapter). It should be noted that Absalom's killing of Amnon in revenge for the rape of his sister, Tamar, reported in 2 Samuel 13, would be regarded as unjustified based on these same laws of vengeance.

Vengeance

Vengeance is usually defined as inflicting punishment on another in return for an offense or injury or the withholding of benefits and kindness from another for the same reason. The Hebrew Bible distinguishes between vengeance that is "proper" and vengeance that is "sinful." Vengeance is "proper" for humankind only in the restricted sense of dispensing justice for a legally punishable crime or sin, meted out in the prescribed manner. The one who inflicts the punishment is thus acting as an instrument of the court of law or, in rare cases, of God's revealed will but *never merely to satisfy personal animosity*. This is a particularly salient point when examining the actions of Simeon and Levi. Biblical examples of "proper" vengeance include "When a man strikes his slave . . . and he dies there and then, he must be avenged" (Exod. 21:20) and "The Lord spoke to Moses, saying, 'Avenge the Israelite people on the Midianites' "(Num. 31:1–2). Similarly, vengeance is appropriate when it is directed in a legally just war against the enemies of the entire people of Israel who are at the same time considered enemies of God: "To execute vengeance upon the nations and punishments upon the peoples" (Ps. 149:7). Again, this situation is not applicable to the actions of Simeon and Levi.

Generally, vengeance is a *divine* prerogative, as the following verses indicate: "For *He* will avenge the blood of His servants, wreak vengeance on His foes" (Deut. 32:43; emphasis added), "*I* will bring a sword against you to wreak vengeance for the covenant" (Lev. 26:25; emphasis added), and "O *Lord God of vengeance*, O God of vengeance, shine forth" (Ps. 94:1; emphasis added). While the rabbis[2] considered the imitation of God's ways, such as mercy, forgiveness, and so on, to be the ethical ideal for man (see, e.g., Sot. 14a; Sif. Deut. 49; Shab. 133b), they did not fail to point out that certain activities attributed by the Hebrew Bible to God, such as vengeance, should *not* be imitated by humans, the reason being that "with a human being wrath controls him, but the Holy One blessed be He, controls His wrath, as it is said, 'The Lord avengeth and is full of wrath' " (the Hebrew is *ba'al hemah*, literally "master of wrath" [Nah. 1:2; Gen. R. 49:8]).

Human vengeance as the expression of personal animosity is explicitly *prohibited* in the Bible in the verse "You shall not take vengeance or bear a grudge against your kinsfolk. Love your *neighbor* [presumably that includes the Shechemites?] as yourself: I am the Lord" (Lev. 19:18). The rabbis offer a precise definition of this passage:

> What is vengeance and what is bearing a grudge? If one said to his fellow: "Lend me your sickle," and he replied "No," and tomorrow the second comes to the first and says: "Lend me your ax," and he replies: "I will not lend it to you just as you would not lend me your sickle"—that is vengeance. And what is bearing a "grudge"? If one says to his fellow: "Lend me your ax," he replies "No," and on the morrow the second asks:

"Lend me your garment," and he answers: "Here it is, I am not like you who would not lend me what I asked for"—that is bearing a grudge. (Yoma 23a; Maim. Yad, De'ot, 7:7, 9; *Sefer ha-Hinnukh*, nos. 247, 248)

Various reasons have been offered by Jewish exegetes for the injunction against vengeance—besides the obvious one that it increases hatred and strife among humankind. One consideration presented by Abraham Cohen (1949) is that a "man" and his neighbor are really "one organic unit" (210), so that one retaliating against the other is analogous to the situation in which one hand slicing meat with a knife slips and cuts the second hand. *Sefer ha-Hinnukh* gives another rationale: one ought always to consider the harm that befalls himself or herself as punishment for sin ultimately deriving from God with the human perpetrator of the injury being merely an unwitting instrument of divine providence. That is, repentance rather than vengeance is called for (*Sefer ha-Hinnukh*, no. 247). Further, Maimonides states that "one should rather practice forbearance in all mundane matters, for the intelligent realize that these are vain things and not worth taking vengeance for" (Maim. Yad, De'ot, 7:7).

There is, according to the Talmud, one notable exception to the injunction *against* vengeance. "Any *talmid hakham* (pious Torah scholar) who does not avenge himself and retains anger like a serpent, is no real *talmid hakham*" (Yoma 22b–23a), the reason being that offense against him entails a slur against the Torah itself. This dispensation granted the *talmid hakham* is, however, highly qualified by the rabbis. It is limited to cases where the scholar has suffered personal rather than monetary injury; the scholar may not take overt action but may merely withhold interference if another takes up his cause, and the dispensation is terminated if the offender seeks forgiveness (Yoma, ibid.; Rashi). In addition, according to Maimonides (Yad, Talmud Torah, 7:13), the special permission granted the scholar applies only to instances where he was publicly reviled, thus involving a gross desecration of the honor of Torah; and finally, the purpose for allowing vengeance in such a case is that it causes the offender to recant, after which he must be forgiven.

In all other instances where one has been wronged, *vengeance in all its forms is forbidden*, *contra* the actions of Simeon and Levi. The ideal, according to the Talmud, is to be of those "who are insulted but do not retaliate with insult, who hear themselves put to shame without replying" (Yoma, ibid.). Concerning such people, the rabbis declare, "he who forbears to retaliate will find forbearance [from God] for all his failings" (Yoma, ibid.; Shab. 88b; RH 17a). Clearly, Simeon and Levi did not fit any of the previously described criteria. As a result, their vengeance is "sinful"—yet no words of reproof from Jacob, the narrator, or the deity.

Was There a Rape?

Recently, scholars have been using a variety of approaches, such as historical, anthropological, or source critical methodologies, to address this narrative. Surprisingly, many of these studies have marginalized the rape committed by Shechem and the arguably even *more* violent acts of mass destruction conducted by Simeon and Levi. For example, according to Gerhard von Rad, the narrative does not report *actual* events in the family life of Leah and Jacob. Rather, it remembers a "prehistoric conflict" in early Israelite tribal history: "The narrative seems to go back to the time when Israelite tribes were not yet settled in Palestine but on their way thither in search of new pasture" (von Rad 1972, 329).[3] In other words, the sole purpose of the narrative is to memorialize the departure of the tribes of Simeon and Levi from the territory around Shechem.

Even more startling to me is the fact that a number of scholars write that the Hebrew text does *not* clearly indicate that Dinah was raped. Rather, they argue, the story suggests "mutual" love, which, after it is consummated, pushes the couple to make their relationship legitimate. For example, Jean-Daniel Macchi (2000) states that the problem for the brothers is not violence against Dinah but the rendering impure of their family. Thus, for Macchi, the story represents an "intra-textual debate about marriages with those who are not part of Israel" (37).

Mayer Gruber (1999) claims that the view that Shechem raped Dinah derives from the Vulgate, which renders the verb in Genesis 34:2 by *rapuit*. He maintains that throughout the Hebrew Bible "take . . . for a wife" means marry a woman. While I agree that the expression "take for a wife" *does* indicate a legitimate sexual relationship, Gruber seems to ignore the fact that verse 2 ("Shechem, the son of Hamor the Hivite, the prince of the country, saw her, took her, laid [no preposition] her, and abused her") does *not* read "took for a wife" but rather three violent verbs, none of which indicates matrimony or matrimonial intent. While Gruber notes that Nahmanides lent support to the view that Genesis 34 is a rape narrative, he argues that

Deuteronomy 22:24 and 21:4 prove the verb means have intercourse with and not rape. He continues,

> [C]ommentators who have treated Gen 34 as a rape narrative, have failed to come to terms with the fact that Shechem's behavior does not correspond to scientifically documented behavior of a rapist: rape is not an expression of love, or even lust, but an expression of anger or demonstration of power. The rapist does not seek to marry his victim. The biblical narrative refers not to rape but to pre-marital sex. Shechem's sin was not that he raped Dinah but that he failed to understand that the children of Jacob interpreted his intermarriage with Dinah not as a legal marriage, but as fornication. (120)

Alice Keefe (1993) explores the relationship between sexual and marital violence in Genesis 34, Judges 19, and 2 Samuel 13 and writes that the violated body of a woman functions as a *metonym* for the social body as it is disrupted by war. Similarly, Lyn Bechtel (1994) views the narrative as one of exogamy/endogamy. She concludes from the group dynamics of the story that Dinah is not raped. Instead, she writes that Genesis 34 portrays Dinah and Jacob as prepared to interact with outsiders (Shechem, Hamor, Shechemites) who are loyal to their own group values and customs in contrast to Simeon, Levi, and the sons of Jacob, who want to maintain strict group purity and absolute separation. She claims that the story challenges this isolationism by demonstrating its potential dangers for the overall group: "Ironically, if there is a rape in this story, it is Simeon and Levi who 'rape' the Shechemites." Characterizing the rape as acceptable intercourse, Bechtel redefines the killing as rape.[4] While I agree with Bechtel's point vis-à-vis Simeon's and Levi's actions, I disagree with that part of her sentence "*if* there is a rape in this story." To my reading, as stated earlier, there are several rapes, and the physical rape of Dinah is undeniable.

In addition, Terence E. Fretheim (1994) observes, "Shechem proceeds to act in a way atypical of rapists: He clings to Dinah ... loves her ... and speaks to her heart.... The latter phrase may cause Dinah's positive response" (323). Even more supportive of Shechem is Ita Sheres (1990): "If one is to find male compassion in the story, one has to turn to Shechem, 'the stranger,' who after the rape falls in love with Dinah and realizes that he must 'console the girl' before proceeding with official, ritualized courtship. ... In fact, it can be easily argued that Shechem's attitude is not only the *most* human but also the *most credible:* how else could he have expected to live with Dinah, whom he had raped, as his wife?" (111ff.; emphasis added). Von Rad (1972) seems to concur in this view: "The figure of Shechem is made more human for the reader" than the brothers who "purify the honor of their violated sister at the cost of a morally ambiguous deed" (328).

My Reading

I see this narrative differently. Shechem rapes Dinah, yet I agree with Sheres that he is certainly not lacking in sympathy. My view of Shechem is based both on the narrator's point of view and on Shechem's own discourse. In describing Shechem, the narrator in the Hebrew text begins with his societal status: Hamor, his father, is "*the* Hivite" (emphasis added) and thus not just *any* Hivite but "the prince of that country" (Gen. 34:2). Within the Hivite community, the narrator tells us, Shechem is "the most honored of all the house of his father" (Gen. 34:19). The purpose of this type of character description, as Adele Berlin (1983, 36) notes, is not to enable the reader to actually visualize the character but rather to establish the character's place in society and to define the character's own particular situation. Now that Shechem is introduced as the son of *the most* important man of a neighboring tribe and is held in particularly high esteem by his fellow countrymen, there are established behavioral expectations. That is, because Shechem is so highly respected and important, he is held to relatively high moral standards.

But a reader can form a contrary opinion of Shechem almost immediately because of the narrator's description of his actions. By specific word choice, the narrator *unequivocally* condemns him because of his assault on Dinah: "Shechem, the son of Hamor the Hivite, the prince of the country, saw her, took her, laid [no preposition] her, and abused her" (Gen. 34:2).

In the preceding verse, the narrator said that Dinah went out to "see" the daughters of the land, an innocent action on her part. The narrator then reports that Shechem "sees" Dinah. Having seen Dinah, Shechem then "took her, laid [no preposition] her, and abused her," a particularly damaging characterization. In biblical Hebrew, the normal grammatical construct *šakab 'im*—(lay *with*) is used to convey *co*habitation, a mutually agreed-upon act. However, *šakab*, or *šakab "et* ("lie" used with a direct object rather than a preposition), is used when the act is forced, a rape. In the Amnon and Tamar narrative, for example, Amnon first tries to seduce his half sister, Tamar, and says, "Come, lie *with* me, my sister" (2 Sam. 13:11). When she refuses, the narrator reports Amnon's actions: he "abused her and laid [no preposition] her [direct object]" (2 Sam. 13:14). This account is in contrast to the story of David and Bathsheba, where the narrator makes it clear, both textually and grammatically, that Bathsheba was *not* raped: "David sent messengers and he took her; and she came in unto him, and he lay *with* her" (2 Sam. 11:4).

Obviously, this verb is problematic. Although in the Bible males do "lie with" females in the context of "legitimate" sexual relations (Uriah's reference to spending the night with his wife [2 Sam. 11:11] and the conception of Solomon [2 Sol. 12:24] are two examples), the vast majority of the uses of the verb *šakab. Šakab* refers to rape (as in this case), incest (e.g., Lot and his daughters [Gen. 19:32, 34, 35]), promiscuity (the activities of Eli's sons [1 Sam. 2: 22]), seduction (the attempts of Potiphar's wife to seduce Joseph [Gen. 39:10, 12, 14]), adultery (the punishment of David that others will "lie with" his wives [2 Sam. 12:11]), and forbidden relationships (such as an unclean woman, father's wife, daughter-in-law, aunt, and homosexual partners [Lev. 20:11–19]).

The verb also has numerous associations with death and defeat. "To die" is to "lie" with one's ancestors (1 Kings 1:21; 2 Kings 14:22; etc.), and the dead are those who "lie" in the grave (Ezek. 32:21; 29; Ps. 88:6; etc.).

Certainly, associations of eroticism and destruction/death have a long literary tradition. Emily Vermeule (1979) points to the "ambiguity of slaughter and sex" and notes that Homer has "a habit, at mocking moments, of treating enemies as lovers, fusing the effects of Eros and Thanatos" (157). Death itself has been described as a lover (McClelland 1964, 182–216) or as a sexually potent goddess (Coogan 1978; Good 1982).

Attraction and revulsion, longing and fear, are coexisting images of sexuality and death in biblical literature as well.[5] Commenting on Songs 8:6 ("Set me as a seal upon your heart, as a seal upon your arm: for love is strong as death, passion is hard as Sheol. Its flashes are flashes of fire, fiercer than any flame"), Marvin Pope (1977, 228–229), for example, notes the association of love with death; Francis Landy (1983) notes that because of the grammatical construction of the verse, Death "inevitably engage[s] Love" (123); and Susan Niditch (1989) emphasizes the metaphoric equation, reading this verse as an assertion that on some level "love is death and death love" (43 n. 5).

There seems to be a philological tradition tying eroticism to death as well. In many languages, the word translated as "to die" is used also to mean "have a sexual climax," especially for a man (e.g., Lat. *morticula;* Fr. *la petite morte*). As Louise Vasvari (1990) notes, it is possible that the associations are multiple: deathlike spasms in the moment of orgasm and vice versa, men about to die often experience an erection, the male organ "dies" after climax, and the like. It seems more than coincidental that in Genesis 34, *šakab* certainly links eroticism and death—on a mass scale.

In this text, the themes of attraction and revulsion, longing and fear, and sexuality and death are in abundance. The three verbs in Genesis 34:2—"take," "lay," and "abuse"—negate any possibility of seduction or mutual consent and imprint the act of violence. The narrator says that from Shechem's perspective Dinah is an object. She is not lain *with* but rather *laid.* Shechem, who is the son of a prince and highly regarded by his fellow Shechemites, has committed rape, and a reader, most appropriately, would be shocked.

But herein lies a problem. In an immediate sequel, the narrator describes Shechem's change of heart. In contrast to the Amnon and Tamar narrative, where the sequence of events is love, rape, and then hate, Shechem first commits a barbarous act and then falls in love with his victim! The three verbs of force, so powerful in the Hebrew text, give way to three equally strong verbs of endearment: "His soul (*nefesh*) "clung" to Dinah, the daughter of Jacob, and he loved the young woman, and he spoke to the heart of the young woman" (Gen. 34:3).

The narrator, in verse 3, presents an inside view of Shechem that shows how Shechem has changed. Because of specific word choice, the narrator seems to guarantee the sincerity of Shechem's emotions. The Hebrew *nefesh* is used here as an intensifying synonym of the personal pronoun. The psychology of this rapist is precisely the *opposite* of Amnon's in 2 Samuel 13 who, after having consummated his lust for his sister by raping her, despises her. Here, the fulfillment of the impulse of unrestrained desire is followed by love, which complicates the moral balance of the story.

We are told that Shechem's soul *dbaq,* or "clung," to Dinah. This verb indicates a permanent bond, not a temporary infatuation. Genesis 2:24, for example, explains that "a man leaves his father and his mother, *dbaq* ["clings"] to his wife, and they become as one flesh." Similarly, the Psalmist says "my soul *dbaq* ["clings"] to you" when referring to God; and Ruth's steadfastness to Naomi is emphasized by the repetition of the word *dbaq*—a leitmotif in that narrative.

The narrator also reports that Shechem "spoke to the heart" of Dinah, a particularly significant phrase since it appears rarely in the

Hebrew Bible and each time in situations putting or showing the speaker in a *positive* or favorable light: to "speak to the heart" is to "comfort," "appease," or "soothe." Thus, Shechem's sincerity and love seem to be emphasized by the use of this expression. The phrase occurs only when a situation is wrong or difficult or when danger is in the air (see Gen. 34:3, 50:21; Judg. 19:3; 1 Sam. 1:13; 2 Sam. 19:8; Isa. 40:8; Hosea 2:16; Ruth 2:13; 2 Chron. 30:22, 32:6), and when the phrase appears, someone speaks to the "heart" of the fearful character to resolve a frightening situation in a larger context of fear, anxiety, sin, or offense. That is, the phrase is used when someone tries to talk against a prevailing negative opinion. Consequently, in this case, Shechem "speaking to the heart" depicts his attempt to change Dinah's (reasonable enough) negative reaction to him and convince her to accept him.

Shechem raped Dinah, and there is no doubt that his action was deplorable. However, despite the fact that verse 3 does not cancel the impact of verse 2, it provides another factor when considering Shechem and the later measures taken by Dinah's brothers. Just as the narrator uses shocking verbs in describing Shechem's actions, the next three verbs suggest the replacement of violent behavior by equally strong positive emotions.

Another problem in this narrative vis-à-vis Shechem and the actions of Simeon and Levi is that the biblical writer plays with the word *lqa*—"take." In describing the rape, the narrator says that Shechem "took" Dinah. Suiting the action to the word, Shechem, in love, asks his father to "take me this child for a wife." "Taking" by force, a reprehensible act, is now opposed to the envisaged "taking" in marriage. The "young woman" referred to by the narrator in verse 3 has become the object of Shechem's love, and he calls her a "child" when speaking to his father, a diminutive term, a term of affection. "Take," which indicated violent action in the narrator's report of the rape, now recurs in a decorous social sense—the action initiated by the father of the groom in arranging a proper marriage for his son. Shechem refers to Dinah as *yaldah*, "girl" or "child," a term that suggests equally her vulnerability and the tenderness he now feels for her. However, in verse 12, when addressing the brothers, Shechem does not refer to Dinah as *yaldah*, "girl," his previous reference to her, but as *na'arah*, the proper term for a nubile young woman. This is coupled by the narrator's reference to *him* as the *na'ar* (boy) in verse 19, the masculine counterpart of the term he used for Dinah in verse

12, suggesting that from the perspective of the narrator, Shechem is probably an adolescent. In this regard, it should be noted that in the text there was no previous indication of Shechem's age.

In examining the characterization of Shechem, there is a dilemma: there was a rape, and that rape cannot be justified. Yet because of Shechem's "change of heart," somehow a reader can feel sympathy for the rapist. This is problematic.

Dinah

Until fairly recently, the major focus of Genesis 34 by biblical commentators has been on Dinah—and many of the commentators view her as the *cause* of both her rape and all the subsequent events.

For example, according to the *Legends of the Jews*, Ginzberg (1911) writes,

> While Jacob and his sons were sitting in the house of learning, occupied with the study of the Torah [!], Dinah went abroad to see the dancing and singing women, whom Shechem had hired to dance and play in the streets in order to entice her forth. *Had she remained at home, nothing would have happened to her. But she was a woman, and all women like to show themselves in the street.* (287; emphasis added)

During the Renaissance, biblical translators and religious exegetes unanimously blamed her for the entire incident. Tyndale, in his Aprologue to Genesis, states that this narrative, like the rest of the Hebrew Bible, sets forth a lesson to be learned, and that lesson is simple:

> Marke also how greate evelles folow of how litle an occasion. Dinah goeth but forth alone to se the doughters of the contre, and how greate myscheve and troble folowed.

Calvin, a major influence on the English translators, reads the rape of Dinah similarly:

> Dina is kidnapped and raped because, having left her father's house, she went away and wandered in greater freedom than belonged to her. She should have stayed quietly at home, as the Apostle advises it (Titus 2:5) and as nature itself teaches it, for this virtue, which a common proverb attributes to women, that they must be keepers of the house, applies to girls. For this reason the fathers are taught to keep their daughters under narrow watch if they want to protect them from all indignity. (qtd. in Tavard 1972, 177)

And according to Henry's *Old Testament Commentaries,*

> Young persons, especially females, are never so safe and well off as under the care of pious parents. Their own ignorance, and the flattery and artifices of designing, wicked people, who are ever laying snares for them, expose them to great danger. They are their own enemies if they desire to go abroad, especially alone, among strangers to true religion. Those parents are very wrong who do not hinder their children from needlessly exposing themselves to danger. Indulged children, like Dinah, often become a grief and shame to their families. Her pretence was, to see the daughters of the land, to see how they dressed, and how they danced, and what was fashionable among them; she went to see, yet that was not all, she went to be seen too. She went to get acquaintance with the Canaanites, and to learn their ways. See what came of Dinah's gadding. The beginning of sin is as the letting forth of water. How great a matter does a little fire kindle! We should carefully avoid all occasions of sin and approaches to it. (Gen. 34:1–19)

According to these commentators, the "Rape of Dinah" is a perfect opportunity to counsel women. Unanimously, they write that Genesis 34 is a transparent narrative that teaches young women to stay at home where they belong, or the consequences will be dire. The consequences in *this* tale were dire in the extreme.

My Reading

Just as I disagree with many of the exegetes on the question of whether there was a rape, I see the representation of Dinah differently as well. First, it seems significant that despite the fact that this narrative features Dinah, the only daughter of Leah and one of the few biblical daughters identified by her mother's name,[6] even feminist readers often have ignored this chapter in the Bible. Dinah is the only female descendant mentioned in the Genesis account of Jacob and his 12 sons (however, Gen. 46:15 mentions both Dinah and *daughters* [plural] of Jacob). The announcement of Dinah's birth (Gen. 30:21) stands out in the narrative both because it presents a female child and because it lacks an explanation of her name, in contrast to that for all the 12 brothers.[7]

Dinah's birth to Leah follows the announcement that Leah had borne six sons to Jacob. With a female, her childbearing comes to an end.[8] Furthermore, the birth of Dinah occupies the pivotal spot in the transition between Leah's childbearing and that of the previously barren but favored wife, Rachel. Once Leah's part of the Jacob family is complete, God "remembered" Rachel and opened her womb for the birth of Joseph.

Second, it seems particularly strange that despite the fact that this narrative is usually referred to as "The Rape of Dinah," Dinah is actually a minor character. She engages in no direct discourse, and the only knowledge we have of her is provided by the narrator. She is described in relational terms, and these relational references are significant when considering this story in the context of violence and Simeon's and Levi's use of the religious requirements imposed upon the Shechemites. The narrator introduces Dinah as the *daughter* of Leah (v. 1). After she is raped, the narrator calls her the *daughter* of Jacob (v. 3) and the *sister* of Simeon and Levi (v. 25). These family ties are maintained throughout the narrative as a rhetorical device. Jacob heard that Shechem had defiled *Dinah his daughter* (v. 5); Shechem had done a disgraceful thing in defiling *Jacob's daughter* (v. 7); Shechem talked to *Dinah's father* and *brothers* (v. 11) who protested that they could not give their *sister* to one who is uncircumcised (v. 14); if their conditions are not met, Simeon and Levi threaten to take their *daughter* and be gone (v. 17); Shechem had delight in *Jacob's daughter* (v. 19); and *Dinah's brothers* slaughtered all the Hivite males (v. 25). Throughout Genesis 34, Dinah's familial references serve to highlight the close bond between members of her family and also to focus on various subrelationships.

Third, Dinah's story deals directly with male/female violence.[9] What makes this story particularly compelling is that although it is reminiscent of the Abraham/Sarah, Isaac/Rebecca brother-sister-foreign male motif (in that a female is placed in danger sexually vis-à-vis a foreign potentate and a brother/half brother is involved), Dinah is not a sister-wife but an unmarried, *childless*, sister/daughter, and the question of sexual possession, and thus violence, looms.

Fourth, and most important with regard to Dinah, is that in this story yet again a woman has no voice. But her silence is neither a natural nor an accidental phenomenon. The primacy of the male voice in Dinah's story can be neither achieved nor maintained without an elaborate narrative strategy which includes the suppression of a female and its subsequent violence. Indeed, throughout Genesis, narratively essential women are defined and described only in terms of their relationship to a male. For example, it is somewhat ironic that in the whole saga of the flood and the ark, in Genesis 6–9, Noah and his sons are continually named, but the identities of the four others saved with them—the grandmother and the three mothers of the whole human race to follow—are neither recorded nor considered in their own right.

This biblical preoccupation with sexuality and violence is highlighted in Simeon's and Levi's question (Gen. 34:31): "Will he treat our sister like a whore?" Although the "he" is not specified, the brothers seem to be railing against Shechem. What must be protected, they argue, is "our view"; that is, the female must conform to a male ideal, and that construct includes the reduction of any possible female complexity or sexuality. But Simeon's and Levi's actions go beyond "protecting" Dinah. They "take" Dinah from Shechem's house without any consideration of her needs and/or desires. Does Dinah now return Shechem's love? Does Dinah *want* to go home? They then kill all the males and "take" the women, children, and property of the Shechemites. Read this way, Genesis 34 represents not only the subjugation of female desire to male rule by means of a continuum of violence but also a continuum of the physical abduction of childless Dinah out of Shechem's house to the metaphysical violence exerted by the text. Throughout the narrative, Dinah and the Shechemites are treated as objects. As Sharon Jeansonne (1990) notes with regard to Dinah, initially, she was attacked by Shechem against her will, and ultimately she is taken away from her new home by her brothers, who do not ask her about her wishes. The same can be said about the Shechemite women.

The Justification for the Vengeance of Simeon and Levi

The narrator of Genesis 34 seems to refrain from questioning the brothers' authority and actions with regard to the subsequent massacre and pillage of the Shechemites. It does not address the brothers' right to act purportedly on their sister's behalf, much less the extent and ferocity of their revenge. Although Jacob rebukes Simeon and Levi for endangering the family's survival in Canaan, he does not mention their decision to take the law into their own hands or its moral/ethical/legal implications.

Sepher Hayashar[10] exonerates the brothers in an interesting, although not textually supported, way:

> Some say that though six hundred and forty-five Shechemite men and two hundred and seventy-six boys were circumcised, yet Hamor had been warned by his aged uncles, and by his father Hadkam, son of Pered, that this breach of custom would vex all Canaan, and that they would themselves raise an army to punish such impiety. Hamor ex-

plained that he had accepted circumcision only to deceive Jacob's sons: at Shechem's wedding feast, when the Israelites lay drunken and at ease, he would give the signal for their massacre. Dinah secretly sent her bondmaid to tell Simeon and Levi of Hamor's plan. They vowed that by the following night no man would be left alive in Shechem, and attacked the city at dawn. Though withstood by twenty bold Shechemites who had evaded circumcision, they killed eighteen: the other two ran and hid in a bitumen pit.

Louis Ginzberg (1911) provides one of the most interesting (and again not supported by the biblical narrative) rationales of the massacre in his *The Legends of the Jews:*

When Jacob heard that Shechem had defiled his daughter, he sent twelve servants to fetch Dinah from Shechem's house, but Shechem went out to them with his men, and drove them from his house, and he would not suffer them to come unto Dinah, and he kissed and embraced her before their eyes. Jacob then sent two maidens of his servants' daughters to remain with Dinah in the house of Shechem. Shechem bade three of his friends go to his father Hamor, the son of Haddakum, the son of Pered, and say, "Get me this damsel to wife." Hamor tried at first to persuade his son not to take a Hebrew woman to wife, but when Shechem persisted in his request, he did according to the word of his son, and went forth to communicate with Jacob concerning the matter. In the meanwhile the sons of Jacob returned from the field, and, kindled with wrath, they spoke unto their father, saying, "Surely death is due to this man and his household, because the Lord God of the whole earth commanded Noah and his children that man shall never rob nor commit adultery. Now, behold, Shechem has ravaged and committed fornication with our sister, and not one of all the people of the city spake a word to him." And whilst they were speaking, Hamor came to speak to Jacob the words of his son concerning Dinah, and after he ceased to speak, Shechem himself came to Jacob and repeated the request made by his father. Simon and Levi answered Hamor and Shechem deceitfully, saying: "All you have spoken unto us we will do. And, behold, our sister is in your house, but keep away from her until we send to our father Isaac concerning this matter, for we can do nothing without his counsel. He knows the ways of our father Abraham, and whatever he saith unto us we will tell you, we will conceal nothing from you."

Shechem and his father went home thereafter, satisfied with the result achieved, and when they had gone, the sons of Jacob asked him to seek counsel and pretext in order to kill all the inhabitants of the city, who had deserved this punishment on account of their wickedness. Then Simon said to them: "I have good counsel to give you. Bid them be circumcised. If they consent not, we shall take our daughter from them, and go away. And if they consent to do this, then, when they are in pain, we shall attack them and slay them." The next morning Shechem and his father came again to Jacob, to speak concerning Dinah, and the sons of Jacob spoke deceitfully to them, saying: "We told our father Isaac all your words, and your words pleased him, but he said, that thus did Abraham his father command him from God, that any man that is not of his descendants, who desireth to take one of his daughters to wife, shall cause every male belonging to him to be circumcised."

Shechem and his father hastened to do the wishes of the sons of Jacob, and they persuaded also the men of the city to do likewise, for they were greatly esteemed by them, being the princes of the land.

On the next day, Shechem and his father rose up early in the morning, and they assembled all the men of the city, and they called for the sons of Jacob, and they circumcised Shechem, his father, his five brothers, and all the males in the city, six hundred and forty-five men and two hundred and seventy-six lads. Haddakum, the grandfather of Shechem, and his six brothers would not be circumcised, and they were greatly incensed against the people of the city for submitting to the wishes of the sons of Jacob.

In the evening of the second day, Shechem and his father sent to have eight little children whom their mothers had concealed brought to them to be circumcised. Haddakum and his six brothers sprang at the messengers, and sought to slay them, and sought to slay also Shechem, Hamor, and Dinah. They chided Shechem and his father for doing a thing that their fathers had never done, which would raise the ire of the inhabitants of the land of Canaan against them, as well as the ire of all the children of Ham, and that on account of a Hebrew woman. Haddakum and his brothers finished by saying: "Behold, to-morrow we will go and assemble our Canaanitish brethren, and we will come and smite you and all in whom you trust, that there shall not be a remnant left of you or them."

When Hamor and his son Shechem and all the people of the city heard this, they were sore afraid, and they repented what they had done, and Shechem and his father answered Haddakum and his brothers: "Because we saw that the Hebrews would not accede to our wishes concerning their daughter, we did this thing, but when we shall have obtained our request from them, we will then do unto them that which is in your hearts and in ours, as soon as we shall become strong."

Dinah, who heard their words, hastened and dispatched one of her maidens whom her father had sent to take care of her in Shechem's house, and informed Jacob and his sons of the conspiracy plotted against them. When the sons of Jacob heard this, they were filled with wrath, and Simon and Levi swore, and said, "As the Lord liveth, by to-morrow there shall not be a remnant left in the whole city."

They began the extermination by killing eighteen of the twenty young men who had concealed themselves and were not circumcised, and two of them fled and escaped to some lime pits that were in the city. Then Simon and Levi slew all the city, not leaving a male over, and while they were looking for spoils outside of the city, three hundred women rose against them and threw stones and dust upon them, but Simon single-handed slew them all, and returned to the city, where he joined Levi. Then they took away from the people outside of the city their sheep, their oxen, their cattle, and also the women and the little children, and they led all these away, and took them to the city to their father Jacob. The number of women whom they did not slay, but only took captive, was eighty-five virgins, among them a young damsel of great beauty by the name of Bunah, whom Simon took to wife. The number of the males which they took captive and did not slay was forty-seven, and all these men and women were servants to the sons of Jacob, and to their children after them, until the day they left Egypt.

When Simon and Levi had gone from the city, the two young men who had concealed themselves in the lime pits, and were not slain amongst the people of the city, rose up, and they found the city desolate, without a man, only weeping women, and they cried out, saying, "Behold, this is the evil which the sons of Jacob did who destroyed one of the Canaanite cities, and were not afraid of all the land of Canaan." (287ff)

But it is not only ancient commentators who exonerate Simeon and Levi. Most of the more recent discussions of Genesis 34 tend to take at face value the story of Dinah's rape and the subsequent avenging by her brothers. Generally, the focus of the discussions has been the motivations of the "good" brothers and their transactions with the rapist.[11] But even exceptional analyses that focus on the relationship between the brothers and their sister interpret the brothers' interference on behalf of Dinah as an act of compassion and devotion. Robert Alter (1996), in his translation and commentary Genesis, writes in reference to Genesis 34:7:

> [F]or he had done a scurrilous thing in Israel by lying with Jacob's daughter, such as ought not be done. It is a technical means for strongly imprinting the rage of Jacob's sons in the presence of their father who has kept silent, and even now, gives no voice to his feelings about the violation of his daughter. (190)

Using a more sociological approach, Clinton Bailey (1991) notes that many aspects of biblical life are similar to traditional Bedouin life as lived by Bedouins today and that, as a result, Bedouin culture can elucidate the episode of the rape of Dinah. He claims that Jacob's sons—desert people—behaved according to "desert logic of law and justice" (20). That is, while every violation of a Bedouin right is viewed with gravity, violation of a woman's honor is most serious. The mutual responsibility of Bedouin for one another is based on common blood; they are very concerned that the people whom they consider patrilineal kin are in fact kin. However, using Bailey's logic, Bedouin culture also explains the behavior of *Shechem*, in that he came directly to Jacob after the rape to mollify him, to pay the highly unusual bride-price (circumcision of the entire tribe), and to marry Dinah. Considering the tribal context that Bailey puts forth, Jacob's rejection of desert logic when he curses Simeon and Levi (Gen. 49:6–7) seems inconsistent.

Esther Fuchs (2000) has an interesting reading: "What Dinah's brothers set out to rectify is the family's damaged honor. Even as they agree that their sister was molested against her will, the word used to describe her ordeal does not convey her physical or emotional suffering but the symbolic stigma attached to a rape victim. What is outrageous to the brothers is the fact that their sister was made into a *zonah*, or harlot (Gen. 34:31: "But they said, 'Should he treat our sister as a harlot?' ")" (211). Thus, according to Fuchs, the references to Dinah as a sister serve to justify the brothers' brutal actions. Read this way, the story of Dinah's rape serves as a prelude to the destruction of Shechem. The more outrageous her victimization, the more justified their bloody reactions. Thus, verse 13 explains that the brothers deceive Shechem and Hamor "because" the former "defiled Dinah their sister." Verse 25, which describes the murderous actions of Simeon and Levi, refers to them as "Dinah's brothers" after having identified them as "Jacob's sons." The description of the brothers' pillaging of Shechem also appears to repeat what is known already, namely, that this repetition is to remind the reader of Dinah's brothers' motivations. The reference to "Dinah" and "their sister" implies that what we are witnessing are not wanton acts of violence but rather expressions of anger and a keen sense of justice and brotherly commitment (Fuchs 2000, 220). As a result, according to Fuchs, the narrative refrains from treating the brothers' personal investment in killing the rapist.

My Reading

I disagree. The information given earlier, that Simeon and Levi were "grieved and very angry" because of what had happened to their sister, raises considerable doubts because the narrator tells us in verse 13 that they spoke *bᵉmirmh*—"deceitfully." Does *bᵉmirmh* attach itself to the brothers' words or beliefs? As discussed later in this chapter, *because* they spoke deceitfully, the proposed negotiations of Simeon and Levi are a camouflage for treachery and violence. They make religious demands, that is, the circumcision of the entire adult male population of Shechem, to give the Shechemites an *impression* of reconciliation and unity, but their real goal is to lull Shechem and Hamor into tranquillity and extract revenge, vengeance to which they were not entitled under the circumstances discussed earlier. Read this way, Simeon and Levi are blatant violators of the covenant made with the Shechemites and thus blatant violators of biblical law.

Because of Shechem's love of Dinah, Hamor suggests an alliance of friendship and marriage between the two tribes: "The soul of my son Shechem longs for your daughter. Please give her to him for a wife" (Gen. 34:8). Hamor addresses them in dignified, familial terms, "your daughter" "for my son." The following is a diagram of the conversation between Hamor and Jacob's sons outlining the terms of the negotiations (based on Leibowitz 1981, 382).

Hamor to Jacob's sons (vv. 9–10)	Jacob's sons to Hamor and Shechem (v. 16)
The soul of my son Shechem longs for your daughter: Please, give her to him to wife.	_____
Make marriages with us.	_____
_____	We cannot do this thing, to give our sister to a man who is not circumcised, for that would be a disgrace to us.
_____	Only in this will we consent to you. If you will be as we are, every male of you circumcised. Then
Give us your daughters	We will give our daughters to you
and take our daughters	and we will take your daughters
And settle among us	And we will settle among you
	and become one people
And the land will be before you.	_____
Settle and trade in it	_____
and acquire property in it.	_____

But the narrator tells us that Simeon and Levi speak *b*ᵉ*mirmh*. The Hebrew Bible attaches a pejorative meaning to *b*ᵉ*mirmh* and its cognates since this adverb is used most often to condemn a character or an act. For example, in Genesis 27:33–35, Isaac, trembling with shock and distressed by the "great and exceedingly bitter cry" of his favorite, says, "Your brother has come *b*ᵉ*mirmh* and taken away your blessing." Because of the constancy of lexical sense within the biblical text, Simeon and Levi claim scruples which they do not in fact have. Perhaps it is not just circumstantial that, as Alter (1996, 191) notes, the same term, *mirmah*, was first attached to Jacob's action in stealing the blessing and then used by Jacob to upbraid Laban after the switching of the brides. Could this be the reason Jacob does not condemn the actions of Simeon and Levi after they slaughter and plunder in direct violation of the pact that they had made?

Significantly, Jacob's sons do not discuss the trade or property when negotiating with Hamor and Shechem. Instead they maintain that under the terms of this treaty, the two tribes will become "one people." The only barrier to this arrangement, they claim, is that Shechem and his fellow Shechemites are uncircumcised. The brideprice they extract from the Shechemites to have their daughter marry Shechem is circumcision, an act *mandated by their religion:* "to give our sister to a man who is uncircumcised, . . . would be a *herpah* (disgrace) to us" (Gen. 34:14). Circumcision for the Shechemites would have been a mark that they now belonged to YHWH's "chosen" community.

The subsequent massacre and looting reveal the true intent of Simeon and Levi. And the revenge does not end with slaughter by Simeon and Levi; they continue on to plunder the city and take the wives and children as prey:

> On the third day, when they were in pain, two of the sons of Jacob, Simeon and Levi, Dinah's brothers, took each man his sword, and came to the city securely, and slew all the males. And Hamor and Shechem his son, they slew with the edge of the sword, and took Dinah out of Shechem's house and went out. The sons of Jacob came upon the slain, and plundered the city, because they had defiled their sister. Their sheep and their cattle and their asses and whatever was in the city and whatever was in the field they took. And all their wealth and all their little ones and their wives they captured, and plundered all that was in the house. (Gen. 34:25–30)

The narrative, which began with "Dinah went out . . . Shechem took her" ends with "they took Dinah out of Shechem's house and went out." Their "rationale" to Jacob is, "Should he deal with our sister as with a whore?" And although Jacob angrily responds "you have troubled me," he provides a purely utilitarian (and self-serving) argument in his words of reproof ("*I* being few in number, they will gather themselves together against *me*, and *I* shall be destroyed, *I* and my house" [emphasis added]).

Simeon and Levi falsely pretended religion and used the religiously mandated covenant of circumcision as a venue to acquire the Shechemites' "sheep and their cattle and their asses and whatever was in the city and whatever was in the field they took. And all their wealth and all their little ones and their wives... and ... all that was in the house." As the Geneva translators note in the marginalia, Simeon and Levi "made the holy ordinance of God a meane to copasse their *wicked purpose.*" Since the demands of Simeon and Levi were made under "false pretences" and only to accomplish their own "wicked purpose," the brothers committed the greater *herpah* by having violated the treaty with the Shechemites as well as the laws pertaining to vengeance in the Hebrew Bible. Thus, unlike Shechem, who rapes but is ultimately reconciled to paying restitution, Simeon and Levi speak "deviously," make a false covenant based on the religious requirements of circumcision, slaughter innocent people, capture women and children, and plunder the city. So much for their religious convictions. So much for the *herpah*—disgrace—associated with Dinah being given to one who is "uncircumcised."

Further, the narrative refrains from any reference to YHWH in this text, and none of the participants in Genesis 34 reveals any awareness of the deity's presence or authority. The omission of the deity in the rape and vengeance scenes is all the more blatant since His name is invoked several times in the narratives that precede and follow it. That is, when Jacob meets Esau after having stolen Isaac's blessing, he offers him gifts and says, " 'No, please; if I find favor with you, then accept my present from my hand; for truly to see your face is like *seeing the face of YHWH*, since you have received me with such favor. Please accept my gift that is brought to you, because *YHWH has dealt graciously with me*, and because I have everything I want.' So he urged him, and he took it" (Gen. 33:10–11; emphasis added). While YHWH appears to be unaware of or indifferent to Dinah's rape and its aftermath, he appears as soon as this ordeal is over ordering Jacob to build for him an altar in Bethel (Gen. 35:1). By completely omitting any references to the deity in this narrative, the text is able to avoid a difficult issue. Thus, any mention of YHWH in this context would likely elicit the question why YHWH has not intervened on behalf of the raped woman, either as redeemer or as avenger, or on behalf of the Shechemites whom Simeon and Levi duped and "seized their children and wives." It certainly brings to mind the similar absence of YHWH when Lot offers his daughters to be gang-raped (Gen. 19:7–8), when Jephthah sacrifices his own daughter (Judg. 11:39), or when the Levite offers his concubine to be raped and killed (Judg. 19:25). On the other hand, YHWH *did* react to stay the hand of Abraham when Abraham was about to sacrifice Isaac *at His own command* (Gen. 22:12). Can it be that only the male offspring of Abraham merit the deity's protection? Are women and foreigners dispensable?

As a last point, how should we deal with Jacob in this text? The deceit practiced so often by the characters in the earlier Genesis narratives predominates in Genesis 34 as well. Jacob, who deceived his father and uncle, now has sons who act in the same manner in regard to Shechem and Hamor.[12] Rather than confront Hamor and Shechem about the rape, Simeon and Levi pretend to be amicable. And Jacob's response? Upset because his sons made him "odious to the inhabitants of the land" (Gen. 34:20) and therefore personally vulnerable to attack by other neighboring tribes because of the insincerity and untrustworthy nature of his word, Jacob subsequently reduces their inheritance (Gen. 49:5–7). However, Jacob also reduces the inheritance of Reuben because Reuben had "defiled his father's bed" by sleeping with Bilhah, his father's concubine (Gen. 35:22). Do the two crimes deserve the same punishment?

Conclusion

Obviously, this is a most disturbing story, in part because of the multiplicity of "rapes" committed. Dinah is raped physically by Shechem, and this act initiates the entire litany of horrendous acts that take place. But Dinah is "raped" thrice more if rape is defined as "violent, destructive, or abusive treatment." First, it could be said that she is "raped" psychologically by the lack of any reaction on the part of her father, Jacob, after Shechem's horrendous act; next, she can be viewed as "raped" metaphorically by her brothers who "take" her out of Shechem's house, thus leaving her husbandless and without possibility of another marriage; and third, she is arguably "raped" by the Hebrew Bible itself in that the only other mention of this violated woman, the only daughter of Jacob, is in Genesis 46:15, which lists the names of all of Jacob's offspring who went to Egypt.

But the "rapes" in the text do not end with Dinah. Simeon and Levi metaphorically "rape" the sanctity of their word when they blatantly violate the terms of the treaty that they negotiated with Shechem and Hamor. Not only do they place their entire family in jeopardy, they mock the very essence of honor by promising one thing and delivering another. Finally, it is not unreasonable to assume from the narrative that when Simeon and Levi "took" the Hivite women they raped them as well.

The rape(s) of Dinah in Genesis 34 are many. What is so disturbing is that the slaughter of the Shechemites is perpetrated in the name of Simeon's and Levi's false religion and vengeance.

Notes

1. This is something unusual in the history of the patriarchs and their progeny in light of Abraham's and Isaac's pandering of their wives in chapters 12 and 20. See Rashkow (1993, 26–48).

2. In this chapter, the word *Rabbis* refers to the particular group of Jewish religious leaders known technically as "the Rabbis." They flourished from the second until approximately the end of the sixth century in Palestine and Babylonia. Growing out of a sect of first-century Judaism, their cultural, social, and religious hegemony over the masses of Jews grew during this period, in which the major literary productions of Rabbinic Judaism—the Midrashim and Talmudim—were produced. Their closest historical cognates are the Fathers of the Church, sometimes referred to as the Patristics.

3. For similar interpretations, see, for example, Davidson (1979, 12–50) and Maher (1982).

4. A similar approach is taken by Bernd Jörg Diebner (1984), who reconstructs the controversy from the perspective of "Jerusalem's orthodoxy" during the second century B.C.E. For a thorough critique of this approach, see Susanne Scholz (2000, 109–112).

5. For a more detailed discussion of sexuality in the Hebrew Bible, see Rashkow (2000).

6. Only here and in Genesis 36:39 does a mother's name identify a daughter. Dinah is "the daughter of Leah," and Mehetabel is "the daughter of Matred, daughter of Mezahab." In Ruth 1:8, Naomi does not explicitly name the mothers of her two daughters-in-law, Ruth and Orpah: "Go back each of you to your mother's house." For a more detailed discussion of the "lack" of daughters in the Hebrew Bible, see Rashkow (1993, 65–84).

7. Because of these features, the authenticity of Dinah's place within a unit of Genesis (29:31–30:24) that lists the birth and names of 11 of Jacob's

sons has been called into question. However, other aspects of Dinah's position in this matriarchal section may mitigate the apparent strangeness of the Dinah verse.

8. As a woman, I would like to think that the seventh position, considering the symbolic value of that number, seems to represent the fulfillment of Leah's maternal role, one that includes at least one female child—but that is another issue.

9. See Fewell and Gunn (1991), Rashkow (1990), and Sternberg (1985) for discussions of this narrative and issues of sexuality and violence.

10. A late twelfth-century heroic Midrash on Genesis, the beginning of Exodus, Numbers, and Joshua, compiled in Spain, written in Hebrew.

11. See the citations mentioned in Fuchs (2000, 201).

12. It should be noted that in the account of the raping of Jacob's daughter Dinah by Shechem and the subsequent revenge on the Shechemites by Jacob's sons in the Testament of Levi 5–6, Jacob *himself* accepts the idea that the Shechemites could be circumcised and then intermarry with his descendants Kugel (1992).

References

Alter, R. (1996). *Genesis: Translation and commentary.* New York: W. W. Norton.

Bailey, C. (1991). How desert culture helps us understand the Bible: Bedouin law explains reaction to rape of Dinah. *Bible Review, 7*(4), 14–21, 38.

Bechtel, L. M. (1994, June). What if Dinah is not raped? (Genesis 34). *Journal for the Study of the Old Testament,* 19–36.

Berlin, A. (1983). *Poetics and interpretation of biblical narrative.* Sheffield: Almond.

Clark, R. (2001). The silence of Dinah's cry: Narrative in Genesis 34 in a context of sexual violence. *Journal of Religion and Abuse, 2*(4), 81–98.

Cohen, A. (1949). *Everyman's Talmud.* New York: Dutton.

Coogan, M. D. (1978). *Stories from ancient Canaan.* Philadelphia: Westminster.

Davidson, R. (1979). *Genesis 12–50.* Cambridge Bible Commentary. Cambridge: Cambridge University Press.

Diebner, B. J. (1984, July). Genesis 34 und Dinas Rolle bei der Definition "Israels." *Dielheimer Blätter zum Alten Testament,* 59–75.

Driver, G. R., & Miles, J. C. (1952–55). *The Babylonian laws* (G. R. Driver & J. C. Miles, Eds.). Oxford: Oxford University Press.

Fewell, D. N. (1997). Imagination, method and murder: Un/framing the face of post-exilic Israel. In T. K. Beal & David M. Gunn (Eds.), *Reading Bible, writing bodies: Identity and the Book.* London: Routledge.

Fewell, D. N., & Gunn, D. M. (1991). Controlling perspectives: Women, men, and the authority of violence in Judges 4 and 5. *Journal of the American Academy of Religion, 58*(3), 389–411.

Fretheim, T. E. (1994). The book of Genesis: Introduction, commentary, and reflections. In L. E. Keck (Ed.), *The new interpreter's Bible* (321–674). Nashville: Abingdon.

Fuchs, E. (2000). *Sexual politics in the biblical narrative: Reading the Bible as a woman.* Sheffield: Sheffield Academic Press.

Ginzberg, L. (1911). *The legends of the Jews* (Vol. 1) (Henrietta Szold, Trans.). Philadelphia: Jewish Publication Society.

Good, R. M. (1982). Metaphorical gleanings from Ugarit. *Journal of Jewish Studies, 35,* 55–59.

Graves, R., & Patai, R. (1983). *Hebrew myths: The book of Genesis.* New York: Greenwich House.

Gruber, M. I. (1999). A re-examination of the charge against Shechem son of Hamor. *Beth Mikra, 157,* 119–127.

Jeansonne, S. P. (1990). *The women of Genesis: From Sarah to Potiphar's wife.* Minneapolis: Fortress.

Keefe, A. A. (1993). Rapes of women/wars of men. *Semeia, 61,* 79–97.

Kugel, J. (1992). The story of Dinah in the testament of Levi. *Harvard Theological Review, 85*(1), 1–34.

Landy, F. (1983). *Paradoxes of paradise: Identity and difference in the Song of Songs.* Sheffield: Almond.

Leibowitz, N. (1981). *Studies in Bereshit (Genesis): In the context of ancient and modern Jewish Bible commentary* (Aryeh Newman, Trans.). Jerusalem: Alpha.

Macchi, J. D. (2000). Amour et violence: Dina et Sichem en Genese 34. *Foi et Vie, 99*(4), 29–38.

Maher, M. (1982). *Genesis.* Wilmington: Glazier.

McClelland, D. C. (1964). *The roots of consciousness.* Princeton: Van Nostrand.

Niditch, S. (1989). Eroticism and death in the tale of Jael. In P. L. Day (Ed.), *Gender and difference in ancient Israel* (43–57). Minneapolis: Fortress.

Pope, M. (1977). *Song of Songs.* Garden City: Doubleday.

Pritchard, J. B. (Ed.) (1969). *Ancient Near Eastern texts relating to the Old Testament* (W. Albright, Trans.). Princeton: Princeton University Press.

Rashkow, I. N. (1990). *Upon the dark places: Anti-Semitism and sexism in English Renaissance biblical translation.* Sheffield: Sheffield Academic Press.

Rashkow, I. N. (1993). *The phallacy of Genesis: A feminist-psychoanalytic approach.* Louisville: Westminster John Knox.

Rashkow, I. N. (2000). *Taboo or not taboo: Sexuality and family in the Hebrew Bible.* Minneapolis: Augsburg Fortress.

Scholz, S. (2000). *Rape plots: A feminist cultural study of Genesis 34.* Bonn: Lang.

Sheres, I. (1990). *Dinah's rebellion: A biblical parable for our time.* New York: Crossroad.

Sternberg, M. (1985). *The poetics of biblical narrative: Ideological literature and the drama of reading.* Bloomington: Indiana University Press.

Tavard, G. H. (1973). *Women in Christian tradition*. Notre Dame: University of Notre Dame Press.

Vasvari, L. O. (1990). A tale of "tailing" in the *Libro De Buen Amor. Journal of Interdisciplinary Studies, 2*(1), 13–41.

Vermeule, E. (1979). *Aspects of death in early Greek art and poetry*. Berkeley: University of California Press.

von Rad, G. (1972). *Genesis: A commentary* (3rd rev. ed.). Philadelphia: Westminster.

CHAPTER 5

The Cain-Abel Syndrome: In Theory and in History

Ricardo J. Quinones

Part One: Cain and Abel as Symbol and Metaphor

The Cain-Abel theme has had an extraordinarily rich, diverse, and even unexpected career. It has given rise to three interpretive traditions and enlisted the talents of some of the West's greatest thinkers and writers. As we examine the core of the story, here in the first part of this chapter, we can see why this is so, but nothing quite prepares us for its greater exemplifications in the masterworks of Dante and Shakespeare, the one representing the older religious interpretations of the theme and the other the possibilities it offers for some social and political rectification in the thought of the High Renaissance.

The appeal of the theme—its durability and its variety—is perplexing when we acknowledge, as we must, that Cain-Abel is in its appearance and even in its inner core a stark and unlovely theme, prompting one writer to call it gloomy.[1] It is marked by murder, bringing with it, as Claudius realizes in *Hamlet*, "the primal eldest curse," that of fratricide. Its motivating emotion, envy, is loathsome and practically inadmissible. Indeed one of the theme's constant functions has been to provide figures and events responsible for the growth of an evil that is reprobate and unregenerate.

The long duration and appeal of the Cain-Abel story may in large part be explained by the potency of its nuclear account, by the power of the words and the graphic actions that strike us undeniably. The

Cain and Abel, by Palma Giovane. Erich Lessing/Art Resource, New York.

language itself is memorable and has echoed resonantly throughout Western literature. "Am I my brother's keeper?" "The voice of thy brother's blood crieth to me from the ground." "A fugitive and a vagabond . . . " "My punishment is greater than I can bear." Whether intact or altered, these lines in the classical languages or in their modern renditions (as the previously cited sixteenth-century English) have the power to arrest attention and to direct it to a new kind of significance. The story of Cain-Abel has generated its own power of allusion throughout literature and history.

The actions themselves, murder and banishment, are highly dramatic, and the issues they provoke are compelling. One of the greatest bequests of Judaism (as well as of Platonism) to the West is a sense of justice, not justice negotiated but justice inviolate. God hears the cry of Abel's blood. There is something in the principle of divinity itself that insists that the victim's voice be heard and that justice be done. A crucial characteristic of the Cain-Abel theme is that it never relinquishes this constitutive part. A murder has been committed, a death has occurred. As Arturo Graf, the great Italian thematologist, insisted at the beginning of the last century, "Sia che si vuole, tu, Caino, hai ucciso il tuo fratello" ("No matter what you say, you Cain have killed your brother").[2] The fact that someone is responsible cannot be swept under the rug. If justice must be served, this means that the theme cannot avoid making a judgment.

This also means that the theme unavoidably contains extensive social ramifications. When God places the mark on Cain, its purpose in protecting him from retaliations is, in the mind of more than one expert, to ensure the end of blood vengeance. The first murder carries in its wake the explosive potential for accelerating reciprocal violence, the vendetta, the feud, the civil war, and as such it will draw the attention of Augustine, the *Beowulf* poet, Dante, Machiavelli, and Shakespeare—obviously one of the theme's more formidable lines of development. The cry is an ancient one, uttered again by the angel in Byron's *Cain*, "Who shall heal murder?"

But the story is based upon other forms of experience that are psychically even more penetrating and enduring. Intrinsically the theme is devoted to presenting the stark and basic fact of *division*, division that is so unyielding as to become part of the essential matter of existence itself. Although this is the fundamental datum that determines many of the component parts of the theme, that theme itself experiences some refinement. The fraternal context of the Cain-Abel story means that division becomes more emotionally vibrant as the *tragedy of differentiation*. Such differentiation is painfully realized at the moment of the offering, when one of the brothers has his essential nature endorsed over that of the other brother. The *arbitrariness of preference* thus compounds the tragedy of differentiation and brings home the fact of division in a way that is particular to the Cain-Abel theme.[3] Furthermore, the division of the brothers within the Cain-Abel rubric shows a great capacity to assume the nature of rival principles and thus enter into great dualistic schemes.

Division, the tragedy of differentiation, the offering, and the arbitrariness of preference have become distinguishing features of the Cain-Abel theme. But there are three other residual forces in the theme that are equally determining and that also deserve to be signaled here. They are violence, envy, and mystery. While serving to set off the Cain-Abel story from allied themes, their abiding presences, in conjunction with the other great issues just indicated, help explain why it is that Cain-Abel has superseded other stories of "rival brothers" within and outside the Bible and has become such a predominant part of the Western imagination.

Cain-Abel is based on facts of sheer division. Unity of whatever sort—familial, tribal, even personal—the virtual starting point of the theme, proves to be elusive and even illusory. However much we may wish them to be so, no two things can ever be equal. "All things being equal," is a phrase born to be contradicted. If two people do the same thing, according to the Latin dictum, those two things can never be the same. Difference is apparent in the very conditions of existence, in the very relationships of couples. That relationship itself promotes asymmetry has been shown by René Zazzo's book on twins (one that incidentally exerted strong influence on the foremost contemporary French novelist Michel Tournier). Even in the minds of identical twins, one of the pair is regarded as predominant.[4] What story is more indicative of this principle, tests it more fully, than the story of brothers? This also shows why it is that in post–romantic literature Cain and Abel must eventually merge with doubles and twins. These latter two acquire the essential characteristics of the Cain-Abel theme.

Difference is also essential to our understanding of time and space. Time is made up by distinguishing one moment from another. In fact, Jacques Derrida regards temporality itself, finitude, as an outright product of violence. Even if space is regarded as mythic—we can come back again to the same place—no two objects can occupy the same space. This shows, as Tournier reasons in *Les meteores*, that because they cannot occupy the same space, even twins must by necessity have different perspectives. Tournier's two major novels (*Les meteores*, 1975, trans. as *Gemini*, 1981, and *Le roi des aulnes*, 1970, trans. as *The Ogre*, 1972) may be fully located amid the issues being discussed here.

More particularly, the durability of the Cain-Abel story is derived from its capacity to confront dire division at the most elementary, even primitive level, that of the falling-out of brothers. The fraternal context of the theme is all-important; brothers serve to intensify, epitomize, and generalize all sorts of discord and division in a particular way. The appeal of the theme is not simply division but division within a context of extraordinary unity. Where the expectations of communion and innocent, un-self-conscious unity have been so great, the facts of difference are all the more startling. This is why we are drawn to use the phrase "the tragedy of differentiation" to describe the intrusions of difference and of destiny into such a unity. Where we had all the more reasons to expect harmony, the varying pulls of individual destinies are all the more painful. Here in this context of fraternal communion and division, the Cain-Abel story does more than express the falling-out of brothers; by means of the brothers it finds occasion to offer powerfully compact tellings about ruptures in life itself. The Cain-Abel theme thus becomes a master story for addressing fundamental divisions in existence and, perhaps even more important, varying ways of response to those differences.

One of the many associations into which the Cain-Abel theme enters in the course of its long career is the foundation sacrifice. But this is more than a casual encounter; it is a meeting that is derived from the core of the theme itself. Augustine was the first to make much of the similarities between the biblical brothers and Romulus and Remus. Despite the difference between them—distinctions he was careful to make—Augustine saw them as archetypally related: each locates the foundation of the city in the blood sacrifice of the brother. In *Les meteores*, Tournier adds to the pairs of brothers involved. Referring to Esau and Jacob, Romulus and Remus, Amphion and Zethos, and Eteocles and Polyneices, Tournier's interlocutor, Father Seelos, speaking to his diminished and beleaguered congregation in the divided and recently walled-in sector of East Berlin, reminds them that these brothers have mysteriously one thing in common: "That thing is a city. A symbolic city that seems every time to demand the fratricidal sacrifice."[5] Tournier's account is indicative because it is clear—as his own works make plain—that over these other pairs, Cain and Abel seem to preside, almost as if their story were the master story, covering in the fullness of its own materials matters that are treated incompletely or less suggestively in the other stories.

That the Cain-Abel theme figures prominently in foundation sacrifice has recently been argued by Hyam Maccoby in his *The Sacred Executioner: Human Sacrifice and the Legacy of Guilt.*[6] To summarize, Maccoby readily allows that the Cain of the Israelite redaction of Genesis is a murderer without any ritualistic or communal associations. However, by capitalizing on textual duplications, resonances, and anomalies and indicating the various cultural levels and accretions in the text, he proceeds to construct a Kenite saga in which Cain, not Adam, is the first ancestor. Cain performs a ritual foundation sacrifice, not of his brother but rather of his son—Abel. Although Maccoby's arguments are plausible, one wonders why Cain and Abel need to be transformed—and at such great lengths—into father and son since as brothers they seem to have done so well. If this is not clear from the biblical narration itself, it is certainly clear from the ways that history has regarded the story.

The brother sacrifice, over which Cain-Abel presides, contains a powerful range of emotional elements—perhaps even more powerful than those of the father and son. In any event, the component parts and energies are different. Brothers are true intimates, coevals and cohorts into whose elementary unity a terrible division and separation must intrude. The sacrificed brother has thus greater possibilities for indicating a lost portion of the self, a self that is abandoned, sundered, the twin, the double, the shadowy other, the sacrificed other that must be gone and yet can never be gone. The sacrificed brother is thus better able to express all the dimensions of some lost portion of life that the foundation sacrifice in its fullest meaning acknowledges.

The primary situation of an original equalness indicates that, better than father and son, the brothers are suited to represent not only individuals in contention but individuals with basically different attitudes toward the very conditions of existence. For instance, when confronted with the facts of existence that blood sacrifice seems to typify, Abel and his followers and heirs separate themselves and seek out purification in atonement. This is prototypically Christian. In the later but less edifying transformation, Abel will be equally devoted to unity, but to a unity based on disregard and unawareness. In their selfishness, Cain and his progeny may create discord, but correspondingly in a later epoch, their very quest for selfhood can lead to a reintegration of the forces that had been so sorely divided. The accrued value of the Cain-Abel story seems to show itself in the larger confrontations and transformations that it prompts.

It is from this elementary pattern of brotherly loss as expressive of the conditions of existence itself that other elements of the Cain-Abel theme—elements that distinguish it from other themes involving brothers—are derived. Although other versions of the brother sacrifice confront the tragedy of differentiation, the Cain-Abel story seems to engage the human family more fully—from early unity to later division—and in more of its relationships. Brotherhood, as we can imagine, is a potent cultural force that the theme presents (in its many variations). But so is fatherhood. In fact, as we shall see, there is a prevailing psychological and social relationship between the presence of the father and altered evaluations of the respective sons. But the father figure plays an even more central and dramatic role, and it is this role that helps distinguish Cain-Abel from the other themes. Difference between brothers is rendered more grievous by what I call the arbitrariness of preference, the fact that some arbiter, divine or paternal but always fatherly—and hence authoritative and decisive—is rendering judgment vis-à-vis the difference. The tragedy of differentiation is aggravated by the arbitrariness of preference, the pathos of which is increased by the sense of earlier unity and unsuspecting innocence.

The tragedy of differentiation and the arbitrariness of preference are powerful presences that are unleashed from within the confines of the story and that reverberate throughout the psyche, as they do throughout history itself. A poignant and powerful emotional center of the story and of the theme is of course the offering by as yet untested, undefined young people. Generations of readers have reflected in pained anguish on the mystery of the offering itself, the careless indifference of it or the heartrending innocent pathos, and then on the terror of rejection, what it means to have one's being invalidated. Of the many authors addressing the theme, it is perhaps John Steinbeck in *East of Eden* who captures the pathos of this moment best. But for many of them the offering is at the center of life—all life is an offering where one is being judged. The Cain-Abel story is potent because it presents the first offering, the first venture out of the self, out of an undifferentiated and unconscious communion, and into an objective world. Brotherhood, where young innocence and communion are epitomized, will increase the pain of difference. The offering quite naturally then forms the first definition of character; it is a fundamental presentation of the self. How vulnerable the offerer is, and how massively crushing can rejection be. This might explain the special appropriateness of the Cain-Abel story within a setting of artists. The ventures of art are distinctive presentations of the self where the totality of one's being is defined and placed on the line.

All the brother stories reflect basic facts of division, but only in the Cain-Abel story does division rise to the level of great dualistic principles in contention. Very early, Cain-Abel lent itself to presentations of large, opposed principles. An extraordinary part of the theme's appeal rests precisely on its dualistic nature and hence upon a contest of values. When one brother rises, as Abel does in the predominantly Christian era, the other falls; but in the romantic and postromantic era, it is Cain who attempts to rise and Abel who most certainly falls. The reason for the emergence of Cain-Abel as a ruling theme may be found in this dualistic scheme; it is at its best when it presents rival principles in opposition.

The Cain-Abel story thrives not only because it is dualistic but because the dualisms to which it lends itself are expressive of the dominant energies in various epochs—here we can refer chiefly to two, the Christian and the romantic, while being mindful, as the second part of this chapter makes clear, the critical moment of change represented by Machiavelli and Shakespeare. A substantial polarity is thus established where each term of the dichotomy represents a powerful and representative amalgamation of forces that are so large and compelling as to be a summary of an epoch. In the classical Christian era, the Cain-Abel story represented the formidable conflict between the conservative, skeptical, and urbane (even urban) pagan intelligence—Cain who is a "citizen"—and the militant, aspirant, religious personality—Abel. When we come to the nineteenth and twentieth centuries, we again see that Cain and Abel are opposing one another across an essential polarity, one that is expressive of the dominant and rival energies of the time. Now, however, it is Cain who becomes "idealistic" and Abel who becomes "realistic"—in the temperamental and typical sense in which Schiller intended the terms. The essential drama that the Cain-Abel theme represents in the modern world is that between a questioning, dissatisfied, probing critical intelligence, keenly aware of division and somehow in search of a better order, and a nonaspirant Abel, who by virtue of some personal accommodation or by simple resignation is more accepting of the contradictions of life. In the case of Abel we witness a figure that had been representative of a revolutionary religious spirit, coming to stand for the consolidation of the religious spirit with the social structure of the day. If Cain and Abel can come to represent large, rival principles, then in the course of time, large opposing principles can find their figures in Cain and Abel.

Violence is crucial to the Cain-Abel story in all its aspects and throughout its history. At its origins, Cain-Abel does not only show difference, it shows division: its dualisms are conflict ridden. The adversarial nature of the subject suggests opposition, and its confrontations are inevitably violent. At the center of the theme is a vortex of emotional fury that is compelling because it is so graphic (as indeed the theme's appeal to visual artists has demonstrated) but also because its consequences are so irreversible. At the same time they may be continuous; that is, the extremity of violent behavior prompts its own duplication. "Who shall heal murder?" is the cry heard again and again because violence breeds its own repetition. Violence calls forth violence and immediately, as we have already seen, locates the subject within the profoundest issues of social justice, even those concerning revolution and the changes of regimes. More primitively, instances of proliferating as well as escalating violence within the theme's tightly drawn nexus of relationship produce for Cain progeny that are monstrous. This development, natural enough given the possibilities of the core account, yields a tradition quite at odds with that of the sophisticated and hence secular Cain.

Violence may thus serve as the basis of larger consequences for the Cain-Abel theme. One such consequence is the theme's tendency to replace Adam and Eve where the concern is the continuity of evil. The proliferating nature of violence, its capacity to breed a response in its own likeness, may be the basis of something that is irreparable in the theme. For this reason the children, Cain and Abel, may become more acceptable surrogates than might the first parents.[7] Moreover, as the great male and female polarities, Adam and Eve are needed to reconstitute the race. Not marked by violence, their lapse— and it becomes only that—betokens reparability. As a sexual fall (and ignoring the theological sense of disobedience), it may be regarded as more human and even more humanistic; that is, it has nothing of the monstrous in it. Interesting later consequences may also follow from these curious distinctions: when the "affective sensibility" of the Enlightenment will place Cain and Abel in decidedly domestic circumstances, that is, will remove Cain from his isolation and provide him with a sister-wife, then the character of Cain himself seems more inclined to regeneration.

Violence is terminal, but it is also decisive. And although moral courage is probably superior to physical courage, there is nonetheless something crucial in acts requiring physical courage. In the development of Cain, such characters as Shane or Will Kane in *High Noon* become "point men," individuals who take on the gravest responsibility at the moment of greatest risk. The key to the presence of violence in the Cain-Abel theme might be precisely its involvement in such critical moments. Cain-Abel persists in showing the dramas of people brought to a crossroads where some kind of radical action is required involving either the community or the self. The theme will invoke the trauma of violence to bring to birth a new moment of being, even a new dimension of the self that leads to a revivification of the community. But all these instances will require some form of violence. Hence, even the double and the twin, when conjoined with the Cain-Abel story, will be compelled to undergo some violent sundering. The theme will find it hard to relinquish its primal rooting in the brother sacrifice.

Along with its other designations, those of *Homo ludens, Homo faber,* and *Homo necans,* humankind is also envious: *Homo invidiosus.*[8] Envy is universal (even chimpanzees evidence sibling rivalry), it is logical (no two things can ever be equal), and it is constitutive (Melanie Klein insists that we take it in with our mother's milk).[9] But the fact that it is endemic to human nature has not kept it from being considered the most repellent of emotions. Francis Bacon has called it a "vile and loathsome affection." In *Billy Budd*, Melville considers envy to be the one inadmissible fault: "though many an arraigned mortal has in hopes of mitigated penalty pleaded guilty to horrible actions, did ever anybody seriously confess to envy?"[10] One of its qualities is a skulking interiority. Most vices are forward moving and fairly outstanding; only envy is recessive, betraying a sulking neediness. For this reason, Aristotle can define envy as a defect for which there is no mean: to be half envious is not a moderate virtue. It broods over feelings of wantingness, of lack; it shows the devastation that is the disease of the shriveled heart. This is all contained in the language. Consequently, the French can say "J'ai envie de," which we translate as "I desire," but in truth what is meant when we say it in English is, "I want that." Envy betrays a wantingness, a great need.[11]

As always, a crucial witness is Dante, and although he will reveal in his *Commedia* this perverse and inadmissible quality of envy, he will show something else: the large extensiveness of envy as a theological and social problem. In some way, when Aristotle denies envy a mean, he is also demoting its importance. In any theocentric worldview however, envy assumes extraordinary proportions. The definition of God in Dante's great poem is that such divine goodness is utterly without envy—"La divina bontà che da se sperne ogni livore." The fact that such an avoidance of envy is most appropriate to divinity might indicate that envy is more suitable for humans; nevertheless, in the *Purgatorio*, that most confessional of poems, the one sin that Dante will only partially own up to is envy (he will quite acceptably spend much more time on the lower terrace where pride is purged).[12] But this compliance with the general reluctance to admit envy is coincidental with another view, that of envy's theological and hence social pervasiveness. We might understand this better by comparing envy with jealousy. Jealousy is immediate, catastrophic, yet circumscribed—Othello is jealous. Envy is subtle but more extensive and pernicious—Iago is envious.[13] In this sense, then, envy was Lucifer's sin, and Wisdom tells us that "by envy of the devil, death entered the world." Lucifer's pride, according to Augustine, made him envious, and this drove him to turn from God and then to destroy God's creation, by which he felt himself to be replaced. The menacing she-wolf that so intimidates Dante at the beginning of his aborted ascent has been set loose from hell by envy. This particular conjunction of envy with the she-wolf exhibits the social extensiveness of what is primarily a theological vice. In the central cantos of the *Purgatorio*, envy slips its narrow mooring within the series of the seven deadly sins and, with the aid of Augustine's discussion in the fifteenth book of *The City of God* (where, incidentally, the large and typical roles of Cain and Abel are described), becomes a major social force, a frustrated expression of that large theology of desire that returns humankind to its divine origins.

Nevertheless, these two aspects of envy, its inadmissibility and its theological and social extensiveness, may be brought together and comprehended when we realize that the Cain-Abel story is not only dualistic but usually triadic. The anger of the sibling is a displaced anger that is really directed against God, against the figure that bestows favor so arbitrarily. What this means is that envy exists in protest against God's grace, against God's favor. At its heart, then, envy is repellent because it lives in opposition to the conditions of existence. The quarrel of envy is ultimately a quarrel with God, its arena, or its facade, is a hatred of those whom God favors. When this animosity is directed toward a sibling or a cohort, we are in the midst of a Cain-Abel story. That the enmity is actually directed against God explains why envy is so reluctant to show its face. When it does, it does so against the secondary object, the naturally unsuspecting Abel, who, after all, committed no wrong and, in Melville's language, does not reciprocate malice. This explains all the more fully why Cain is so ulterior and divided and why Abel is so innocent. The reason for the offense is beyond his comprehension as well as beyond any reply. *Un coeur sans defense.* This also explains why, although the larger motif of *freres ennemis* enjoys universal recurrence, the theme of Cain-Abel can enjoy a long and revealing history only in a theocentric culture, which means a Judeo-Christian culture.[14]

Through all its historical alterations, an inherent suitability persists between the Cain-Abel theme and envy. This has to do with closeness of relationship as well as enclosed space. Envy is a directed emotion that involves comparison among approximates. From Hesiod on, we have been instructed that the potter envies only another potter.[15] It would be crazy to envy the flight of the eagle or the dolphin's plunge. As Miguel de Unamuno, that remarkable clinician of the soul, informs us, "Envidia es una forma di parentesco" ("Envy requires a relationship"). Consequently, brothers may be called on to represent the prototypal situation of envy. One is naturally drawn to make invidious comparisons between brothers.

The situation of envy also requires a constant physical presence. Envy might be allowed to dissipate itself if some kind of spatial distancing were possible. One does not envy someone in the next village (again Unamuno). Envy requires physical proximity, and brotherhood can provide the closest of physical relationships. This is why the Cain-Abel theme finds such ready shelter aboard ship (think only of *The Secret Sharer, Billy Budd,* and *The Caine Mutiny*). As Melville tells us in *Billy Budd,* "[T]here can exist no irritating juxtaposition of dissimilar personalities comparable to that which is possible aboard a great warship fully manned and at sea. . . . Wholly there to avoid the sight of an aggravating object one must needs give it a Jonah's toss or jump overboard himself." But there is a larger significance to this importance of physical closeness. As it serves to aggravate antipathy, it also tends to make inevitable the imminent clash. Consequently, the lonely isolation of the brothers, the fact that they go out to the field alone, is a structural and physical component of the theme that is morally required. The tight closeness of brotherhood in the spiritual and physical sense lends to the theme its aura of unavoidability, in fact, of necessity.

The Cain-Abel story, from the first, was enveloped in mystery. This might be seen on the level of story itself; from the original spare telling to the most prolix and elaborate *Finnegans Wake*, there is reticence, if not confusion, not only as to the question of *why* it has happened but even as to *what* has happened. We must also acknowledge that at the heart of the theme is radical differentiation at so fundamental a level, that of siblings, as to defy further explanation. The story is mysterious because it confronts such essential irreducibility. In these circumstances one looks to some kind of ultimate causation. Kent, compelled to acknowledge the difference between Lear's daughters, can only return causation to the stars, as well as the basic inclination of temperament derived therefrom. In this attribution Shakespeare was like many of his age, including Francis Bacon:

> It is the stars,
> The stars above us, govern our conditions;
> Else one self, mate and [make], could not beget
> Such different issues.

In the Cain-Abel story, the sisters in *King Lear* may provide female counterparts to the brothers. Consequently, these considerations are aggravated when the differences are profoundly moral. The tragedy of differentiation leads to the larger reflection on the mystery of iniquity. "Is there any cause in nature that makes these hard hearts?" (3.6.81–82). This point of such apocalyptic questions is that they are unanswerable, that they lead to the blank wall of the irresolvable. But we must look at the kinds of conditions that provoke such questions. And the Cain-Abel story, for reasons mentioned and to be demonstrated, presents such conditions.

But beyond that of a tragic and irreducible division in human experience itself, mystery has another and not unrelated meaning, one from which we derive our sense of "mystical." The Cain-Abel theme is part of a *mysterium*, an arcanum of knowledge that some could penetrate and understand should they possess the proper key or clues. The Greek *musterion* indicates a secret thing or ceremony, one that can be entered only by the *mustes*. In terms of action, of course, Abel is the passive partner, but in terms of understanding he may be the exalted one, the one who is searching for the higher meaning in the earthly drama. Abel, then, becomes the type for Christ, who will finally and for all time provide the key to the *mysterium:* his revelation is the crucial piece that makes sense of the otherwise decipherable puzzle. It is curious that this meaning of mystery is not different from the modern version of what we call a mystery novel, which requires the final clue or the last deciphering for everything that is present to become clear and fall into its rightful place. But such a grand design requires a remarkable designer. We come to see that the vindication of Abel rests upon the eternal fatherhood, and indeed traditionally, throughout the course of the theme, this tight link between Abel and the overarching control of the father will be critical. Envious Cain's war is in actuality directed against the father, and in the remarkable transformation that the theme undergoes in the epoch of romanticism and later, the vindication of Cain will be strongly dependent upon the demotion of Abel, to be sure, but even more clearly upon the absence of the father.

Myth, as it were, is a cover letter whose purpose is to disclose inner reserves and energies not immediately apparent in the literal account of the story itself. It contains in order to release; it formalizes in order to set loose. As we shall see, there are large historical relevancies of the Cain-Abel theme, but on the more intimate as well as universal level of myth, what the retold and revised story releases are those pressures showing the interactions of unity and disruption, of communion and the processes of individuation. The Cain-Abel story lent itself to many versions of the varying pulls of unity and of division. In a creational, monistic view of the world, one dominated by the ideal of unity, Cain can stand forth as the malefactor who not only abhors but actually destroys unity. Division is a tragic product of Cain's actions, and he, unlike Abel, is content to live in its midst. But there is another version of the story, one that would regard the sense of unity as illusory, as belonging to myths of the early age of the race and of the individual, where we are integral and at peace. Such a unity never existed; instead, the individual is confronted with the facts of difference, with individual consciousness, and with the needs of selfhood. Where in the first case division threatened community, here in the second individuation must be rescued from an unawareness that is complicit with conformity. This act of separation, consciously and unconsciously pursued, calls to mind an act of violence, even murder. And this must be the other inner psychological need to which the Cain-Abel story responds and feeds. The violence of Cain against his brother comes to represent necessary physical and psychical facts of individuation, the flight from an undifferentiated communion that either is stagnant or does in fact serve only to conceal a real disruption. The physical slaying of the brother ensures the coming into being of the self. If the urge toward unity and the necessary relegation of Cain to the role of malefactor is typical of the classical Christian era, then this possible regeneration of Cain is typical of the Byronic and post-Byronic epochs.

This reason why the coin may be turned over and the reverse employed where the obverse had stood is that a compact of issues radiates from the center of the Cain-Abel story: disruption and community, union and separation, individuation and unawareness. These are the powerful forces that the theme contains and discloses. The particular value of the theme as a cultural indicator is derived from the fact that at its core these forces are so highly dynamic and ready to lend themselves to such startling transformations.

In its structural components and, more important, in its secret reserves and hidden resources, the Cain-Abel story is admirably suited to reflect the complexities and shifts of a revolutionary age. In the post-Byronic age, which was responsive to the waves set in motion by the French Revolution, Cain has become the quester, the metaphysical rebel, the force in search of new ideas and new modes of being. As in Augustine's *City of God*, this is still a story *contra paganos*, but now the daring one is Cain, and the subservient, even stagnant one, shall we say, the citizen, is Abel. Abel becomes conservative, as the ethical imperatives that he has come to represent have been conventionalized. This conventionalization of the ethical that leads to the progressive pejoration of the qualities of Abel is one of the most stunning cultural facts of the modern world and is central to any discussion of the post-Enlightenment versions of the Cain-Abel story. But the demotion of Abel does not automatically mean the elevation of Cain. It has the effect of removing a stable moral center and guide from the endeavors of the theme. This gives us some clue as to the purposes of Cain. Through his character, his thoughts and responses, the author will struggle to assert, and this with evident difficulty, a new moral and ethical code. This is why the Cain-Abel story is such a powerful one in the literatures of the nineteenth and twentieth centuries. It is perfectly poised to acknowledge any dissatisfaction experienced with the more traditional religious and moral values, hence the demotion of Abel, and to dramatize the struggle on the part of a character, offended by the conventional moral code, to create a new moral center that has a basis that is violent, dire, and problematic, as paradoxical and contradictory as the character of Cain himself. The Cain-Abel theme provides a perfect locus for the fuller ramifications of this moral ambiguity in the modern world, and those works that treat most fully both aspects of the dialectic, that of liberating possibility as well as the presence of guilt, the role of the ethical and the role of destiny, seem to be the works that receive our respect and are ranked among the great works of the modern epoch.

Involved in violence, burdened by guilt, Cain seems to be a greater figure than the boisterously enterprising Ulysses, as adapted by Tennyson, or the largely passive and suffering Ulysses of Joyce. He does act, and his actions are based upon a laudable quest for freedom, for dignity, for some form of human worth; but these very actions seem implicated in violence and call forth the shouldering of some harsh destiny and necessity. An element of dire intractability will never be absent from the theme, but this also means that the theme issues a call for an encounter with reality, with history and its consequences. This is no Promethean theme, no projection of an absolute will, but rather one that shows the will meeting reality, and this dire and dual confrontation will be true from beginning to end.

In its broadest sense, and we shall raise this argument again and again, the Cain-Abel story involves an encounter with history, oppressive, inevitable history, or history transcended and transformed but never ignored. In fact, perhaps the greatest contribution of the theme will be the program it provides for scrutiny of the ambiguities of human action, understood in the full complexities of historical change.

Part Two: Cain as Sacred Executioner

As already suggested, however briefly, citizen Cain and monstrous Cain constitute two well-known traditions of the Cain-Abel story. Each comes surrounded by a repertoire of common qualities and familiar patterns that will continue to have a part—large and small—in later versions of the theme. But there is another tradition, an unexpected and powerful one that will have an even more active part in the changes of Cain in the modern world, one that more fully reflects its complexities and problems. This is Cain as Sacred Executioner. The phrase, already utilized in the preceding section, is borrowed from Hyam Maccoby's *The Sacred Executioner: Human Sacrifice and the Legacy of Guilt.*[16] The Cain we have in Genesis 4 is perhaps only implicitly a Sacred Executioner, but the Cain that we have come to possess, the one that history and the theme's own potent resources have created for us, earns such a designation in a much fuller sense.

That complex and lengthy cultural period that we call the Renaissance was responsible for many new attitudes that were crucial in the formation of the modern West. One such fundamental concept undergoing change was that of time. Even historians of science and economic historians today acknowledge that the concept of time emerged in the Renaissance and was instrumental in shaping a new set of attitudes, attitudes that could be called "proto-industrial." What the Renaissance promoted, and here the economic historians Nathan Rosenberg and L. E. Birdzell are right, was a change in attitudes that permitted a "growth-system" conducive to innovation.[17] Essentially what the Renaissance introduced was a changed attitude toward change itself.

The Cain-Abel story seems to fit into and benefit from these new attitudes toward historical change. Although, in its essential elements, expressive as they are of violence and disruption, the Cain-Abel story is not a conservative myth, traditionally, it had lent itself to accounts of degeneration, and this is as true of citizen Cain as it is of the monster-spawning Cain. But of course in a different epoch, there is no reason why Cain and Abel could not come to stand equally for regeneration. What we will come to witness is a new citizen Cain, this time not viewed from the perspective of religious "atonement" but rather one willing to live within the contradictions of history, for whom history can be only a cracked mirror, but whose motives and actions are directed toward peace and social order. We are of course alluding to Machiavelli's New Prince, who has the courage to enter into historical change and out of this dynamic and difficult moment to create viable and enduring institutions. It is not so much that the Cain-Abel story is utilized in these accounts but that its own internal dynamics are in accord with this new historical moment and themselves undergo reflective alteration because of the changes brought about in other modes of thought. It should be emphasized, however, that such alteration does not occur simply within a generalized frame of thought; it is expressed in such critically pertinent stories as Romulus and Remus and in Shakespeare's great brother dramas, where, indeed, the Cain-Abel story is present by name in important instances.[18] The changes in Renaissance thinking not only comply with but actually foster the possibilities for change and innovation contained in the Cain-Abel story.

We must remember that this is not a Faustian or a Promethean theme; in its basic components, and in the questions it provokes the Cain-Abel story is social, and, as a consequence, its ways are modulated. If Cain (or his Roman counterpart, Romulus) is vindicated, it is because each is able to guarantee a rule of law, or place a limit on personal willfulness, in the same way that ritual might be utilized to dispel the envy of the gods against required acts of human violence. The way to historical innovation is validated because these actions, we come to realize, are dominated not by heedlessness but by a serious attempt to satisfy the powers that be. These twin motivations, endemic but submerged in the Cain-Abel story, of violent disruption and yet the assumption of guilt, of action and yet of conscience, are responsible for the appeal of the theme in the Renaissance and, especially, beyond in the postromantic era.

Although it is a cliché of Italian and modern cultural criticism to juxtapose Dante and Machiavelli, if Cassirer's work is any indication, such a conjunction can prove to be enormously effective and revealing.[19] For as much as Dante may be looking backward, and indeed his mythos is conservative, he was responding precociously to developments that would only gain force in the modern world. For instance, his Ulysses in *Inferno* 26 is a potent presentation because, in that figure, Dante anticipated the energetic expansionism of Western man—indeed the occidental expansion. And if his superior creation has created problems for later criticism, it is only because Dante's own evaluation of his character was superseded by the events that he anticipated. And as Ulysses' cohort in Hell is Guido da Montefeltro, who by his own admission was more of the fox than the lion, we can see that some of the code words of the Machiavellian Prince were not unknown to Dante—indeed they are Ciceronian and classical.

But there are other, more important reasons for linking the two. Max Weber is certainly correct in his argument, made in "Politics as a Vocation," that both politics and religion preside over and represent two methods of response to the same event: a "dark event," the foundation sacrifice. Dante and Machiavelli, two Florentines of the early and High Renaissance, are among the purest instances of the religious and the political solutions, but solutions to the same problem, an originary act of violence that seems to be at the foundation of the city and state if not of existence itself.

Like Augustine, Dante was not unaware of the meaning of foundation sacrifice; as we have said, he simply came to deplore it. The consequences of civil war were such that Dante came to realize that society required for its peaceful functioning not a foundation myth based upon blood sacrifice but rather a divinely ordered myth based upon justice and charity. If the Sacred Executioner was to put an end to accelerating violence and to undifferentiation, Dante found that, contrary to expectations, those were the very products of civil war and that civil war has its own foundations in a modern ritual sacrifice. As we have had many occasions of late to learn, long-lasting strife produces such an interlocking system of charge and countercharge that culpability becomes universal. This is a condition of moral chaos, where all are guilty and no one can speak for justice. With undifferentiation, the voice of justice is silenced. The Buondelmonte murder, the origin of then contemporary Florentine history, is purposefully described by Dante as such a sacrifice, an act of propitiation to the God of War, which instead of being regenerative turned out to have the opposite effect. Civil war, its causes and consequences, is the basic reality that Dante must encounter, and in so doing he explores the deepest recesses and specific realities of Citizen Cain, and even of his later, reformed version, the Sacred Executioner.

Dante, although depending on Augustine in many ways and particularly, as we shall see, on book 15 of the *City of God*, carries no built-in opposition to the city. Even in the *Paradiso*, in the celebrated encounter with Charles Martel, Dante takes as a basic assumption, one not requiring proof, that life would be worse if humankind did not live in cities (8.115–17). And even in the Earthly Paradise, Dante is promised he will only be a "silvano" (or "forester") for a short period of time: his true destination is to arrive at the city and be a citizen in that city where "Christ is a Roman" (*Purgatorio*, 32.100–2). Accordingly, we should not be surprised that Dante's Cain is not a Citizen Cain but rather a monstrous one that is the more monstrous because he is so real. History itself has bred its own flavor of monstrosity. Dante's *Commedia* is a poem of civilization: the danger is the feud, not the sophisticate (although some deleterious aspects of urbanity certainly infect Dante's bad counselors). The feud that leads to civil war has a way of unleashing monstrosities that are more horrible than are all the monsters. The accelerating reciprocal violence, the undifferentiation and replication, all mean that it is impossible to distinguish rights and wrongs. Where all are guilty, as in Shakespeare's first historical tetralogy, the series of plays culminating in *Richard III*, justice itself is the primary casualty. Rather than serving to limit undifferentiation and reciprocal violence, the foundation sacrifice is its sanctioned progenitor, its original cause. For this reason, then, Dante must take current actions back to their sources, the foundation sacrifice, and in the debilities of the source, any conception of a Sacred Executioner must also suffer.

The Cain that we first encounter in *Purgatorio* 14 is a Cain different from others we have known. Although bursting on the scene in the terraces of envy, he does not fit the conventional epitomes of envy. Rather, as an admonitory example, he enters crying out line 14 from Genesis 4, "Everyone that findeth me shall slay me" ("Anciderrami qualunque m'apprende"; 1.133). Although he arrives as a lightning bolt and departs amid a detonating report of thunder, he is an awful, a terrible, but not a monstrous Cain—such as we will witness in the lower Inferno. In fact, Cain makes his appearance there not simply as the prototype of the first murderer, the killer of his brother, but as the representation of the fuller social consequences of that and of similar actions in history. That is, he is so terrible because he must continue to live as the first victim of the personal horror brought about by the atmosphere of reciprocal violence, the vendetta, that he helped introduce. His context is decidedly historical since he comes following Guido del Duca's heartrending account of the degradation of his native Romagna. A cursed land is followed by the first cursed criminal, who is the titular head of the deterioration that the Romagna has come to know. Hence, Cain is presented not as the epitome of envy but rather as the initiator of violence who turns out to be its natural and retributive victim, living in dread of retaliation.

This is a picture of Cain the terrorized, not Cain the terrible. And this is his legacy—and that of envy in its larger social implications—to the ravaged Romagna.

In the Caina, the first section of the Cocytus, we encounter a fuller picture of the consequences of civil war and its terrible, unrelenting divisions. Another disastrous effect of civil war is undifferentiation, whereby antagonists—victors and victims—come to resemble one another. This results in another significant alteration in the Cain-Abel story. Within the experience of civil war or its more primitive antecedent, the feud, the Cain-Abel theme loses its polarities. Everyone comes to be contaminated by the spreading guilt of reciprocal violence. The more pernicious effect, of course, is that no one can speak for justice (which is why one of Dante's persistent questions concerns the presence of any just people amid the ruins of the divided city). So it is, then, that in the Caina, that initiatory and determining stage in the downward and degenerative processes of Cocytus, the true gateway to Hell, the brothers are victim-culprits, so bound together by mutual animosity as to be practically indistinguishable. The brothers are so constricted because, like Cain and Abel, they are from the same womb, "d'un corpo usciro." But there is more than poignancy at brotherly division here in the lower Inferno. The Alberti brothers are actually locked together in a ferocity that mimics their earlier and pacific unity as innocent children. The very structure of brotherhood makes up a situation of doubleness and hence of reciprocity. In the cruel intensity of Cocytus' infernal punishment, they are perversely compacted. The very links that should have bound them together in an ideal of brotherhood are here reinforced with a terrible vengeance, that of undifferentiation. If the feud is the opposite of reciprocity, then undifferentiation is the travesty of communion. The brothers reflect the political divisions of the time: one, Napoleone, was a Ghibelline, and the other, Alessandro, was a Guelph. The division was exacerbated by the arbitrariness of parental preference: to Napoleone, their father left only the *decimas*, or tenth of the patrimony. The brothers literally killed each other, and the feud continued when Alberto, the son of Alessandro, killed Orso, the son of Napoleone.

Ever since my essay "Ulysses' Brother: The Cain-Abel Theme in Dante's *Commedia*," I have belabored the significance of the changes that Dante brings to the Cain-Abel story. What the feud and civil war or, rather, Dante's explorations of their consequences have done is to convert the differentiated Cain-Abel into the larger motif of *freres ennemis.* By means of the processes of civil war, there is little possibility of differentiating one brother from the other. But, Dante feels, this is the inevitable logic of Citizen Cain. In a startling transformation, Cain, rather than representing the limited but genuine values of the earthly city, now becomes a monster; Citizen Cain has been transformed into his own monstrous progeny. Indeed, as we shall have occasion to reiterate, when history becomes a nightmare, the Cain is a monster, both presiding over and reflecting the consequence of undifferentiation. When the antagonists of Cain have become his counterparts and not his opposites, this means that the values of Abel have been lost to the city. However, this does not mean that the values of Abel have been lost completely, that Abel is not germane. Rather, his agents have become those rare instances of single just men and women—dear to Milton as well as to Dante—who stand in isolation against the overwhelming and preponderant deterioration of their times. Historically, the values of Abel have been banished from the city, and the only alternative left to any Abelite figure is separation, the time-honored condition of pilgrimage. From the depths of his own personal experience, Dante transforms exile into the purposive and positive religious experience of pilgrimage. This means of course that (what had been so potently present in Heb. 11:15–16 and in the remarkable meditations of Philo) earthly citizenship is no longer viable; it becomes the debased alternative to genuine belonging in the City of God, the intermediary stage to which is real viability, or pilgrimage.

Through his spokesman, Marco Lombardo, in *Purgatorio* 16 Dante argues that the disintegration of moral polarities—the very possibility of justice itself—is the direct product of the larger confusion of Church and Empire. The encroachment of the one upon the legitimate powers of the other has meant for each a loss of its purpose, the larger undifferentiation. Although this means ideally that disaster, historically caused, is not necessary, realistically the patterns of events indicate that it has become typical and preponderant. If disaster does make historians of us all, this reality drives Dante back to seek out the origins of his own and his city's debacle. When Dante turns to the original event of modern Florentine history, he finds a murder—the Buondelmonte murder of 1215—that he deliberately casts as a blood sacrifice. Although Dante had clear conceptions of the real and theoretical possibilities of a just society, the tenure of such a society is all too brief. It stands exposed not only to historical change and human malfeasance but also to its own blood beginnings, which await their moments of opportunity to spring and reassert their primitive sway. This means that the city does not do, cannot do, what it was intended to do. Founded to preserve humankind from the brutalities of existence, it does exactly the opposite, unleashing them on an unsuspecting and vulnerable society in a more horrid and monstrous way. If the ultimate contest of the story of Cain is with blood origins, with the capacity to overcome those origins, violent though they may be, and thus elude the closing grip of history, then Dante sees little possibility for regeneration. Rather, like Augustine, he sees the city trapped in the divisions of its origins, and such original sin always manages to reassert itself.

Cacciaguida's historical chronicle of the happier, more primitive days of the Florentine commune leads up to the former grandeur of the Amidei family, one of whose daughters was jilted by Buondelmonte and who then retaliated by murdering the young man as he rode in a carriage to church. The civil war that follows destroyed the Amidei family. And for the Buondelmonti, who were latecomers to the city, it would have been better had they been thrown into the Ema River rather than be actors in such fateful events. The *but* or *ma* of the concluding tercet is forceful, like a vast historical sigh at what was not to be:

> Ma conveniesi a quella pietra scema
> ché guarda il ponte che Fiorenza fesse
> vittima nella sua pace postrema.

> (But it was needful that to the wasted stone which guards the bridge
> Florence should offer a victim in her last days of peace.)
> *Paradiso*, 16.145–47[20]

The wasted stone was the statue of Mars that stood at the entrance of the Ponte Vecchio. Here, Buondelmonte's carriage was assaulted on Easter Sunday. The feast of the Resurrection following the sacrifice of Christ stands in ironic contrast to the consequences of the Buondelmonte murder. What Dante has done in this tercet is to call attention to two different versions of blood sacrifice, the one of the earthly, the other of the heavenly city.

It is for this reason that I wish to concentrate on Dante's description of the original event, the origin of Florence's troubles: the murder of Buondelmonte and the origins of the civil war that can be traced to the division of the feuding families. The tercet in which Dante describes this even is in itself among the most powerful in the entire *Commedia*—this by virtue of its compact poetic density and its radiating scope of reference; the murder of Buondelmonte on Easter Sunday 1215 is described in terms of a foundation sacrifice that yielded far-from-beneficent effects. This description brings Dante to other, far more profound interpretations of the divided city.

René Girard has written compellingly in *La violence et le sacré* of the sacrificial murder as a kind of self-regulating device whereby society stabilizes and maintains itself. The scapegoat absorbs the blows of society, bundles them up, and carries them away with him. The net effect of this process of "unanimous victimage" is the prevention of precisely that kind of accelerating reciprocal violence and undifferentiation that the feud and its heir, the civil war, seem to engender. Hence the importance of this primitive "dark event" at the origin of what was for Dante modern Florentine history. It was to put a halt to the wheeling exchange of violence that foundation sacrifice was established. This may have been in Mosca dei Lamberti's mind when he uttered the pernicious advice that became so notorious, "Capo ha cosa fatta" ("What's done is done"), and thus persuaded the Amidei not merely to hurt the offending Buondelmonte but to kill him (*Inferno*, 28.107). Mosca is rightly punished in Hell for this bad counsel. His advice was nefarious because it did not put an end to hostilities but rather initiated the extraordinary long and bloody cycle of hostilities, of attack and counterattack, that came to typify proceedings of Guelphs and Ghibellines and subsequently the replication of these procedures in the antagonisms of White and Black Guelphs. This advice was the "mal seme," the bad seed for the Tuscan people: its tendency was to proliferate and reproduce its own repeated chain of likenesses. The advice brought its own power of retributive replication, as Dante was inspired to remind Mosca: "la morte di tua schiatta," the death of his own line. What is produced is a kind of retaliatory ferocity, of the same kind with which Farinata in *Inferno* 10 is able to respond to Dante, reminding him of how difficult he will find it to return to Florence. The end result of this original sacrificial act is the kind of accelerating reciprocal violence, marked by indistinguishability and undifferentiation, as aggressors become victims and are obliged to undergo the pain to which they had put their erstwhile opponents. How much of twentieth-century history might be told in these terms, where victims become aggressors and victims in their turns. The replicative mirror effect of these actions is indeed maddening, and their greatest victim, particularly of the self-justifying mutual recriminations, is justice.

In the same way that the strife between Whites and Blacks is not the beginning, so it is not the end. There is a worse horror, a more infernal product of the processes of undifferentiation: degradation, a downward cycle of pejoration resulting finally in a terrible reversal. Here I would like to refer to Walter Burkert's *Homo necans*, man the hunter.[21]

In Burkert's theory, the practices surrounding the hunt—hunting, killing, distributing, pleading, propitiating, cleansing—all were related to and in some way the dim ancestor of the foundation sacrifice. Both Girard and Burkert—whose respective works appeared coincidentally in 1972—recognize at the heart of society a "dark event" that is violent, and each recognizes this dark event as somehow necessary to existence and even social life.[22] Each acknowledges, consequently, a tragic basis to existence.

Dante turns things around. The foundation sacrifice does not result in the organized prevention of cycles of recurrent violence. This is not to be seen as a violation of Girard's theory, only the recognition that his schema of ritual origins undergoes elaboration in history, as he himself argues.[23] Similarly, the rites of *Homo necans* do not precede ritual sacrifice; rather, in Dante's experience of history, they follow it. The end product of the sacrificial victimization of Buondelmonte was Fulcier da' Calboli, the hunter of the remaining White Guelphs in Florence.

This description occurs in the canto of the *Purgatorio* (14) parallel to that of Cacciaguida in the *Paradiso*. Another father figure of an earlier generation laments the mutability and decline that have afflicted his region, in this case the Romagna. Guido del Duca, like Cacciaguida, rehearses the litany of names that were once great and are now obscured; he too bemoans the process of bastardization that has taken place. Most families are better off who do not seek to reproduce themselves in such degenerate times.

Dante begins this encounter by having Guido del Duca describe the flow of the Arno to the sea as a process of bestial deformation: the inhabitants along the river's course in turn pejorate from pigs, to dogs, to wolves, to foxes (ll. 29–57). The foxes are, as we shall see, the Pisans, and the wolves are the Florentines. In this capacity, they are of course far from innocent, and that is one of the consequences of the long-lasting civil war: a general distribution of guilt. But even Dante must express his horror when the triumphant Blacks in effect hire a professional soldier, Fulcier da' Calboli, to be their willing instrument of extirpation. Guido foresees the arrival of Fulcier, the "cacciator di quei lupi " ("the hunter of those wolves"; ll. 58–66). In 1303, Fulcier assumed the post of *podesta* of Florence—a post he was to reassume in other towns of central Italy in the course of his rather long and evidently prosperous career. He hunted down the families of the Whites and brutally killed them (Dante, in fact, regards him as a hireling, a bounty hunter who is reimbursed for his activities by being extraordinarily reappointed to a second semester as *podesta* beyond the usual single term of six months). The entire episode reeks of the slaughterhouse, as indeed the victims are described as "antica belva," old cattle ready for market. Calboli as hunter emerges covered with blood. "Sanguinoso esce dala trista selva" ("Bloody he comes out of the wretched wood"). Dante rightly casts the Buondelmonte murder as the mythic reenactment of an ancient rite in which an immolated victim is offered to the mutilated statue of the God of War. But this did not turn out to be a propitiatory rite but rather one that led to more carnage, in fact, the very undifferentiation that the scapegoat sacrifice was intended to avoid. In this process of reversal, monsters are bred. The hunter as butcher emerges from the carnage. *Homo necans* is the result of the original murder. The blood beginnings of existence are not atoned but rather are made all too patent. But there is an even more important reversal. The *citta partita* has become the *trista selva*. The city itself has regressed to the savage place that its very foundation was intended to transcend. Its mean streets have become the savage wood, and man has reverted in his nature to being a hunter. Far from representing a refuge from savagery, the city, in its blood sacrifices and carnage, seems dedicated to reproducing the *selva oscura* that Dante first intended to elude. This is why his false start at the poem's beginning must be corrected by another commencement. His regeneration requires that he be brought right up against the thigh of the beast.

Rather than resolving these antagonisms, the closed confines of the city seem to aggravate them. The wall of preservation has become a mechanism for entrapment. The citizens, like rats, gnaw at one another within its confines. Consequently, the ultimate statement of this process of undifferentiation and degradation, the ultimate act of reversal whereby the *citta partita* becomes the *trista selva*, must be cannibalism. Charles Singleton has urged us to dismiss anthropophagal speculations in *Inferno* 33 as unworthy.[24] But why should they be unworthy? From all that we have learned, there is nothing unknown to human conduct in that practice. Even the chimpanzees do it. To acknowledge the anthropophagal implication of the Ugolino episode is not to infer that Dante condones such practice but merely to underscore the extreme processes of undifferentiation, degradation, and reversal that the political vehemence of the time seems to have unleashed.

This Massacre of the Innocents is the nadir of the hopelessness that Hell must finally promote. As in Shakespeare's *Richard III*, nearly a century of civil war has given birth to undifferentiation. No one can speak for justice in the terrible tangle of charge and counteraccusation (as the Ugolino-Ruggiero struggle would illustrate). The massacre of the children is an indication of the closing of the future, as a final source of innocence is removed. In his condemnation Dante has recourse to a classical city: Pisa is a "novella Tebe," a new Thebes, which itself was divided by several brother murders and, as a consequence, worthy of invocation as a negative ideal by means of which Pisa's own transgression may be measured. In some ways there is a connection between Thebes—the brother murder, the divided city— and cannibalism. If we see why the foundation myth of the brother murder is at the origin of the divided city and, for Dante was well as for Augustine, results in the terrible process of undifferentiation, we also see it is not only implied but intellectually necessary that this same process should involve cannibalism. The divided city—and this explains Dante's vituperative invocation of Thebes—results not only in undifferentiation but also in reversal; the products of life itself are turned against their roots. Cannibalism is the end of this process and the true inverse of fraternity, both of which prospects are contained within the Cain-Abel story.

When Cain makes his distraught appearance in *Purgatorio* 14, he is attended by a group of familiars. His entrance takes place on the terrace where envy is purged. Moreover, the central moral question of these cantos derives its answer verbatim from Augustine's book 15 of the *City of God* and from the very section where Cain is introduced to carry the rubric of the earthly city. In this canto, so marked by a sense of civic decline, Guido del Duca laments his own sin of envy but then turns to humankind to bemoan a common affliction: "O human kind," he cries out, "why do you set your hearts where needs must be exclusion of partnership?" ("O gente umana, perche' poni 'l core la'v'e mestier di consorte divieto?"). In the subsequent canto this question is resumed by Dante and answered (in Augustinian language) by Virgil:

Perché s'appuntano i vostri disiri
dove per compagnia parte si scema,
invidia move il mantaco a'sospiri.
Ma se l'amor dela spera suprema
torcesse in suso il disiderio vostro,
non vi sarebbe al petto quella tema;
ché, per quanti si dice púi tí "nostro"
tanto possiede piú di ben ciascuno,
e piú di caritate arde in quel chiostro.

(It is because your desires are fixed where the part is lessened by shar-
ing that envy blows the bellows to your sighs; but if the love of the
highest sphere bent upward your longing, that fear would not be in
your breast. For there, the more they are who say ours, the more of
good does each possess and the more of charity burns in that cloister.)
(15.48–57)

The two points for discussion here—the provenance of the passage from book 15 of the *City of God* and the extraordinarily large
social role of envy—are actually connected. In chapter 5 of book
15, Augustine makes some necessary distinctions: unlike Romulus
and Remus, Cain and Abel are not motivated by the same desires,
"[f]or Abel was not solicitous to rule in the city which his brother
built."[25] This means, on the other side, that Cain did not kill his
brother out of fear for his own safety or in defense of his own provisions; rather, "he was moved by the diabolical, envious hatred
with which the evil regard the good, for no other reason
than because they are good while themselves are evil." This is a
theological scheme whereby evil is radical and by its nature irreducible to further explanation. The passage that follows is the one
on which Dante relies:

> For the possession of goodness is by no means diminished by being
> shared with a partner (*"consorte"*) either permanent or temporarily
> assigned; on the contrary the possession of goodness is increased to the
> concord and charity of each of those who share it. In short, he who is
> unwilling to share this possession cannot have it; and he who is most
> willing to admit others to a share of it will have the greatest abundance
> to himself. (482)

The fact that Dante has clearly used this remarkable passage from
Augustine is less important than is the total context of the Cain-Abel
story, the earthly city, social discord, and envy that are at the heart of

the larger vision that inclines Dante toward Augustine and that he finds corroborated by his personal and public experiences. The earthly city is defined by the actions of Cain, and his motivation is envy, which is here translated into a problem with enormous social repercussions.

We anticipate here a large change in the meaning and associations of envy. Harry Stack Sullivan suggests that envy may be "the active realization that one is not good enough."[26] Even though the concept has been internalized and made dependent on the subject's sense of his own worth, it does not conceal the explosive social ingredients of envy: how precisely does one live with the realization that one is not good enough? How does society, and the informing mythos of any social structure, assuage or sublimate such realizations? Immediately we sense the larger social significance not only of envy but of its placement in the Cain-Abel story. Dante's conception of envy goes beyond Sullivan's in that he specifically locates it in a moral philosophy with strong social and ethical connections.

As Marco Lombardo explains in canto 16, it is because the Church and the Empire have lost respect for each other's separate but coordinated function that the vision of any higher ideal has been lost. If the Church, in its institutional being and in its leading representatives, is seen to be striving for the same things as ordinary natural man, then the particular vision of which the Church is guardian will itself be discredited. Moreover, if the Church intervenes and thwarts the power of the Empire, then the secular power devoted to maintaining social order will find itself thwarted. The Church and the Empire have become tangled up, as undifferentiated in their actions and goals as have the political parties of the day, the religious orders, and the individuals, such as the Alberti, who are so ferociously interlocked in the Caina.

Envy exists, Dante means, because the vision of any higher purpose and goal has been discredited. But the particular vehemence with which people strive for the unworthy goals and particular horrors perpetrated are explained by Dante's sense of humankind possessing an innate, powerful and undeniable urge to return to God. When this desire is frustrated, the mimetic energy still remains active but misdirected, and the violent reversals of which the lower Inferno bears witness are the result. This is an extraordinarily condensed version of the theology of desire that motivates Dante's thinking. It does explain, however abridged, why envy can be so massively destructive as a social force.

The *Inferno* is meant to depict the Hell that the city can become (in our own day, the power of the American cinema has brought this realization home). In Dante's poem, the Cain-Abel theme, rather than being different from Romulus and Remus, actually enters into the same association with foundation sacrifice that Augustine first suggested. This means that the qualities of Abel are exempted from the Inferno and that brothers become as undifferentiated in their new violent attachments as were Romulus and Remus: They become subsumed under the rubric of *freres ennemis*, and indeed, in this new format, Cain becomes monstrous. Foundation sacrifice is not only the foundation myth; it becomes the prevailing myth of the earthly city, the primitive act from which the city can never seem to shake free. Committed, then, to processes of devolution, Citizen Cain can only terminate in cannibalism, the ultimate end of any society in an advanced state of corruption.

In order to realize his qualities, Abel must escape the confines of the earthly city and find his true nature by means of pilgrimage, by which he hopes to atone for the lost brotherhood of the foundation sacrifice and reconstitute the true brotherhood of the heavenly city. For this reason, brotherhood, so disfigured in the *Inferno*, is recaptured in the *Purgatorio*, the canticle whose dominant mode is fellowship on the way of pilgrimage. But the brotherhood is that of a spiritual brotherhood, a new confraternity that joins together those who have set loose from their native confines. For instance, the sublime meeting with Forese Donati in cantos 23 and 24 (along with canto 8, the most representative cantos of the *Purgatorio*) is informed by the sense of spiritual recognition in the face of physical disfigurement. In fact, the separate locations of the Donati family, forming one of the crucial triptychs of the poem, are an expression of the disintegration of the social world that the *Purgatorio* so poignantly records. Personal destinies divide families, and while Piccarda will be a touchstone for Paradise and Forese will make his way in Purgatory, the wayward and headstrong Corso is hell-bent for destruction, where intimations of his death suggest his own disfigurement, when he will be left "vilmente disfatto." Earthly life is a process of undoing for which, then, the brother sacrifice is a fitting metaphor. Amid the damage and the terror, a new calling is issued to a better brotherhood. This means of course that the *Purgatorio* is itself steeped in blood, the blood that is shed and the blood that is generously offered, that is, the discipleship of the blood.

In canto 5, for instance, two violent deaths recall vividly the bloodshed at the death agony. Jacopo del Cassero, wounded in desperate flight, watches his lifeblood leave him: "e lí vid' io / delle mie vene farsi in terra lago" ("and there I saw a pool growing on the ground from my veins"; ll. 83–84). Buonconte da Montefeltro, wounded through the throat, describes his own death flight: "fuggendo a piede e'nsanguinando il piano" ("flying on foot, and bloodying the plain"; 1.99). But the same violent shedding of blood finds its counterpart in the Christian sacrifice. At the gates of Purgatory, the third step of recovery was colored porphyry: "si fiammeggiante, / come sangue che fuor di vena spiccia" ("so flaming red as blood that spurts from a vein"; 9.102–3). And we can comprehend some of the moral trauma in this process when Provenzan Salvani frees himself from pride and liberates a friend, when, begging for ransom money in the square at Siena, he brought himself to tremble in every vein ("si condusse a tremar per ogni vena"; 11.138). The warrant of this blood discipleship is indicated by Forese when he explains to Dante why it is that the souls flock to the tree of abstinence; it is the same desire that led "Cristo lieto" to call out to the Father, "quando ne liberò con la sua vena" ("when he made us free with his blood"; 23.73–75). The *Purgatorio* thus counters the myth of foundation sacrifice so dominant in the *Inferno* by virtue of its prevailing mythos of a renewed brotherhood of the spirit joined in pilgrimage and based on the blood sacrifice of Christ.

As a member of a genuine community, however, Dante never relinquished his hopes for eventual reconstitution of the earthly city itself, and not only any earthly city but the Florence that he knew and loved as a child and that nurtured and fed his talents and development as a young man. We should bear this in mind when we say that we do not demote the remarkable presentations of brotherhood and fellowship that prevail in the *Purgatorio* by stating that Dante's highest quest is for fatherhood. In fact, brotherhood as such (*fratellanza*) is a phrase employed only once in all of Dante's works, indicating a kind of alliance of arms and as a consequence an inheritance from the system of loyalties and obligations of the feudal nobility.[27] To be sure, Roman thought gives little expression to brotherhood, and this is as it should be if the city itself was founded on fratricide.[28] Virgil indicates as much when he portrays Aeneas, whose association is familial and genealogical, as carrying father and leading son and when he confirms that the foundation of the line that led to Rome's greatness was dependent upon exclusion, the death of Turnus. Christianity also preserved brotherhood for the monastic orders, and its own controlling myths were genealogical: Father, Son, and Holy Ghost. Christ could have no brother (despite the recordings of history), and nowhere does Dante mention his own.

The overarching quest of Dante's poem is for fatherhood because Dante's heroic energies are directed at reconstituting the fallen and sundered human community. In this enterprise the sustaining figure is the father, primarily because he has the encompassing vision that is able to contain the terrible, rival energies of life and that converts rivals by intellectual justice into complementary forces; that is, he makes brothers into sons. The great plague of Dante's time was that component parts had become adversarial: Church versus State, love versus knowledge, Franciscan versus Dominican, and Guelph versus Ghibelline. Opposites had become exclusive rather than mutually defining. Only the father, not the brother, has the capacity to rise to the level of the higher vision and restore mutuality. In fact, for Dante, and this is essential for our story, brotherhood depends upon fatherhood and would be lost without it. This explains why the central encounter in each of the canticles is with a large father figure, Brunetto Latini (*Inferno*, 15), Guido del Duca-Marco Lombardo (*Purgatorio*, 14–16), and Cacciaguida (*Paradiso*, 15–17).

It would of course be inappropriate here to manufacture another dualism, one of brotherhood versus fatherhood. But, subdued though it may be, a kind of tension exists between the two ideals. They are not, after all, twin ideals. It is only in the modern world that brotherhood comes to the front with a conceptual and ideological force quite different from the prior two traditions, that of the blood brotherhood and that of the discipleship of the blood. These two forces themselves actually required the presence of lord or Savior. The third historical emergence of brotherhood occurs only at the cost of the real or symbolic death of the father, that is, after the French Revolution.

In the greatest mutations along the way of the Cain-Abel story, Machiavelli's role is truly revolutionary despite the fact that he refers to Cain and Abel in only a very minor poem.[29] Machiavelli is so momentous because he turned Augustine's—and Dante's—views upside down and effected a return to the prior pagan conception, where Romulus—who enjoyed archetypal association with Cain in Augustine's account—becomes a Sacred Executioner from whose actions many good things accrued to Rome. Machiavelli's horizons are unmistakably historical and political. Where Augustine builds on two cities, a procedure that almost necessarily demotes the earthly city, Machiavelli limits the horizons of his perspective to humankind in history to one city. In this sense, his contributions may be said to re-paganize the theme, to de-theologize it. In Machiavelli's advice to the prince, the fate of the innocent Abel is all too evident: the unarmed prophet perishes with no claim on any higher restitution.

If in Machiavelli's thought the foundation crime may in certain circumstances be overcome, that is, if history itself can be transcended, this can be done only within history and not without pain and difficulty. Machiavelli's supreme myths have to deal with necessary conflict and decision. Since he, like almost everyone else before him, accepts as a political fact that only one person can rule or found a state, it is almost necessary that mythical and real brothers are pitted one against the other in the dire dilemma of political power. His vision of power is exclusive, requiring that the brother be discarded—precisely the exigency that Augustine and Dante wished to transcend in their vision of the inclusiveness of charity, where all the losses of life may be restored.

Nevertheless, despite these conditions that are grim and even harsh, they are acceptably so, as Machiavelli still embraces the Renaissance vision of possibility: some founding figures have emerged and can emerge who have the capacity to enter into historical change and out of its ambiguities and necessities restore human order. The quandary with which Machiavelli confronts the New Prince is far more difficult than that facing Plato's philosopher-king. Machiavelli has brought the traditional dilemma into history, into crucial moments of choice and power. By the very means of actions that are morally ambiguous, if not evil, Machiavelli's Prince must produce institutions that are viable and that contribute to the order and the welfare of the state. We can see why these changes brought about by the most important political philosopher of the modern world not only contribute to future arguments on which Cain-Abel, as a theme, depends but also appeal to the deepest energies and resources of the theme. This is primarily so because Machiavelli gives impetus to a closer scrutiny of historical change, to the intricate complexities of human life, and to a realistic assessment of the role of violence in effecting change or development of any sort. One should not imagine that because it is based on a vision of the world that assumes division and violence such scrutiny is immoral. Rather, what it seeks to establish are sound bases for evaluating genuine and long-lasting principles of change—change that is regenerative rather than degenerative.

Machiavelli effects this possible rehabilitation of an original act of violence by creating "space" around the event, or a larger forum for discussion and evaluation. Here *space* of course means greater breadth of judgment, but it also implies greater intricateness, even a kind of inextricability between event and consequence. Because means and ends are placed on the same continuum, it is erroneous to state that this is arguing that the end justifies the means. What Machiavelli does is enlarge the domain of what we call the "event." Rather than separating intention, act, and consequence into discrete units, he sees them as part of a larger duration where indeed they are part of a single unrolling phenomenon. Judgment, then, is not confined to act but must include intention, which, however, might only be retrospectively revealed by later actions. Machiavelli does not look to one act or event but rather to a series that includes intention, event, and further acts. At decisive moments in history, new individuals are called to acts that might be ambiguous, but the meanings of these acts are revealed by later acts that themselves help reveal intentions, or persistent purposes. The fundamental question that Machiavelli asks is, Was the New Prince violent in order to destroy or violent in order to mend? Was he dominated by private ambition or by the common good? In Romulus' case—and this makes Romulus the realistic yet heroic model for the New Prince—it becomes clear that the Roman founder had acted for the common good and not out of private ambition.[30] This is demonstrated by the fact that he immediately organized a Senate, reserving to himself only wartime powers as commander in chief of the army and the power to convoke the Senate. He submitted his individual will to the rule of law and the general good, actions that are vindicated by the fact that the institutions that he established continued to exist even in the time of the Republic. Where Augustine would present us with an earthly city that was irretrievably marred in its very foundation, Machiavelli shows us a revolutionary foundation act that may be legitimized.

With this important emphasis on intention; with the creation of space around the event; in fact, with the enlargement of what constitutes the event to a larger complex of interrelated forces that are difficult to separate; with the possibility that a "murderer" might even be a hero—a Sacred Executioner who endures evil in order to save the state—we can see what a contribution Machiavelli has made not only to the political account of Romulus and Remus but also to its archetypally joined parallel story, that of Cain and Abel. We can anticipate Joseph Conrad's *The Secret Sharer*, where Leggatt's act—

the so-called murder of the surly mate, the act that brands him as
Cain—is inextricably connected to his saving the ship and where,
moreover, the young captain's appropriation of the vagrant otherness
of Leggatt is instrumental in his own revitalization of the sagging
structures of authority. The pattern of political legitimation provided
by the Sacred Executioner has bold implications for the regeneration
of Cain and points to a new and potent revolution in attitudes toward
change. We further see what contributions Machiavelli made to the
legitimation of new regimes in the early modern period. Rather than
justifying any kind of takeover or conduct on the part of the New
Prince, Machiavelli's main contribution was in the program of
greater scrutiny that he advanced to judge complex bases of action.
If he wrote that the unarmed prophet perishes, he did not write that
the armed butcher triumphs but that the armed prophet may be victorious. The problem, as always, seems to be one of distinguishing
which is which.

These political and thematic lessons were not lost on Shakespeare.
In his second tetralogy of English history plays (*Richard II* to *Henry
V*), Henry Bolingbroke is himself seen to be Machiavelli's early modern prince, the founder of a new house at a decisive moment of historical change, a Sacred Executioner who enters into evil and not
only overthrows his monarch but is ultimately responsible for his
death. Shakespeare makes clear reference to the blood beginnings at
the foundation of a new state when, at the end of *Richard II*, the
already weary usurper, confronted with the corpse of his predecessor,
protests that he is full of woe "that blood should sprinkle me to make
me grow."[31] Accusatory blood that blighted the earth it at first
drenched is actually a necessary condition for his growth. Later, in *2
Henry IV*, when his efforts are redeemed in the good resolutions of his
son (who shows his own respect for law and the submission of individual ambition and caprice to principles of good government),
Henry IV then recognizes that he is indeed a Sacred Executioner as
well as a *bouc emissaire*. With his death, all the "soil of the achievement," the necessary and unavoidable acts that went into the reestablishment of order, will go with him into the earth (4.5.189–190). He
is the original founding prince who enters into the dilemma of historical change and with good purpose succeeds in renewing the state.
His revolutionary acts in the second tetralogy will be contrasted with
a similar revolution of the Yorkists in the first tetralogy, and by these
contrasts Shakespeare himself will add to the scrutiny of moral purpose amid historical change.

This line of argument can help us place in sensible relationship the two grand historical tetralogies (the first culminating in *Richard III* and the second in *Henry V*) that occupied so much of Shakespeare's interests in the 1590s. Rather than a single cycle of eight plays, they are instead two interrelated attempts to deal with the same problem, the one that Machiavelli signaled as the most crucial of the early modern period. The essential problem is that of historical change, even revolution, and when and upon what principles original revolutionary acts may or may not be validated. This problem enters fully into the dynamics of the Cain-Abel theme, which will be concerned with scrutinizing with extraordinary care the limits and possibilities of violence in effecting historical change.

The revolution of the Yorkists, which dominated the actions of the first tetralogy, failed when Richard III became a nemesis turning the principles of his house against his house. This denouement retrospectively exposed the original principles on which Yorkists framed their regime to be faulty. Instead of stability, cycles of repeated crime and reciprocal violence emerged. The question that is asked—and that is always being asked in the larger social dimensions of this study—is, "Who shall put an end to murder, and by what means?" This is why the processes of curse, replication, and undifferentiation are so crucial: they indicate that the original actions may not be justified but instead merely reproduce their own abhorrent likenesses— with a vengeance. The original actions of the House of York could not result in the establishment of any principles of justice. Indeed, there is a strong Marlovian strain in the Yorkist rulers, one that exposes an eagerness to possess the golden round of the kingship, but without any corresponding virtues or principles that would be conducive to good government. In short, their original acts of violence contained no principles—other than self-aggrandizement—for the sake of which such actions could be undertaken. In reality, then, no positive political ethic, nor even any principle of justice, can emerge from within the contents of the first tetralogy: the great deliverer, Henry of Richmond, the future Henry of Tudor or Henry VII, was whisked away from England when a youth and thus was exempt from the evil that contaminated an entire society.

Providing as it does a program for scrutiny of the complex bases of action in history, the Sacred Executioner and, by extension, Cain-Abel provide devices of legitimation as well as of denunciation. Where the Yorkist actions fail to gain validation, the Lancastrian program arrives at legitimation. In fact, the contrast is intended and precise, thus showing that the two tetralogies are much closer in purpose than has been heretofore thought. The Lancastrian revolution itself begins with a violent disruption, the "dark event" of Richard's deposition, with proliferating revolution, and with the possibility that Prince Hal would become another Richard II, thus providing a mocking replicative curse on Henry's early actions. The curse, so active in the first tetralogy, is present potentially in the second. If Henry fails, then the hold of the historical past is irreversible, and humankind's capacity for resolute but difficult actions effecting change is denied. The primary dramatic question is, Will Henry and his son, unlike York and his sons, be able to surmount the original sin and evolve stable principles of government, and have they legitimized revolution and historical change?

There is no question that Henry's actions are ambiguous. Although it is true that Richard II misunderstood the bases of power, was emotionally manic in his responses, and was as guilty of abdication as Henry was of usurpation, nevertheless Henry, while submitting in principle to Richard, did return with a show of force that (although technically formed to restore his patrimony) struck at the very heart of Richard's authority. Of even greater ambiguity are Henry's ultimate goals for England. These must all be clarified in the course of his struggle to secure his rule and eventual peace.

In the issues they raise, these plays may be compared with a yet greater series, Aeschylus' Oresteia, itself dependent upon two revolutionary acts of violence: one condemned and the other eventually legitimized (in fact, resulting, as does 2 Henry IV, in the triumph of law itself).[32] Each of the series is bound to explore principles of legitimation. Each addresses the question of replication and undifferentiation and the abiding question of how to act so as not to add to the series of crime and accusation. Clytemnestra's act of killing Agamemnon is not the act to end the previous cycles of reciprocal violence. Contrary to her expectations, she simply adds one more link to the chain of repeated crime, in fact, one that calls forth another act of violence. Her motives themselves are ambiguous: although she claims she is seeking justice for the murder of her daughter, she also needs to protect her relationship with Aegisthus. Subsequent actions do nothing to vindicate her original revolutionary act. She feels no guilt or sorrow but rather brazenly challenges the compunctious chorus of elders; she dismisses her children, she cannot throw off her attendant bad dreams, and she presides over a land where fear reigns. Retrospectively there is nothing her regime can produce to justify her original intentions and to legitimize her actions. Rather than being separate, her later actions are revealed to be part and parcel of her general unworthiness for rule.

The second and comparable revolutionary act, that of Orestes, has a different motivation, a different psychology, and a different outcome. The urging of Apollo elevates Orestes' motivation. Nevertheless, the event itself is still terrible. But unlike Clytemnestra, Orestes is overcome by guilt (which of course is different from her experience of fear). As Jacqueline de Romilly has so intelligently argued, the onset of Orestes' anguish marks the beginning of expiation.[33] The very fact of guilt indicates that his first act had not been in defiance of the gods and that his intentions are still within the frame of a moral order that guilt itself acknowledges. Orestes' actions, then, are moved to the larger plane of contest between the forces of illumination, hope, and positive change (Apollonian) and the darker chthonic powers of unyielding moral principle. Necessarily by the closest of margins, the progressive forces are triumphant. In fact, their victory serves to establish the rule of law and not to abrogate it.

Henry IV's sense of guilt is, then, of paramount importance in distinguishing his actions—his revolution—from that of the Yorkists. Unlike them, Bolingbroke does not exult in his triumph over his enemies but rather is overcome with guilt and nearly spent by his own sense of the burdens and the responsibilities of rule. In addition, his concern for the kind of ruler his son will be shows his overriding solicitude for the fate of his land. This concern with later consequence—that his son be a just ruler—retrospectively clarifies and legitimizes his original intentions. In fact, it reveals the qualities of the original enterprise and shows them to be valid. Despite earlier comparisons with Richard II, Hal does manifest his worthiness—in fact, he is obliged to prove it twice, once by showing his sense of honor on the field of battle and the other by showing his respect for law. Each of these reformations derives from a significant encounter with his father, and in each Hal proves himself by revealing his own sense of the burdened responsibilities of rule. This, as it turns out, is a major point of contrast with the Yorkists.

Out of a revolutionary act, a regime of law has been reestablished. An original act of violence is not necessarily condemned to see its own image repeated in a chain of actions and reactions. In this way, if history itself may be transformed, the ultimate contest is over the possibility of regenerative change. During the Renaissance, Machiavelli and Shakespeare, unlike Augustine and Dante, sought to make their keenest contributions to the problems and needs of their times the formulation and the dramatization of the possibility that some original acts of violence might be legitimized. In this sense, the Sacred Executioner and a regenerate Cain share a mutual and inter-related interest. The Cain-Abel theme, in one of its predominant aspects in the modern world, fits in with a new mode of appraisal and judgment. The central motive is the validation of change itself in con-test with the dark forces of history, but perhaps an even greater con-tribution and meeting point between the two allied interests is the program of scrutiny that they each provide, that is, the search for a realistic basis for analyzing and assessing actions in the extremely complex yet compelling arena of historical change.

The chapter in which Machiavelli justifies Romulus' action is titled "How a man must be alone to found a new republic or to reform com-pletely its ancient institutions." The necessary sacrifice of the brother seems to be required by such dire exclusivity. But this sacrifice is a metaphor for the general loss of the other, the divisiveness and changes of life itself. In *1 Henry IV*, the emergence of Hal is actually dependent upon the defeat of Hotspur, his cohort-rival in the contest to determine what qualities are to be representative of the newly developed modern England:

> Two stars keep not their motion in one sphere.
> Nor can one England brook a double reign
> Of Harry Percy and the Prince of Wales. (5.4.65–67)

Clearly, Hotspur is not qualified to lead the new nation that England was becoming. His honor-bound code is anachronistic, recalling an outmoded chivalric society. He seems single-minded and, as such, incapable of coping, as Hal does, with the multiple and complex lev-els of new English society. In fact, what Shakespeare has presented in the character and conduct of Hal is not only a figure suited to be king but also, looking far into the future, a glimpse into the protoindustrial mind, one already conditioned to control the energies of existence and, by manifesting such control, to master Nature and the condi-tions of life.

At the end of the nineteenth century and even earlier, such a tri-umph had come to be too one-sided, and critics mistakenly came to regret the loss of the energies that Hotspur contributed. This lament is mistaken as far as the histories are concerned, but when it comes to the later tragedies, particularly *Antony and Cleopatra*, a new per-spective is introduced. The sacrifice of the other in these historical bouts of dire exclusivity is regarded as too costly. Unlike the histories, the tragedies are concerned not with the virtues of the winners and the reasons for the defeat of the losers but rather with the defects of the winners and with the qualities of the losers, whose absence detracts from the very achievement of the winners. It appears that the very virtues of the winners disqualify their victory since they have no basis in fecundity or in any conditions for the sake of which actions are undertaken. In this sense, the means that are instrumental to success have become ends in themselves, and any deeper sources of conduct as well as grander goals seem to be avoided.

The conflict of Antony and Octavius must be regarded in the light of this readjusted vision. It would appear that in Shakespeare (and in this he is similar to Dante), the triumph of the Sacred Executioner has bred its own antitype. Lamenting the dire exclusivity to which the contest for rule has brought them, the victorious Caesar uses language similar to that employed by Hal in his conflict with Hotspur: "We could not stall together / In the whole world." The fatal development of the Roman Empire had room for only one rule. Although recognizing this necessity, Caesar still regrets it:

> But yet let me lament
> That thou, my brother, my competitor
> In top of all design, my mate in empire,
> Friend and companion in the front of war,
> The arm of mine own body, and the heart
> Where mine his thoughts did kindle—that our stars,
> Irreconcilable, should divide
> Our equalness to this. (5.1.40–48)

This striking repetition involves a revision. The facts of conflict and exclusivity remain the same, but their evaluations alter. We can recognize Octavius' true aptitudes for rule and yet also be sharply cognizant of the deficiencies of these very qualities when they are obtained at the cost of the virtues that Antony possesses. The organization of world empire seems to have been gained not only at the cost of spontaneity, individual courage and heroism, generosity, and loyalty but also by the more serious loss of the fructifying powers of life that give meaning to conquest and to achievement. The larger question of "to what end?" has been set aside for the purposes of instrumentalism.

The ramifications of this revision for modern versions of the Cain-Abel story are enormous. In *Antony and Cleopatra*, division is still seen to be endemic and necessary, and the other, the mysterious brother, who here represents vital qualities and energies, must once again be sacrificed. But this is not a wholesome encounter; the virtues of the sacrificed brother are not incorporated into a new and rejuvenated caliber of being, which is the larger justification of such sacrifice (be it the Christian sacrifice of the Mass or any of the sacrifices that are present in the accounts of regenerate Cain, where somehow the lost brother is brought back into greater fullness of being). Such expansion does not occur here; rather, a constriction of being does. This new and painful division Schiller will address in his *Naïve and Sentimental Poetry*, in which he discusses the "idealist" and "realist" types that would come to dominate the nineteenth century. Such division would hold vital resonance for the Cain-Abel story, but with a startling shift. In the postromantic, modern world, it is the regenerate Cain who becomes the aspirant quester and Abel the contented domesticated personality—that is, the pagan—but who by virtue of his very acquiescence comes to manage and represent the powers of society. In this context of Abel's demotion and Cain's promotion, we are left to contemplate the casualties of another terrible division, particularly when Abel's social victories seem to be at the cost of the total loss of the essential powers now figured by the dispossessed and uprooted Cain.

There are many lessons, models, and examples to be extracted from the Cain-Abel syndrome, nearly all of them hazardous. But two such extractions might be valuable. The first is that while division, some original act of violence, resides at the heart of the human experience, both religion and politics are the human means derived to remediate this dire situation. The religious invokes the better principles of a spiritual brotherhood, the political that of a realistic and somewhat benevolent figure who is capable of entering into the ambiguous arena of historical change and bringing about regeneration. The enemy of each seems to be undifferentiation, the accelerating violence so dependent upon charge and countercharge, a kind of moral no-man's-land, where nobody can speak for justice because all are guilty and victims alike, a condition so sadly reflected in our contemporary world.

Notes

1. Eli Weisel, "Cain and Abel: The First Genocide," in *Messengers of God: Biblical Portraits and Legends*, trans. Marion Weisel (New York: Random House, 1976), 37–64.

2. Arturo Graf, "La poesia di Caino," *La Nuova Antologia* 134 (March–April 1908): 440.

3. Auguste Brieger, *Kain und Abel in der deutschen Dichtung* (Berlin: Walter de Gruyter, 1934), locates "two centers" to the theme—sacrifice and fratricide—and these two centers turn out to be determinants of a dualism that Brieger calls variously "das religiose Moment" and "das menschliche Moment." The religious moment, or structure, revolves around the sacrifice and the humanistic around the fratricide. But each of these moments can have further historical spin-offs, with the humanistic, for instance, revealing a struggle between Man and God or between Man and Man that results in an "erotic" moment that may involve incest or a brother conflict for possession of the mother (1–2). Brieger's discussions are quite valid, but perhaps he may go wrong in not allowing for other component parts and not seeing more of these parts as active within the various moments.

4. René Zazzo, *Les Jumeaux, le couple et la personne*, 2 vols. (Paris: Presses Universitaires de France, 1960), chapter 8, "Les asymétries du couple," 614 ff., and "Dernières remarques": "La différenciation de deux partenaires par l'influence de l'un sur l'autre s'opere meme dans le cas défavorable a l'extrême ou les deux partenaires sont identiques, génétiquement" ("This differentiation of two partners by the influence of one on the other is active even in the most unfavorable of cases where the two are genetically identical"; 707).

5. Michel Tournier, *Les meteores* (Paris: Gillimard, 1975), 514–516, and *Gemini*, trans. Anne Carter (Garden City: Doubleday, 1981), 429–430.

6. Hyam Maccoby, *The Sacred Executioner: Human Sacrifice and the Legacy of Guilt* (London: Thames and Hudson, 1983), 7–40.

7. Philippe Sellier, "Le mythe de Cain," comments, "l'histoire de Cain, souvent mise en rapport avec celle de la Tour de Babel, symbolise infiniment mieux le déesastre de la transgression que ne fait l'anodin vol d'une pomme" ("The story of Cain, often related to that of the Tower of Babel, is an infinitely better symbol of the disaster of the Fall than any harmless theft of an apple"; 17). Martin Buber also writes, "It [Cain-Abel] and not the former [Adam and Eve] is the story of the first 'iniquity.'" *Good and Evil* (New York: Scribner, 1953), 81. Buber does, however, stress the "perspective founded on the combination of the two tales" (82).

8. See Helmut Schoeck, *Envy: A Theory of Social Behavior*, trans. Michael Glenny and Betty Ross (New York: Harcourt, Brace and World, 1969), 4, and throughout for a comprehensive study of envy. Rather than sociological, Schoeck's volume is a work of moral philosophy with a special thesis: envy is at the basis of democratic egalitarianism and is thus either sanitized (a work may be *enviable*) or unacknowledged (he notes its absence in the language of modern social scientists and even in the works of literary critics who discuss *Billy Budd*!). From our perspective, we can note the curious bibliographical lack of Cain and Abel studies in relation to *Billy Budd* and *East of Eden*. See also Peter Walcot, *Envy and the Greeks* (Warminster: Aris and Phillips, 1978), and Leslie H. Farber, "Faces of Envy," in *The Ways of the Will: Essays toward a Psychology and Psychopathology of Will* (New York: Basic Books, 1966), and "On Jealousy," *Commentary* 56 (1973): 50–56.

9. Melanie Klein, *Envy and Gratitude and Other Works, 1946–1963* (New York: Dell Publishing, 1975), 176–235.

10. Francis Bacon, "Of Envy," included in the *Essays* of 1625 and *Billy Budd, Sailor (An Inside Narrative)* by Herman Melville (New York: The Library of America, 1984), 1384. In light of future associations of Cain and monstrousness, it is revealing that Melville's address to Envy is preceded by the rhetorical question, "Is Envy then such a monster?"

11. Envy derives from the Latin *in-videre*, indicating a looking onto that is external; it is thus a primitive emotion associated with the eyes and vision (it knows nothing of *respicere*, the looking again that results in respect, or of *ad-mirare*, the looking up and outward that results in admiration).

12. Interesting enough, Dante's conception of envy is more like *Schadenfreude*, that is, more of a delight in another's misfortune than fear of another's success. This might reflect the powerful direction of his own personality. If, as Schoeck argues, envy is appropriate to democratic societies, then Dante's weakness of pride is more appropriate to his own concern with *gentilezza*, or nobility. In this sense, Dante's society, like Shakespeare's, is not threatened by a leveling resentment but rather by emulation, the energetic activity that aspires to be like the great. It is "ascencionist."

13. For discussions of envy and jealousy, se Schoeck, *Envy*, 95–97. Such distinctions are of course sliding and slippery. We might try another tack: if envy is the correlational opposite of admiration ("admiration is happy self-abandon, envy, unhappy self-assertion," says Kierkegaard, as quoted by Schoeck, 172), then envy might be dissolved by admiration, but the problems of jealousy would not be solved by admiration. Othello's problems would not be less severe if he admired Cassion, as in weakened moments he is brought to do. Iago's envy would be resolved if he brought himself frankly to admire Othello.

14. This quarrel with God the Father explains the later role of Cain as revolutionary figure. The easy transformation is understood by Albert Camus in his *L'Homme revolte* when he writes, "The history of rebellion, as we are experiencing it today, has far more to do with the children of Cain than with the disciples of Prometheus. In this sense it is the God of the Old Testament who is primarily responsible for mobilizing the force of rebellion." *The Rebel*, trans. Anthony Bower (New York: Vintage Books, 1956), 32.

15. This passage occurs in the *Works and Days* immediately after Hesiod distinguishes between two kinds of strife (Eris), the bad Eris that leads to destruction and the good Eris that leads to competition and improvement.

> This strife is good for mortals.
> Then potters eye one another's success and craftsmen, too;
> The beggar's envy is a beggar, the singer's a singer.

From *Hesiod*, trans. Apostolos N. Athanassakis (Baltimore: The Johns Hopkins University Press, 1983), 67. This incentive to work should not surprise us, given the title as well as the fact that the exhortation is addressed to his brother!

16. In August 1985, Professor Harold Fisch, himself profiting from Maccoby's suggestive arguments, delivered a paper, "Cain as Sacred Executioner," to be reprinted in *Byron, the Bible, and Religion: Essays from 12th International Byron Seminar* (Newark: University of Delaware Press, 1990). Judging from his précis, wherein Byron's Cain is described as a rebel and a Promethean seeker after knowledge and Cain's crime, like Adam's, as "an event in salvation history, a kind of *felix culpa*," there might be some divergences in our uses of the phrase "sacred executioner."

Sections from the material on Dante in this chapter (but also including other aspects of Cain) have already appeared in R. Quinones, "Ulysses' Brother: The Cain and Abel Theme in Dante's *Commedia*," in *Renaissance Studies in Honour of Craig Hugh Smyth*, (Florence: Giunti Barbera; 1985), and in a related piece, R. Quinones "Foundation Sacrifice and Florentine History in Dante's *Commedia*," *Lectura Dantis* 4 (1989): 10 ff.

17. Nathan Rosenberg and L. E. Birdzell Jr., *How the West Grew Rich: The Economic Transformation of the Industrial World* (New York: Basic Books, 1986), 20–34. See also my *Renaissance Discovery of Time* (Cambridge: Harvard University Press, 1972), and, for a general summary of the main lines of that book, "The New Dynamic of Time in Renaissance Literature and Society," in *Time: The Greatest Innovator*, ed. Rachel Doggett (Washington, D.C.: Folger Shakespeare Library, 1987), 25–37. Although in such a work as this—one that seeks to show significant changes—it is proper to emphasize the innovative elements that will in time become dominant, it should be remarked that in large part Renaissance treatments of Cain and Abel were traditional. Francis Bacon allied Abel as shepherd with the contemplative life and Cain as tiller of the soil with the active life. Judy Z. Kronenfeld, in a paper delivered at a Modern Language Association session in 1977, "Abel, the Contemplative Shepherd, and Renaissance Pastoral," described the ways by which the traditional association of Abel with religious trust and contentment entered into the presentations of the life of the shepherd. In the July eclogue of *The Shepheardes Calender*, Edmund Spenser likens the ideal shepherd to Abel. John Donne, in "The Progresse of the Soule," describes Abel "as white, and milde as his sheepe were, / (Who, in trade, of Church, and kingdomes, there / Was the first type) " (stanza 41). It is surprising that in Chaucer's work there is only one reference, none in Philip Sidney, and none in Ben Jonson. In the same epoch, special attention should be directed to Agrippa d'Aubigne's *Les Tragiques*, the long Protestant epic poem anticipatory of *Paradise Lost* but without Milton's classical conceptual power, where Cain is the haunted malefactor unable to find any rest and thus punished by a fate worse than death. Apparently in the same epoch of religious wars, Thomas Lecoq wrote his *Tragedie representant l'odieus et sanglant meurtre commis par le maudit Cain a l'encontre do son*

frere Abel. See the highly intelligent defense of this play by Enea Balmas, "La Tragedie de Cain de Thomas Lecoq," in *Melanges a la memoire de V. L. Saulnier* (Geneva: Droz, 1984), 651 ff. In an admittedly waggish mood—as designated poet he felt obliged to introduce a merrier note to a solemn theological discussion—Erasmus concocted another fable, one whereby Cain, ever the con man, managed to persuade an angel guarding the gates of the earthly Paradise to allow him to pilfer a few seeds. This "Promethean" Cain was thus punished even more terribly, and the gullible angel was sacked. See *Opus Epistolarum Desiderii Erasmi Rotterdami,* ed. P. S. Allen (Oxford: Clarendon Press, 1906), 1, 268–271.

18. I am thinking particularly of *Richard II* and *Hamlet,* where two significant references in each call to mind the issues of Cain and Abel. *Richard II,* 1.1.104 and 5.1.43; *Hamlet,* 3.3.37 and 5.1.85.

19. See Ernst Cassirer, *The Myth of the State* (New Haven: Yale University Press, 1946), 156–162.

20. The Italian text from *La Divina Comedia,* 2nd ed., rev. ed. Natalino Sapegno, 3 vols. (Florence: La Nuova Italia, 1968), and the English from *The Divine Comedy of Dante Alighieri,* rev. ed., trans. John D. Sinclair (New York: Oxford University Press, 1958).

21. *Homo Necans,* trans. Peter Bing (1972; reprint, Berkeley and Los Angeles: University of California Press, 1983); Burkert's contributions to *Violent Origins* (see n. 22) are also invaluable.

22. Helpful discussions of the "dark event," as well as a general summary of Girard's arguments and those of Burkert, occur in the volume *Violent Origins,* ed. Robert G. Hammerton-Kelly (Stanford: Stanford University Press, 1987), esp. 118–129.

23. See also Girard, *Des Choses cachées depuis la fondation du monde,* with J. Oughourlian and G. Lefort (Paris: Grasset, 1978), where the specific notion of the antimyth is developed with the purpose of countering the foundation sacrifice, and *Le Bouc emissaire* (*The Scapegoat*) (Paris: Grasset, 1982), trans. Yvonne Freccero (Baltimore: The Johns Hopkins University Press, 1986) esp. 89–94.

24. See his essential commentary *The Divine Comedy,* Bollingen Series 80, 3 vols., trans. Charles S. Singleton (Princeton: Princeton University Press, 1970). In addition to the larger logic, numerous anthropophagal references support the argument of cannibalism.

25. Augustine, *The City of God,* trans. Marcus Dods (New York: Modern Library, 1950), 482.

26. Harry Stack Sullivan, *The Interpersonal Theory of Psychology* (New York: W. W. Norton, 1953), 347.

27. See the *Enciclopedia Dantesca* (Rome: Istituto del' Enciclopedia Italiana, 1970). The word *frate,* a term of address indicating a spiritual brotherhood and fraternal equality in the ways of pilgrimage, is employed 13 times in the *Purgatorio.* Ulysses calls his comrades "O frati," but this is

an appeal to the brotherhood of warfaring and adventure. It should be obvious that although brotherhood calls forth issues of fatherhood, this in no way is intended to slight the roles of Beatrice, or Mary, or the feminine principle itself.

28. See Livy, *The History of Rome* (Cambridge: Harvard University Press, 1935), 1:16, as well as Horace's regret that this foundation myth constitutes something of a curse, which itself leads to civil war. *Epode VII:*

> Sic est: acerba fata Romanos agunt
> scelusque fraternae necis,
> ut immerentis fluxit interram Remi
> Sacer nepotibus cruor.
>
> (So this is how it is: harsh Fate drives Romans on
> To kill their brothers,—
> And so has it always done since sinless Remus' blood
> Became a curse on all his lineage.)

Charles E. Passage, trans., *The Complete Works of Horace* (New York: Frederick Ungar, 1983), 107–108.

29. "Dell'ambizione," *Tutte le opere di Niccolo Machiavelli*, 2:714 (see n. 30). See Sebastian de Grazia, *Machiavelli in Hell* (Princeton: Princeton University Press, 1989), 67, 74, 77, 80.

30. See the fundamental book 1, chapter 9, in "Discorsi sopra la Prima Deca di Titi Livi," in *Tutte le Opere di Niccolo Machiavelli*, 2d ed., ed. Francesco Flora and Carlo Cordie (Florence: Mondadori, 1968), 1:119–121, and the Discourses in *The Portable Machiavelli*, ed. and trans. Peter Bondanella and Mark Musa (New York: Penguin Books, 1979), 200–203. In the same edition, the editors remind us that the crucial phrase from *The Prince*, "si guarda al fine" ("one must consider the final result")—preeminently sound advice—should not be translated into the phrase "the end justifies the means," which, they add, is "something Machiavelli never wrote" (135).

31. All quotations conform to *The Riverside Shakespeare*, ed. G. Blakemore Evans et al. (Boston: Houghton Mifflin, 1974).

32. See my *The Renaissance Discovery of Time*, 334.

33. Jacqueline de Romilly, *La Crainte et l'angoisse dans le theatre d'Eschyle* (Paris: Les belles Lettres, 1958).

CHAPTER 6

AUGUSTINE: THE VICIOUS CYCLE OF CHILD ABUSE

Donald Capps

If psychologists have generally been reluctant to apply their theories, concepts, and interpretive frameworks to Jesus, they have found in Augustine's *Confessions* fertile ground for psychological theorizing. Some of the best-known names in psychology of religion and related fields contributed to a symposium on the *Confessions* in the *Journal for the Scientific Study of Religion* (*JSSR*) in 1964–1965. Another generation of psychologists of religion contributed to a second symposium in the same journal in 1986–1987. Several studies from both eras, plus others originally published in other journals and books, were republished in 1990 in *The Hunger of the Heart: Reflections on the Confessions of Augustine* (Capps & Dittes, 1990).

Many of these studies focused on Augustine's relationship with his mother, Monica, and, either explicitly or implicitly, on the relative absence or insignificance of his father, Patricius, in his life and in the formation of his personality. But in all these studies, there was no sustained discussion of Augustine's relationship to his son Adeodatus, and references to his son were only in passing. The one possible exception was a very brief article in the original *JSSR* symposium by David Bakan (1965), who views Augustine as having the mind of an adolescent insofar as the relational entailments of the self and attitudes toward sexuality are concerned. He suggests that this is perhaps best reflected in Augustine's acknowledgment of his role in the sinful conception of Adeodatus but not in the formation of his personality. Augustine failed, in Bakan's view, to accept the responsibilities of fatherhood.

As the father of a teenage son myself, I was prompted to address the issue of Augustine's relationship to Adeodatus, both because it had been neglected in all the other psychological studies based on the *Confessions* and because I was not convinced that Bakan's view, based on a single quotation from the *Confessions* ("I had no part in that boy, except the sin"), was entirely accurate. After all, Adeodatus remained a part of Augustine's household even after Augustine's wife and Adeodatus' mother were sent back to northern Africa so that he could marry a Milanese heiress (which, however, never took place because of Augustine's conversion to Christianity and vow of sexual chastity). Was it then a matter of failing to accept the responsibilities of fatherhood? Or could it have been that Augustine sought to reverse or at least minimize the consequences of his son's illegitimate birth by an *excessive* attention to his paternal obligations?

I presented my reflections on this question in an essay titled "The Scourge of Shame and the Silencing of Adeodatus" in *The Hunger of the Heart* (Capps, 1990). I later revised this essay into a chapter titled "Augustine: The Vicious Cycle of Child Abuse" in *The Child's Song: The Religious Abuse of Children* (1995). In the introduction to this book, I alluded to Alice Miller's account in *Banished Knowledge* (1990a) of her experience of happening onto a Saint Nicholas celebration while walking through a forest in Switzerland one day in early December. I recount this experience here—in some detail—because it has direct bearing on the following analysis of Augustine's relations with Adeodatus.

A number of families had come with their children to the edge of the forest, where they lit candles in anticipation of an appearance of Saint Nicholas. By tradition, young mothers inform Saint Nicholas prior to the celebration about the behavior of their children. So, when he appears, he carries with him a big book that lists precisely the vices and the virtues of each child. This enables him to speak to each of them as if he is all-knowing.

When Saint Nicholas appeared, there was a hush, and then he began to call on the children, one by one, chiding them for their misdeeds and praising them for their good deeds. Vera was called on first: "Where is little Vera?" Vera, a small girl, barely two years old, with a trusting, expectant look, came forward. She gazed with candid curiosity into the saint's face. He spoke to her:

I must say, Vera, Saint Nicholas is not at all pleased that you don't always like to put away your toys by yourself. Mommy is too busy. You're old enough to understand that when you've finished playing you must put away your toys and also that you should share them like a good girl with your little brother and not keep everything for yourself. Let's hope next year will see an improvement. (14)

He then proceeded to enumerate the good things that Vera had been doing and then asked, "Well now, Vera, have you also learned a little song for Saint Nicholas?" But Vera stood there too scared to utter a sound, so her mother sang the song that Vera had prepared for Saint Nicholas, and Vera was given a small package from his sack.

Little Stefan, who was about two and a half years old, was next. As he came forward, Saint Nicholas addressed him:

Well, well, Stefan, you're still using a pacifier; you're much too big for that, you know. If you brought along your pacifier you might as well give it to Saint Nicholas right away. (At this suggestion, the other children burst into laughter.) No, you haven't got it with you? Then tonight you will put it on your bedside table or give it to your little brother. You don't need a pacifier anymore, you're much too big for that. Saint Nicholas has also noticed that you're not always a good little boy at the table, always interrupting when the grown-ups are talking; but you must let the grown-ups talk, you're still much too small to be constantly interrupting the others. (15)

Miller noticed that little Stefan seemed on the verge of tears. He stood there looking thoroughly scared, shamed in front of all the others. So she intervened in his behalf. She said to Saint Nicholas, "A minute ago you were telling him he's too big for a pacifier, and now you say he's too small to speak up at the table. Stefan himself will know very well when he no longer needs his pacifier." Immediately, some of the mothers interrupted her. One mother said, "Here it's up to Saint Nicholas to say what Stefan must do." So Miller held her peace, and the celebration continued as it had begun, leaving *her* to suffer in her quiet anguish. "No one," she writes, "noticed the cruelty, no one saw the stricken faces (although the fathers were constantly taking flash pictures). No one noticed that each of the reprimanded children *ended up not being able to remember the words of the little poem or song;* that they couldn't even find their voices, could hardly say thank you; that none of the children smiled spontaneously, that they all looked petrified with fear" (15–16; emphasis added).

In the episode witnessed by Alice Miller, Saint Nicholas reduced the children to silence. When he was through declaring to them their faults and virtues, they were unable to sing the song or say the poem they had prepared just for him. In this chapter on Augustine and his son Adeodatus, I will focus attention on another episode in which a child, Adeodatus, was also silenced by well-meaning adults. Only this time the child was prohibited from mourning the loss of his beloved grandmother.

Adults' efforts to prohibit children from openly grieving are common. What makes this particular episode stand out from many others is that the child was the son of Saint Augustine, the man who—with the possible exception of Saint Paul—has done more than any other mortal to shape and define the Christian faith. His story has been told again and again. For many Christians, it is an inspiring story of a man who yielded to the power of the gospel and dedicated his life to the church of Christ. But I want here to tell the story of his unsung son, the boy who tried to mourn his grandmother Monica's death and who himself died shortly thereafter. Unlike his father, who was 75 years old when he died, Adeodatus was only 17 when he died, too young to make his mark in the world. I write of him because his story enables us to explore the subtle ways in which religion, including the Christian faith, may crush the spirit of a child.

To place his story in context, we need to go back in time to his father's childhood and lift up an episode that has direct bearing on what was eventually to become of Adeodatus.

A Little One, but with No Little Feeling

In his *Confessions* (1960), Augustine relates how, as a child, he was severely beaten by his teachers at school. His account of these beatings reflects the fact that we adults, in looking back on our childhood sufferings, have very mixed reactions and responses to those persons who were the agents of these sufferings. That this account is addressed to God—with whom he, as an adult, is now on speaking terms—adds a further complexity.

The interpretive frame that he chooses for his account of these beatings is deception and deceit: "O God, my God, great was the misery and great the deception that I met with when it was impressed upon me that, to behave properly as a boy, I must obey my teachers. This was all that I might succeed in this world and excel in those arts of speech which would serve to bring honor among men and to gain deceitful riches." The boy did not know that he was being prepared for an adult life based on the illusions of this world. He had not the slightest notion that what was occurring in school was for some unknown purpose in the very distant future: "I was sent to school to acquire learning, the utility of which, wretched child that I was, I did not know. Yet if I was slow at learning, I was beaten" (51).

The adult Augustine does not believe that his teachers acted from personal malice. After all, "this method was praised by our forebears, many of whom had passed through this life before us and had laid out the hard paths that we were forced to follow." But he cannot resist noting that all of this is the consequence of Adam's original sin: "Thus were both toil and sorrow multiplied for the sons of Adam." As a son of Adam, the adult Augustine (51) can accept the fact that he and other children were doomed to suffer, for suffering is a fact of life. Yet if Adam is ultimately to blame for the fact of our suffering, is there anything that God might do to alleviate the suffering, to soften the blows? As children, "we discovered, Lord, that certain men prayed to you and we learned from them, and imagined you, as far as we could, as some sort of mighty one who could hear us and help us, even though not appearing before our senses." Thus, "while still a boy, I began to pray to you, my help and my refuge, and in praying to you I broke the knots that tied my tongue. A little one, but with no little feeling, I prayed to you that I would not be beaten at school" (51–52). So, two well-established traditions—the beating of children and the praying to God for deliverance—converged. As his teachers turned to the former, Augustine, the child, resorted to the latter.

But God did not heed his prayers, nor did his parents. "When you [God] did not hear me—and it was 'not to be reputed folly in me'— my punishments, which were then a huge and heavy evil to me, were laughed at by older men, and even by my parents who wished no harm to befall me" (52). While we might have expected Augustine to ask why God did not respond to his entreaties—thus taking the side of the child—he centers instead on his parents' decision not to intervene in his behalf, and he offers a religious justification for this. Supposing, he says, that there is a person of "so great a soul, who clings to you with so mighty love" that he "so devoutly clings to you and is thus so deeply affected that he deems of little consequence the rack, the hook, and similar tools of torture." And supposing that he deems these tools of torture insignificant despite the fact that he "loves those who dread such things most bitterly." Such love for God, that one would deem the sufferings of another as of little consequence, may explain why "our

parents laughed at the torments we boys suffered from our teachers."
Of course, "in no less measure did we fear our punishments, and no
less did we beseech you to let us escape" (52).

By drawing this analogy between beatings he suffered as a child
and the torturing devices used against adults, the adult Augustine
recognizes just how severe the children's sufferings were. Yet in providing a legitimation for his parents' failure to intervene, and a religious one at that, he spares the parents and absolves them of any
responsibility for what has occurred. Moreover, he goes on to
acknowledge that the children brought their suffering on themselves:
"Yet we sinned by writing, reading, and thinking over our lessons less
than was required of us." That we as children did not do as well as we
should was not God's fault either, for "there was in us no lack of
memory or intelligence, for you willed that we should have them in
sufficient measure for our years" (52). If the children's behavior can
be defended at all, it is only because they were doing what adults also
do: "Yet we loved to play, and this was punished in us by men who did
the same things themselves. However, the trivial concerns of adults
are called business, while such things in children are punished by
adults." So he returns to the issue of the delusion—the meaningless-
ness—of the whole scenario: "Perhaps some fine judge of things
approves my beatings for I played ball as a child." Yet in playing ball,
all that he did was to resist "learning arts by which, as an adult, I
would comport myself in still more unseemly fashion." By what right,
then, did his teachers beat him? "Did the very man who beat me act
different from me? If he was outdone by a fellow teacher in some tri-
fling discussion, he was more tormented by anger and envy than I
was when beaten by my playmate in a ball game" (52).

The bottom line, though, is that Augustine and the other boys
sinned "by going against the commands of my parents and of those
teachers." After all, he was able, later on, to "put to good use the
learning that they wanted me to acquire, no matter with what purpose in my regard." And "I was disobedient, not out of a desire for
better things, but out of a love for play. I loved to win proud victories
in our contests" (53). As a child, he prayed for deliverance from the
beatings inflicted by his teachers. Now, as an adult, he prays for deliverance from the love of trivial pursuits, including the same trivial
pursuits to which his teachers were captive: "Lord, in your mercy
look down upon these things and deliver us who now call upon you.
Deliver also those who do not yet call upon you, so that they may call
upon you and you may deliver them" (53). If God is a God of deliver-

ance, it is not—as he thought as a child—that God delivers us from suffering but that he delivers us from the illusions to which we were subject as children and to which our readers were also subject. If our teachers erred, it was in the fact not that they beat us but that we were beaten for the wrong reasons. And if our parents refused to intervene, this was not because they were unfeeling—as we thought at the time—but because they clung to God with such a mighty love that they could resist their children's pleas, secure in the knowledge that the torments their children were suffering were for their own good (Miller, 1984).

The Scourging God

The beatings that Augustine suffered as a boy have received little scholarly attention. Readers of this remarkable exercise in self-disclosure have paid far more attention to his account of his involvement in the stealing of a farmer's pears when he was a teenager. The boyhood beatings are passed over as if they are of little significance. However, two scholars—E. R. Dodds and Leo Ferrari—have taken note of the fact that Augustine was beaten by his teachers, and both believe that the beatings left permanent scars on his psyche. Dodds (1927–1928) notes that Augustine "has none but painful memories" of his earliest schooling at the small country town of Thagaste. He resisted being compelled to acquire mechanically information whose value was not apparent to him, and "like other proud and sensitive children, he resented the cane still more. He tells us that he would pray to God with a passion disproportionate to his age that he might not be beaten in school; and he rightly blames his parents for laughing at his prayer, pointing out that the suffering which amuses the adults may be agony to the child." Also, "he never forgave the schoolmaster who beat him for faults which he habitually committed himself." These beatings had lasting effects, for "it is a fair inference from his language that these beatings produced what psychologists call a *trauma*, a permanent injury to his personality." Their lasting effects were reflected in his compensatory behavior: "For the humiliations of the classroom it seems that he sought compensation in dominating his fellows. Black jealousy tortured him if he so much as lost a game of ball. Puny, delicate and weak-voiced, he had not the physical qualities of a leader; but when he could not make friends otherwise, he bribed them with stolen sweetmeats, and when he could not win games otherwise, he won them by cheating" (462).

Note that Dodds claims that Augustine "blamed" his parents for laughing at his prayers when, in fact, as we have seen, he offers a theological explanation for why his parents did not sympathize with him. It was not that they were callous or unfeeling but that they were responding to a greater love than that they felt for their own beloved child. On the other hand, Dodds is quite right that the beatings Augustine suffered were traumatic and produced a "permanent injury to his personality," and the evidence that Dodds offers for this—a compensatory need to dominate others—is entirely plausible.

Ferrari (1974) offers a much more extensive interpretation of the beatings and their impact on Augustine's personality. He focuses on Augustine's tendency throughout his adult years to engage in excessive self-reproach, on his pervasive sense of sadness and hopelessness, and on his tendency to be mistrustful of others. Ferrari believes that all these traits can be attributed to the beatings he suffered as a child. As he points out, "There is ample evidence for the enduring influence of these early floggings, not only upon his most important formative years, but also upon his outlook as a mature man" (3).

Like Dodds, Ferrari believes that Augustine as a boy was of a uniquely sensitive nature and "was thereby all the more susceptible to being profoundly disturbed by his first whippings." What neither he nor Dodds considers is the likelihood that it was the whippings that made Augustine so sensitive. Also, in stressing his sensitivity, both seem to imply that some children, those who are less sensitive, might not be traumatized by beatings. On the other hand, Ferrari stresses the severity of the beatings, as suggested by the fact that the adult Augustine compared them to the worst devices of torture known to humankind.

For Ferrari, whether Augustine was thrashed at home prior to beginning school is an open question since he does not imply this in his *Confessions* or elsewhere. Yet Ferrari notes that Augustine's father Patricius was a man given to violent anger and that only the tact of his wife, Monica, saved her from the wife beating that was traditional in the village. As a young married man, Augustine's father beat several servants who were the source of rumors injurious to his wife: "Whether his frustrated anger could also have been released upon his children is not known. Certainly, the infant Augustine must have been at least the transfixed spectator to his father's rages, even if not the subject of his irate thrashings" (4).

In any case, Ferrari believes that Augustine's parents refused to intervene in his behalf because they were extremely ambitious for him from his earliest years, and they considered education to be the means whereby he would later make a name for himself in the world. But "[c]onsidering the traumatic circumstances under which the sensitive infant was so early in life goaded on to seek worldly fame and wealth through his oratorical talents, it is the less surprising that he later so violently rejected all these worldly ambitions. Further, it would seem credible too that here in the first floggings administered by some grim tyrant of a schoolmaster, together with the mocking laughter of his very own parents at the painful stripes which he bore home, lay the first seeds of disenchantment with the adult world. Aided by other factors, this could later ripen into renunciation of the world and of worldly pursuits" (5–6).

In Ferrari's judgment, his parents' mocking laughter also had an enduring effect on Augustine's personality, especially in the fact that he was very sensitive to being the object of any kind of ridicule: "Humor there is in Augustine, but it always seems to be directed at something other than himself. A master of grinding irony when vanquishing some unfortunate opponent in public debate, he is nevertheless consistently serious about himself and his intentions" (6).

Thus, the beatings' long-term effects are reflected in his tendency toward excessive self-reproach, his rather sorrowful temperament, his disenchantment with the world of adult pursuits, and the seriousness with which he took himself. Especially concerned with the tendency toward excessive self-reproach, Ferrari explains this in religious terms, noting that "cruel and terrifying as were the beatings which the young Augustine suffered at school, in his mature years through the light of his faith he was able to view these scourgings as the work of God Himself. . . . Seen in the larger perspective of eternal salvation, the scourgings of school days are merely an apprenticeship to the sufferings of life, by which God calls wandering and wayward souls back to Himself" (6–7).

Noting Augustine's many references in his *Confessions* to the scourges of God, Ferrari suggests that "the irate schoolmaster of Augustine's infancy therefore becomes the scourging God who purifies his soul through the many punishments of life." There are some twenty references in the *Confessions* to the scourgings or floggings suffered at the hand of God. These range from the derision he endured when the Manichaeism to which he had devoted nearly a decade of his life was proven a sham to God's redoubling of lashes of fear and shame; to bring him to conversion; to the grievous loss of his mother in death. The flip side of this belief in the scourging God was his conviction that he deserved these scourgings, for he was very much a sinner. Moreover, the fact that he was the object of God's scourging was a hopeful sign, for "just as the father loves a child when punishing it, so too God's scourges are a sign of his love." Ferrari concludes, "There are grounds for arguing that the traumatic terror of his first floggings as a very young schoolboy contributed to an enduring sense of culpability and the formation of a temperament disposed to self-reproach and suffering." Ferrari believes that this led Augustine to overemphasize the stern Jehovah of the Old Testament at the expense of the merciful and loving God of the New, but he thinks the end result was positive, for "just as the floggings of his first schoolteachers drove him to the study of literature in which he was to excel as a professional orator, so too in the school of life, the later scourges of God impelled him to a profound study of the Bible upon which he became a peerless authority and the principal interpreter for the Western Christian tradition. Without the boyhood beatings which affected him so profoundly, there may well have been no Saint Augustine" (14).

But I am not so sanguine. I share Alice Miller's view that nothing good comes from the abuse of children and that the cases of great historical figures offer no grounds for suggesting otherwise. As she says of Nietzsche (Miller, 1990b), his greatness as a philosopher was not because of but despite the fact that he was abused, and the fact that he was a seriously flawed philosopher—however brilliant—is largely owing to the abuse he suffered as a child. The same applies to Augustine. It is a tenuous argument to say that Augustine would not have become a peerless authority on the Bible had he not felt himself to be the object of the scourgings of God, and Ferrari himself suggests that his interpretation of the Bible was one-sided (and therefore flawed) precisely because he was the victim of beatings as a child.

Yet we are concerned here not with Augustine's contribution as a Father of the Church but with what his childhood experience of being beaten meant for his relationship to his son Adeodatus and especially with how it happened that Augustine did to Adeodatus what his teachers had done to him. If Dodds and Ferrari are correct that the beatings he suffered as a child had a lasting effect on his personality, then we should want to explore these effects on his role not only as Father of the Church but also as the father of Adeodatus. Key to these effects is the fact that the beatings prompted him to pray and that in praying "I broke the knots that tied my tongue." Ferrari takes this statement to mean that the beatings happened when Augustine was so young that he "learned to talk by begging God not to allow him to be beaten at school." Rather, I take it to mean that, in being inflicted with beatings that he had no power to defend against, he began to speak to God, pleading with God to exercise his power to stop the beatings. Thus, the beatings caused him to pray, and from this time forth Augustine interpreted his sufferings within a religious frame of reference. The experience of being beaten and the impetus to pray are forever linked in his psyche. Furthermore, if he was unable to cry out during the beatings for fear that he would be beaten even more severely, prayer to God was a means of untying his tongue, of giving vent to his feelings of frustration and rage. In this way, God became more than his potential deliverer, for God also became the one on whom he could vent his rage, the scourging God to whom he could talk back, though always in a carefully modulated manner, lest he anger God and invite retaliation. Perhaps this explains the fact that his praise of God in the *Confessions* is often accompanied and some-what undermined by an undertone of veiled criticism against God (Bakan, 1965). Even his decision to become a rhetorician may, in this sense, be related to his childhood beatings, for rhetoric is the skill of speaking on more than one level at once, of implying more than is lit-erally spoken. All this has direct bearing on the fate of Adeodatus, who was the indirect victim of the beatings Augustine suffered at the hands of his teachers.

"As She Breathed Her Last, the Boy Began to Wail"

Adeodatus makes an important, if seldom noticed, appearance in Augustine's account of his own mother's death. The fact that Augustine concluded his account of his life not with his conversion to the Christian faith but with the death of his mother is significant, for with the account of her death his narrative comes full circle, back to its initial starting point in his account of being beaten by his teachers.

In recounting the event of his mother's death, he recalls that, as he closed her eyes, "a great wave of sorrow surged into my heart. It would have overflowed in tears if I had not made a strong effort of will and stemmed the flow, so that the tears dried in my eyes. What a terrible struggle it was to hold them back!" Then, as she breathed her last, "the boy Adeodatus began to wail aloud and only ceased his cries when we all checked him. I, too, felt that I wanted to cry like a child, but a more mature voice within me, the voice of my heart, bade me keep my sobs in check, and I remained silent. For we did not think it right to mark my mother's death with weeping and moaning, because such lamentations are the usual accompaniment of death when it is thought of as a state of misery or as total extinction. But she had not died in misery nor had she wholly died. Of this we were certain, both because we knew what a holy life she had led and also because our faith was real and we had sure reasons not to doubt it" (Augustine, 1961, 201).

When they had succeeded in quieting Adeodatus, Evodius, a friend of Augustine's, took up a psaltery and began to sing Psalm 100—"Of mercy and justice my song shall be; a psalm in thy honor, Lord"—and the whole house sang in response. As funeral preparations were being made, Augustine remained in another room, "conversing with friends on matters suitable to the occasion, for they did not think it right to leave me to myself." He continued to control his emotions, so much so that his friends "thought that I had no sense of grief." How little they knew, for throughout the day, "I fought against the wave of sorrow and for a while it receded, but then it swept upon me again with full force. It did not bring me to tears, and no sign of it showed in my face, but I knew well enough what I was stifling in my heart. It was misery to feel myself so weak a victim of these human emotions, although we cannot escape them, since they are the natural lot of mankind, and so I had the added sorrow of being grieved by my own feelings, so that I was tormented by a twofold agony" (201).

During the day, he "found comfort in the memory that as I did what I could for my mother in the last stages of her illness, she had caressed me and said that I was a good son to her. With great emotion she told me that she could not remember ever having heard me speak a single hard or disrespectful word against her" (200). When her body was carried out later in the day for burial, he continued to keep control of his emotions: "I went and returned without a tear. I did not weep even during the prayers which we recited while the sacrifice of our redemption was offered for my mother and her body rested by the grave before it was laid in the earth, as is the custom there. Yet all that day I was secretly weighed down with grief. With all my heart I begged you to heal my sorrow, but you did not grant my prayer. I believe this was because you wished to impress upon my memory, if only by this one lesson, how firmly the mind is gripped in the bonds of habit, even when it is nourished on the word of truth" (201). At night, though, when he lay alone in bed, his feelings about his mother came back to him, little by little, and he began to cry. "The tears which I had been holding back streamed down, and I let them flow as freely as they would, making of them a pillow for my heart. On them it rested, for my weeping sounded in your ears alone, not in the ears of men who might have misconstrued it and despised it" (202).

In publicly admitting that he wept that night, he is aware that those who read his account will interpret it as they will. So be it: "Let him understand it as he will. And if he finds that I sinned by weeping for my mother, even if only for a fraction of an hour, let him not mock at me. For this was the mother, now dead and hidden awhile from my sight, who had wept over me for many years so that I might live in your sight. Let him not mock at me but weep himself, if his charity is great" (203). And so his account of his mother's death ends on a note of defiance: "You may say that I sinned in weeping for my mother, but do not mock me, for in mocking me, you mock the woman who shed so many tears for her good son, the son who never spoke a single hard or disrespectful word against her" (203).

I suspect that many of us reading his *Confessions* today, if we were inclined to mock, would mock his herculean efforts to control his emotions and would view with relief the fact that he was able to weep, finally, if only for a fraction of an hour. But his use of the word "mock" calls to our minds the episode with which he began the story of his life and specifically the fact that his parents mocked him when he showed them the stripes on his back and sought their sympathy. Out of such mockery was born a son who was good to his mother, a son who never dared to speak a single hard or disrespectful word against her.

But what of Adeodatus? Once Augustine and his friends succeeded in silencing him—suppressing his cries of grief with the singing of a psalm—we hear nothing more of him. Father and friends repaired to a room where they conversed together on topics suitable for the day. Whether Adeodatus joined them, Augustine does not say. Later, when they took the body out for burial, Adeodatus was surely in the company of mourners, but again his father makes no mention of the fact. After he was silenced, he disappears from the text. He who had dared to weep openly is thenceforth stricken from the record.

Who was this Adeodatus? What do we know about him? Almost all our information about him comes from his father's *Confessions*. He was conceived when Augustine was 19 years old and living as a university student in Carthage, the largest city in northern Africa,[1] and had found himself a mistress. Writing briefly about his son's birth in book 4 of his *Confessions*, he mentions this illicit relationship, noting that he was ever faithful to this woman who was not his wife, and then adds, "With her I learned at first hand how great a distance lies between restraint of a conjugal covenant, mutually made for the sake of begetting offspring, and the bargain of a lustful love, where a child is born against our will, although once born he forces himself upon our love" (Augustine, 1960, 94). He does not elaborate on the statement, "born against our will," but it is evident that, at least initially, Adeodatus was unwanted. In his biography of Augustine, Peter Brown (1969) suggests that the conception and birth of Adeodatus "may well have had the 'sobering' effect which Augustine would later recommend to young husbands." But this is Augustine the older teacher, making a moral point about how a serious mistake may bring a young man to his senses. For the young man of 19 years, the conception and birth of Adeodatus was a matter of deep, overwhelming shame: a young girl was pregnant, and he was the father. Had his mother not warned him, just a couple of years earlier, to "keep from fornicating," and had he not ignored her, for "such words seemed to be only a woman's warnings" (68)?

He had gone to Carthage and had sought love there, and indeed he found it, in a woman's arms. But love had its costs, and God saw that he would suffer for it: "I plunged headlong into love, whose captive I desired to be. But my God, my mercy, with how much gall did you sprinkle all that sweetness of mine, and how good you were to do it! For I was loved, and I had gained love's bond of joy. But in my joy I was bound about with painful chains of iron, so that I might be scourged by burning rods of jealousy, and suspicion, and fear, and anger, and quarreling" (77). The young intellectual with a bright future before him was now possessed of a "wife" who was his social inferior and a son whom neither of them desired. They named the child Adeodatus, "gift of God," as if to suggest that they could somehow make it right by giving credit (or blame) to God.

While Adeodatus managed to "force himself upon our love," to make them love him despite the circumstances of his conception, he was still and always associated in Augustine's mind with the shame he experienced as a 19-year-old youth who had sought the joys of love but discovered, too late, that these joys are accompanied with the scourgings of God. Moreover, while Augustine and this nameless woman remained together for nearly 15 years, they never had another child.

Augustine also mentions Adeodatus in his brief account of his "wife's" return to Africa, though only in passing. She "returned to

Africa, vowing that she would never know another man, and leaving me with our natural son" (153). Adeodatus was 15 years old by now, and the three of them had been together all this time, having spent a year in Augustine's native Thagaste shortly after Adeodatus' birth, then seven years in Carthage, followed by a year in Rome and nearly two in Milan. She was now being sent back to northern Africa, perhaps to Carthage, because his mother, who had recently arrived in Milan, had arranged his engagement to marry into a wealthy Milanese family. (He would have to wait a year or so, however, because his fiancée was underage, i.e., not yet 12 years old.) His "wife's" vow never to know another man may suggest, as his biographers have assumed, that this was a selfless expression of religious piety or, if not this, at least a willing acceptance of current social conventions regarding women in second-class marriages. Yet her vow "never to know another man" and the act of "leaving me with our natural son" may also suggest her anger that she could be so callously dismissed after nearly 15 years of life with Augustine and their son Adeodatus and for such dubious reasons. While Augustine speaks of his love for her and says her leaving "was a blow which crushed my heart to bleeding," he says nothing about the impact of all this on Adeodatus, who was, after all, losing his mother.

Adeodatus is next mentioned in the account of their baptisms into the Christian faith on Easter Sunday a year later. Augustine notes that he and his close friend Alypius were joined in baptism by Adeodatus, who was "born of me in the flesh out of my sin. Well had you made him: he was almost fifteen years old, and in power of mind he surpassed many grave and learned men. O Lord my God, creator of all things most powerful to reform our deformities, to you do I confess your gifts. For in that boy I owned nothing but the sin. That he was brought up by us in your discipline, to that you and none other inspired us" (214). Augustine then goes on to describe the book that he and Adeodatus had produced together: "This is one of our books which is entitled *On the Teacher*, and in it he speaks with me. You know that his are all the ideas which are inserted there, as from the person of the one talking with me, when he was in his sixteenth year. I had experience of many still more wonderful things in him. To me his power of mind was a source of awe. Who except you is the worker of such marvels?" (214).

Here, in this passage, Augustine refers to his son in the past tense. This is because Adeodatus was no longer alive. After the death of Augustine's mother, Augustine and Adeodatus returned to

Augustine's native town of Thagaste in North Africa. Three years later Adeodatus died. Peter Brown notes that Augustine was, in fact, twice bereaved that year. Besides the death of Adeodatus, Augustine experienced the death of a longtime friend, Nebridius, who had returned with him to Africa and had gone to live with his mother in his country house near Carthage. Brown (1969) observes, "This double-blow is one of the most significant blanks in Augustine's life," for nothing is known about Augustine's reaction to these deaths (135).

Just because the two deaths are a major "blank" in our knowledge of his life does not mean that they had identical effects. Augustine's refusal to travel to see his dying friend Nebridius would indicate that the two deaths were experienced very differently. We may assume that Augustine was physically present when his son Adeodatus died, and we may further assume that Adeodatus' mother, the only woman whom Augustine had loved, was absent. No doubt, Augustine's brother and sister were there to share his grief, and undoubtedly there were several close and loving friends. But these could not take the place of the mother of Adeodatus and of Augustine's own mother as he grieved for his son.

A major blank in our knowledge about the death of Adeodatus is the cause of death. We may assume that he died of natural causes (there were certainly many such causes from which to die in northern Africa); and, given the esteem in which Augustine held medical doctors,[2] we may also assume that he was greatly frustrated by their failure to save his son. But the cause and circumstances of Adeodatus' death are inaccessible to us. All that we do know is that Augustine viewed the death of his son as an unanticipated act of God ("Quickly you took his life away from the earth") and that now, writing his *Confessions* some seven years after his son's death, "I remember him with a more peaceful mind, for I have no fear for anything in his childhood and youth, and none at all for him as a man" (214). Nor is there any mention of his having shed tears over the loss of his son on the day of his death, for he concludes his remembrance of Adeodatus with this statement:

> We made him our companion, in your grace no younger than ourselves. Together we were ready to begin our schooling in your ways. We were baptized, and all anxiety over the past melted away from us. The days were all too short, for I was lost in wonder and joy, meditating upon your far-reaching providence for the salvation of the human race. The

tears flowed from me when I heard your hymns and canticles, for the sweet singing of your Church moved me deeply. The music surged in my ears, truth seeped into my heart, and my feelings of devotion over-flowed, so that the tears streamed down. But they were tears of glad-ness. (214)

Again the psalms and canticles successfully blocked and contained the emotions of grief. Here, in this passage, his rhapsodic testimony to the "voices of your sweet-singing Church" replaces any account that we might have expected of the death itself. If, on the occasion of Augustine's mother's death, Adeodatus was silenced by Augustine and his friends, now, in his own death, Adeodatus is textually silenced, as the day of his passing is neither described nor com-mented on.

Of course, there is no reason in principle why Augustine should be expected to say more than he has in his *Confessions* about his son's death. He has already written a very self-revealing book, and it may seem impertinent for the modern reader to want or expect more. But the fact that we are left in the dark about Adeodatus' death neverthe-less frustrates our natural desire to know how Augustine felt about himself as a father and what light he could have shed on Adeodatus' own feelings about his experiences as son of Augustine. Can it be that the statement "For in that boy I owned nothing but the sin" is a full and accurate summation of Augustine's fatherly role and of the mean-ing that it finally had for him? Without an account of his son's death and its meaning for him, there is no way to tell.

Yet the very fact that Adeodatus was born in shame, that he was an "unwanted" child, makes this an important question to ask, espe-cially since his life was over almost before it began. Does Augustine suspect that the shameful circumstances of his son's conception are somehow responsible for his early death? Were his fears about his son's spiritual fate owing, in part, to concern that he himself would be to blame if Adeodatus were to suffer eternal torment? Is he relieved that his son did not live long enough to commit the sins and errors of his own youth and that, as far as Adeodatus' "adulthood" was concerned, it was a clean and unblemished slate? That the whole course of events set in motion by the conception of Adeodatus has finally come to an end?

Augustine's comment "For in that boy I owned nothing but the sin" is intended as praise for God, who was the author of everything good in Adeodatus. Yet it also suggests that he continues, even now, seven or more years after his son's death, to identify the boy with the circumstances of his birth and therefore to associate him with his own personal shame. To be sure, their project together—the dialogue between student and teacher—communicates the father's delight in his son's intellectual prowess and contrasts quite dramatically with Augustine's own sixteenth year, when *his* father admired his emerging sexuality. Yet the dialogue itself, while occasionally spirited, conveys a father-son relationship in which the father is very firmly in control. When Adeodatus is offered the last word, he tells his father what he knows his father wants to hear ("I have learned by your warning words") and is appropriately submissive ("You have taken up and resolved all the difficulties I was prepared to urge against you; you omitted nothing at all that caused me to doubt") (Augustine, 1953, 69–101).

Thus, the child had been *born* in shame, but Augustine seems determined that the living child will not be the *source* or *cause* of shame either to Augustine or to himself. Brought up in God's discipline, Adeodatus would never be allowed to give his father cause for anxiety. He would be a son to whom Augustine could point with fatherly pride, even put on display, and the basis for this pride would be the son's "power of mind" in which "he surpassed many grave and learned men." What his son would not be allowed to exhibit is deep and genuine emotions: wailing over the death of his grandmother while his father and his father's friends succeed manfully in controlling their own emotions. How do we know that Adeodatus did not die the victim of such control? Bereft of his mother and now of his grandmother too, he may well have died not of heartbreak—though surely this was present—but of the inability to express openly and freely how he felt. Is there not also a deep irony in the fact that the father's testimony to his son's legitimacy centers on a book in which Augustine is the teacher, doing to his son in verbal form what his teachers did to him through physical beatings: controlling and exacting obedience and deference? The difference is in the fact that teacher and parent are one and the same person, so the boy in this case has no one to turn to for solace. Even God is inaccessible to him, for his father—unlike his father's teachers—is so clearly identified with God that there can be no hope or illusion that God would side with the son against his father. Adeodatus is utterly, painfully alone and on his own. For him, there is no enlightened witness (Miller's term for adults who support children by validating through their words and actions the children's own perceptions of reality when these are being undermined by other adults).

To Silence Is to Shame

And so we come full circle. The story that began with the cries of a young boy in pain—from being beaten by teachers—ends with the cries of another boy who was experiencing another kind of pain, grief over the loss of his grandmother (and, no doubt, the reactivation of the grief he felt when his mother was taken from his side). In both instances, the adults turned a deaf ear and refused to hear the child's cries. Ironically, the first boy is numbered, at the end, among the adults who will not hear, apparently because he has learned to muffle the cries of the child within himself. As he heard the cries of his own son, he too "felt that I wanted to cry like a child, but a more mature voice within me, the voice of my heart, bade me keep my sobs in check, and I remained silent" (Augustine, 1960, 200). What is this but the silencing of children's emotions by adult codes of conduct? And what is this silencing but a subtle form of shaming? So the more things change, the more they remain the same, and the lessons that Augustine learned about shame as a child are forgotten by him, now an adult. If there is a moral to the story, it is that an otherwise praiseworthy act of self-revelation—the *Confessions*—has legitimized the shaming of defenseless children. And for this, it seems to me, no amount of self-reproach could possibly be excessive.

But Augustine has lived his life. There are no more lessons for him to learn from the silencing of Adeodatus. We, however, have much to learn from it if we will. Let us return to the room where Monica breathed her last breath: the mother dies, the grandson cries, the boy is rebuked, and the father and his friends sing a psalm. Does this scene communicate or signify what our lives—yours and mine—are all about? Is this, the final episode in Augustine's narrative, the climax of the story, the event to which everything that went before is pointing, for which everything that precedes it was preparation? Our last image of Augustine, as the narrative comes to a close, is that of the father joining in the silencing of his son so that he and his friends may sing their praises to God. I suggest that the tragedy of human life is captured in this pathetic scene. Is this the dead woman's legacy, the faith for which she fought so hard? As the cries of Adeodatus are muffled and the voice of Evodius gains strength and resonance, surely one feels that something is terribly wrong with this world, that the scene no doubt discloses some deep flaw in the universe itself. It should not have happened this way. Father and son, bereft of the women who were more to them than any other, should be joining in shared lamentation. Yes, the dying of Monica was sad and worthy of grief, but even more tragic was the rebuke and the silencing of Adeodatus.

Others, of course, may not react to this deathbed scene as I have reacted, and, since the silencing of Adeodatus has not been commented on by other interpreters of this scene, I am aware that my reaction may be totally idiosyncratic. The point, however, is that this is the episode in Augustine's narrative of his life where I experience a shift from reading his text to being read by it (Ricoeur, 1976, 92–95). And I find that, when this shift occurs, the episode depresses rather than inspires me and causes me to take no pride in the fact that I, like Augustine, am a Christian. Rather, it fills me with a sense of the tragic limitations not only of Augustine's life and his insights into his life but of human life in general and of our capacity to understand ourselves. As I consider his struggle with the problem of whether to shed tears or to contain them, I feel shame for him, and I feel the undeniable truth of Helen Merrell Lynd's (1958) observation that "the import of shame for others may reach even deeper than shame for ourselves" (57). How trivial and yet how tragic that Augustine would experience this dilemma—to cry or not to cry—as a reflection of who he is as a person and as a faithful Christian. And yet was this not the very issue he confronted as a boy being beaten at school—to cry or not to cry—and did not everything, including his very selfhood, depend on which course he took? Is it any wonder, then, that he should come to view his comportment in the death room of his mother as a test of who he is both as a person and as a child of God?

Then the shame that I feel for him I begin to feel for myself as I sense that I am no less concerned to "do it right" not only or primarily in grieving but in all areas of my life where I feel that others are observing me. As I reflect on past scenes, trivial by any objective standards, where I struggled so manfully to play my own part oh-so correctly or demanded of my own son that he act so as not to embarrass me, I realize that I am no different from Augustine. The shame I feel for him comes back to me, and I am left feeling very much exposed and ashamed. In this shame there is a deep sense of loneliness, of being without God in the world, for my God—as for

Augustine too—has been a God who discloses himself in the order and quiet dignity of our lives. I have known him, as did Augustine, in the psalms and canticles I have sung on occasions such as this. Although not without feeling, these songs have not much to do with primitive cries of pain and chaotic, unmanageable emotions but with maintaining control. Surely I am not alone in feeling as I do, ashamed for my obvious skill in keeping emotions in check, but the weight of Christian tradition after Augustine is against those of us who feel this way, and this only increases our sense of loneliness.

The "Death" of Augustine

Now let us return to the schoolroom in Thagaste, where Augustine, the boy's father, was mercilessly beaten by his teachers. Tell me if I am not correct in asserting that the tragedy began there: a boy cried out to his Father in heaven for deliverance from the pain that was crushing his spirit, but his Father in heaven did not respond. What the boy learned from this nonresponse was that he must learn to control himself, to muffle his cries, to learn to hold his peace even—or especially—when in pain. Something died in that boy in that classroom in northern Africa, and this death, unlike that of his son, *is* recounted in his *Confessions*. Only it is not presented as a death, for it appears at the beginning of the narrative, and it would be absurd for an autobiography to presume to give an account of the death of its primary subject and author. Moreover, even if this had been a biography and not an autobiography, so that the primary subject's death could be related and described, we would not look for the account of his death in the first pages of the book, in a chapter on the childhood of a man who lived to his seventy-fifth year.

Still, I submit that a death did occur in that classroom and that no one mourned because no one realized that it happened. We too experienced a kind of death in similar settings in school, in church, at home, on the playing fields—wherever—as we too learned to muffle our cries and as we too allowed the adults to interpret our pain for us. Moreover, like Augustine, we have learned to take the adult's perspective on what occurred, and we have turned to religion to find therein the legitimations for adults' assault against the spirit of the child. In so doing, we have allowed ourselves to be deceived, as when Augustine claims that it was the "more mature voice within me" that was "the voice of my heart" when, in truth, it was his desire to "cry like a child" that voiced his heart, now crushed and broken.

It is time to resurrect the child's perspective, whether or not it is able to command religious support and respect. If the psalms composed by others communicate our feelings too, then, by all means, let us sing the psalms. But, if not, let the psalms go unsung, and let us hear instead the cries that come truly from the heart.

Notes

1. Carthage was well known in the ancient world as a city that engaged in the ritual sacrifice of children. Augustine himself comments on this practice in *The City of God*, noting that the God to whom children (usually small boys) were sacrificed was Saturn, who mutilated his father and devoured his children. That northern Africans sacrificed their children to the god Saturn was widely commented upon in classical and patristic writings. Especially noteworthy in this regard is Minucius Felix's comment that "in some part of Africa infants were sacrificed to [Saturn] by their parents, and their cries smothered by endearments and kisses for fear of a victim being sacrificed in tears." This prohibition against crying over a loss has relevance to our later discussion of Adeodatus' reaction to his grandmother's death. For classical and patristic references to child sacrifice (see John Day 1989, 86–91).

2. In discussing the fact that he believed many things without proof, Augustine (1960) offers the following examples: historical events, places he has never seen, facts about personal friends, and "so many things about physicians" (139). The specificity of this last example indicates that there is, for him, something quite special about medical doctors.

References

Augustine. (1953). *Augustine: Earlier writings* (J. H. S. Burleigh, Ed.). Philadelphia: Westminster.

Augustine. (1960). *The Confessions of Saint Augustine* (J. K. Ryan, Trans.). Garden City: Image Books.

Augustine. (1961). *The Confessions of Saint Augustine* (R. S. Pine-Coffin, Trans.). Baltimore: Penguin Books.

Bakan, D. (1965). Some thoughts on reading Augustine's *Confessions. Journal for the Scientific Study of Religion 5*, 149–152.

Brown, P. (1969). *Augustine of Hippo*. Berkeley: University of California Press.

Capps, D. (1990). Augustine's *Confessions:* The scourge of shame and the silencing of Adeodatus. In D. Capps & J. E. Dittes (Eds.), *The hunger of the heart: Reflections on the Confessions of Augustine* (69–92). West Lafayette: Society for the Scientific Study of Religion, Monograph Series No. 8.

Capps, D. (1995). Augustine: The vicious cycle of child abuse. In *The child's song: The religious abuse of children* (21–36). Louisville: Westminster John Knox.

Capps, D., & Dittes, J. E. (Eds.). (1990). *The hunger of the heart: Reflections on the Confessions of Augustine.* West Lafayette: Society for the Scientific Study of Religion, Monograph Series No. 8.

Day, J. (1989). *Molech: A god of human sacrifice in the Old Testament.* New York: Cambridge University Press.

Dodds, E. R. (1927–28). Augustine's *Confessions:* A study of spiritual maladjustment. *Hibbert Journal 26*, 459–473.

Ferrari, L. (1974). The boyhood beatings of Augustine. *Augustinian Studies 5*, 1–14.

Lynd, H. M. (1958). *On shame and the search for identity.* New York: Harcourt, Brace & Company.

Miller, A. (1984). *For your own good* (2nd ed., H. Hannum & H. Hannum, Trans.). New York: Farrar, Straus, and Giroux.

Miller, A. (1990a). *Banished knowledge: Facing childhood injuries* (L. Vennewitz, Trans.). New York: Doubleday.

Miller, A. (1990b). Friedrich Nietzsche: The struggle against truth. In *The untouched key* (H. Hannum & H. Hannum, Trans., 71–133). New York: Doubleday.

Ricoeur, P. (1976). *Interpretation theory: Discourse and the surplus of meaning.* Fort Worth: Texas Christian University Press.

CHAPTER 7

TERRORIZING THE SELF TO SAVE THE SOUL: THE DESTRUCTIVE POWER OF LEGALISTIC CHRISTIANITY

Donald E. Sloat

Terrorist Attacks

On September 11, 2001, Mohammad Ata carefully guided the huge Boeing 767 across the New York skyline and with planned deliberation crashed it headlong into the World Trade Center. Thousands died.

An intense, committed Christian carefully placed his homemade bomb next to the Atlanta abortion clinic in the early morning hours. When it exploded minutes later, the front of the building was in shambles, but no one died.

An intelligent, top-of-his-class Israeli rabbi was determined to keep the Jewish faith pure and intact by killing the "Christian" church leaders. Many died until God knocked him to the ground on the road to Damascus.

"I don't wanna go to Sunday School!" Britany wailed to her neatly manicured mother, who bent down and softly insisted, "Britany, don't say that! You don't mean that! You want to go to Sunday School. You want Jesus to be proud of you. Tell Jesus you want to go to Sunday School!" No one died.

Four different situations, four individuals, four places in time. What do these have in common? Why start this chapter with these vignettes, you wonder? At first glance, it is easy to see how the first three events share a common theme. Each individual deliberately

An airplane crashing into the World Trade Center, September 11, 2001. AP/Wide World Photos.

planned and carried out violent action against other people and/or property. They wanted to destroy, hurt, and make an impact. And they did.

They also shared an underlying principle that was anchored in their particular religious beliefs: each believed that he was supporting God's cause, and therefore God's purposes in the universe supersede individual feelings and life itself. The eventual outcome was worth any price, even innocent human life, because it advanced God's agenda.

But what about Britany and her mother? Please consider this thought. For many years, I have worked with damaged Christians and written about spiritual abuse. I have observed the lack of safety in conservative churches and Christian families, and I have witnessed many struggles. However, only since 9/11 have I realized that legalistic Christian teaching is actually a terrorist attack on the person's real self and the core of unique individuality.

Britany's mother committed a violent act against her daughter that was no less damaging than the other examples, except her behavior is sanctioned by the church, wrapped up in a spiritual disguise, and there is no blood on the floor when she has concluded her attack. I will show in this chapter how the Christian church has devised a systematic methodology designed to terrorize in order to save.

Foundation for Violence: Good News Lost

To gain a perspective, what is the Good News that has been lost, and how could its absence contribute to violence? If we consider the thousands of years and billions of human beings who have populated this earth, we observe the ongoing human struggle to find personal meaning, to manage healthy/destructive urges, and to find a religious belief system that is personally meaningful and makes sense of one's existence. Ellens (2003) insists that while human beings are busy living and trying to develop a religious belief to placate the gods, the early Hebrews' God has staked out His position vis-à-vis humanity:

> The Bible sounds a clear and singular trumpet, whose notes convey singularly good news. ... It is the good news that God accepts us as and where we are for the sake of what we can, therefore, become. It is the good news about healing and wholeness for the pathological, inadequate, distorted, and lost persons of the world. It is the word about the only chance for the likes of us. In sum, the theology of grace asserts that God is in the healing business. (52)

Allison (1972) also is convinced that Christianity is a religion of redemption, not of control. It is not to be equated with superego and civilization. It is a very personal, individualized message that declares, "There is no rejection!"

> No matter how evil we may feel that we are, God reckons us good in Jesus Christ. This is what is good about the Good News ... [which is] directed fundamentally to the ego and the self. As simple as this propo-

sition is, the fact remains that many within and without the Christian church have never discovered it. . . . Yet it is the only foundation that will allow us to accept the demands of civilization without sacrificing our nature. (34, 50)

One would think that this amazingly simple yet profound truth would trigger a human stampede of gigantic proportions in God's direction. Historically, this has not happened. So how did the Good News lose its appeal and become lost somewhere in seldom-used archives? How could this have happened? How could so many spiritual people, saints, and theologians be wrong? Allison's (1972) comments put his proposition into perspective:

> One of the reasons why this simple but fundamentally important foundation of the Christian faith is little known and rarely discovered is that Christianity tends in each epoch to be "domesticated" and acclimated to the contemporary culture, subsumed under the establishment's need for controls, and seduced by the powers of civilization to be its servant. The most obvious example is that of Constantine, officially recognizing Christianity first as a legitimate religion and then as a legal one. This latter recognition put the church in the position of being the guardian and custodian of civilization, a position she has largely maintained since that time. This custodial, traditional, controlling responsibility was often urged upon the church by rulers who have always needed religious sanctions for the structure of ethics and justice in a society. Hence, the church was given power, prerogatives, prestige, and a vested interest in the given culture. Of course, these are generalizations and there are many examples of the Christian prophetic spirit being a catalyst and a cause of cultural upheaval, social change, and transition in a civilization. However, the vast preponderance of the Christian role was seen to be, overwhelmingly, that of control rather than redemption. . . . A religion of nagging—of exhorting and rebuking, of law and control, of condemnation and fussing-at—is a big part of the picture presented as Christianity, not merely by popular distortions but within the very citadels of scholarly learning. (34–35, 37)

Within the church, devotional materials are written to support and guide one's personal relationship with God. If we examine the traditional devotional materials that have been written since the middle of the seventeenth century, we should discover what the church has considered important. Allison determined that most of the church has emphasized a version of Christianity similar to that of Jeremy Taylor, a popular devotional writer of the seventeenth century.

For Jeremy Taylor, Christianity was a promise of pardon, acceptance, and forgiveness *on condition that* a person first fulfill the demands of the law. He effectively turned the New Testament upside down, apparently ignoring the scriptural statements "While we were yet sinners Christ died for us" (Rom. 5:8 KJV) and "Not that we loved God but that he loved us" (1 John 4:10 KJV). The New Testament clearly states that it is the weak, the wicked, the sick, and the sinner whom God loves and for whom Christ died:

> This message always appears threatening to those responsible for the structures of morality and civilization, and their continual temptation is to turn the Gospel from being good news to the self, pulled as it is between the opposing sides of nature and civilization, to a *promise* of good news *when* the demands of civilization are met. What is important is not merely the fact that this religion of control was Taylor's presentation of Christianity in the seventeenth century, ... but this misrepresentation of Christianity has rarely been criticized since then. ... (36–37)

Foundation for Violence: Pagan Rituals and Control

When grace is stripped from Christianity, a set of pagan rituals is all that remains. God is a frightening Being who must be pleased, although one never knows for sure if He is pleased *enough*. So the emphasis switches to controlling behavior, our own and others. Since the desire to control is typically grounded in fear and much of the human need is to reduce personal anxiety (Ellens, 1982), the fear/control system makes intuitive sense. Such a system is at the heart of all other religions.

When grace is not totally stripped form Christianity, we have a modified version of the pagan base with the promise of "grace" if we behave sufficiently as promoted by Jeremy Taylor in the previous discussion. Of course, this grace is no grace at all if it has to be earned. And if a person can behave well enough to believe he has earned it, then he is deluded for sure.

Obviously, we need to have control in our personal lives and in our society in order to live normal, healthy, peaceful lives. Although control can be misused, it also is essential to life. But the lack of balance in certain segments of Christianity has pushed grace aside, which is a corruption of the original Abrahamic covenant, and sets the stage for all kinds of complications and distortions.

As Allison observes, civilization has domesticated the church and seduced it into being its servant to control behavior in society. Girard (1987) fleshes out a segment of this domesticating process by describing the three essential elements in the mimetic process of employing violence to reduce dissonance in order to maintain peace in the face of the natural human tendency to dissonance, chaos, and disorder:

1. The codification of control structures or prohibitions
2. The creation of rituals for enacting both the redemptive violence event and the patterns of required conformity within the society
3. The killing of the scapegoat

When we examine any organized religion that has a legalistic bent, these principles jump out at us. Islam has tight rules on appropriate behavior, dress codes for men and women, and the acceptable practice of killing an adulterous female who has shamed the family. Catholics regulate diet, birth control, and methods of worship rituals. Protestants prohibit Sunday activities, hair length, and women in leadership. Hindus cannot eat cow's flesh. The Amish prohibit advanced education, using modern technology for "personal convenience," and "kill the scapegoat" with their practice of shunning.

The Role of Self

The world and all societies at their lowest denominator consist of individuals. So when we talk about society and maintaining order, we are ultimately concerned with individual behavior and how each person's behavior affects the group. When people agree, there is consensus and harmony. When one individual's thoughts, desires, goals, and actions interfere with another individual's thoughts, desires, goals, and actions, we have dissonance or conflict. The ongoing tension can increase if the social group encourages individual development as a priority because diversity can be unsettling to the social order.

This is a problem people have struggled with since the beginning of civilization: what is the best way to govern a society that maximizes personal uniqueness without creating social chaos? At least some civilizations have struggled with it. Others were simply dominated by the individual who was able to dominate the society. It is easy to see how religion (Christianity) naturally fits the role of regulating individual behavior by appealing to a higher deity and a higher purpose than the government itself.

Adolf Hitler delivering an address in Nuremberg, 1934. Library of Congress.

On the political level, this concept of control produces totalitarian governments that imprison independent thinkers who do not comply with the leaders' pronouncements. Those in control have a list of rules that spell out acceptable behavior. Within this framework, behavior is judged not by its own merit but by the degree with which it complies with the stated goals of the leaders. Not obeying the delineated rules can result in extremely negative consequences.

Since all behavior and thoughts spring forth from individuals, the person who wants to control must stifle dissent, independent thought, willfulness, and resistance to his wishes by either getting rid of individual human beings (reference Milosevic in Kosovo, Stalin in the Soviet Union, and Hitler in Germany). Killing the human scapegoat is equivalent to killing a self or a group of "selves."

My point is that the individual is the essential component in all this, and each individual is a unique self. The Judeo-Christian tradition believes each self has inherent significant value, and therefore violence against the self is abhorrent because life has value. Compare this to Iraq under Saddam Hussein where life was cheap and the leaders killed and maimed their own citizens at will.

Since the church is a microcosm of society, the principles described here also apply to the church community and the Christian homes within it. Rules are codified, rituals are developed to either contain or express death to the self, and systematic programs are designed to stifle or silence the self. All this is packaged as a desirable, God-sanctioned program that is doing the right thing even if it does not make sense.

I find it very distressing that the organized Christian dysfunctional package is deliberately taught to adults and children. Most other dysfunctional practices happen by default (the alcoholic parent is not intentionally drinking to teach "Adult Child of Alcoholics" [ACA] concepts to his children), but the distorted Christian system has four-color curriculum materials, training classes to train the trainers, reward systems for the students, systematized punishment for dissenters (scapegoats), and mass rallies to keep people in the program. It is a carefully designed package with very specific goals.

The "Master List"

The Christian focus on control instead of grace sets the stage for pathological actions and what Girard calls "codification of the rules." Personal openness and growth are actively discouraged in a controlling, shaming atmosphere. Compliance and submission, rather than creative ideas and personal development, are rewarded.

When control is the primary Christian emphasis, the following scenario is likely: the unacceptable behaviors are defined, a motivational system of fear and guilt is established to ensure compliance, appropriate rewards and punishments are set up as reinforcers, and this entire structure is justified by Scripture.

Sin, unacceptable behavior in the legalistic church, is generally defined in two ways. First, there is a specific master list of sins, but there is also a second "list" of vague and implied sins, generally including anything that is "selfish." The second category seems to be a catchall for anything not specifically on the master list. The behaviors to avoid are usually related to sin being operationally defined as moral badness. I am referring to the everyday definition and not the official theological statements in the major confessions (Sloat, 1990, 1999).

The master list plays a crucial role in the control system and causes all sorts of confusion for Christians who are told that they are saved by grace through faith but then must, for some reason, keep the rules to maintain their standing with God. Allison (1972) cites one reason for this conflicting theological practice:

> Indeed, Roman Catholicism in the sixteenth century and most of Anglicanism and English-speaking Protestantism in the seventeenth century made a tragic mistake, with sinister pastoral results, by essentially defining sin as being only conscious and deliberate, in spite of the biblical, patristic, and medieval traditions to the contrary. This pushed the root problems of the human heart underground and left the confessional and pulpit dealing with the symptoms of sins, theologically isolated from their deeper, demonic, and often unconscious roots. The expectation, that a man's will can be changed by exhortations to control, was the essence of Pelagius's heresy, yet it has become a commonplace of traditional and establishment Christianity. (40)

Even though I grew up in northern Indiana thousands of miles from seventeenth-century Protestantism, I can see the truth of Allison's observation in my holiness church's theology. The master list included smoking or chewing tobacco, drinking alcohol, dancing, bowling, movies, cards, and, of course, such things as lying, stealing, and not going to church. Other sins included wearing jewelry, open-toed shoes, and short hair for women as well as flashy clothes and so on. Television was just starting to get off the ground, and it was often referred to as a tool of hell. The emphasis was very much on specific behaviors to avoid.

Although master lists have many points in common, they vary according to denomination and geographic location. A Lutheran fellow from St. Louis moved to a conservative area in western Michigan. Accustomed to mowing his yard on Sunday, he innocently broke the Sunday morning silence with his noisy lawnmower. After stern looks and remarks from his neighbors, he gradually began realize he was violating the community's master list regarding Sunday behavior. Desiring to be a good neighbor, he stopped mowing on Sunday.

After considerable debate, two Christian families who had cottages adjacent to each other on a lake resolved the problem of what each family could do on Sunday. One family decided they could sit in their lawn chairs if they only faced the lake but did not go into the water. The other family decided they could also sit outside, but they had to have their backs to the water.

In some families the definition of sin becomes so narrow that one's personal nature is stifled and a sense of guilt is strengthened as unre-

alistic goals are set for "holy" living. A woman who had grown up as
a minister's daughter told me that as part of her early Christian training her godly grandmother had repeatedly drilled into her the verse
in James, "Therefore, to him who knows to do good and does not do
it, to him it is sin" (4:17). This verse had a deep effect and influenced
her life from the time she was a youngster. For example, there were
occasions when walking through the house she was tempted to simply ignore some lint on the carpet. As she approached the lint, however, this admonition entered her mind and threw her into conflict.
She knew that picking up the lint would be the right thing to do and,
therefore, that to just walk past without picking it up would be sin.
However, as she searched her heart, she did not feel like picking it up,
and this trivial matter became a choice between obedience and sin—
a heavy and unnecessary choice for a young child.

Another woman in her thirties told me that she still feels guilty
using scissors on Sunday mornings, even to trim a loose thread from
her daughter's dress. Until recently, if she had to use scissors on
Sunday, she selected a pair with plastic-wrapped handles as insulation
for her hand from the lightning she expected. Although she knew
rationally that this was not necessary, she did it anyway.

It is tempting to narrate the humorous things Christians sometimes do as they attempt to keep within the bounds of the list but still
do what they really want to do. Is it okay to get the Sunday paper if
it is delivered Saturday before midnight? Should we put the television
antenna in the attic (this was an issue in the 1960s) so others do not
know we have it? May we eat out on Sunday if it is far enough away
from home so no acquaintances can see us and be offended as the
weaker brothers?

In churches like the one in which I grew up, a person could lose salvation by not attending to the rules. Obviously, making a wrong
move could mean eternal damnation, something no sensible-minded
person would want to risk. I have friends from other churches that
believe in eternal security who worry that they may not have been
saved in the first place, so their security is no more certain than that
of their Armenian friends.

A Moral or Relationship Problem

There is a related emphasis of conservative Christian thinking
regarding the fall story in Genesis 3 that serves as the linchpin on
the side of control instead of grace (Sloat, 1990). Christians gener-

ally believe Adam's sin created a moral problem (meaning human nature is bad or shameful or evil) as well as a relationship problem (meaning human beings are out of relationship with God, themselves, and others). The practical implications of emphasizing one over the other of these points are significant in terms of everyday Christian practice.

There is no doubt that people commit evil actions, but what is the answer to the human dilemma? Do we emphasize an inherently shameful inner self that is immoral and "wormlike" and tell people how bad they are? Or do we emphasize healing the broken relationships with God, self, and other people? If we emphasize the moral problem, we will try to contain the evil self, which places Christianity in the control position Allison has described. On the other hand, if we believe people's self-centeredness is increased *as the result* of a relationship problem, then we will see grace as the remedy for healing the relationship.

The moral emphasis surfaces in sermons when the minister wants to drive home the point that evil is rampant in humanity. "We are born in sin," the pastor insists. "It is born right in us. The other day my three-year-old son lied and said he had not hit his sister when I saw him do it. Nobody had to teach him to lie. It is in him. And at the age of three, his sinful nature is showing itself."

The Evil Self

It is a fact that many churches promote dislike of self as a desirable spiritual trait, suggesting that to think of oneself as a worthwhile person is sinful and self-centered. Such thinking has been enshrined for centuries in Christian literature. Referring again to Girard's paradigm, we see the ritual of "self-hate" threaded through the church to ensure that individuals conform to the desired behavior patterns. This not only reduces social conflict but also increases one's chances of pleasing God and saving one's soul.

Carter and Narramore (1979) touch on this as they discuss the integration of psychology and Scripture and point to the distinction between biblical *fact* and biblical *interpretation*. They assert that large portions of the Evangelical church have been influenced by the Keswick Movement, which taught a morbid form of self-denial and debasement as part of a deeper spiritual life. They observe that such teaching can stir neurotic feelings of guilt and self-devaluation and offer this quote from Hession as an example of this negative teaching:

> Those who have been in tropical lands tell us that there is a big differ-
> ence between a snake and a worm when you attempt to strike at them.
> The snake rears itself up and hisses and tries to strike back—a true pic-
> ture of self. But a worm offers no resistance; it allows you to do what
> you like with it, kick it or squash it under your heel—a picture of true
> brokenness. Jesus was willing to become just that for us—a worm and
> no man. And he died so, because that is what he saw us to be, worms
> having forfeited all rights by our sin, except to deserve hell. And he now
> calls us to take our rightful place as worms for him and with him. (24)

Can we seriously believe that Jesus became "a worm and no man" for
us and that we are supposed to "take our rightful place as worms for
him and with him"? When Philippians 2:5–7 states that Christ chose
to take the form of a servant even though He was God, this is not
wormlike action. The very notion is degrading and hardly fits the
larger Christian message.

This problem of negative Christian teaching about the self is also
tackled by Robert H. Schuller (1982), who touches on this worm theology being promoted by Hession:

> One reason many Christians have behaved so badly in the past two
> thousand years is because we have been taught from infancy to adult-
> hood "how sinful" and "how worthless" we are. The self-image will
> always incarnate itself in action. A negative diagnosis will become a
> self-fulfilling prophecy. The most difficult task for the church to learn
> is how to deal honestly with the subject of "negativity," "sin," and "evil"
> without doing the cause of redemption more harm than good. (61)

Within the church there appears to be lack of consensus about what
constitutes proper perception of self and how the sense of self fits
into the Christian life. The concept of self-esteem for Christians has
been popularized in recent years by Robert Schuller through his
books and television programs. In comparison to the messages I
heard growing up, his ideas are a refreshing breath of fresh air
because they bolster my self-worth.

Some people take exception to the idea that Christians should have
good self-esteem because they equate positive self-esteem with sin.
Recently, I was discussing this point with a prominent layman. In
response to his statement that Schuller's notion of self-esteem is sinful, I asked, "Do you mean I should say that I am a worm?" "Of
course!" was his instant reply.

The point in the moral emphasis is clear. The human self is evil,
and if left unattended it will blossom like the wild thistles and briars

that spoil the idyllic meadow. Just as society must guard itself against unscrupulous individuals, conscientious Christian parents must protect their growing children from the children's own inherent evil self that is itching to break out in rampant, nasty behavior. But not just behavior today—the real fear is that the beloved children will rush down the broad road to hell and eternal damnation. Suddenly, the stakes are high, yes, high beyond human comprehension, and this reality stokes the parents' indescribable terror. What is worse for Christian parents than to visualize their children spending eternity in hell's flames?

The Value and Necessity of Self

Although I do not intend to resolve this complicated issue here, I believe many people are confusing self-esteem or self-image, a part of our psychological equipment, with our inability to earn salvation, a spiritual concept. I can have good self-esteem and still recognize that "my righteousness is as filthy rags." Conversely, calling myself a worm is not going to earn any spiritual points, either. Often I see Christians beating themselves on their heads, putting themselves down, and treating themselves horribly in the name of God:

> The truth is that self-belittling is not true Christian humility and runs counter to some very basic teachings of the Christian faith. The great commandment is that you love God with all your being. The second commandment is an extension of the first—that you love your neighbor as you love yourself. We do not have two commandments here, but three: to love God, to love yourself, and to love others. I put *self* second, because Jesus plainly made a proper self-love the basis of a proper love for neighbor. The term *self-love* has a wrong connotation for some people. Whether you call it self-esteem or self-worth, it is plainly the foundation of Christian love for others. And this is the opposite of what many Christians believe. (Seamands, 1981, 70–71)

Abby is a middle-aged Christian woman who learned several years ago that she is diabetic, but even though she knows enough about diabetes to write a book on it, she fails to eat properly or take her insulin regularly. On one occasion she began a diet that she knew could lead to an insulin reaction, and even her physician advised against it. As a result, she became quite ill at work when her sugar dropped to a precipitous level, almost requiring hospitalization. Her doctor referred her

for psychotherapy because her eating habits were potentially dangerous for her physical health. As we discussed her life, it became obvious
that she carried lots of shame and had a low sense of personal worth.

She had become a Christian at the age of 13 at an Evangelical
church, and that church's training, along with her non-Christian
mother's constant criticism, affected her self-image. She did not really
care if she died, although she had no intentions of killing herself.
Consistently, she put everyone else ahead of her own feelings or needs
since she enjoyed doing things for others. After listening to her, I
remarked, "Instead of loving others as you love yourself, you treat
other people better than you do yourself. For you, we should turn
Jesus' statement around and tell you to love yourself as much as you
do other people."

I am convinced that teaching children to give up things before they
have learned to possess them (renunciation) or to put themselves last
before they have mastered self-assertion creates feelings of low self-
worth and shame. Carried to an extreme, this restricted upbringing
can cause some people to even doubt their existence, let alone experience worth:

> It is by daring to express his desires, tastes, and opinions, and through
> feelings that they are respected, that the child becomes aware that he
> exists, of being a person distinct from other persons. It is a violation of
> the person of the child to try to direct him in everything according to
> what his parents think best, without heeding his own preferences. He
> comes to the point where he no longer knows what his desires, tastes,
> and opinions are, and an individual without any personal desire, taste,
> or opinion does not feel that he exists, either. This can be observed in
> families with high moral or religious pretensions. The parents are so
> sure they have a monopoly of absolute truth that any other view than
> their own can only be a grievous error in their eyes. They are so sure
> of their judgement in all matters, that they impose it on their chil-
> dren—for their own good they think.
>
> This often goes along with the teaching of self-abnegation. While
> still young the child must learn to forget himself, to disregard his per-
> sonal desires, to behave in accordance with the requirements of others,
> seeking always to please them rather than himself. Of course the par-
> ents head the list of the "others" who must be pleased and have con-
> stant service rendered to them, whereas they themselves scarcely ever
> bother to gratify any of the child's pleasures which they look upon as
> mere selfish whims. And they accuse him of selfishness if he manifests
> any personal aspirations. (Tournier, 1968, 107–108)

Church leaders and ministers often treat Christians in the same fashion as the parents in this quote treat their children. They do not allow the parishioners to ask questions and to assert their own opinions. The implication is that only the minister or parent is capable of making correct decisions, while the child or parishioner is inferior and must be told what to do. As a result, shame is promoted, and a faulty concept of self-assertion inhibits people from fully experiencing and knowing themselves:

> The irony of this is that in the name of God well-intentioned parents and ministers lay a foundation which makes Satan's work easier: Satan's greatest psychological weapon is a gut-feeling of inferiority, inadequacy, and low self-worth. This feeling shackles many Christians, in spite of wonderful spiritual experiences, in spite of their faith and knowledge of God's Word. Although they understand their positions as sons and daughters of God, they are tied up in knots, bound by a terrible feeling of inferiority, and chained to a deep sense of worthlessness. (Seamands, 1981, 49)

Terrorizing the Self

When we look specifically at families in the legalistic Christian community, we often see an external focus that is uniquely Christian. The focus is on correct behavior at the expense of children's emotions. I realize that Christian families are not the only ones who emphasize correct behavior, but there is a unique quality here simply because it *is* Christian. This emphasis includes powerful spiritual truths, but these truths can either be helpful or have definite negative effects. Christian parents can invoke God and spiritual truths in their desire to control their children, a weapon unavailable to non-Christians. The goal to encourage children to live godly lives is laudable, but the method can be emotionally devastating.

Parents who hear the "evil self" teaching emphasis and accept it are going to see evil selves in their children. Consequently, they will ratchet up their control and try to extinguish any signs of budding "sinful" behavior. In their family, they will emphasize control at the expense of grace or redemption in the family system. This control emphasis leads to an oppressive atmosphere that stifles individual freedom and openness. In the name of God, the parents introduce rigid goals to obtain the desired result in their children.

Because the parents fear their children's potential for evil, many will go to any lengths using fear, guilt, shame, and manipulation with Scripture to keep their children in line. By this standard of thinking, self-esteem and personal security are expendable commodities that pale by comparison to the potential evil that children may commit. Containing the immoral potential is the only acceptable spiritual goal, and there is little room or need for grace.

Even though I have been counseling Christians for almost 40 years and have been writing about the dysfunctional practices that stifle the inner self for the past 20, the events of 9/11 rattled my perspective on terrorism in general. It gradually dawned on me that these legalistic demands and stifling controls are an assault on the precious inner soul, the part of the person made in the image of God, and the intent is to kill or at least silence the self in order to save the person's soul—to stop him or her from sinning or sinning in a particular way. Saving a child's soul from eternal damnation is the highest principle, and individual feelings pale by comparison to this significant truth.

A disturbing example of how a concerned Christian is trying to literally silence a child's self to save his soul came to my attention as I finalized this chapter. A nurse in a local hospital talked to a Christian woman whose grandson was in the pediatric intensive care unit. As they discussed the child's physical status, the grandmother expressed her heartfelt concern this way: "I pray that God will let him die before he can grow up and commit some evil that would keep him out of heaven."

The Evangelical Rules

In order to accomplish this important task of controlling the potentially evil self, the parents and church need a system that will (1) get rid of or silence the evil self and (2) keep the child as well as adults on the right path. The answer is a dysfunctional, legalistic control system that is wrapped in spiritual language, but it is a subtle terrorist attack on the real self.

As mentioned earlier, most dysfunctional family patterns happen by default: the destructive patterns simply flow out of the parents' personality dynamics. The alcoholic father is not trying to teach his children the three rules (Black, 1982, 31–49) of the alcoholic home: (1) don't talk, (2) don't trust, and (3) don't feel. Growing up in an alcoholic home is a difficult task because there are so many unhealthy elements and destructive patterns, but in the dysfunctional Christian home, it is no picnic, either. In fact, it is worse because there are so many heavy spiritual truths intertwined with the family dysfunctions that complicate recovery.

For example, in the legalistic Christian environment, there is a deliberate intent to teach the destructive ideas that I have named the Evangelical Rules (Sloat, 1990, 105–146). These rules are similar to the alcoholic home rules, except the Evangelical Rules proscribe the desired behavior. In fact, the Evangelical Rules are often harder to contend with than the alcoholic rules because it appears God sanctions them. They are backed up with Scripture and can determine one's eternal destiny. These are mighty issues for a young person to handle, and the secular alcoholic rules pale by comparison because they lack the weighty spiritual dimension.

The Evangelical Rules are listed here to help you visualize them. Notice how they are divided from left to right. All the "Don't dos" are on the left, and the "You're supposed to do" admonitions are on the right. To help your visualization, lean back from this page and concentrate your focus on the two columns:

Rule #1: "Don't talk . . . Do say . . . "
Rule #2: "Don't trust . . . Do trust . . . "
Rule #3: "Don't feel . . . Do feel . . . "
Rule #4: "Don't want . . . Do want . . . "

All the emphasis on the left is against the self, and the focus on the right is toward others, doing what parents/God want us to do. The Evangelical Rules define how a person must silence the real self and replace it with whatever the rules say is "holy" or acceptable according to the prevailing Christian standard. The rules also determine the direction of a person's focus. Instead of an internal focus regarding self-development and awareness, a person must adopt an external focus that is concerned with surviving and trying to maintain personal safety in their fearful environment.

The Rules Silence the Self

Consider how these rules relate to normal, emotional development of the self. In order to move through the healthy stages, a child must have a solid attachment with caregivers which serves as a solid foundation for the subsequent stages. Feeling unconditionally loved, a child can move confidently through the various stages knowing their parents are supporting them all the way (see Figure 7.1).

Healthy Development	Unhealthy Development
Unconditional Love	**Conditional Love**
⇓	⇓
Attachment	Isolation
⇓	⇓
Separation	Fusion
⇓	⇓
Integration	Splitting
⇓	⇓
Adulthood	Childlike

Figure 7.1   Developmental Stages

The attachment stage is critical, and if the attachment is *conditional*, the child lives in an unsupported disconnected state of fearful isolation. If the child obviously has to earn any love or caring, having one's own thoughts will not please the parents who emphasize control ("Say what I want to hear"). So to please and avoid punishment, the child's only alternative is to enter the fusion stage. This means the youngster fuses with the parents by taking on their ideas and values as his or her own. Setting the true self aside in an attempt to avoid parental rejection, the parental demands and wishes are adopted as one's own in an attempt to gain acceptance and at least some attachment. For the child who is in survival mode at this stage, earned love is better than no love at all, even if it means selling off the self.

This in turn leads to the next unhealthy stage of splitting, where decisions are not made on the basis of the child's personal self but rather on what will please the person handing out the love. The things that please the parent are kept because it feels safe to have these ideas and thoughts, while the behavior and thoughts that bring rejection are split away. Unable to form a separate identity and become independently responsible, the individual builds an exterior shell of a person and lives childlike in relationship to other people and adults. You can see from this progression how the Evangelical Rules very effectively silence the self (Cloud, 1993).

In this system, a thread of fear overshadows individual lives, and children must pursue the unhealthy developmental side in hopes of finding some security in an unsafe setting. As Joe, a character in

Cloud's narrative, summed it up, "In my family, if any emotion or something came up, I had to put it away. My folks couldn't accept it. 'Just laugh it off!' they told me when kids pushed me in school. So I had to put part of me away." The unacceptable aspects of a person must be gotten out of the way in order to have a relationship with the feared person who is in control and has the love one so desperately wants to receive.

Tournier's (1968) description of the typical legalistic home so aptly summarizes what takes place as a child grows up under these rules:

> A child brought up in an environment like that in which all worldly pleasures are frowned upon, will forswear dancing, flirtation, theatre-going, alcohol, tobacco, nice clothes, and any interest in good food. He will retain perhaps for the rest of his life the idea that everything plea-surable is forbidden, and a sin. . . . A negative education of this kind destroys a child's self-confidence and pushes him into neurosis, because it blocks the spontaneous force of life within him. . . . Many people do not like life. Their upbringing has left them with a prohibition inside of them, which says: "Living prohibited." . . . To put a brake on this vital impulse on the excuse of teaching the child wisdom or Christian humil-ity, is to fail to understand the rhythms of Nature implanted by God. (115–116, 128–129)

The High Cost of "Holiness"

In this legalistic system, the only way to be "holy" is to pay a huge price—not the ultimate price of one's physical life but a price that in many ways is worse in terms of extended suffering. It is the loss of one's real self. The high cost of being "holy" is being internally dead to one's real self, yet the body is alive, involved in life and trying to please others. It means to live disconnected to one's true feelings, preferences, goals, activities, and so on. If I want to be loved, I must be sure that my actions and thoughts conform to the image I am expected to portray. The Evangelical Rules function as a guide for doing this. It is a huge price to pay in order to gain a "holiness" that does not exist and that God does not require.

The scapegoat assumes the ultimate responsibility for the problem in Girard's view. I suggest that the "self" is seen as the ultimate prob-lem in human nature and the church and that the human reflex of violence Ellens (2003) describes is used to cleanse the individual as well as society of the evil inherent in the self. In the process, humans reject the covenantal offer of grace and revert to a pagan, barbaric, violent method that has been dressed up and socialized to look spiritual in modern times. Modern religion is deadly when it rejects grace as its core.

Now before you decide that I am throwing too much of the baby out with the dirty bath water, understand that I am not saying that the points on the right are in error or should not be part of the Christian picture. The Bible does talk about obeying parents, self-denial, fear of God, and so on. It would be absolutely foolhardy for parents to stop teaching biblical values and principles to their children because they need these values as a foundation for their development. However, these teachings must be taught with a proper balance and understanding that takes the personal stages of development into account. Biblical principles value and build the self as a necessary part of spiritual development and personal wholeness.

A person who has not worked with abuse survivors may wonder if I am stretching the truth when I insist that Christian parents and churches often terrorize the inner self. To bring this truth into clearer focus, I am including a first-person narrative that details how a Christian father used God and scripture to devastate his daughter's inner self. Terri is a Christian woman in her fifties. Her father was physically, emotionally, and spiritually abusive, and she has suffered from posttraumatic stress disorder. Incidentally, her father was an upstanding member in the community and the local church. As you read her story, notice how her father's fear-based theology has placed huge obstacles in her personal path.

A Victim's Story

It comes as no surprise to the victim of abuse that the perpetrator seldom uses only one type of abuse. For example, if a father abuses his child physically, chances are he will also abuse her psychologically, verbally, emotionally, and so on. My father was no exception. And whereas each and every type of abuse leaves its telltale marks and scars, I believe the most insidious type of abuse is spiritual. Perhaps this is because the damage is done to the innermost part of the child, her very soul. In addition, when the child matures and realizes that her feelings about God are markedly different than those her pastor describes, she develops an enormous guilt load and fears for her very salvation.

Spiritual abuse can occur *without* the actual use of Scripture. Just a few choice words can harm a sensitive child. Even as a small child, I was usually too frightened to misbehave. When I did, however, I was not told I was being "naughty." I was told that I was "wicked" and "evil." These are very scary words to a small child.

In Scripture, God is referred to as "our Heavenly Father" (Matt. 6:26, 32; Luke 11:11–13; John 1:12). We become His children by the process of adoption (Rom. 8:15; Gal. 4:5–7; Eph. 1:5). In Psalm 103 we are told that God forgives our sins, heals all our diseases, redeems our lives, and crowns us with love and compassion. He is said to be merciful, gracious, and slow to anger. Later in this chapter (v. 13), God again compares Himself to our earthly father.

But when experience teaches us that our earthly father is hostile, unfair, judgmental, unpredictable, hurtful, violent, cruel, vindictive, hypocritical, and demanding of perfection, the comparison to "God the Father" breaks down. It is impossible to picture a loving and compassionate "God the Father" when our human father is the very opposite. And without "God the Father," our God is incomplete. There can be no Trinity (God the Father, God the Son, and God the Holy Spirit). This is a terrible dilemma for a Christian. I finally solved it for myself by renaming the Persons of the Trinity as follows: God the Creator, God the Son, and God the Holy Spirit.

Psalm 111:10 reads, "The fear of the Lord is the beginning of wisdom." The phrases "the fear of the Lord" and "fear the Lord" are repeated in the Bible a multitude of times. "Fear" was translated to me (quite literally at times) as "terror." The concept of fear/terror permeated nearly every biblical "truth" I was taught. I have lived my entire life in fear:

Fear that I might *do* something I should not

Fear I might *not* do something I should

Fear that my judgment of right and wrong was faulty

Fear of the judgment promised in so many passages

My father often misquoted verses to enhance the fear I felt. For example, the verse "It is a fearful thing to fall into the hands of the living God" (Heb. 10:31 KJV) was consistently misquoted to me as "It is a fearful thing to fall into the hands of an *angry* God." I didn't realize the correct wording until I was well into adulthood. I must have read that verse incorrectly dozens of times.

In the twenty-fifth chapter of Matthew's gospel, Christ uses the parable of the sheep and the goats to illustrate to his followers the separation of believers and nonbelievers at the final judgment (vv. 31–46). God puts the believers (His sheep) on His right and the nonbelievers (goats) on His left. He then passes out the appropriate reward (Heaven) or judgment (Hell) to each group. I vividly remember being firmly led by the arm into our family room and very pointedly made to sit at my father's left side. I was retold the parable with the proper emphasis being placed on the extreme wickedness and evil living of the "goats," resulting in their being in the place of dishonor (the left) and their coming judgment. With my having earned a place at his left side, my father would offer long, pious prayers, pointing out to God my wickedness and imploring God to show me my many shortcomings and to turn my heart from the path of transgressions to the way of repentance. I was then made to go to my mother and beg for forgiveness for having been such a shameful person and such a sorrow to her (reference Prov. 29:15 KJV). The irony of all this is that dad's actions were based on some minor transgression that I cannot remember. What I do remember is the deep sense of shame and indescribable terror as my dad placed me so confidently with the goats.

I cannot begin to list all the Bible verses used as weapons, that is, excuses to explain disciplinary measures. The list is much too long. But here is a sampling:

> Do not withhold discipline from a child; if you beat him with a rod, he will not die. (Prov. 23:13 KJV)

Translation: Spare the rod, spoil the child.

> Foolishness is bound up in the heart of a child; but the rod of correction will drive it far from him. (Prov. 22:15 KJV)

Translation: Children are foolish/bad: beat it out of them with a rod.

> Chasten your son while there is hope, and let not thine heart spare for his crying. (Prov. 19:18 KJV)

Translation: This verse seems to leave no room for mercy.

> Honor thy father and thy mother that thy days may be long upon the land which the Lord thy God giveth thee. (Exod. 20:12 KJV)

Translation: Honoring your parents means obeying them and have a "good attitude" while doing it. A "good attitude" consists of working with a smile, *never* questioning "Why?" and under *no* set of circumstances *ever* frown, argue, or offer a differing opinion. If you follow this command, God will allow you to live a long life—but disobey, and you *die*!

And if you think only Old Testament verses can be twisted and used as weapons against a child, read on:

"Children, obey your parents in the Lord, for this is right" (Eph. 6:1 KJV). If you feel that the words "in the Lord" leave you a loophole, the next verse closes it.

"Children, obey your parents in all things; for this is well-pleasing unto the Lord" (Col. 3:20 KJV). The three little words "in all things" very efficiently close any imagined loophole of the previous verse.

As you see here, you can make the Bible say or mean nearly anything you desire if you take a verse out of context and change a word here or there. And when it comes to quoting Scripture, what young child can (or dares) compete with an adult who has been hearing and reading the Bible for his entire lifetime? The damage done to a young soul may take an entire lifetime to heal. But the scars remain. And so does the pain of the ongoing struggle with faith, trust, and the concept of a loving and compassionate Heavenly Father.

I have cited here only a very small sampling of the Bible verses that were twisted to control me. My father is no longer living, and I am finding it easier to forgive him as time goes by. He, too, was a human being, with all the faults and failings that human beings have. I just wish he could have loved me and accepted me as the person I was. What a different foundation I would have had for my life and for my spiritual development.

In the Name of God

The 9/11 World Trade Center and Pentagon attacks were shocking and devastating and wasted thousands of human lives. The magnitude of the flames, the taped images of the towers falling in slow motion, and the endless list of victims forced Americans to stop whatever they were doing and face this epic human tragedy.

The spiritual abuse described here is hardly noticed. This is a tragedy of unspeakable proportions that CNN does not cover and *Time* magazine does not feature. But every day in my consulting office, I am witness to struggling human beings who have experienced terrorist-like attacks on their inner souls. This is an ongoing devastation that is carried on in the privacy of nice-looking families and expensive church education buildings and promoted by trained ministers. The irony is that this horrible damage is done in the name of God.

Did not Mohammad Ata carry out his attack in the name of God?

References

Allison, C. F. (1972). *Guilt, anger, and God: The patterns of our discontents.* New York: Seabury.

Black, C. (1982). *It will never happen to me.* Denver: M.A.C. Printing and Publishing Division.

Carter, J. D. & Narramore, B. (1979). *The integration of psychology and theology: An introduction.* Grand Rapids: Academie Books, Zondervan.

Cloud, H. (1993). *Decisions that heal: How to understand your past to ensure a healthier life.* Grand Rapids: Zondervan Publishing House. This book provides an excellent description of the developmental stages from a Christian perspective.

Ellens, J. H. (1982). *God's grace and human health.* Nashville: Abingdon.

Ellens, J. H. (Ed.). (2004). *The destructive power of religion: Vol. 1 Sacred scriptures and psycho-social violence.* Westport: Praeger.

Girard, R. (1987). *Things hidden since the foundation of the world.* (S. Bann & M. Metter, Trans.). Stanford: Stanford University Press.

Schuller, R. H. (1982). *Self-esteem: The new reformation.* Waco: Word Books.

Seamands, D. A. (1981). *Healing for damaged emotions.* Wheaton: Victor Books.

Sloat, D. E. (1990). *Growing up holy and wholly.* Brentwood: Wolgemuth & Hyatt.

Sloat, D. E. (1999). *The dangers of growing up in a Christian home* (2nd ed.). Grand Rapids: Mandy Press.

Tournier, P. (1968). *A place for you.* New York: Harper & Row.

CHAPTER 8

Imposed Shame: The Origin of Violence and Worthlessness

Donald E. Sloat

The Deliberate Perpetrator

Terri's father, Dick, apparently liked to impress his friends with his child-rearing philosophies because he had a graphic gesture that expressed his true heartfelt feelings toward his firstborn:

> He had another favorite speech that really shows what he was thinking. I used to hear this almost every time he had friends over to our house for Sunday dinner. "I wanna tell ya, I know what I'm talking about. You don't see my kids acting up, do ya? I'm telling ya, be firm, don't give an inch. You've got to CRUSH their spirits before they get big enough to give you any trouble!" He uttered the word "CRUSH" with a gleeful intensity, and for additional emphasis, he fiercely twisted the toe of his foot into the pavement as if he were grinding out a discarded cigarette butt.
>
> I don't think he really ever realized just how accurate that action was. I always felt like that imaginary cigarette butt under his toe. He made me feel as feel as worthless as a cigarette butt someone had tossed on the ground. Just thrown away. I could never figure it out, but I knew there must have been something about me that was basically flawed.

It is amazing and sad that Terri's "Christian" father so clearly declared his deliberate goal of committing violence against her spirit. He intended to destroy her spirit and impose into her psyche a self he had fashioned in his mind. Many well-intended Christian parents use destructive legalistic practices on their children because it is all they know, but Dick was not mistreating Terri out of misinformed good intentions.

Dick was evil, elevating himself above God and acting out his narcissistic nature. He announced to himself and anyone who would listen that he had the right to take his daughter's real self, made in God's image (Gen. 1:26), and deliberately crush it. He continued this cruelty by declaring that he was going to construct a self in his daughter that was superior to the original equipment that God had given her. This is a graphic example of what Shengold (1989) calls "soul murder."

The Worthless Self

When a child's internal self is stifled, frightened into hiding, or crushed, as Dick described it, something must fill the space or fulfill the function that the self was intended to accomplish. Terri's father intended to fill that space inside her with a self that suited his purposes. He wanted her to think as he wanted her to think. He wanted her to feel the feelings he deemed appropriate. He wanted her to want the things he wanted her to want. He wanted her to internalize his notion of self as her own. This is typical of the legalistic "Christian" mentality that rejects grace and wants to use Fundamentalist Evangelical codes to shape children (Sloat, 1990).

Instead of feeling loved and worthwhile, children like Terri develop a shame-based identity (Bradshaw, 1988). As Terri wrote, "There must have been something about me that was basically flawed." In my clinical work, I have observed that the feelings are deeper and more destructive than merely feelings of being flawed. The inescapable, deeper feelings produce a deep sense of worthlessness. It is the internal haunting voice that insists, "If you really knew me, you wouldn't love me!" The real self that was created in God's image has been replaced with a false, worthless self that feels unlovable and insignificant (Masterson, 1988).

The Driving Force

Shame drives such destructive human behavior. Shame is an integral part of human nature and colors everything we do. If we look behind Dick's abuse, we will find residual shame in him driving it. If we explore Terri's worthless feelings, we will discover shame. There is a shame connection between the perpetrator and the victim. How does this work? How can shame drive both behaviors? Can we understand why this abusive behavior makes sense to Dick? How is shame connected to his destructive behavior toward his daughter's self? Is it possible for him to change?

How can the victim-survivor get rid of this crippling worthlessness? How does she protect herself against this assault on her essential nature? Does it require extensive cognitive restructuring? What does she do with this "worthless self?" Where does she put it inside her psyche?

In this chapter, I offer my perspective, based on extensive clinical observation, on the interactions between shame and destructive behavior, with an emphasis on the shame link between perpetrator and victim. These are clinical concepts that I employ in therapy to help survivors sort through their worthless feelings and make sense of their inner confusion.

The Three Types of Shame

Some authors and clinicians use the generic or general term "shame" when they describe shame-based behavior. I find that breaking shame into three different categories (Bradshaw, 1988; Broucek, 1991; Green & Lawrenz, 1994) more accurately reflects the reality of the human condition and makes it easier to understand the connection between shame and behavior (see Fossum & Mason, 1986). The three types of shame may be described as follows:

1. Natural shame—the normal human condition of being imperfect.
2. Moral shame—the bad feelings people experiences when they act contrary to the natural laws and personal values. It is sometimes referred to as healthy shame.
3. Imposed shame—the shame that is generated when we refuse to accept personal ownership and responsibility for our natural shame and moral shame. This might also be called borrowed shame.

The terms "imposed shame" and "borrowed shame" imply that the shame in this category does not belong to the persons who have it in their possession. I prefer the term "imposed shame" because it clearly describes the fact that the perpetrator has imposed his shame upon the victim. This is the toxic shame that makes a person feel worthless and is destructive of the human spirit and relationships (a thorough explanation of shame may be found in Kaufman, 1985).

The Natural Psychospiritual Forces

In order to understand shame and its implications, we must appreciate the natural psychospiritual forces that function in the universe and are inherent to human beings. These principles are certain and predictable, much like the laws of physics and chemistry. We know that the earth revolves around the sun, gravity is always down, and light travels at 186,000 miles per second. We can count on it.

These natural psychospiritual forces are invisible principles and values that are constitutive to the nature of every human being regardless of culture, religion, race, and geography and are in operation even if the person is unaware of their existence. They operate outside human control, and we cannot insulate ourselves from their effects and influence.

These natural psychospiritual dynamics are the following:

- Love is the ultimate psychospiritual principle in the universe.
- Human life is the supreme value in the world.
- Relationships constitute the source of meaning in life.
- We are all responsible for our choices and their consequences.

Jesus clearly included two of these principles in his summation of the divine commandments and implied the other two. He said, "Love God with your entire being, and your neighbor as yourself." Some may argue that these Judeo-Christian concepts do not apply to all cultures. I believe that most humans, regardless of religious orientation, would acknowledge these four psychospiritual principles. These principles serve as the underpinnings for all relationships among humans and are the foundation for understanding the dynamics of shame.

The Ultimate Principle of Love

Some might say that claiming love as the ultimate structural principle in the universe seems to substitute it for God. There was a time when I might have thought so as well. However, I believe that truth is often obscured by the use of inadequate metaphors. Many humans fear God more than they feel loved by him. They have been taught to think of God in metaphors which cause fear, guilt, and shame rather than security and well-being. Someone like Terri who was brutalized by a parent, as a sensitive child threatened by the hellfire of a revival meeting, or as a young girl taught to deny herself and substitute her honest thoughts for those her parents believed Jesus wanted her to feel is a person with a destructive set of metaphors for God.

Aurelius Augustine was not spared from childhood perpetrators of imposed shame, though he pleaded for God's intervention. As an adult, the childhood scars complicated his attempts to establish a trusting relationship with the God who had apparently ignored his childhood pleas (Capps & Dittes, 1990). Augustine never resolved his childhood trauma, and his residual shame shaped his theology.

The Bible declares that God is love, not just that God loves. "God" and "love" are synonymous. So saying that love is the highest principle in the universe is an exact corollary to saying that God is the supreme being in the universe. Love is the active expression of God's essence. Humans long for love and relate to it.

The Supreme Value of Human Life

The Judeo-Christian tradition that God created humans in his own image has established the supreme value of human life as a principle in Western culture as well as in most others. Those of us who live in the United States tend to value human life as a matter of course, often forgetting that some other cultures do not share our beliefs. The preamble to the U.S. Constitution emphasizes individual value and guarantees personal rights. As Americans, we are often surprised when other cultures show minimal regard for human life. Of course, they tend to look at our culture and wonder how we have been willing to intentionally kill 75 million unborn babies since 1965, 400,000 each quarter of a year. Life is fragile and rare and cannot be replaced. Each person receives only one life, and when one's life ends, there is no going back to what was. Life is precious. This principle is endemic in the universe and is inherent to all humans everywhere.

The Ultimate Meaning in Relationships

There are four relationships at work in this force in the universe:

- An individual's relationship to love (God)
- An individual's relationship to self
- An individual's relationship to another person's self
- An individual's relationship to the rest of organic and inorganic creation

All of life is a complex network of relationships that extend in vertical, horizontal, and inward directions—three dimensions, so to speak. We all have a relationship with our inner self, with our concept of a higher power in the universe, with other persons and groups, and with the created world. Human beings are relational by design. Because each human being's essence is a unique, priceless self, the relational network that connects these priceless selves is precious. Mainly, the relationships consist of interactions between two selves. The way two people treat each other can either honor the other person's intrinsic value or dishonor and damage it. The same is true for one's relationship to one's self and one's relationship to the higher power as well as to the universe. So if we apply the natural principle of love, we will relate in a healthy manner to our internal self, to another individual's self, to the God of love, and to God's world.

The relationships inherent in this psychospiritual paradigm are simple in concept but profound and complicated in operation. People in general have had a hard time comprehending this principle in relationships, to say nothing about enacting it well and wisely. The evening news is a descriptive summary of how humans wreak harm on one another by violating relationships. We see this in the politics of our work setting. We see the harried person passing us impatiently on the highway. We hear of the suicide bomber in Israel. Much of history is an accounting of how people have damaged each other in their respective relationships.

Life is sacred. Therefore, relationships are sacred. Any violation of these damages the dynamics of love. Borrowing loosely from the field of economics, our entire relationship network constitutes an intangible commodity that has infinite value, vast inventories, unlimited investment opportunities, and patchwork regulatory systems. It is the arena of ultimate value and opportunity. The measure of a person is determined by his or her conduct within each of these four relationships.

The Fact of Individual Responsibility

The human race consists of generation after generation of unique individual selves, each with inestimable value. As each one of these selves confronts his or her existence and searches for meaning in life, each individual must ultimately choose his or her own course of action. At the deepest level, our quality of life and meaning will depend on how we handle the four psychospiritual principles. As

Adam and Eve Driven Out of Paradise. Library of Congress.

members of the human race, we are accountable for how we relate to love as the highest principle in life, how we relate to ourselves, how we choose to relate to others, and how we relate to the universe. In each of these relationships, life has natural consequences, positive or negative. The consequences always belong to the person who is responsible for the particular behavior that led to the consequences.

For example, if I treat a stranger with courtesy, I feel an inner warmth and sense of satisfaction. If I say a hurtful word to my wife, I feel guilty and a nagging sense of not liking myself. The psycho-spiritual principle is in force even when we intentionally deny any responsibility for our behavior. This factor is critical to our understanding of shame.

The Condition of Natural Shame

None of us is perfect. Natural shame is the appropriate consequence of the human condition of being flawed. As flawed or incompletely evolved creatures, we are capable of choosing destructive attitudes and behaviors. Presumably, a perfect human being would have healthy behaviors driven by healthy motives and would never impose shame on another person. The Judeo-Christian tradition describes the origin of natural shame in the Genesis 3 story of Adam and Eve.

Living in perfect Eden, they were given the freedom of choice, and this led to the chain reaction of events that ended in their feelings of shame. Perfection was forfeited. Flawed human existence became endemic and universal. Even if the story were literally a historical report, it could not be more truly descriptive of the human condition. However, natural shame does not destroy a person's worth and create deep, worthless feelings. Natural shame is not toxic shame. The Judeo-Christian tradition does not teach that the self is worthless. The Bible insists that each self has inestimable value. Natural shame is a fact of life, a state of being, and a product of imperfection or incompleteness in our selves. Therefore, each human being is capable of good behavior as well as bad behavior. That is just the way it is.

The Consequence Is Moral Shame

Responsible behavior is living by the four psychospiritual principles. If we were perfect, we could make perfect choices and live flawlessly. However, natural shame is our normal condition, so we are destined to violate the natural laws as a matter of course, no matter hard we try. Moral shame is the legitimate consequence of irresponsible behavior. It is the uncomfortable feeling that "I don't like the way I feel when I use people to get what I want." Moral shame produces a warning signal of internal distress that reminds us of our flawed nature when we have made a bad decision. Moral shame does not bring a feeling of worthlessness. Some refer to moral shame as "healthy shame" (Bradshaw, 1988).

Complex human beings, with physical, emotional, social, psychological, and spiritual needs, are born into a complicated culture consisting of other like-minded people. The built-in goal is to thrive and develop within this cultural system where the psychospiritual principles are working silently in the background. This is a daunting task for the grown-ups in the system, but the newborns must start from primitive beginnings and discern rather quickly how to manage. The new humans must master this daunting enterprise with internal equipment that is permanently flawed. This means they are capable of making unhealthy and harmful choices and will inevitably do so in the experimentation necessary to discern how to manage. Since these neonates are free agents and use their flawed or limited reasoning to make personal choices, they will make decisions that violate the principle of love, the highest principle. They will violate their own relationship to themselves through choices that are shortsighted and counterproductive. They will take shortcuts that feel good but prove to be damaging. They will violate relationships with others, using them for their own purposes, saying and doing things that hurt. The principle of personal responsibility reigns as they receive the logical and natural consequences of their choices. The psychospiritual system is comprehensive and inviolable, but all the players are genetically flawed, so everyone in life is going to violate the structural forces part of the time or all of the time.

The Link between Responsibility and Moral Shame

The crucial point to understand about moral shame is that we who choose and perform irresponsible behavior own the consequences. Except in rare cases, we also experience the consequences, though sometimes they fall only on others, and we do not even notice. We still own that part of the total system of dynamics. It belongs to us. If we are responsible in handling our irresponsible behavior, we accept ownership and take the consequences we deserve. This may involve restitution, apology, embarrassment, loss of status, bad feelings, or the like. We accept the consequences and deal with them.

Authentic and appropriate moral shame is one of the consequences of irresponsible or dysfunctional behavior, and it belongs to the person who chooses the behavior. The person who chooses the harmful behavior owns the behavior by choosing it, and the fact of choosing the harmful behavior automatically links responsibility for the behavior to the person who chose it. It is the self-awareness of knowing that "I did it!" that empowers us to experience the legitimate moral shame and its painful affect. Responsibility and moral shame are irrevocably linked. This fact is a critical point for understanding imposed shame.

The Impossible Pragmatic Solution

So we have a flawed physical universe that includes disease, accidents, pollution, and death. We have millions of flawed people grouped in various geographic locations, playing out their agenda with genetically impaired decision making. All this is governed by a set of natural psychospiritual forces everyone is doomed to violate, and everyone is going to hurt and be hurt by others. It is inevitable.

How can this possibly work? With great difficulty at best. Outlining the way it works helps us understand what is really happening.

Let us return, briefly, to the principle of responsibility. We have behavioral options that can empower this entire flawed system to function with significantly less complication and difficulty. We can do the following:

1. Accept the fact that we are all flawed
2. Be aware of internal warning signals when we violate the system dynamics
3. Respond to these signals and others' reactions by acknowledging our dysfunctional behavior
4. Make appropriate amends for violating the system and each other

If we all assume responsibility for our actions, the system could remain relatively clear of endogenous reinfection. I could admit I was irresponsible toward you, and you could see how you had hurt me. I would not blame you for my bad decisions, and you would not blame me for your decision to violate the universal principles of relationship. I would have my moral shame in response to my choices, and you would have yours. The key to making this system work is the appropriate assigning and accepting of responsibility. This is the hinge upon which life works or fails.

There is a contemporary example of this approach being used to resolve a very flammable political situation. When South Africa transferred political power to Nelson Mandela and dissolved the long-standing apartheid governmental structure, Mandela and other officials faced a very difficult situation. During apartheid, the white government had sanctioned the killing and brutalizing of many black people. What should the new government do with the known governmental perpetrators? How could the new government help the victims heal? How could they restore trust in the government?

Mandela refused to grant blanket amnesty. What he did propose was a novel approach. To receive amnesty, the perpetrators had to appear before the South African Truth and Restoration Commission (TRC) and admit the details of their violence and killings. They were not required to apologize, only to say what they had done. The victims also appeared before the TRC (1995) and told their stories. Although the results have not met everyone's expectations, it has been a proactive approach to a volatile situation. It has helped avoid additional conflict and violence by asking individuals to take responsibility for their actions.

Former South African President Nelson Mandela speaks in Johannesburg February 2003. AP/Wide World Photos.

Imposed Shame

Imposed shame is legitimate shame that has been misplaced. It often happens as follows. We decide, consciously or unconsciously, to violate the psychospiritual system. We declare by our behavior that the rules do not apply to us, that we are not flawed and do not make mistakes. If our behavior seems wrong to someone else, it is obviously some else's fault. We are not responsible. We will do as we wish when we wish. We can trust our own judgment and desires.

Just as gravity is unaffected by our opinions about it, so are the psychospiritual forces in the universe. Despite our behavioral protestations to the contrary, we continue to live under these natural laws. We are flawed persons who are predisposed to choose irresponsible behavior that harms the fabric in all four relational spheres. As we do so, we generate moral shame as a logical consequence of our choices. So far, the principles are operating normally. Our next step should be that of recognizing the moral shame warnings and accepting responsibility for the irresponsible behavior that has damaged the relational fabric.

When this does not happen, we reject the responsibility that rightfully belongs to us and shift it to the person we have hurt. We insists either implicitly or directly, "You made me do it!" Classic examples are the husband who tells his wife, "If you didn't burn the eggs, I wouldn't have to hit you," and the wife who assaults her husband with, "If you had returned home on time every day, I would not have had the affair with the house painter."

We easily make the injured party the one to blame. To say that this is confusing is an understatement. It is predictable if the perpetrator or the perpetrator and the victim have grown up with this style of relating. Reality is shattered as the thought flashes through the victim's mind, "Maybe that is true!" At times there is a fragment of logic that says, "Yes, I guess if I had not. . . . Maybe I am at fault." Responsibility has been shifted. The perpetrator is now further empowered in his or her narcissism. The normal and appropriate moral shame, which is an integral component of the transaction, has been translated into imposed shame and placed on the victim (Mellody, 1989).

The perpetrators assume the "better than" position to avoid feeling their own moral shame and to reject personal responsibility for irresponsible behavior. From their superior position, their behavioral statement is, "I am better than you. You are worth less than I am. I am giving you the responsibility for this situation. I can treat you anyway I want. You are worthless."

When our personal responsibility with its attendant moral shame is passed to our victim, the victims experiences our moral shame as their own, and it enters the victims as worthless feelings. They feel worthless because they feel responsible for causing this hurtful situation but see no way that they could have avoided it since they had no control over the dynamics. They have been persuaded that it is their fault, and even though they are unsure of how it is their fault, it definitely feels to them like it is their fault. They feel like worthless persons for causing all this. If they were as they should be, this would not have happened. The one who gets the blame, gets the shame. Locate where the perpetrator has placed the responsibility for his behavior, and you will discover the perpetrator's moral shame, now translated into toxic imposed shame residing in the victim's soul.

Why would people assume this stance and become perpetrators of imposing shame on others? Typically, their parents or other perpetrators imposed his or her shame on them. They are also carrying imposed shame from someone else, and it feels intolerably toxic to them when added to their own legitimate natural and moral shame. In order to not feel so toxic and worthless, they deny personal responsibility for what they do and refuse to accept their natural and moral shame. They already feel overwhelmed with all the imposed shame others have imposed upon them in the past and have no psychic energy left to carry normal moral shame; thus, they develop a defensive process to ward off their normal and natural shame by imposing it upon their victims.

Some call imposed shame by other terms, such as "carried shame," "borrowed shame," or "toxic shame." The victim is feeling responsible for the other person's behavior and is carrying or borrowing the perpetrator's moral shame. The perpetrator has imposed his responsibility and shame upon his or her victim. Many victims become perpetrators, and the process continues from generation to generation. This is strongly evident recently in the pedophilia scandal among Roman Catholic priests who are, themselves, victims of molestation as younger persons. Of course, not all violence and human abuse of humans are shame induced. Brain injuries, organic diseases, chemical imbalances, and substance abuse also spark dysfunctional and sometimes violent behavior. As brain research advances in the coming years, I believe we are going to learn that brain dysfunction contributes to more dysfunctional behavior than we have accounted for in the past. However, whatever the source of the destructive energy, the shame dynamics we have here described nonetheless prevail in the psychosocial and psychospiritual system.

The Shame Connection: Imposed Shame and the Perpetrator

As discussed previously, people who are able to accept the reality of the natural psychospiritual principles that reign in life and who

accept their human condition will make amends for the rips and ruptures they make in the fabric of their relationship. Sure, damage is
done, but when the individual acknowledges responsibility, healing
can take place for the perpetrator and the victim. In addition, the biblical concept of grace, God's unconditional forgiveness and acceptance, reckons the person perfect despite being a flawed work in
progress. The biblical message indicates that from the divine perspective, spending our psychic energy on guilt, fear, or shame is an
enormous and unacceptable waste. Divine grace is unconditional forgiveness and acceptance intended specifically to stop that waste and
empower us to invest our psychic energy instead in growth within
the dynamics of the psychospiritual system of life (Ellens, 1982). The
spirit of God will work in those people who focus on working out the
complications of living life as a flawed person within the dynamics of
the existing system.

However, it requires considerable maturity to take a stand and
declare, "Yes, I did hurt you. I was irresponsible!" If we have grown
up in an abusive system of relationships, we are already loaded with
imposed shame from other perpetrators. Because the affect that
accompanies worthlessness is so utterly painful, we easily decide we
will not be hurt that badly again. Usually it is the strong-willed person who makes this decision because his natural tendency is to take
action against his environment anyway. Narcissists, whose pathology
is an inherited condition, are particularly at risk to become perpetrators of imposed shame on others.

Thus, to avoid the painful affect, we deny that we possess a flawed
nature that can harm the relationship fabrics in our lives, push grace
aside, and start down the path of violence in its many forms. This
implies that we believe we are better than others and can treat them
as suits our needs, with little sense of responsibility or empathy. We
essentially elevate our personal self-interest above others' feelings
and do what is comfortable or convenient to us regardless of its effect
on others. If we can bolster this position with some sacred scripture
or a higher principle, our forward momentum into evil behavior
accelerates. This evil behavior or violation of others can take many
forms, as we all know from the excessively real tragedies of history.
Usually, the form of the reaction is determined by the individual personality style, pathology levels, and characterological structure
(Bradshaw, 1988; Horney, 1945; Middleton-Moz, 1990).

This defensive-aggressive behavior places the perpetrator's
responsibility and moral shame on the victim who receives them in

the form of imposed shame. Thus, the loop is complete. The perpe-trator and his victim are linked through the shared dynamic of imposed shame. This link can often become an addictive constellation of destruction.

Imposed Shame and the Victim

This shame connection is subtle, and many abused people do not see it or understand it. They believe the worthlessness they feel is their true identity. When they look inside themselves, all they see is the toxic shame and all the blame they have collected through the years. Even though they may cognitively believe they have value, their unconscious or subconscious sense of the truth does not believe it. This worthlessness can become the primary force that decides how they think about themselves and life itself.

To provide perspective as well as hope for the survivors who is feel-ing worthless, I frequently describe, in clinical interventions, the three types of shame, emphasizing the imposed shame dynamic. Then I draw a circle on the easel and write in it, "Real Self, True Self, Image of God." Then I explain that this represents the original self that was made in God's image. This is the self with opinions, preferences, goals, feelings, and the like. I explain how the moral shame of the per-petrator is imposed shame for the victim-survivor. I then take a paper patch and attach it over the circle representing the original self. This represents the perpetrator's moral shame imposed on the survivor. It is a layer of shame, and it covers the real self. Every time people are abusive or hurt others and do not take responsibility for it and repair it, they put another layer of imposed shame on the survivor. More patches illustrate this. The pile of patches grows, and it becomes apparent how difficult it becomes to discern the real self, hidden under these layers of other people's shame. I point out that this is the shame that makes us feel worthless. The good news is that it does not belong to us, the survivors! We can give it back to the person who owns it. I illustrate this by removing the patches one at a time, sym-bolically giving one to dad, one to mom, two to the neighbor kid, three to the hellfire preacher, and the like, until the original circle representing the true inner self is exposed. Our true self that has value was buried beneath this toxic shame that felt like it belonged to us, but it did not!

Witnessing this exercise does not, by itself, release the survivors from their toxic imposed shame, but it does provide a perspective that there is a valuable inner self waiting to be discovered and that the debilitating worthless feelings belong to someone else. The healing has begun.

The Summation

Solving this human dilemma has engaged theologians for centuries and psychologists for the past century and a half. Even a cursory review of history reveals the enormity of the problem and the inevitable fact that human nature has a proclivity to consistently run afoul of the principle dynamics of life. Healing can occur on an individual level, but changing the broader social order appears impossible to achieve. So what can we do? The short answer is assigning responsibility where it belongs and holding each other accountable. This can begin to unload the toxicity of the imposed shame by means of simple reality orientation. In addition, it is imperative that we recognize that the dynamics which a true expression and acceptance of grace affords humans is the one indispensable factor in making the healing of the system work. Unconditional grace, both divinely and humanly mediated to us, is the sine qua non for turning the downward spiral of human destructiveness upward into a spiral of renewal and healing. The force of this grace alone has the inherent ingredients to support and redeem life as flawed humans work out their issues within the principles of psychospiritual dynamics (Allison, 1972; Ellens, 1982).

Ironically, the worthless feelings, or the imposed shame, drive the various methods that the perpetrating persons can choose to protect themselves against further hurt. In carrying out this self-protection, they create more imposed shame for the next person or the next generation, who in turn must struggle with its own worthlessness and destructive defensiveness. Untreated, imposed shame eats silently away at the souls of the perpetrators and their victims, creating infections of conflict and erosion of healthy personality dynamics throughout the society, the long-term consequences of which are recorded in the enormous wreckage of history (McWilliams, 1994; van der Kolk, McFarlane, & Weismaeth, 1996).

References

Allison, C. F. (1972). *Guilt, anger, and God: The patterns of our discontents*. New York: Seabury.

Bradshaw, J. (1988). *Healing the shame that binds you.* Deerfield Beach: Health Communications.

Broucek, F. J. (1991). *Shame and the self.* New York: Guilford Press.

Capps, D. & Dittes, J. E. (Eds.). (1990). *The hunger of the heart: Reflections on the Confessions of Augustine.* West Lafayette: Society for the Scientific Study of Religion, Monograph Series No. 8.

Ellens, J. H. (1982). *God's grace and human health.* Nashville: Abingdon Press.

Fossum, M. A. & Mason, M. J. (1986). *Facing shame: Families in recovery.* New York: W. W. Norton.

Green, D. & Lawrenz, M. (1994). *Why do I feel like hiding? How to overcome shame and guilt.* Grand Rapids: Baker Books.

Harper, J. M. & Hoopes, M. H. (1990). *Uncovering shame.* New York: W. W. Norton.

Horney, K. (1945). *Our inner conflicts.* New York: W. W. Norton.

Kaufman, G. (1985). *Shame: The power of caring.* Cambridge: Schenkman Books.

Masterson, J. F. (1988). *The search for the real self.* New York: Free Press.

McWilliams, N. (1994). *Psychoanalytic diagnosis.* New York: Guilford Press.

Mellody, P. (1989). *Shame: A gift from God; the legacy of abuse.* San Diego: Encore Cassettes.

Middleton-Moz, J. (1990). *Shame and guilt: Masters of disguise.* Deerfield Beach: Health Communications.

Shengold, L. (1989). *Soul murder: The effects of childhood abuse and deprivation.* New York: Fawcett.

Sloat, D. E. (1990). *Growing up holy and wholly.* Brentwood: Wolgemuth & Hyatt.

South African Truth and Reconciliation Commission. (1995). "Promotion of National Unity and Reconciliation Act, No. 34 of 1995." (http://www.doj. gov.za/trc).

van der Kolk, B. A., McFarlane, A. C., & Weismaeth, L. (Eds.). (1996). *Traumatic stress.* New York: Guilford Press.

CHAPTER 9

HELL, MARTYRDOM, AND WAR: VIOLENCE IN EARLY CHRISTIANITY

Grant R. Shafer

The history of Christianity presents us with a paradox. Jesus of Nazareth is best known as a preacher of nonviolence. Yet Christians, in persecutions of other religions, in wars about religion, and in wars of conquest, have perhaps been more violent than members of any other religion except Islam, the other product of ancient Israelite religion. This chapter explores the roots of Christian violence in the period when Christians were the least violent, when they were an outlawed minority in the Roman Empire, and when Christians first practiced large-scale violence, immediately after they conquered that empire. This treatment briefly discusses three topics as understood by early Christians: hell, martyrdom, and war. It argues that although the Christians were not overtly violent, their understanding of these things betrays a love as well as a fear of violence, a desire for revenge, and ambivalence about socially sanctioned violence. This is not to say that early Christians were extraordinarily violent, but their unique social and historical setting produced a great frustrated anger that was put into action not so much by themselves as by their spiritual descendants, who persecuted enemies within and attempted to conquer enemies outside their societies.

Exposition

Hell

The Christian concept of hell has its roots in Jewish eschatology, which, in turn, seems to have emerged in contact with

Zoroastrianism. Zoroastrianism, which became the religion of Persia, taught that all time is divided into four 3,000-year periods in which Ahura Mazda, the good creator of the universe, and Angra Mainyu, the creator of demons and creatures of darkness, alternately coexist and fight over the universe. At the end of the last trimillennium, Ahura Mazda will defeat Angra Mainyu, and the dead will be raised and judged.[1] After three days in heaven or a vividly described hell, all the dead will share blissful eternity with Ahura Mazda, and Angra Mainyu and his demons will be annihilated. So, in Zoroastrianism, hell, although sadistic, is not eternal.[2]

In reading a few of the later passages of the Hebrew Bible, life after death comes to mind. The destruction of the kingdom of Israel and the exile of the kingdom of Judah undermined the idea that the righteous would be rewarded in this life, and the experience of martyrdom in the struggle against Antiochus IV Epiphanes made the hope of a reward after death essential to many Jews. The book of Isaiah can be divided into two parts: chapters 1 to 39 can be assigned to Isaiah, who prophesied between 742 and 687 B.C.E., and chapters 40 to 66 belong to the time of the Persian Empire. Thus, it is perhaps significant that in 25:8, in the midst of an eschatological section, Isaiah says, "[God] will swallow up death forever." This is reminiscent of Canaanite mythology, and it is difficult to interpret other than as a belief in immortality. Ezekiel was a priest whose prophecies were given between 593 and 563 B.C.E., thus just before, and for a generation after, the destruction of Jerusalem by the Babylonians. Ezekiel says (37:1) that God brought him to a valley full of dry bones. God directed him to command the bones to be restored to life, and so it happened (vv. 4–10). God said that the bones were "the whole house of Israel" (v. 11). God said to Israel that he would "open your graves, and raise you from your graves" (vv. 12–13). Finally, God says "I will place you in your own land" (v. 14). Despite the vivid language of restoration to life, this seems to be a metaphor for the restoration of the nation rather than a teaching about the resurrection of individuals.

During the Jewish exile in the sixth century, the folktale of Job, who loses his wealth, family, and health but is afterward rewarded for his virtue, became the setting for a discussion about the justice of God. Job says, "For I know that my Redeemer lives, and at last he will stand upon the earth; and after my skin has been thus destroyed, then from my flesh I shall see God, whom I shall see on my side, and my eyes shall behold, and not another" (Job 19:25–26). Although on the face of it this seems to express a hope of life after death, the text of verse 26 is corrupt, and many doubt that an afterlife is here affirmed. During the war with Antiochus Epiphanes (ruled 175–164 B.C.E.), stories of the Jewish exile in Babylon were written under the name of Daniel, who is commended in Ezekiel 14:14 and 28:3. In chapter 11, Daniel predicts the fall of the Persian Empire to Alexander the Great, the division of his empire among his generals, the wars among them and their heirs, and particularly the acts of Antiochus Epiphanes, followed by future predictions that were not fulfilled. Chapter 12 speaks of the end of the world; verse 2 says, "[M]any of those who sleep in the dust of the earth shall awake, some to everlasting life, and some to shame and everlasting contempt." Here we have a definite reference to life after death, but overwhelmingly the Hebrew Bible is concerned with this life.

The eternity of punishment in hell is also suggested in Daniel 12:2, which says that "some [shall awake] to shame and everlasting contempt." 4 Maccabees 9:9, 10:11, 15, and 12:12 also threaten Antiochus with eternal tortures. This concept is found in Greek mythology, where the punishment of Ixion, Sisyphus, and Tantalus in Tartarus is eternal. Tartarus is mentioned in the Septuagint of Job 40:15 (40:20 RSV), where Behemoth plays with beasts in Tartarus; of Job 41:23 (41:32 RSV), where Leviathan considers Tartarus of the abyss a prisoner and the abyss as a stroll; and of Proverbs 24:51 (30:16 RSV) in a list of things that do not say "Enough." Thus, in the Septuagint, Tartarus seems only to mean a deep place of the underworld. In a variant reading[3] of 1 Enoch 20:2, the archangel Uriel rules Tartarus. In 2 Peter 2:4, the verb *tartaroo* is used to describe how sinful angels were thrown into hell. This usage shows the influence of Greek mythology on early Christian eschatology.

For the New Testament, the life after death of Jesus is axiomatic. The oldest surviving Christian writing is Paul's first letter to the Thessalonians. In 4:14–17, Paul says that Jesus rose from the dead, the Christian dead will rise, and the Christians who have not died will join Jesus and the resurrected Christians. In 1 Corinthians 15:5–8, Paul gives a list of those to whom the risen Jesus appeared. The gospels add the detail that Jesus' tomb was found empty.

Resurrection is a mixed blessing. Daniel 12:2 says that some dead will awake to everlasting life, some to everlasting contempt. Christian resurrection was likewise of two kinds. Paul says, "[I]n Christ shall all be made alive," (1 Cor. 15:22), but along with the "saved," he speaks of the "perishing." (1 Cor. 1:18; 2 Cor. 2:15, 4:3) Elsewhere in the New Testament, the fate of the "perishing" is given in more detail.

Matthew 25:31–46 is an account of the last judgment with the inspiring detail that what is done to the "least" of Jesus' brethren is done to him (v. 40). However, there is nothing inspiring in store for those who have not helped the "least"; their fate is "the eternal fire prepared for the devil and his angels" (v. 41) and "eternal punishment" (v. 46). In Mark 9:48, Jesus describes *gehenna* as "where their worm does not die, and the fire is not quenched." This is a reference to Isaiah 66:24, where it is the fate of the corpses of rebels against God to endure an eternal torment. In the parable of the rich man and Lazarus, the rich man goes to "Hades" and calls out, "Father Abraham, have mercy upon me, and send Lazarus to dip the end of his finger in water and cool my tongue; for I am in anguish in this flame" (Luke 16:24). Abraham refuses. Jesus says that the lost will weep and grind their teeth (Matt. 8:12, 13:42, 50, 22:13, 24:51, 25:30; Luke 13:28). Twice (Matt. 13:42, 50) this takes place in a furnace, three times (Matt. 8:12, 22:13, 25:30) in "outer darkness." James 5:3 says to the rich, "Your gold and silver have rusted, and their rust will be evidence against you and will eat your flesh like fire." Revelation 19:20, 20:10, 14, 15, 21:8 speak of a lake of fire and sulphur into which any one whose name is not in the book of life and various other sinners will be thrown; 14:9–11 says, "If any one worships the beast and its image, and receives a mark [of the beast] on his forehead or on his hand, . . . he shall be tormented with fire and sulphur in the presence of the holy angels and in the presence of the Lamb. And the smoke of their torment goes up for ever and ever; and they have no rest, day or night." The devil, the beast (Antichrist), and the false prophet will also be tormented forever in the lake of fire (Rev. 20:10), and the same goes presumably for the rest of the damned, who also go into the lake of fire (Rev. 20:15, 21:8). The eternity of this punishment is also stated in Matthew 18:8: "it is better for you to enter life maimed or lame than with two hands or two feet to be thrown into the eternal fire," 25:41 ("eternal fire"), 46 ("eternal punishment"), and in Jude 7: "Sodom and Gomorrah and the surrounding cities, . . . serve as an example by undergoing the punishment of eternal fire"; 13: "the nether gloom of darkness has been reserved for ever" for false Christians; and suggested in Mark 3:29: "but whoever blasphemes against the Holy Spirit never has forgiveness, but is guilty of an eternal sin"; 9:48: "their worm does not die, and the fire is not quenched"; 2 Thessalonians 1:9: "They shall suffer the punishment of eternal destruction"; Hebrews 6:2: "eternal judgment" is part of "elementary doctrine"; and Jude 6: sinful angels "in eternal chains."

Martyrdom

The belief in life after death in Judaism arose in the experience of martyrdom. The Jewish tradition of martyrdom can be thought to begin with the war against Antiochus Epiphanes. Antiochus, who ruled Palestine as one of the successors of Alexander the Great, replaced the Jewish high priest, Jason, with Menelaus. When it was rumored that Antiochus was dead, Jason attacked Jerusalem. Antiochus mistook this for a revolt and took Jerusalem, killing many and looting the Temple. He then decided to replace Judaism with Greek religion. A war between Antiochus and Jewish traditionalists erupted.

Biblical Perspectives on Martyrdom

The book of Daniel, written in this period, has two stories relevant to martyrdom. In Daniel 3, Nebuchadnezzar, king of Babylon, sets up a huge golden image and commands everyone to fall down and worship it on pain of being thrown into a burning furnace. Three Jewish governors of Babylon, Hananiah, Azariah, and Mishael (also known as Shadrach, Meshach, and Abednego), refused to worship the image and were thrown into the furnace. They emerged unharmed, although their executioners were killed by the heat, and the three were promoted by Nebuchadnezzar.

In Daniel 5:30–31, Darius the Mede overthrew the Babylonians. Darius made Daniel one of three presidents over the entire Persian Empire and planned to "set him over the whole kingdom" (Dan. 6:1–3). Daniel's colleagues and subordinates were jealous and, knowing that Daniel prayed to God, persuaded Darius to decree that anyone who petitioned anyone but Darius for 30 days would be thrown to the lions (vv. 4–9). Daniel was caught praying to God, and after trying to save Daniel, Darius regretfully threw Daniel to the lions (vv. 10–18). After a night with the lions, Daniel was unharmed, and Darius threw Daniel's accusers and their wives and children to the lions (vv. 19–28). The detail that the children were thrown to the lions and that the lions broke all their victims' bones before they reached the bottom of the den and the death of the executioners of Hananiah, Azariah, and Mishael shows the sadism and vengefulness sometimes associated with martyrology.

2 Maccabees, written in the first century B.C.E., also tells of the war against Antiochus. Mothers who circumcised their sons were killed with them, Sabbath observers were burned, and the writer explains

A scene of martyrdom from Maccabees, book 2. The Art Archive/Bibliothèque Municipale Valenciennes/Dagli Orti.

that these events were manifestations of God's mercy since God punished Israel before its sins became as bad as those of the Gentiles (2 Macc. 6:10–17). 2 Maccabees 6:18–31 tells of the martyrdom of the prominent scribe Eleazar. He was forced to eat pork but spit it out. The sacrificers urged him to bring kosher meat and pretend it was pork. He refused because he feared misleading the young. He also said that he feared the punishment of God (vv. 26, 30).

2 Maccabees 7 tells the story of a mother and her seven sons who refused to eat pork. One by one they were dismembered and fried but refused to eat. They professed a belief in resurrection (vv. 9, 11, 14, 23, 29, 36), which would not be granted to Antiochus and his follow-

ers (v. 14), who would be punished by God (vv. 17, 19, 31, 35, 36). The martyrs also maintained that God was punishing them (vv. 18, 32) and their nation (v. 38). The last of the brothers prayed God "by afflictions and plagues" to make Antiochus acknowledge God (v. 37), which was fulfilled in 9:5–28, where Antiochus was struck with worms and rotting flesh and honored the Jews and their God. What is interesting here is the violence of the martyrs' God. Eleazar's fear of God's punishment moves him to submit to torture. Both the atrocities of Antiochus—including the torture of the seven brothers and their mother by Antiochus, which were a sign of the mercy of God since they would have been worse had God let the Jews continue to sin—and the illness of Antiochus are punishments from God.

3 Maccabees, written in the first century B.C.E., is similar to Daniel in that Jews are marked for death but are miraculously saved. After a victory over Antiochus III, Ptolemy IV Philopator (221–203 B.C.E.) visited Jerusalem but was miraculously prevented from entering the Holy of Holies (1:1–2:24). Angered by this, Ptolemy tried to force the Jews in Egypt to worship Dionysus (2:25–30). When the majority of the Jews refused, Ptolemy gathered them in the hippodrome and prepared elephants to trample them (2:32–5:4). It is noteworthy that the persecuted Jews prayed God to foil "with vengeance" (5:8) the attack upon them. Consequently, when the time for the elephant stampede came, God caused Ptolemy to oversleep (5:11–12). The next day, which Ptolemy had next planned for the trampling of the Jews, Ptolemy forgot what he had planned (5:27–33). Likewise, on the third occasion for the Jews' destruction, the priest Eleazar prayed for deliverance, recounting how God had "destroyed" Pharaoh, "broke in pieces" Sennacherib, and diverted the fire from Shadrach, Meshach, and Abednego "against all their enemies," and the Jews were saved by two angels and the repentance of Ptolemy, and the elephants attacked Ptolemy's soldiers (6:1–7:9). Upon their deliverance, the Jews successfully requested permission to punish those Jews who had obeyed Ptolemy's order to worship Dionysus (7:10–15). Here we see in the prayers for deliverance and attacks on Ptolemy's soldiers and apostate Jews the element of vengeance in Israelite religious traditions.

4 Maccabees is an argument on the preeminence of reason, written between 20 and 54 C.E., using the martyrdom of Eleazar and the seven brothers. 1.11 says, "[T]hey became the cause of the downfall of tyranny over their nation." 7:4 compares Eleazar to a city that holds out against siege and his reason to a shield. In 6:29, Eleazar says, "[T]ake my life in exchange [*antipsukhos;* cf. 17:21, Ignatius of

Antioch] for theirs [the Jews']." In 6:23, 9:1 (cf. 2 Macc. 7:30), the martyrs ask their tormentors, "Why do you delay?" 9:9 threatens "eternal torment by fire" to Antiochus.

The first of the brothers said to the others, "Do not leave your post in my struggle.... Fight the sacred and noble battle for religion. Thereby the just Providence of our ancestors may become merciful to our nation and take vengeance on the accursed tyrant" (9.24). The second brother said, "How sweet is any kind of death for the religion of our fathers! Do you not think, you most savage tyrant, that you are being tortured more than I, as you see the arrogant design of your tyranny being defeated by our endurance for the sake of religion? I lighten my pain by the joys that come from virtue, but you suffer torture by the threats that come from impiety. You will not escape, most abominable tyrant, the judgments of the divine wrath" (9: 29–32). The third brother said to Antiochus, "[Y]ou . . . will undergo unceasing torments" (10:11). The fourth brother swore by "the eternal destruction of the tyrant" (10:15). He told Antiochus to "[c]ontrive tortures" (10:16). The fifth brother said, "I have come of my own accord, so that by murdering me you will incur punishment from the heavenly justice" (11.3). He calls Antiochus "hater of mankind" (11.4), throwing back the standard accusation against the Jews.[4] He says, "Tyrant, they are splendid favors that you grant us against your will, because through these noble sufferings you give us an opportunity to show our endurance for the law" (11:12). The sixth brother said, "So if you intend to torture me for not eating defiling foods, go on torturing!" (11:16), "and I myself will bring a great avenger upon you" (11:23), and "Your fire is cold to us [cf. *Martyrdom of Polycarp* 2.3], and the catapults painless, and your violence powerless. For it is not the guards of the tyrant but those of the divine law that are set over us" (11:26–27); 12:1 says he "died a blessed death." The seventh brother said to Antiochus, "[J]ustice has laid up for you intense and eternal fire and tortures, and these throughout all time will never let you go.... Surely [my brothers] by dying nobly fulfilled their service to God, but you will wail bitterly for having slain without cause the contestants for virtue . . . on you [God] will take vengeance both in this present life and when you are dead" (12:12, 14, 18). The text continues, "After he had uttered these imprecations, he flung himself into the braziers and so ended his life" (12:19).

Chapter 13:12 says, "Remember whence you came, and the father by whose hand Isaac would have submitted to being slain for the sake of religion"; 13:13–16 is instructive: "[L]et us use our bodies as a bulwark for the law. Let us not fear him who thinks he is killing us [cf. Matt. 10:28; Luke 12:4–5], for great is the struggle of the soul and the danger of eternal punishment lying before those who transgress the commandment of God. Therefore let us put on the full armor of self-control" (cf. Eph. 6:11–17); 14:20 says, "But sympathy for her children did not sway the mother of the young men; she was of the same mind as Abraham"; 15:27–28 says, "She did not approve the deliverance which would preserve the seven sons for a short time, but as the daughter of God-fearing Abraham she remembered his fortitude." Chapter 17:6 says to the mother, "For your sons were true descendants of father Abraham"; 15:8 says, "[Y]et because of the fear of God she disdained the temporary safety of her children"; 16:14 calls her "soldier of God in the cause of religion." She told her sons, "Fight zealously for our ancestral law" (16:16), and, "For [God's] sake also our father Abraham was zealous to sacrifice his son Isaac, the ancestor of our nation; and when Isaac saw his father's hand wielding a sword and descending upon him, he did not cower. Daniel the righteous was thrown to the lions, and Hananiah, Azariah, and Mishael were hurled into the fiery furnace and endured it for the sake of God" (16:20–21); 16:25 says, "They knew also that those who die for the sake of God live in God," and 17:1 says, "Some of the guards said that when she also was about to be put to death she threw herself into the flames so that no one might touch her body."

We read in chapter 17:20–22 that "because of them our enemies did not rule over our nation, the tyrant was punished, and the homeland purified—they having become, as it were, a ransom [antipsukhos] for the sin of our nation. And through the blood of those devout ones and their death as an expiation, divine Providence preserved Israel that previously had been afflicted." Chapter 17:23–24 says, "For the tyrant Antiochus, when he saw the courage of their virtue and their endurance under the tortures, proclaimed them to his soldiers as an example for their own endurance, and this made them brave and courageous for infantry battle and siege, and he ravaged and conquered all his enemies"; 18:4–5: "Because of them the nation gained peace, and by reviving observance of the law in the homeland they ravaged the enemy. The tyrant Antiochus was both punished on earth and is being chastised after his death. Since in no way whatever was he able to compel the Israelites to become pagans and to abandon their ancestral customs, he left Jerusalem and marched against the Persians"; 18:22: "For these crimes divine justice pursued and will pursue the accursed tyrant."

Another aspect of 4 Maccabees is the description of the torture of the martyrs. "[Eleazar's] flesh was being torn by scourges, his blood flowing, and his sides were being cut to pieces" (6:6). The guards "poured stinking liquids into his nostrils" (6:25); Eleazar "was now burned to his very bones and about to expire" (6:26). "The wheel was completely smeared with blood [of the first brother], and the heap of coals [burning him] was being quenched by drippings of gore, and pieces of flesh were falling off the axles of the machine" (9:20). "These leopard-like beasts tore out [the second brother's] sinews with the iron hands, flayed all his flesh up to his chin, and tore away his scalp" (11:28). "Enraged by [the third brother's] boldness, they disjointed his hands and feet with their instruments, dismembering him by prying his limbs from their sockets, and breaking his fingers and arms and legs and elbows. Since they were not able in any way to break his spirit, they abandoned their instruments and scalped him with their fingernails in Scythian fashion. They immediately brought him to the wheel, and while his vertebrae were being dislocated upon it he saw his own flesh torn all around and drops of blood flowing from his entrails" (10:5–8). "[The mother of the seven] watched the flesh of her children consumed by fire, their toes and fingers scattered on the ground, and the flesh of the head to the chin exposed like masks" (15:15); "[she] saw the flesh of children burned upon the flesh of other children, severed hands upon hands, scalped heads upon heads, and corpses fallen on other corpses. . . . Neither the melodies of sirens nor the songs of swans attracted the attention of the hearers as did the voices of the children in torture calling to their mother" (15:20–21); 18:21 says that Antiochus "pierced the pupils of their eyes and cut out their tongues." 4 Maccabees shows us the Jewish reaction to all this in military images, the martyrs' desire for death, their desire for vengeance, eternal punishment of the persecutor, the martyrs' fear of God's punishment, and a sadomasochistic relish for torture.

Lactantius' *Persecutors* 21 likewise recounts, "[Galerius] began this mode of execution by edicts against the Christians, commanding that, after torture and condemnation, they should be burnt at a slow fire. They were fixed to a stake, and first a moderate flame was applied to the soles of their feet, until the muscles, contracted by burning, were torn from the bones; then torches, lighted and put out again, were directed to all the members of their bodies, so that no part had any exemption. Meanwhile cold water was continually poured on their faces, and their mouths moistened, lest, by reason of their jaws being parched, they should expire. At length they did expire, when, after many hours, the violent heat had consumed their skin and penetrated into their intestines."[5] This detailed description of torture also suggests sadomasochism.

The martyrology of the New Testament has both similarities and differences relative to what we have seen of the Old Testament. Jack Miles comments on the martyrdom of the seven brothers in 2 Maccabees 7 and Jesus' ethic of nonresistance: "In the Books of Maccabees, moral resistance does not preclude military resistance but only pursues it by other means, like propaganda or "psy-op" (psychological operations) in modern warfare. In the Gospels, moral resistance entirely replaces military resistance."[6] John the Baptist can be considered a martyr, but his story does not exhibit the elements of other martyrologies. Jesus is the supreme martyr in the New Testament and Christianity. Jesus differs in two ways from the seven brothers in 2 Maccabees 7. One is that Jesus seemed reluctant to die. This detail is plausible for two reasons. One is that the church is unlikely to have invented it since it casts doubt on Jesus' divinity. The other is that it is attested by the synoptic gospels (Matt. 26:37–44; Mark 14:33–39; Luke 22:41–44), John 12:27 (though this seems to be misplaced from Maundy Thursday to Palm Sunday), and Hebrews 5:7. The second difference between Jesus and the seven brothers is the tradition that Jesus forgave his executioners (Luke 23:34), although this detail is missing from most of the best manuscripts. A similarity between Jesus and the seven brothers is that their deaths were planned by God, that is, God was punishing the brothers (2 Macc. 7:18, 32), and Peter says that Jesus was "delivered up according to the definite plan and foreknowledge of God" (Acts 2:23). Paul says, "[God] did not spare his own Son" (Rom. 8:32). 1 Corinthians 5:7 says, "For Christ, our paschal lamb, has been sacrificed." Jesus foretells his own death (Matt. 16:21, 17:22, 20:18–19; Mark 8:31, 9:31, 10:33–34; Luke 9:22, 44, 18:32–33). This shows that Jesus' death was desired by God. Jesus said, "The Son of man goes as it is written of him, but woe to that man by whom the Son of man is betrayed! It would have been better for that man if he had not been born" (Matt. 26:24; Mark 14:21; cf. Luke 22:22). This prophecy is partly fulfilled in Matthew 27:5, where Judas hangs himself, and in Acts 1:17, Judas "bought a field with the reward of his wickedness; and falling headlong he burst open in the middle and his bowels gushed out." This illustrates the martyrological element of vengeance.

A saying of Jesus applicable to martyrdom is found in Matthew 10:28 and Luke 12:4–5: "And do not fear those who kill the body but cannot kill the soul; rather fear him who can destroy both soul and body in hell." This is comparable to 4 Maccabees 13:14–15: "Let us not fear him who thinks he is killing us, for great is the struggle of the soul and the danger of eternal punishment lying before those who transgress the commandment of God," thus illustrating the martyr's fear of God's punishment.

In the "little apocalypse," Jesus predicts that his followers will be persecuted: "[F]or they will deliver you up to councils; and you will be beaten in synagogues; and you will stand before governors and kings for my sake, to bear testimony [*marturion*] before them. . . . And brother will deliver up brother to death, and the father his child, and children will rise against parents and have them put to death" (Mark 13:9, 12; cf. Matt. 10:17–22, 24:9–14; Luke 21:12–19). In Matthew 10:38–39 (cf. 16:24–25; Mark 8:34–35; Luke 9:23–24, 14:27, 17:33; John 12:25), Jesus says, "[A]nd he who does not take his cross and follow me is not worthy of me. He who finds his life will lose it, and he who loses his life for my sake will find it."

Another reference to martyrdom is found in Matthew 20:20–23 and Mark 10:35–39. James and John, the sons of Zebedee, or their mother, ask Jesus to sit at his right and left hand in his glory. Jesus asks whether they can drink from his cup or be baptized with his baptism. They affirm that they can. Jesus says that they will drink from his cup and be baptized with his baptism, which suggests that James and John were to be martyred. Indeed, Acts 12:2 reports that James was executed by Herod Agrippa. John the son of Zebedee was traditionally identified with the Beloved Disciple of the Gospel of John, and the Beloved Disciple was expected to survive until the return of Jesus (John 21:20–23), but the identification is doubtful, so John the son of Zebedee may have been executed. Matthew 20:20–23 and Mark 10:35–39, with the prophecy of the death of the sons of Zebedee, suggest that, like the deaths of the seven brothers and that of Jesus, the death of the sons of Zebedee was planned by God.

John 13:36–37: "Simon Peter said to him, 'Lord, where are you going?' Jesus answered, 'Where I am going you cannot follow me now; but you shall follow afterward.' Peter said to him, 'Lord, why cannot I follow you now? I will lay down my life for you.' " In John 21:18–19, Jesus says to Peter, "[W]hen you are old, you will stretch out your hands, and another will gird you and carry you where you do not wish to go." The evangelist comments, "This he said to show by what death he was to glorify God." Here again martyrdom is a fulfillment of prophecy, perhaps foreordained by God. Peter's death also glorifies God.

Stephen is thought to have been the first Christian martyr, and his story has several parallels with the death of Jesus. Like Jesus (Acts 2:22), Stephen performs "wonders and signs" (6:8). Jesus was accused of saying that he could destroy the Temple and rebuild it in three days (Matt. 26:61, 27:40; Mark 14:58, 15:29; cf. John 2:19–21); Stephen is accused of saying that Jesus will destroy the Temple (Acts 6:14). Before the Sanhedrin, Jesus speaks of the Son of Man sitting at the right hand of God (Matt. 26:64; Mark 14:62; Luke 22:69); before the Sanhedrin, Stephen says that he sees the Son of Man standing at the right hand of God (Acts 7:56). Finally, in some manuscripts, Jesus asks God to forgive Jesus' executioners (Luke 23:34); Stephen asks Jesus to forgive Stephen's executioners (Acts 7:60). These details stand in sharp contrast to the desire for vengeance found in many martyrologies.

In Acts 12:2, Herod Agrippa I, king of Judaea, beheads James the son of Zebedee. Herod then jails Peter, but "[t]he very night when Herod was about to bring him out," presumably for execution, Peter is freed from prison by an angel (12:3–19). Then Herod goes to Caesarea, where he is hailed as a god. As punishment "he was eaten by worms and died" (12:20–23). The implication here is a sense of desired vengeance in this narrative of martyrology.

Revelation 6:9–11 exhibits a like spirit. The souls of martyrs ask God how long it will be before he will avenge them; verse 11 indicates that there is a fixed number of martyrs who must be killed before they all can be avenged. So here again martyrdom is foreordained by God. That martyrdom was a real possibility is attested by Revelation 2:10, "Do not fear what you are about to suffer. Behold, the devil is about to throw some of you into prison, that you may be tested, and for ten days you will have tribulation. Be faithful unto death, and I will give you the crown of life," and by 2:13, which speaks of the martyr Antipas; 12:10–11 says that "our brethren . . . loved not their lives even unto death." In 13:15, "[T]hose who would not worship the image of the beast" are killed; 20:4 says, "I saw the souls of those who had been beheaded for their testimony to Jesus"; 14:13 declares, "Blessed are the dead who die in the Lord henceforth. Blessed indeed, . . . that they may rest from their labors, for their deeds follow them!" In 17:6, the harlot, Rome, is said to be "drunk with the blood of the saints and the blood of the martyrs of Jesus"; 18:24 observes that "in her was found the blood of prophets and of saints"; and 18:6 tells us to "[r]ender to her as she herself has rendered, and repay her double for her deeds; mix a double draught for her in the cup she mixed. As she glorified herself and played the wanton, so give her a like measure of torment and mourning"; 18:20: "Rejoice over her, O heaven, O saints and apostles and prophets, for God has given judgment for you against her!" Chapter 19:2–3 says, " '[A]nd [God] has avenged on her the blood of his servants.' Once more they cried, 'Hallelujah! The smoke from her goes up for ever and ever.' " Revelation strongly exemplifies the element of vengeance in martyrology.

The second epistle to Timothy was not written by Paul but was written early in the second century. However, it may reflect historical knowledge of Paul's death: 4:6 says, "For I am already on the point of being sacrificed; the time of my departure has come." Paul's execution is seen as a sacrifice. Martyrdom is an offering to God, perhaps required by God.

These biblical references exhibit three common elements. First, God wants the martyr to die. The seven brothers testify that God is punishing them and their nation. It is God's will that Jesus die. Jesus predicts his own death and those of Peter, James, and John. Revelation teaches that there is a predetermined number of martyrs. Paul's death is an offering to God. Second, the martyr wants to die because the alternative is eternal punishment. Eleazar submits to torture and death because he is afraid of God's punishment. 4 Maccabees 13:14–15 advises us not to fear the persecutor because of the eternal punishment for those who disobey God. Jesus says not to fear those who can kill the body but him who can destroy both body and soul in hell. Third, the martyr wants revenge on persecutors. Shadrach, Meshach, Abednego, Daniel, the seven brothers, the martyrs of Revelation, and even Jesus have or will have the satisfaction of seeing their persecutors punished, although Stephen and perhaps Jesus magnanimously forgo this.

Extrabiblical Perspectives on Martyrdom

Josephus, *Antiquities of The Jews* 20.9.1, reports that in 62 C.E., James "the brother of Jesus who was called Christ"[7] was stoned at the instigation of the High Priest Ananus. Hegesippus, cited in Eusebius, *Historia Ecclesiastica* (*HE*) 2.23, gives a more detailed account of James' death. What is notable is that Hegesippus says that after the execution of James, the Romans besieged Jerusalem. Actually, the Jewish revolt was four years later, but Hegesippus makes the destruction of the Jewish polity God's vengeance for the death of James. Eusebius' *HE* 3.5.3 also says that God avenged violence against Christ and the apostles by destroying the people of Judaea.

In 64 C.E., Rome burned. Tacitus' *Annals* 15.44.2–8 reports that many blamed the fire on Nero. To deflect suspicion from himself, Nero executed Christians. What is relevant here is that Tacitus says that the Christians were convicted not so much of arson as of "hatred of the human race."[8] While this sort of accusation was leveled against Jews and might have been attached to Christians because they originated as a Jewish sect, it could also point to Roman awareness of Christian ideas about the destruction of unbelievers.

Ignatius, the bishop of Antioch, is interesting in psychological terms. On his way to execution in Rome, he wrote to the Roman church asking them not to attempt to save him. Ignatius shows his eagerness for suffering and death; he will force the beasts to attack him and says, "Let there come on me fire and cross and conflicts with wild beasts, wrenching of bones, mangling of limbs, crushing of the whole body, grievous torments of the devil, may I but attain Jesus Christ."[9] If the desire for revenge in other martyrologies manifests a certain sadism, Ignatius seems masochistic. In any case, there is a relish for violence. Ignatius wishes to be "a sacrifice to God," which indicates that God wants his death.

The Martyrdom of Polycarp,[10] narrating events of 156 C.E., is also instructive. It is said that the other martyrdoms in the same persecution have happened "in accordance with the will of God," who is said to have power over all things (2.1; cf. 1.1, 7.1). Polycarp is likened to a ram for sacrifice and a whole burnt offering and calls himself "a rich and acceptable sacrifice" (14.1–2). Polycarp says that God made ready and foretold and brought to pass his martyrdom (14.2). The text says that his martyrdom took place "according to the gospel of Christ" (19.1). This all suggests that the Christians considered martyrdom to be willed by God.

It is also reported, "Cold to them was the fire of the cruel tormentors [cf. 4 Macc. 11:26]; for they kept before their eyes their escape from the fire that is everlasting and is never quenched"; (2.3) Polycarp said to the governor, "You threaten the fire that burns for an hour, and after a little while is quenched; for you are ignorant of the fire of the judgment to come, and of everlasting punishment reserved for the ungodly." These statements hint that martyrdom was thought a way of escaping God's punishment and that vengeance on the persecutors was expected.

It is said of Germanicus that "in his eagerness to be released the sooner from . . . unrighteous and lawless mode of life he used force to the wild beast and pulled it on himself" (3.1). However, the text reports that one who had "forced both himself and others to come forward of their own accord" denied the faith to avoid death when he saw the beasts. Therefore, the text continues, "we do not commend those who surrender themselves" (4.1). Although some Christians desired martyrdom, the church did not always encourage Christians actively to seek it. Under torture, a slave boy betrayed Polycarp, who was conveyed to the stadium so that he might "fulfill his own appointed lot, and that his betrayers might undergo the punishment of Judas himself" (6.2). This illustrates a Christian desire for revenge, even on a boy who broke under torture.

One detail from Polycarp's martyrdom (15.2–16.1) evokes Daniel 3:25–27 (cf. Prayer of Azariah and the Song of the Three Young Men 26–27). Like Shadrach, Meshach, and Abednego, Polycarp is not consumed by flames; he has to be stabbed with a dagger. In any case, the martyrology of Polycarp illustrates God's will that the martyrs die, the martyrs' desire for death, their fear of hell, and their desire for vengeance.

The Letter of the Churches of Lyons and Vienne (Eusebius, *HE* 5.1.11)[11] reads, "[S]ome were manifestly ready for martyrdom, and fulfilled with all zeal the confession wherein they gave witness." In 5.1.25–26, Biblis, who had denied the faith, retracted her denial when she was again tortured to induce her falsely to accuse others because the torture brought to her mind the tortures of hell. 5.1.27 says that the Lord willed some to die in prison to manifest his glory; and 5.1.40, 51, and 56 say that martyrs were "sacrificed"; 5.1.11 calls them lapsed "abortions"; 5.1.44 calls them "dead"; 5.1.45–46 tell how Christians who apostasized were forgiven by the martyrs, recovered their faith, and were executed; 5.1.46 quotes Ezekiel 33:11 to the effect that God does not desire the death of the sinner; 5.1.63 quotes the persecutors as saying that the martyrs met their deaths with joy. Christians in jail asked for prayers that they be martyred. (Eusebius, *HE* 5.2.3). That passage also speaks of "martyrs, whom Christ deemed worthy to be taken up in their confession." In summary, the *Letter* tells that God willed the death of the martyrs, the martyrs wanted to die, and the martyrs feared that they would go to hell if they apostasized, but no desire for revenge is indicated. The Scillitan martyrs (180 C.E.) thanked God for their sentence, indicating that God and they desired their death.

The Martyrdom of Perpetua and Felicitas[12] 2.1 says that they and their companions "were to be sacrificed on the emperor's birthday." The other martyrs, "Revocatus, Saturninus, and Saturus uttered threatenings against the gazing people about this martyrdom. When they came within sight of [the governor] Hilarianus, by gesture and nod, they began to say to Hilarianus, 'Thou judgest us, but God will judge thee.' At this the people, exasperated, demanded that they should be tormented with scourges as they passed along the rank of the venatores. And they indeed rejoiced that they should have incurred any one of their Lord's passions" (6.1). "But Perpetua, that she might taste some pain, being pierced between the ribs, cried out loudly, and she herself placed the wavering right hand of the youthful gladiator to her throat. Possibly such a woman could not have been slain unless she herself had willed it, because she was feared by the impure spirit" (6.4). This martyrology includes God's desire for the martyrs' death, the martyrs' desire for death, and the martyrs' desire for vengeance.

Tertullian's *To Scapula* 5 says that when Arrius Antoninus, governor of Asia, persecuted the Christians, all the Christians in the province confessed before him. Tertullian's *De Spectaculis* 30 betrays the vengefulness of early Christians: "But what a spectacle is that fast-approaching advent of our Lord, now owned by all, now highly exalted, now a triumphant One! . . . that last day of judgment, with its everlasting issues; that day unlooked for by the nations, the theme of their derision, when the world, hoary with age, and all its many products, shall be consumed in one great flame! How vast a spectacle then bursts upon the eye! What there excites my admiration? What my derision? Which sight gives me joy? Which rouses me to exultation?—as I see so many illustrious monarchs, whose reception into the heavens was publicly announced, groaning in the lowest darkness with great Jove himself, and those, too, who bore witness of their exaltation; governors of provinces, too, who persecuted the Christian name, in fires more fierce than those with which in the days of their pride they raged against the followers of Christ! What world's wise men besides, the very philosophers, in fact, who taught their followers that God had no concern in ought that is sublunary, and were wont to assure them that either they had no souls, or that they would never return to the bodies which at death they had left, now covered with shame before the poor deluded ones, as one fire consumes them! Poets also, trembling not before the judgment-seat of Rhadamanthus or Minos, but of the unexpected Christ! I shall have a better opportunity then of hearing the tragedians, louder-voiced in their own calamity; of viewing the play-actors, much more 'dissolute' in the dissolving flame; of looking upon the charioteer, all glowing in his chariot of fire; of witnessing the wrestlers, not in their gymnasia, but tossing in the fiery billows; unless even then I shall not care to attend to such ministers of sin, in my eager wish rather to fix a gaze insatiable on those whose fury vented itself against the Lord. 'This,' I shall say, 'this is that carpenter's or harlot's son, that Sabbath-breaker, that Samaritan and devil-possessed! This is He whom you purchased from Judas! This is He whom you struck with reed and fist, whom you contemptuously spat upon, to whom you gave gall and vinegar to drink! This is He whom His disciples secretly stole away, that it might be said He had risen again, or the gardener abstracted, that his lettuces might come to no harm from the crowds of visitants!' "[13] These passages show the Christians' eagerness for martyrdom and desire for vengeance on their persecutors.

Cyprian (258 C.E.) also thanked God for his death sentence (*Acta Proconsularia of St Cyprian* 4). *Acta Proconsularia* 5 also says that when Cyprian was sentenced, the Christian crowd said, "Let us also be beheaded with him."[14] *Acta Proconsularia* 5 says that a few days after Cyprian was executed, the proconsul who sentenced him died. Cyprian's *De lapsis* 5 said of the persecution of Decius (ca. 250), "It has pleased the Lord to prove his family; . . . the divine judgment awakened our faith from a declining, and, should I so speak, an almost slumbering state; and whereas we deserved yet more for our sins."[15] Of apostates, Cyprian's *De lapsis* 8 writes, "[T]hey hasted to death of their own will." He calls apostasy "undoing," "destruction" (ibid.), "ruin" (ibid., 9). He says, "The altar where he went to perish, was it not his funeral pile? Ought he not to shudder at and flee from an altar of the Devil . . . as from the death and sepulchre of his existence? Why bring an offering with you, wretched man, why present a victim? You are yourself an offering at the altar, you are yourself come as a victim; you have slaughtered there your own salvation, your hope."[16] Cyprian indicates that the persecution is a punishment from God, that many Christians were eager for death but wanted revenge on their persecutors, and that apostasy means damnation.

Lactantius' *On the Deaths of the Persecutors* 11.3 says, "[T]he Christians were wont with eagerness to meet death."[17] *Persecutors* 2 says, "[Nero] it was who first persecuted the servants of God; he crucified Peter, and slew Paul; nor did he escape with impunity; for God looked on the affliction of His people; and therefore the tyrant, bereaved of authority, and precipitated from the height of empire, suddenly disappeared, and even the burial-place of that noxious wild beast was nowhere to be seen."[18] Chapter 3 says, "After an interval of some years from the death of Nero, there arose another tyrant no less wicked (Domitian), who, although his government was exceedingly odious, for a very long time oppressed his subjects, and reigned in security, until at length he stretched forth his impious hands against the Lord. Having been instigated by evil demons to persecute the righteous people, he was then delivered into the power of his enemies, and suffered due punishment. To be murdered in his own palace was not vengeance ample enough: the very memory of his name was erased. For although he had erected many admirable edifices, and rebuilt the Capitol, and left other distinguished marks of his magnificence, yet the senate did so persecute his name, as to leave no remains of his statues, or traces of the inscriptions put up in honor of him; and by the most solemn and severe decrees it branded him, even after death, with perpetual infamy."[19]

In chapter 4, Lanctantius informs us, "It seems as if [Decius] had been raised to sovereign eminence, at once to rage against God, and at once to fall; for having undertaken an expedition against the Carpi, who had then possessed themselves of Dacia and Moefia [*sic*], he was suddenly surrounded by the barbarians, and slain, together with a great part of his army; nor could he be honoured with the rights of sepulture, but, stripped and naked, he lay to be devoured by wild beasts and birds, a fit end for the enemy of God."[20] The following chapter tells how the persecuting emperor Valerian was captured by Shapur I, king of the Sassanian Persians. Shapur made Valerian serve as a stool for Shapur to mount his horse or carriage. Valerian's son, the emperor Gallienus, did nothing to save or avenge his father. When Valerian died, he was skinned, and his skin placed in a Persian temple. In the very next section, we read that Aurelian "by deeds of cruelty irritated the divine wrath" and "[h]e was not, however, permitted to accomplish what he had devised; for just as he began to give a loose to his rage, he was slain . . . by his familiar friends."[21]

Chapter 31 says, "From Maximian [Diocletian's coemperor, who had plotted against other emperors and been forced to suicide], God, the avenger of religion and of his people, turned his eyes to Galerius, the author of the accursed persecution [the greatest, 303–313], that in his punishment also He might manifest the power of His majesty."[22] Thereafter, Lanctantius (33 and 35) happily details the illness of Galerius that persuaded him to stop persecuting Christians: "[N]ow, when Galerius was in the eighteenth year of his reign, God struck him with an incurable plague. A malignant ulcer formed itself low down in his secret parts, and spread by degrees. The physicians attempted to eradicate it, and healed up the place affected, but the sore, after having been skinned over, broke out again; a vein burst, and the blood flowed in such quantity as to endanger his life. . . . He grew emaciated, pallid, and feeble, and the bleeding then stanched. The ulcer began to be insensible to the remedies applied, and a gangrene seized all the neighbouring parts. It diffused itself the wider the more the corrupted flesh was cut away, and everything employed as the means of cure served but to aggravate the disease. . . . Already approaching its deadly crisis, [the disease] had occupied the lower regions of his body: his bowels came out, and his whole seat putrefied. The luckless physicians, although without hope of overcoming the malady, ceased not to apply fomentations and administer medicines. The humors having been repelled, the distemper attacked his intestines, and worms were generated in his body. The stench was so foul as to pervade not only the palace, but even the whole city; and no wonder, for by that time the passages from his bladder and bowels, having been devoured by the worms, became indiscriminate, and his body, with intolerable anguish, was dissolved into one mass of corruption. . . . They applied the warm flesh of animals to the chief seat of the disease, that the warmth might draw out those minute worms; and accordingly, when the dressings were removed, there issued forth an innumerable swarm: nevertheless the prolific disease had hatched swarms much more abundant to prey upon and consume his intestines. Already, through a complication of distempers, the different parts of his body had lost their natural form: the superior part was dry, meagre, and haggard, and his ghastly-looking skin had settled itself deep amongst his bones; while the inferior, distended like bladders, retained no appearance of joints. These things happened in the course of a complete year; and at length, overcome by calamities, he was obliged to acknowledge God, and he cried aloud, in the intervals of raging pain, that he would re-edify the Church which he had demolished, and make atonement for his misdeeds; and when he was near his end, he published an edict [tolerating the Christians]. . . . Galerius, however, did not, by the publication of this edict, obtain the divine forgiveness. In a few days after, he was consumed by the horrible disease that had brought on an [*sic*] universal putrefaction."[23]

"The wicked plan [of persecution] having been carried into execution, Diocletian, whom prosperity had now abandoned,"[24] fell gravely ill and resigned (chapter 17). Lanctantius tells us (42) of the end of Diocletian. "At this time, by command of Constantine, the statues of Maximian Herculius were thrown down, and his portraits removed; and, as the two old emperors were generally delineated in one piece, the portraits of both were removed at the same time. Thus Diocletian lived to see a disgrace which no former emperor had ever seen, and, under the double load of vexation of spirit and bodily maladies, he resolved to die. Tossing to and fro, with his soul agitated by grief, he could neither eat nor take rest. He sighed, groaned, and wept often, and incessantly threw himself into various postures, now on his couch, and now on the ground. So he, who for twenty years was the most prosperous of emperors, having been cast down into the obscurity of private station, treated in the most contumelious manner, and compelled to abhor life, became incapable of receiving nourishment, and, worn out with anguish of mind, he expired."[25]

We are informed (49) similarly of the end of Maximin Daia, who had planned a great persecution of the Christians but for prudential reasons mutilated and killed only a few: "[In Tarsus following his defeat by Constantine's ally, Licinius] being hard pressed both by sea and land, he despaired of finding any place for refuge; and in the anguish and dismay of his mind, he sought death as the only remedy of those calamities that God had heaped on him. But first he gorged himself with food, and large draughts of wine, as those are wont who believe that they eat and drink for the last time; and so he swallowed poison. However, the force of the poison, repelled by his full stomach, could not immediately operate, but it produced a grievous disease, resembling the pestilence; and his life was prolonged only that his sufferings might be more severe. And now the poison began to rage, and to burn up everything within him, so that he was driven to distraction with the intolerable pain; and during a fit of frenzy, which lasted four days, he gathered handfuls of earth, and greedily devoured it. Having undergone various and excruciating torments, he dashed his forehead against the wall, and his eyes started out of their sockets. And now, become blind, he imagined that he saw God, with His servants arrayed in white robes, sitting in judgment on him. He roared out as men on the rack are wont, and exclaimed that not he, but others, were guilty. In the end, as if he had been racked into confession, he acknowledged his own guilt, and lamentably implored Christ to have mercy upon him. Then amidst groans, like those of one burnt alive, did he breathe out his guilty soul in the most horrible kind of death."[26]

Lactantius (50–51) apparently does not think that the horrible death of Galerius exhausts God's wrath against him: "Thus did God subdue all those who persecuted His name, so that neither root nor branch of them remained; for Licinius, as soon as he was established in sovereign authority, commanded that Valeria [Galerius' widow] should be put to death . . . Licinius commanded that Candidianus also should be put to death. He was the son of Galerius by a concubine, and Valeria, having no children, had adopted him. On the news of the death of Daia, she came in disguise to the court of Licinius, anxious to observe what might befall Candidianus. The youth, presenting himself at Nicomedia, had an outward show of honour paid to him, and, while he suspected no harm, was killed. Hearing of this catastrophe, Valeria immediately fled. The Emperor Severus left a son, Severianus, arrived at man's estate, who accompanied Daia in his flight from the field of battle. . . . Long before this time, Candidianus and Severianus, apprehending evil from Licinius, had chosen to remain with Daia; while Valeria favoured Licinius, and was willing to bestow on him that which she had denied to Daia, all rights accruing to her as the widow of Galerius. Licinius also put to death Maximus, the son of Daia, a boy eight years old, and a daughter of Daia, who was seven years old, and had been betrothed to Candidianus. But before their death, their mother had been thrown into the Orontes, in which river she herself had frequently commanded chaste women to be drowned. So, by the unerring and just judgment of God, all the impious received according to the deeds that they had done. Valeria, too, who for fifteen months had wandered under a mean garb from province to province, was at length discovered in Thessalonica, was apprehended, together with her mother Prisca, and suffered capital punishment. Both the ladies were conducted to execution; a fall from grandeur which moved the pity of the multitude of beholders that the strange sight had gathered together. They were beheaded, and their bodies cast into the sea."[27]

Lactantius (chapter 52) concludes his work: "I thought it proper to commit them to writing exactly as they happened, lest the memory of events so important should perish, and lest any future historian of the persecutors should corrupt the truth, either by suppressing their offenses against God, or the judgment of God against them. . . . Where now are the surnames of the Jovii and the Herculii, once so glorious and renowned amongst the nations; surnames insolently assumed at first by Diocles and Maximian, and afterwards transferred to their successors? The Lord has blotted them and erased them from the earth."[28] These passages amply show the desire for vengeance of the leading Christian author of the time.

Violence and Nonviolence in the Worldview of Early Christians

The belief that God wanted the martyrs to die, the desire of the martyrs to die, the martyrs' fear that if they apostasized they would be damned, some obsession with torture by writers of martyrologies, and martyrs' desire for vengeance are attested in much early Christian literature. Put otherwise, the martyrs' God desired the suffering and death of the martyrs, would send them to hell if they denied him, and would punish their persecutors. Although the early Christians did not resist persecution with physical violence, violence was very much on their minds. This is understandable given their circumstances. They lived under a death sentence, although it was seldom carried out, and the God of the Hebrew Bible, whom the Christians adopted, was not a pacifist, so it is not surprising that violence was on their minds. Paradoxically, the Christian policy of nonviolence was prudent, given the overwhelming power of the Roman government, illustrated in the suppression of several revolts of the Christians' cousins and competitors, the Jews.

So the obsession with violence in the cult of martyrdom was accompanied by a general practice of nonviolence among the early Christians. However, there are elements of violence in the teaching attributed to Jesus. The parable of the wicked husbandmen ends with the Lord of the vineyard killing them (Matt. 21:41; Mark 12:9; Luke 20:16). One version of the parable of the wedding feast includes the king sending his armies, killing those who murdered his servants, and burning their city (Matt. 22:6–7; Luke 14:16–24 omits these details). Jesus spoke of the cost of discipleship as follows: "[W]hat king, going to encounter another king in war, will not sit down first and take counsel whether he is able with ten thousand to meet him who comes against him with twenty thousand? And if not, while the other is yet a great way off, he sends an embassy and asks terms of peace" (Luke 14:31–32). Jesus is supposed to have said, "[A]nd if any one forces you to go one mile [Roman soldiers could require civilians to carry their packs], go with him two miles" (Matt. 5:41). When Jesus is arrested and warns Peter to sheathe his sword, Jesus adds that he could summon 12 legions of angels (Matt. 26:53).[29] Jesus said that he had not come to bring peace but a sword (Matt. 10:34); prior to his arrest, Jesus instructed his disciples to buy swords (Luke 22:36) and drove the tradespeople out of the Temple (Matt. 21:12; Mark 11:15–16; Luke 20:45; John 2:14–16). An enigmatic saying is Matthew 11:12: "From the days of John the Baptist until now the kingdom of heaven has suffered violence, and men of violence take it by force." And Luke 16:16: "The law and the prophets were until John; since then the kingdom of God is preached, and every one enters it violently."

Nevertheless, when one of his disciples cut off the ear of one of the arresting gang, Jesus instructed him to sheathe the sword (Matt. 26:52; John 18:11) and declared that all who take the sword will die by the sword (Matt. 26:52; cf. Rev. 13:10). Luke 22:51 says that Jesus healed the wounded man. This story is consistent with a saying of Jesus: "You have heard that it was said, 'An eye for an eye and a tooth for a tooth.' But I say to you, Do not resist one who is evil. But if any one strikes you on the right cheek, turn to him the other also" (Matt. 5:39; cf. Luke 6:29). Finally, the attitude toward violence of some early Christians is expressed in Jesus' words to Pilate: "My kingship is not of this world; if my kingship were of this world, my servants would fight" (John 18:36).

Biblical Preferences of Military Metaphors

Whatever was Jesus' attitude toward violence, the New Testament is somewhat favorable to Roman soldiers. Luke 3:14 says that soldiers asked John the Baptist what they should do. John replied, "Rob no one by violence or false accusation, and be content with your wages." Jesus is also reported to have healed a centurion's servant, commending the centurion's faith (Matt. 8:5–13; Luke 7:2–10), and when Jesus was crucified, it was a centurion who declared him a son of God. (Matt. 27:54; Mark 15:39; "innocent" in Luke 23:47) The first gentile to whom the gospel was preached was a centurion (Acts 10).

Paul has a rather positive orientation to things military in general and to the Roman army in particular. Romans 6:13 says, "Don't offer your members as weapons [*hopla* can also mean "tools"] of wrong to sin, but offer . . . your members as weapons [*hopla*] to God." Verse 23 says, "For the wages [*opsonia*, "military pay"] of sin are death." Here we find a military term in a negative context. Paul said that the magistrate does not bear the sword in vain and is God's servant (Rom. 13:4). In Romans 13:12, Paul tells his readers to put on the armor of light; 16:7 calls Andronicus and Junia "my fellow prisoners of war." 1 Corinthians 9:7 avers, "Who serves as a soldier at his own expense?" 1 Corinthians 14:8 informs us that "if the bugle gives an indistinct sound, who will get ready for battle?" In 2 Corinthians 6:7, Paul says that the servants of God have the weapons of righteousness; 10:3–5 says that "though we live in the world we are not carrying on a worldly war, for the weapons of our warfare are not worldly but have divine power to destroy strongholds. We destroy arguments and every proud obstacle to the knowledge of God, and take every thought captive to obey Christ." 2 Corinthians 11:8 says, "I despoiled [*sulao*, "to strip off the arms of a slain enemy"] the other churches, taking supplies [*opsonion*, "supplies for an army"] to serve you." Philippians 2:25 calls Epaphroditus "my fellow soldier." 1 Thessalonians 5:8 says, "[L]et us be sober, and put on the breastplate of faith and love, and for a helmet the hope of salvation." Philemon 2 calls Archippus "our fellow soldier"; 23 calls Epaphras "my fellow prisoner of war."

Paul says nothing to the Philippian jailer about changing his job (Acts 16:23–34). When Paul was in danger of ambush, he informed his Roman guards (Acts 23:12–35), and when Paul's ship was sinking, the centurion refused to follow custom and kill Paul (27:42). Acts 18:3 says that Paul was a tentmaker; the Greek (*skenopoios*) suggests a leather worker. It is likely that some of the leather goods that Paul made were bought by the Roman army.

In Ephesians 4:8, a follower of Paul quotes Psalm 68:18: "When he ascended on high he led a host of captives," and 6:11–17 commands us to put on the whole armor of God (cf. 4 Macc. 13:16), specifying breastplate, shield against missiles, helmet, and sword. Colossians 4:10 calls Aristarchus "my fellow prisoner of war." In 1 Timothy 1:18, a later follower of Paul says, "I give you this [*parangelia*, "military"] command . . . that you wage a good warfare." 2 Timothy 2:3–4 urges us, "Share in suffering as a good soldier of Christ Jesus. No soldier on service gets entangled in civilian pursuits, so that he may please the one who enlisted him." A military term, *aikhmalotizo*, "to make prisoner of war," is used of the deception of women in 2 Timothy 3:6.

The book of Revelation is replete with military elements. In 1:16, out of the mouth of the heavenly Jesus "issued a sharp two-edged sword," and in 2:12, Jesus is the one "who has the sharp two-edged sword." The Greek word, *nikao*, meaning "to conquer," is used 16 times in Revelation. In 2:16, Jesus threatens that he will "war against them with the sword of my mouth"; 2:23 says that Jesus will strike dead the children of "Jezebel," a false prophetess; 2:27—he who "conquers" will rule the nations with an iron rod as when pots are smashed; 6:2–8 introduces the "Four Horsemen of the Apocalypse."

The first is armed with a bow and goes out to conquer. The second "was permitted to take peace from the earth, so that men should slay one another; and he was given a great sword." The fourth was "given power . . . to kill with sword and with famine and with pestilence and by wild beasts of the earth"; 9:3 tells how locusts stinging like scorpions come from the bottomless pit to torment the godless; 9:7–9 describes them: "In appearance the locusts were like horses arrayed for battle . . . they had scales like iron breastplates, and the noise of their wings was like the noise of many chariots with horses rushing into battle." Chapter 9:16–19 tells how two hundred million cavalry on fire-breathing horses with poisonous snakes for tails help to kill one-third of mankind; 11:5 says that God's two witnesses, with powers of Moses and Elijah, with power to send "every plague," defend themselves by breathing fire. In 11:18, it is said that the time came "for destroying the destroyers of the earth"; 12:5 indicates that Jesus will rule all nations with an iron rod; 12:7–9 tells of war in heaven between the archangel Michael and the Devil and their angels, while 12:17 says that the Devil began "to make war" on the Christians.

In Revelation 13:4, men say of the Antichrist, "Who is like the beast, and who can make war against it?" In 13:7, the apocalyptic narrative tells us that the beast "was allowed to make war on the saints and to conquer them." One ambiguous possibly pacifistic statement is found in 13:10: "[I]f any one slays with the sword, with the sword must he be slain," while 13:14 declares that the beast "was wounded by the sword and yet lived"; and in 14:19–20, "[T]he angel swung his sickle on the earth and gathered the vintage of the earth, and threw it into the great winepress of the wrath of God; and the wine press was trodden outside the city, and blood flowed from the wine press, as high as a horse's bridle, for one thousand six hundred stadia." God attacks his enemies in this great apocalypse. In 16:2, God inflicts "foul and evil sores" on the worshippers of the beast and in 16:3–4 turns the waters of the earth to blood, in 16:8 the sun scorches mankind, in 16:18–20 the greatest earthquake in history strikes, and in 16:21 great hailstones fall. The counterattack comes in 17:14, which indicates that 10 kings "will make war on the Lamb, and the Lamb will conquer them"; in 17:16–17, "[The beast and the 10 kings] will make [Rome] desolate and naked, and devour her flesh and burn her up with fire, for God has put it into their hearts to carry out his purpose." Chapter 19:11–15 describes Jesus as follows: "[B]ehold, a white horse! He who sat upon it . . . makes war. . . . He is clad in a robe dipped in blood . . . and the armies of heaven . . . followed him. . . . From his mouth issues a sharp sword with which to smite the nations, and he will rule them with a rod of iron; he will tread the wine press of the fury of the wrath of God Almighty." In 19:17–21, "[A]n angel . . . called to all the birds that fly in midheaven, 'Come, gather for the great supper of God, to eat the flesh of kings, the flesh of captains, the flesh of mighty men, the flesh of horses and their riders, and the flesh of all men, both free and slave, both small and great.' And I saw the beast and the kings of the earth with their armies gathered to make war against him who sits upon the horse and his army. And the beast was captured, and with it the false prophet. . . . These two were thrown alive into the lake of fire that burns with sulphur. And the rest were slain by the sword of him who sits upon the horse, the sword that issues from his mouth; and all the birds were gorged with their flesh." Chapter 20:7 says, "Satan . . . will come out to deceive the nations which are at the four corners of the earth, that is, Gog and Magog, to gather them for battle; their number is like the sand of the sea. And they marched up over the broad earth and surrounded the camp of the saints and the beloved city; but fire came down from heaven and consumed them and the devil who deceived them was thrown into the lake of fire and sulphur."

Before leaving the New Testament, we should consider two stories in Acts. In Acts 13:11, Paul temporarily strikes blind the magician, and false prophet Elymas bar Jesus. In Acts 5:1–11, a couple named Ananias and Sapphira sell some property, keep part of the money, and give part of it to the church. Peter accuses Ananias of lying to God, presumably because Ananias pretended to give all the money to the church, and Ananias falls dead. Sapphira arrives later, ignorant of her husband's death, and lies to Peter about the transaction. Peter asks her why she has lied and tells her that those who buried her husband are at the door and that they will carry her out, and Sapphira falls dead. It is not at all clear that Peter is the executioner here, but like the blinding of Elymas, it is a violent episode for a pacifist group.

As we noted previously, the New Testament uses military imagery. John the Baptist, Jesus, and Peter get on surprisingly well with soldiers, admittedly except for Jesus' execution. Paul is depicted as working for, appealing to, and being saved by Roman soldiers. Nowhere does the Christian scripture instruct soldiers to give up their profession. Not only did early Christians use military language to express their spiritual struggles, but, as is God in the Hebrew Bible, Jesus is unequivocally depicted as a warrior in Revelation 2:16,

17:14, 19:11–15, and 21. Less familiar is the homicidal Jesus of some apocryphal gospels. For example, in the *Infancy Gospel of Thomas*, the child Jesus strikes dead two other children.[30]

Peter Brock says that no source has Christians objecting to military service before 170 C.E. and that Julianus [*sic*] Africanus was not a pacificist.[31] Some Christians did avoid military service. Some Christian communities instructed soldiers not to perform executions or take the military oath and excommunicated Christians who enlisted. (Hippolytus, *Apostolic Tradition* 2.16.17, 19) There are, however, questions whether *Apostolic Tradition* should be ascribed to Hippolytus, whether its present form is accurate, and whom Hippolytus represents since he was a rigorist and antipope.[32] Helgeland draws several conclusions from this passage. The context seems to be idolatry, following priests and keepers of idols. Execution is forbidden, but killing in battle is not mentioned. "A soldier who is in authority . . . a military governor or a magistrate of a city" are mentioned, indicating that Christianity was not confined to the lower classes. The military oath, recited three times a year, was probably considered idolatrous. Since this is the only place in Hippolytus' work which deals with the army, it seems not to have been important to him, which makes attributing pacifism to him problematic.[33]

Although most Christians would not serve in the army, many early Christian writers do not speak of soldiers as if their work was sinful. Clement of Rome, in his *First Corinthians* 37:1–3, reads, "Let us serve in our army, brethren, with all earnestness, following his faultless commands. Let us consider those who serve as our generals, with what good order, habitual readiness, and submissiveness they perform their commands. Not all are prefects, nor tribunes, nor centurions, nor in charge of fifty men . . . or the like, but each carries out in his own rank the commands of the emperor and of the generals."[34] Ignatius' *To Polycarp* 6.2 uses Roman military terms: "Be pleasing to him in whose ranks you serve, from whom you receive your pay [*opsonia*]—let none of you be found as a deserter. Let your baptism remain as your arms, your faith as a helmet, your love as a spear, your endurance as your panoply, let your works be your deposits (*deposita*) that you may receive the back-pay (*accepta*) due to you."[35] The *Letter of the Churches of Lyons and Vienne* (Eusebius, *HE* 5.1.17–18, 43) refers to martyrs as "combatants."[36]

Tertullian, *Apology* 39, says, "We meet together as an assembly and congregation, that, offering up prayer to God as with united force, we may wrestle with Him in our supplications. This violence God delights in."[37] *Apology* 50 describes martyrdom in military terms: "Well, it is quite true that it is our desire to suffer, but it is in the way that the soldier longs for war. No one indeed suffers willingly, since suffering necessarily implies fear and danger. Yet the man who objected to the conflict, both fights with all his strength, and when victorious, he rejoices in the battle, because he reaps from it glory and spoil. It is our battle to be summoned to your tribunals, that there, under fear of execution, we may battle for the truth. But the day is won when the object of the struggle is gained. This victory of ours gives us the glory of pleasing God, and the spoil of life eternal. But we are overcome. Yes, when we have obtained our wishes. Therefore we conquer in dying; we go forth victorious at the very time we are subdued. Call us, if you like, *Sarmenticii* and *Semaxii*, because, bound to a half-axle stake, we are burned in a circle-heap of faggots. This is the attitude in which we conquer, it is our victory-robe, it is for us a sort of triumphal car. Naturally enough, therefore, we do not please the vanquished."[38] *Apology* 30.4 reads, "[W]ithout ceasing, for all our emperors we offer prayer. We pray for life prolonged; for security to the empire; for protection to the imperial house; for *brave armies* [emphasis added], a faithful senate, a virtuous people, the world at rest—whatever, as man or Caesar, an emperor would wish.[39] *Apology* 37.3 says, "We are but of yesterday, and we have filled every place among you—cities, islands, *fortresses* [emphasis added], towns, market-places, the very *camp* [emphasis added], tribes, companies, palace, senate, forum—we have left nothing to you but the temples of your gods."[40] In *Apology* 42.2–3, we have this declaration: "We sail with you, and *fight* [emphasis added] with you, and till the ground with you."[41]

It can be seen that part of Tertullian's objection to military service by Christians is the idolatrous military religion. *Apology* 16.8 (cf. *Ad Nationes* 12) informs us, "The camp religion of the Romans is all through a worship of the standards, a setting the standards above all gods."[42] The *Treatise on Idolatry* 19 shows the mixture of monotheism, pacificism, and military imagery in Tertullian's argument against military service: "But now inquiry is made about this point, whether a believer may turn himself into military service and whether the military may be admitted into the faith, even the rank and file, or each inferior grade, to whom there is no necessity to take part in sacrifices or capital punishments. There is no agreement between the divine and the human sacrament [military oath], the *standard of Christ* [emphasis added] and the standard of the devil, the *camp of light* [emphasis added] and the camp of darkness. One soul cannot be due to two [lords]—God and Caesar. And yet Moses carried a rod [like a centurion]; Aaron wore a buckle [the belt was symbolic of military service], and John (Baptist) is girt with leather; and if you really want to play around with the subject, Joshua the son of Nun leads a line of march; and the People warred. But how will [a Christian man] war, nay, how will he serve even in peace, without a sword, which the Lord has taken away? For albeit soldiers came to John, and had received the formula of their rule; albeit likewise, a centurion had believed; the Lord afterward, in disarming Peter, unbelted every soldier. No dress is lawful among us, if assigned to any unlawful action."[43]

Tertullian, in his *Treatise on the Crown*, tells how a Christian soldier was punished, probably by death, for refusing to wear a crown during a military ceremony. The essay praises the soldier's decision and explains why. Most of this writing argues that the crown is idolatrous. Tertullian calls the martyr a "soldier of God" and chides other Christian soldiers that they did not emulate him (chapter 1).[44] Military imagery follows: "At once he put away the heavy cloak, his disburdening commenced; he loosed from his foot the military shoe, beginning to stand upon holy ground; he gave up the sword, which was not necessary either for the protection of our Lord; from his hand likewise dropped the laurel crown; and now, purple-clad with the hope of his own blood [being shed], shod with the preparation of the gospel [cf. Eph. 6:15], *girt with the sharper word of God* [emphasis added; compared to a sword in Eph. 6:17; Heb. 4:12; cf. Rev. 1:16, 2:16, 19:13, 15, 21], *completely equipped in the apostles' armour* [emphasis added], and crowned more worthily with the white crown of martyrdom, he awaits in prison the largess of Christ" (chapter 1).[45] That this writing dates from Tertullian's Montanist period is suggested by this statement: "It is plain that as they have rejected the prophecies of the Holy Spirit [mediated by Montanus], they are also purposing the refusal of martyrdom" (chapter 1).[46] That Scripture was no longer sufficient to Tertullian as a Montanist is implied as follows: "Nor do I doubt that some are already turning their back on the Scriptures, are making ready their luggage, are equipped for flight from city to city. For that is all of the gospel [Matt. 10:23: "When they persecute you in this city, flee to the other] they care to remember" (chapter 1).[47]

There is evidence that Tertullian's objection to military service was not pacifistic. In *On the Resurrection* 16, Tertullian distinguishes between murder and killing in battle: "And as for the sword drunken with murders, is there anyone who will not expel it from his whole house, not to speak of his bed-chamber or his pillow-head, under the impression, I suppose, that his dreams could not help but be the remonstrances of the souls which would oppress and disquiet one who had taken to his bed their own blood? On the other hand . . . a sword nobly bloodied in war, a man-slayer of a better sort, will have its credit rewarded by consecration."[48] In his *Treatise on the Crown* 11, Tertullian does make a number of pacifistic points: "Shall it be held lawful to make an occupation of the sword, when the Lord proclaims that he who uses the sword shall perish by the sword? And shall the son of peace take part in the battle when it does not become him even to sue at law? And shall he apply the chain, and the prison, and the torture, and the punishment, who is not the avenger even of his own wrongs?"[49] Immediately following, Tertullian enumerates different objections to military service: Sabbath breaking, guarding pagan temples, taking "a meal where the apostle has forbidden" (presumably in a temple), protecting "by night those whom in the day-time he has put to flight by his exorcisms [pagan gods], leaning and resting on the spear with which Christ's side was pierced," carrying "a flag, too, hostile to Christ," asking "a watch-word from the emperor" after receiving "one from God," being "burned [cremated?] according to camp rule, when he was not permitted to burn incense to an idol, when to him Christ remitted the punishment of fire . . . carrying of the name over from the *camp* [emphasis added] of light to the camp of darkness" (chapter 11).[50] "Lo! the yearly public pronouncing of vows [chapter 12], what does that bear on its face to be? It takes place . . . in the temples. In addition to the places, observe the words also: 'We vow that you, O Jupiter, will then have an ox with gold-decorated horns.' What does the utterance mean? Without a doubt the denial [of Christ]. Albeit the Christian says nothing in these places with the mouth, he makes his response by having the crown on his head."[51] Then Tertullian returns to pacifistic argument: "Is the laurel of the triumph made of leaves, or of corpses? Is it adorned with ribbons, or with tombs? Is it bedewed with ointments, or with the tears of wives and mothers?—it may be of some Christians too; for Christ is also among the barbarians" (chapter 12).[52]

After this expression of nonviolence, Tertullian finishes with military imagery (chapter 15): "To him who conquers He says, 'I will give a crown of life.' Be *you*, too, faithful unto death, and fight *you*, too, the good fight, whose crown the apostle feels so justly confident has been laid up for him. The angel also, as he goes forth on a white horse, conquering and to conquer, receives a crown of victory. . . . Why condemn you to a little chaplet, or a twisted headband, the brow of which has been destined for a diadem? . . . You have a flower in the Branch of Jesse . . . by choosing which the good soldier, too, has got promotion in the heavenly ranks. Blush, ye fellow-soldiers of his, henceforth not to be condemned even by him, but by some soldier of Mithras, who, at his initation in the gloomy cavern, in the camp, it may well be said, of darkness, when at the sword's point a crown is presented to him, as though in mimicry of martyrdom, and thereupon put upon his head, is admonished to resist and cast it off, and, if you like, transfer it to his shoulder, saying that Mithras is his crown. And thenceforth he is never crowned; and he has that for a mark to show who he is, if anywhere he is subjected to trial in respect of his religion; and he is at once believed to be a soldier of Mithras if he throws the crown away."[53] We see that pacifism is only part of Tertullian's problem with the Roman army and not the most important part. Tertullian says, "But now, as they put forth also the objection: But where are we forbidden to be crowned? I shall take this point up, as more suitable to be treated of here—being the essence, in fact, of the present contention" (chapter 1).[54] Indeed this question of idolatry seems to be the essence of Tertullian's objection to military service, as he devotes almost the entire essay (chapters 1–12) to idolatry. Service in the Roman army could involve a number of religious exercises which made it problematic for Christians.

If we did not know the religious nature of the Roman army from Tertullian, we should learn it from the *Feriale Duranum*, a list of religious observances in the Roman army in 226 C.E. In the first nine months of the year, 17 public prayers and 44 animals (all but one a sacrifice of cattle) were offered.[55] One can see that there were many occasions on which a soldier's loyalties to Christ and Caesar could conflict, as the anonymous hero of Tertullian's *Treatise on the Crown* could attest. Helgeland suggests that Christians who survived their 20- or 25-year enlistment did it by Christian polytheism: "Mars is for victory, spring nymphs are for fresh water, Jupiter Dolichenus is for weapons that do not break in combat, and Christ is for when your weapon does break and you die."[56]

Lactantius' *Persecutors* 10 shows how some Christians coped with their mandatory presence at sacrifices" "[W]hile [Diocletian] sacrificed, some attendants of his, who were Christians, stood by, and they put the *immortal sign* on their foreheads. At this the demons were chased away, and the holy rites interrupted. The soothsayers trembled, unable to investigate the wonted marks on the entrails of the victims.

They frequently repeated the sacrifices, as if the former had been unpropitious; but the victims, slain from time to time, afforded no tokens for divination. At length Tages, the chief of the soothsayers, either from guess or from his own observation, said, 'There are profane persons here, who obstruct the rites.' Then Diocletian, in furious passion, ordered not only all who were assisting at the holy ceremonies, but also all who resided within the palace, to sacrifice, and, in case of their refusal, to be scourged; and further, by letters to the commanding officers, he enjoined that all soldiers should be forced to the like impiety, under pain of being dismissed [*sic*] the service."[57]

Tertullian's *Apology* 5.6, *Ad Scapulam* 4 (cf. Eusebius' *Chronicle* 238 olymp. 13, pp. 206–7, *HE* 5.5.3 ff.) showed a less negative attitude toward the military in mentioning the story of Legion XII *Fulminata*, called the "Thundering Legion" by Eusebius, that was suffering thirst during a battle near the Danube. Christians in the legion purportedly prayed successfully for rain and saved the legion. Cassius Dio 82.8.1–10.5 tells substantially the same story but gives the credit to Arnuphius, an Egyptian magician. The column of Marcus Aurelius also tells the story with Marcus praying successfully to Juppiter Pluvius. Hornus calls the story "either apocryphal or of doubtful authenticity"; refers to the detail of a legion "composed entirely of believers"[58] as legendary; alludes to authors who "recognized that there was no historical basis for the tale of a *Christian* legion which prayed for rain, had its prayer heard, and *for that reason* had received the name *Fulminata*"; and is astonished that those authors "nevertheless concluded that the account proved that during that period there were numerous Christians in the army."[59] Hornus devotes surprisingly little space to the story, perhaps because it does not support his pacifist position. Helgeland recognizes difficulties in the Christian version but thinks that part of the legion was with Marcus, who drew his Danubian force from Europe and North Africa, and that Christians were in the legion, whose base, Melitene, was in a "highly Christian" neighborhood.[60] Apparently this legion was saved by a sudden storm, and Christians tried to take credit for it. That Tertullian tells the story shows that his attitude toward Christians fighting for Rome when he wrote his *Apology* was less negative than when he wrote the Montanist *Treatise on the Crown* and suggests that there were many Christians in the army, as does Lactantius' *Persecutors* 11, in which Diocletian said to Galerius that in order to protect the empire, "it would be enough for him to exclude persons of that religion from the court and the army."[61]

Cyprian, like other Christians, uses military language. *Letter* 10 calls Christ the commander of the soldiers. Cyprian's *On the Exhortation to Martyrdom* 10 says that the devil commands an army against them. Cyprian's *Letter 25* says that while the imperial army drills soldiers, the church drills the soldiers of Christ. Cyprian/6, *Letter* 50 writes, "For this, moreover, is another confession of your faith and praise; . . . to seek anew the same camp whence you went forth, whence with the most vigorous strength you leapt forth to the battle to subdue the adversary. For the trophies from the battle-field ought to be brought back thither whence the arms for the field had been received, lest the Church of Christ should not retain those glorious warriors whom Christ had furnished for glory."[62] Cyprian's *Letter 55* says, "Should the battle first come, strengthened by us he will be found armed for the battle."[63] presumably referring to persecution. Reporting the martyrdom of Pope Sixtus II, Cyprian writes, "I ask that what I have reported be made known to our colleagues in the episcopate, so that by their exhortations our communities may be encouraged and ever more prepared for the spiritual combat. This will stimulate them to consider not so much death as the blessings of immortality, and to consecrate themselves to the Lord with ardent faith and heroic fortitude, to delight and not to fear at the thought of testifying their faith. The soldiers of God and of Christ know very well that their immolation is not so much a death but a crown of glory. To you, dear brother, my greetings in the Lord" (*Letter* 80).

Cyprian expresses antiwar sentiments along with positive images drawn from war. *To Donatus* 6 says, "When individuals slay a man, it is a crime. When killing takes place on behalf of the state, it is called a virtue."[64] In *On the Patience of Goodness* 14, Cyprian says, "[A]fter the reception of the Eucharist the hand is not to be stained with the sword and bloodshed."[65] However, Cyprian's *On Mortality* 2 appears to believe that wars are unavoidable.[66] Cyprian's *To Demetrian* 3 (cf. 17) says, "The husbandman fails and languishes in the fields, the sailor at sea, the soldier in the camp; honesty fails from the mart, justice from the tribunal, love from friendships, skill from the arts, and discipline from conduct,"[67] suggesting that soldiering is as legitimate as any other vocation. *Letter* 73 says, "It is the task of a good soldier to defend the camp against traitors and enemies of the emperor. It is the task of a glorious leader to preserve the standards entrusted to him."[68] This is an odd statement given the idolatrous devotion directed to the standards. *To Fortunatus* 13 says, "If it is a glorious thing for soldiers in the world to return home in triumph after defeat-

ing the enemy, how much more impressive and glorious is man's triumphant return to paradise following the devil's defeat."[69]

Athenagoras' *Plea for the Christians* 1.4 declares, "We have learned
not to return blow for blow or to take to court those who rob or plunder us. What is more, if they strike us abusively on one side of the
head, we have learned to offer the other as well and to give our cloak
to anyone who takes our tunic,"[70] espousing nonviolence. However, in
37.2–3 he seems to concede the right of the emperor and the army to
use force: "We pray for your reign in order that the succession may
pass from father to son, as is most fitting, and that your sway may
increase as everyone becomes subject to you [presumably by con-
quest]."[71]

An assertion of the church's peaceful character that is interesting
because couched in military language is found in Clement of
Alexandria's *Exhortation to the Greeks* 11.116–7: "When the blaring
trumpet sounds, it calls the troops together and proclaims war. Will
not Christ Himself who has played a melody of peace to the very ends
of the earth, gather together his own soldiers of peace? He did, indeed,
O man, assemble a bloodless army by means of his blood and his word,
and to that army he entrusted the Kingdom of Heaven. Christ's trumpet is his gospel. He blew it, and we heard. Let us put on the armor of
peace 'donning the breastplate of integrity' and taking up 'the shield
of faith' and putting on 'the helmet of salvation.' Let us whet 'the
sword of the spirit which is the word of God' (Eph. 6.14–17, Thess. 5.8).
In this fashion does the Apostle arrange us on the battlefield of peace.
Armed with invulnerable weapons like these, let us take our position
against the evil one."[72] In his *Miscellanies* 4.4.14, Clement says that
Christians venerate the martyrs just as the Greeks did their war dead,
so 6.14.112 approvingly likens Christians to soldiers, and *The Teacher*
compares Christ to the leader who "directs his troops on the line with
an eye to their safety."[73] *Exhortation to the Greeks* 10.100.2 narrates, "If
you are a farmer, we say, till the earth, but acknowledge the God of
farmers; if you love seafaring, sail on, but remember to call upon the
celestial Helmsman. If you were in the army when you were seized by
the knowledge of God, obey the commander who gives just commands."[74] What does it mean that Clement tells the farmer and the
sailor to continue their trades but omits to tell the soldier that? The
passage sounds a little like 1 Corinthians 7:17–31, in which Paul says
that everyone should remain in the state in which one came to Christ,
circumcised or not, slave or free (though Paul says that if a slave can
become free, the slave should do it), married or not, but one should live

as if one were not in the state in which one is, "[f]or the form of this world is passing away." On the other hand, Clement writes of the trades of the farmer and sailor in the present tense but of that of the soldier in the past. Clement leaves it unclear whether the soldier is to remain a soldier.

To Celsus' criticism as to who would defend the Roman Empire if all were Christians (Origen, *Against Celsus* 8.68), Origen rejoined, "Indeed let everyone do the same as I in rejecting Homeric teaching [i.e., that the god Kronos confers temporal power] but preserving the notion of the divine right of the emperor and obeying the injunction, 'Honor the king' (1 Peter 2.17). If this were to happen, the emperor would not be 'left alone or be deserted and earthly affairs be in the hands of the most lawless and uncivilized barbarians.' If, as Celsus says, everybody followed my lead, it is clear that the barbarians themselves, once converted to God's word, would become most law-abiding and civilized. All cults would be done away with and only the Christians' would survive. Someday Christianity will be the only cult because the Word is ceaselessly *conquering* [emphasis added; note the military term] more and more souls.[75] Further, "[i]f all the Romans were convinced and prayed, they would be superior to their enemies, or would not even fight wars at all, since they would be protected by divine power" (*Against Celsus* 8.68–70).[76]

Nevertheless, Origen seems a pacifist: "[Jesus] considered it contrary to his divinely inspired legislation to approve any kind of homicide whatsoever" (*Against Celsus* 3.8).[77] Like most early Christians, he concedes that the wars of the Israelites were approved by God but holds that that permission no longer applies: "Denying to the Jews of old, who had their own socio-political system and their own territory, the right to march against their enemies, to wage war in order to protect their traditions, to kill, or to impose some kind of punishment on adulterers, murderers, and others who committed similar crimes would have been nothing short of consigning them to complete destruction when an enemy attacked their nation because their own Law would have sapped their strength and would have forestalled their resistance. But Providence, which in an earlier time gave us the Law and now has given us the Gospel of Jesus Christ, did not want the Jewish system perpetuated and so destroyed the city of the Jews and their temple along with the divine worship that was celebrated there through sacrifices and prescribed rites" (*Against Celsus* 7.26).[78]

However, Origen, in *Homilies on Joshua* 15, also interprets Old Testament wars symbolically: "Unless those carnal wars [i.e., of the

Old Testament] were a symbol of spiritual wars, I do not think that the Jewish historical books would ever have been passed down by the Apostles to be read by Christ's followers in their churches. . . . Thus the Apostle, being aware that physical wars are no longer to be waged by us but that our struggles are to be only battles of the soul against spiritual adversaries, gives orders to the soldiers of Christ like a military commander when he says, 'Put on the armor of God so as to be able to hold your ground against the wiles of the devil' (Eph. 6.11)."[79] Origen, in *Against Celsus* 2.30, is thankful for the Roman Empire precisely because it has brought peace: "It is well known that Jesus was born in the reign of Augustus, who, one might say, brought the mass of mankind under a single sovereignty. The existence of many kingdoms would have hindered the spread of Jesus' teaching over the whole world not only for the reasons already cited but because everywhere men would have been forced to serve in the army and to go to war on behalf of their country. . . . How could this peaceful teaching, which prohibits a man from avenging himself even against his enemies, have gained sway if the whole world situation at the time of Jesus had not been made more peaceful."[80] *Against Celsus* 8.73 endorses the defense of the empire: "Indeed, the more pious a man is, the more effective he is in helping the emperors—more so than the soldiers who go out in the lines and kill all the enemy troops that they can," and since pagan priests do not serve in the army, Christians, who pray "taking up the whole armor of God . . . for those who fight in a righteous cause and for the emperor who reigns righteously, in order that everything which is opposed and hostile to those who act rightly may be destroyed," thereby "fight on behalf of the emperor" and form "a special army of piety"[81] and should not be in the imperial army. Origen's military language is typical for early Christians, but his concession that the empire ought to be defended and its enemies destroyed makes his pacifism questionable.

Arnobius, in *Against the Pagans* 1.6, takes the position that for Christians it is preferable "to shed one's own blood rather than pollute one's hands and one's conscience with the blood of another."[82] However, responding to the accusation that the Christians had brought disaster on the empire, Arnobius states that in the three centuries of the church's existence, "there were countless victories over conquered enemies, and nations which had never been heard of were brought under *our* [emphasis added] control,"[83] suggesting his loyalty to Rome. That not all early Christians were pacifists is also suggested by the Christian appeal to the Roman government against

Paul of Samosata. After Paul was condemned by the church, he refused to vacate the church building. In response, the church petitioned the emperor Aurelian, who evicted Paul in 272 (Eusebius, *HE* 7.30.19).

As we leave the period before Constantine, in which Christian aggression was overwhelmingly verbal, it is profitable to consider what Harnack says: "Priests and warriors, monks and warriors—one can place the whole history of the world under these headings, as Hans Delbrück has shown in a spirited presentation. They are opposites, or poles, which at once repel and attract. If the forms of the military estate are transferred to the higher religions, it appears that what is warlike is turned around and changed into its strict opposite or transformed into a mere symbol. But the form has its own logic and its necessary consequences. At first unnoticeably, but soon ever more clearly, the warlike element which was accepted as a symbol ushers in the reality itself, and the 'spiritual weapons of knighthood' become carnal. Even where the process does not go so far, a warlike mood enters which threatens the norm of gentleness and peace. The bellicose champion of orthodoxy is as well known in the history of the church as the aggressive ascetic and pietist. They believe that they are fighting the battles of the Lord, and they try to inflict frightful wounds. The history of 'the watchmen of Zion' (*der Zionswächter*) is the darkest chapter of church history."[84] Harnack also says that the apocalyptic vision of "the war at the end of days" prevented a complete Christian abstention from war[85] and that the concept of spiritual warfare prepared the way for holy war.[86]

Besides the theoretical, one should examine the practical way in which Christians dealt with military service. We have already had one instance of this in the soldier who occasioned Tertullian's *Treatise on the Crown*. Helgeland presents five accounts of military martyrs which he considers genuine. Around 260 C.E., St. Marinus was about to be promoted to centurion; thus, he must have been under arms for a considerable time; Eusebius (*HE* 7.15) says that he "had been honoured with many posts in the army."[87] A soldier who wanted the promotion for himself denounced Marinus as a Christian who would not sacrifice to the emperors. Given three hours to renounce Christianity, during which he was advised by the bishop of Caesarea, Marinus refused and was beheaded. Paradoxically, this account makes clear that Christians could survive and thrive in the army since Marinus was about to be promoted after long service. The bishop does ask Marinus to choose between a copy of the gospels and his sword, but if pacifism were the issue, it seems that the bishop would have presented the choice earlier in Marinus' career.

In the *Acts of Maximilian* (Mauretania, 12 March 295), Helgeland thinks that the issue was "the religious symbolism involved in the military, in particular the lead seal, which probably had the bust of the emperor struck on it."[88] But Maximilian says before the seal is presented, "I cannot serve because I am a Christian."[89] He does object to the seal, but in terms of opposition between Christ and the world. When Dion, the proconsul, points out that other Christians are in the army and asks what wrong they commit, Maximilian answers that Dion knows, leaving us in the dark as to what Maximilian's objection to the Roman army was. Maximilian was perhaps an extreme case: he was not asked to renounce Christianity, and he and his father thanked God for his death sentence.

The *Acts of Marcellus* describe an incident that took place on 30 October 298; they say, correctly, that the Augusti were Diocletian and Maximian but give the Caesars as Constantine and Licinius, who took office in 305 and 308, respectively, after the resignation of Diocletian and Maximian. Marcellus was a centurion of the first cohort, "indicating that he had been centurion long enough and had a clean record in order to be promoted that high."[90] Marcellus had thrown down his centurion's staff, belt, and sword before the legionary standards during a birthday celebration for the emperors and said, "[T]hat I could not fight by any other oath, but solely for the Lord Jesus Christ, Son of God almighty . . . it is not proper for a Christian, who fears Christ the Lord, to fight for the troubles of this world."[91] Another version has Marcellus saying, "I serve in the army of the eternal king, Jesus Christ, and from now on I cease to be a soldier of your emperors. And I disdain the worship of your gods made out of wood and stone because they are images that are deaf and dumb."[92] Since it is not clear that Marcellus' fighting for Jesus would include killing, perhaps we have in Marcellus a Christian pacifist. However, he may not have been a pacifist at all but rather a soldier who refused the idolatry of emperor worship in the form of idolizing the military standards bearing the emperor's portrait or bust. This seems to be the greater likelihood.

Dasius was beheaded for refusing to sacrifice to Diocletian and Maximian. As does Marcellus, Dasius says, "I do not fight for any earthly king but for the king of heaven."[93] As with Marcellus, this may imply pacifism. But Dasius has another motive, too. After all, as he was marched to execution and the guards tried to force him to sacrifice, Dasius scattered the incense, threw down the emperors' images, stomped on them, and crossed himself. Antipathy to idolatry as much as to killing may have been Dasius' motive. Dasius' executioner was Ioannes Anicetus. Does the name Ioannes indicate Christianity?

Julius the Veteran was beheaded in 303 for refusing to sacrifice to the gods. It is difficult to present Julius as a pacifist. Julius testifies to the judge: "In all the twenty-seven years in which I made the mistake, so it appears, to serve foolishly in the army, I was never brought before a magistrate either as a criminal or a trouble-maker."[94] Julius shows some regret along with pride for his long army service. Julius' next sentence is even less amenable to a pacifist position: "I went on seven military campaigns, and never hid behind anyone nor was I the inferior of any man in battle."[95] Julius' next statement, taken with those just quoted, is likewise incompatible with Christian pacifism: " 'I was in the army,' answered Julius, 'and when I had served my term I reenlisted as a veteran. All of this time I worshipped in fear the *God who made heaven and earth* (Acts 4:24), and even to this day I show him my service.' "[96] So here we have a man who for more than a quarter century was simultaneously a brave and *deadly* ("nor was I the inferior of any man in battle") soldier and a self-defined Christian. He seems to have retained the esteem of his comrades even in his rejection of the army cult: "[E]veryone kissed him."[97] Julius seems also to have been preceded in his martyrdom by one fellow soldier and followed by another, both of whom approved of Julius. A legitimate question is how Julius dealt with the army cult in the 27 years before his rejection of it, which resulted in his execution. In the places and time (ca. 276–303) in which Julius served, nonparticipation in the military cult was perhaps winked at. Surely the persecution initiated by Diocletian (303–313) reversed a limited toleration of Christian soldiers.

It has been suggested that in the early Christian period, Roman army service did not imply killing, that service only implied police work,[98] but Helgeland rightly objects that police work was not nonviolent; it included "raids on people's homes, battles against robbers, and the questioning (torture) of suspects."[99] I would only add that police work would presumably include capturing, guarding, and conveying prisoners for execution.

Lactantius, in his *Divine Institutes* 6.20, appears to begin as a pacifist: "For when God forbids us to kill, He not only prohibits us from open violence, which is not even allowed by the public laws, but He warns us against the commission of those things which are esteemed lawful among men. Thus it will be neither lawful for a just man to engage in warfare, since his warfare is justice itself, nor to accuse any one of a capital charge, because it makes no difference whether you put a man to death by word, or rather by the sword, since it is the act of putting to death itself which is prohibited. Therefore, with regard to this precept of God, there ought to be no exception at all; but that it is always unlawful to put to death a man, whom God wished to be a sacred animal."[100] In 6.6, he characterizes war as a zero-sum game in which there is no virtue: "[F]or what are the interests of our nation, but the inconveniences of another state or nation?—that is, to extend the boundaries which are violently taken from others, to increase the power of the state, to improve the revenues,—all which things are not virtues, but the overthrowing of virtues: for in the first place, the union of human society is taken away, innocence is taken away, the abstaining from the property of others is taken away."[101]

Co-opted by the Empire of Constantine and His Imperial Church

However, in *Deaths of the Persecutors*, Lactantius' orientation to war has been changed by the conversion of Constantine. Chapter 16 addresses the confessor (a Christian who suffered but did not die for the faith), Donatus: "[I]n nine combats you subdued the devil and his chosen soldiers . . . how pleasing the spectacle to God, when he beheld you a conqueror, yoking in your chariot not white horses, nor enormous elephants [a reference to the victory parade of a Roman general], but those very men who had led captive the nations! . . . and this it is to be a soldier of Christ; a soldier whom no enemy can dislodge . . . from the heavenly camp."[102] Lactantius' conclusion (chapter 52) also uses military language: "Let us therefore with exultation celebrate the triumphs of God, and oftentimes with praises make mention of His victory; let us in our prayers, by night and by day, beseech Him to confirm for ever that peace which, after a warfare of ten years, He has bestowed on His own."[103] In this work Lactantius becomes a virtual cheerleader for Licinius and Constantine, who espoused the Christian cause.

Lactantius sees the victories of Constantine and Licinius as divinely ordained. *Divine Institutes* 1.1 was written after Constantine's vindication of the church, while the pacifist passages date from before that: "For when that most happy day had shown upon the world, in which the Most High God raised you to the prosperous height of power, you entered on a dominion which was salutary and desirable for all with an excellent beginning, when, restoring justice which had been overthrown and taken away, you expiated the most shameful deed of others. In return for which action God will grant you happiness, virtue, and length of days, that even when old you may govern the state with the same justice with which you began in youth, and may hand down to your children the guardianship of the Roman name, as you yourself received it from your father."[104]

Persecutors 18, praising Constantine, notes his military skill: "Constantius also had a son, Constantine, a young man of very great worth, and well meriting the high station of Caesar. The distinguished comeliness of his figure, his strict attention to military duties, his virtuous demeanour and singular affability, had endeared him to the troops, and made him the choice of every individual." In *Persecutors* 44, before the battle of Milvian bridge, Constantine's affiliation with Christ is stressed: "Constantine was directed in a dream to cause *the heavenly sign* to be delineated on the shields of his soldiers, and so to proceed to battle. He did as he had been commanded, and he marked on their shields the letter X, with a perpendicular line drawn through it and turned round thus at the top, being the cipher of CHRIST. [*sic*] . . . The hand of the Lord prevailed, and the forces of Maxentius were routed."[105] Chapters 46 to 47 give in much more detail the role of the Christian God in the battle between Licinius and Maximin Daia: "The armies thus approaching each other, seemed on the eve of a battle. Then Daia made this vow to Jupiter, that if he obtained victory he would extinguish and utterly efface the name of the Christians. And on the following night an angel of the Lord seemed to stand before Licinius while he was asleep, admonishing him to arise immediately, and with his whole army to put up a prayer to the Supreme God, and assuring him that by so doing he should obtain victory. Licinius fancied that, hearing this, he arose, and that his monitor, who was nigh him, directed how he should pray, and in what words. Awaking from sleep, he sent for one of his secretaries, and dictated these words exactly as he had heard them: 'Supreme God, we beseech Thee; Holy God, we beseech Thee; unto Thee we commend all right; unto Thee we commend our safety; unto Thee we commend our empire. By Thee we live, by Thee we are victorious and happy. Supreme Holy God, hear our prayers; to Thee we stretch forth our arms. Hear, Holy Supreme God.' Many copies were made of these words, and distributed amongst the principal commanders, who were to teach them to the soldiers under their charge. At this all men took fresh courage, in the confidence that victory had been announced to them from heaven. . . . Accounts came that Daia was in motion; the soldiers of Licinius armed themselves, and advanced. A barren and open plain, called *Campus Serenus*, lay between the two armies. They were now in sight of one another. The soldiers of Licinius placed their shields on the ground, took off their helmets, and, following the example of their leaders, stretched forth their hands towards heaven. Then the emperor uttered the prayer, and they all repeated it after him. The host, doomed to speedy destruction, heard the murmur of the prayers of their adversaries. And now, the ceremony having been thrice performed, the soldiers of Licinius became full of courage, buckled on their helmets again, and resumed their shields . . . so the two armies drew nigh; the trumpets gave the signal; the military ensigns advanced; the troops of Licinius charged. But the enemies, panic-struck, could neither draw their swords nor yet throw their javelins. . . . Then were the troops of Daia slaughtered, none making resistance; and such numerous legions, and forces so mighty, were mowed down by an inferior enemy. No one called to mind his reputation, or former valour, or the honourable rewards which had been conferred on him. The Supreme God did so place their necks under the sword of their foes, that they seemed to have entered the field, not as combatants, but as men devoted to death. . . . One half of [Daia's] army perished in battle, and the rest either surrendered to the victor or fled."[106]

Eusebius (*HE* 9.9.5–8, cf. also Eusebius, *Life of Constantine* 1.39) is even more explicit in his approval of Constantine's military activities: "Just as in the time of Moses himself and the ancient God-fearing race of Hebrews the chariots and army of Pharao [*sic*], the pick of his horsemen, were hurled by God into the Red Sea and were drowned there and covered by the depths (Ex. 15.4–5), so, too, Maxentius 'plunged into the depths like a stone,' together with his soldiers and bodyguard as he was in the act of retreating before the divine power accompanying Constantine and was crossing the river in front of him. He himself had spanned this river quite effectively with pontoon boats and in doing so had wrought his own destruction. Thus, we might apply to him the words, 'He dug a pit, hollowed it out and fell into the hole he had made. His efforts shall come back on his own head and his wrongdoing shall fall upon himself' (Ps. 7.15–16). . . . [All of this was done] so that those who had received a victory from God might fittingly emulate, in deed if not in word, the followers of the great servant Moses and sing the same hymns that were recited of old against the ungodly tyrant: 'Let us sing to the Lord. He has covered himself in glory; horse and rider he has cast into the sea. The Lord is my helper and protector; he is my salvation' (Ex. 15.1–2). And, 'Who is like you, magnified in holiness, marvelous in glorious deeds, worker of wonders?' (Ex. 15.11)."[107]

In *Life of Constantine* 1.6 (cf. 1.46), Eusebius points out that Constantine's final victories came *after* his conversion to Christianity: "He accomplished this and publicized it like a good and faithful servant, openly proclaiming himself a slave and freely acknowledging that he was subject to the Ruler of All. God soon rewarded him by making him lord and master, the only victor among all those who had held power who was unconquered and unconquerable. God made him such a consistently triumphant ruler and glorious victor over his enemies that no one ever heard the like of him in human memory. Beloved by God and supremely blessed, he was so reverent and fortunate that he subdued with greatest ease more nations than any previous emperor, and he kept the realm intact up to the very end."[108] Indeed Constantine calls Christ "his ally" in *Historia Ecclesiastica* 9.9.2.[109]

It seems that once the emperor Constantine espoused Christianity, Christian objections to military service evaporated, suggesting that they were situational rather than principled. But according to Hornus, Canon 3 of the Council of Arles in 314, "[a]bout these who throw away their arms in peace, it is right that they be kept away from communion," forbade Christians from deserting the army in peacetime but tacitly allowed them to refuse to fight. According to Hornus, in order to avoid conflict with the church's patron, Constantine, the church banned desertion in peacetime but was silent on the more important prohibition on killing in battle.[110] This interpretation makes the bishops at Arles a bit cowardly and hypocritical. They tell Christian soldiers not to desert in order to avoid conflict with the emperor, but they say nothing about killing in battle, which, on Hornus' reading, the bishops thought could bring damnation on the soldier.

Indeed once Christians controlled the state, they so enthusiastically embraced violence that great crimes in the name of Christ cast doubt on the Christian message. They began by fighting each other. The Donatists, who refused to accept repentant clergy who had formerly given way to apostasy when persecuted, appealed to the government against the Catholics and resorted to violent rebellion when the government ruled against them. The Donatists appealed to Constantine to remove Caecilian as bishop of Carthage.[111] Constantine ruled against[112] and persecuted the Donatists.[113] The persecution lasted about one year, and within a decade the Donatists felt strong enough to seize the Catholic basilica in the city of Constantinople.[114] Purpurius of Limata, a Donatist bishop, killed two nephews and threatened to kill all his opponents.[115]

From the Donatists arose the Circumcellions. These violently obstructed both the collection of debts and the distribution of imperial charity. They also threw masters from their chariots and forced them to run ahead of their slaves, now placed in the chariots. They also tied masters to mills and forced them to turn them. Some Circumcellions pursued "martyrdom" by inducing others to kill them or by jumping off mountains or into water. Augustine also speaks of their "massacres."[116] Donatists called for the assassination of Augustine.[117] The Donatist bishop Primian had a priest thrown down a drain, sent a gang to destroy houses, incarcerated clergy and had them stoned, had lay ministers beaten, was protected from interview by police, and seized properties by force and by official support.[118]

Beginning with Constantine, the Catholics persecuted the Donatists. Referring to Acts 23:12–35, in which Paul informs his Roman guards of a plot against him, and appealing to the *Theodosian Code* 16.5.21, the Council of Carthage in 404 asked the emperors to persecute the Donatists.[119] Augustine's *Letter* 93.5, 17–18, argues that coercion of heretics is valid because in a parable (Luke 14:16–24) the master tells his servants to compel people to come to his banquet, because God used coercion to convert St. Paul, and because Augustine's experience shows that coercion can make good Catholics out of heretics. The Donatist Petilian complained that the Donatists were persecuted and that the secular rulers were not to be trusted.[120] Augustine, in his *Petilian* 2.92.203–13, points out that the Donatists appealed to the apostate emperor Julian for return from exile, a sure sign of their heretical nature, deserving repression by Orthodox Christians.

Augustine set forth the doctrine of the *just war*, in which Christians could serve in good conscience. In the particular case of Boniface, the Roman governor, who wanted to become a monk on the death of his wife, the 67-year-old Augustine traveled more than 600 kilometers to urge Boniface in person to remain a soldier. Augustine also considered the question of war primarily in three of his writings. In *Against Faustus*, he answered the Manichaean criticism of the Israelite God for having commanded war contrary to Jesus' pacifism. The wars of the Israelites and of the Christian Roman emperors show that God controls earthly goods. The deaths of Christ and his followers show that earthly goods should be given up for heavenly goods. War is morally neutral. Death, being inevitable, is troubling only for the coward. The evil of war is only in lust for power, ferocity, savagery, and cruelty. Rulers and soldiers can fight for God.[121] Boniface asked Augustine whether the Donatists should be persecuted. Augustine replied that a Christian ruler should treat religious schism as he would political revolt. Christ authorized force in the parable of the wedding guests who were forced to attend and used force to convert Paul.[122]

Augustine expressed his most complete understanding of war in *City of God*, book 19. One city is formed by love of self, the other by love of God. They are not coterminous with the Roman Empire and the church, which contained both the chosen and the damned. Earthly peace is the goal of the earthly city and a foreshadowing of heavenly peace, which will exist in the Kingdom of God. "Christians will engage in war to secure the earthly peace and will suffer war as a means to heavenly peace."[123]

Although the violence between the Donatists and Catholics is well documented, there are numerous other examples of Christian coercion in the late Roman period. In 348, Firmicus Maternus' *De Errore Profanarum Religionum* 29.1.2 quoted Deuteronomy 13:6–10, which prescribes the death of idolaters, in advising the emperors to eradicate paganism. Priscillian, bishop of Avila, was perhaps the first to be executed by Christians for heresy (385). *Codex Theodosius* 3.7.2 and 9.7.5 (388) prohibited marriage of Jews with Christians, 16.10.10 (391) prohibited pagan worship and imposed fines on officials who participated, and 16.5.21 (392) prescribed fines for free men and whipping and exile for slaves who participated in or permitted heretical meetings. Libanius' *Pro Templis* 8,9 (390) complains of monks who destroy temples. A Christian mob destroyed the Alexandrian lending library (391), the Serapion, murdering Olympius and his followers, and another murdered the notably beautiful and famously erudite Hellenistic Neoplatonist philosopher, Hypatia (415). They dragged her from her chariot into the church on a fatal day in the holy season of Lent (Socrates, in his *Historia Ecclesia*, cf. also Gibbon, *Decline and Fall*, 816–817), stripped her naked on the altar, slaughtered her with weapons of broken pottery, and set her quivering remains on fire.

There were after Constantine some Christians who espoused pacifism. St. Martin of Tours served in the army for over 20 years. When

the commander, later emperor, Julian made a donative to his troops
on the eve of battle, Martin announced that as a Christian he would
not accept the gift or fight. Julian accused Martin of cowardice, so
Martin offered to break through the enemy line without weapons or
armor. He was put under guard so that he would have to make good
his offer, but the next day the enemy surrendered.[124] It is interesting
that Martin's pacifism is vindicated in a bloodless victory. Again we
see the *ambivalence* of Christian pacifism.

From Persecuted to Persecutor

The transformation of the early Christians from persecuted to persecutors set the stage for the later church. The conversion of the
Saxons, the last German pagans, was due less to the ministry of St.
Boniface and more to the campaigns of Charlemagne, called the
"Butcher of Saxons." The Crusades proper were perhaps not culpable
in principle. After all, the Muslims had taken the Holy Land and
other Christian areas by force, but the execution of the Crusades was
appalling. Since crusaders were going to kill non-Christians in
Palestine, they often started by killing Jews at home. When the crusaders captured Jerusalem in 1099, they killed Muslims, Jews, and
native Christians indiscriminately. Actually this reflects military
practice going back to Old Testament times. Deuteronomy 20:10–18
prescribes that when the Israelites come against a city outside the
Promised Land, they should enslave the inhabitants if they surrender.
If the city resists, the "males" should be killed, but "the women and
the little ones, the cattle, and everything else in the city" can be taken
as "booty." However, in Palestinian cities the Israelites should "save
alive nothing that breathes." In Roman and medieval sieges the
inhabitants of a captured city could expect mercy only if they surrendered quickly. The longer the resistance, the greater the massacre
of the citizens. However, the Muslims were less bloodthirsty; when
Saladin recaptured Jerusalem in 1187, he enslaved rather than killed
the Christians. In contrast, Richard the Lion-Hearted massacred
thousands of noncombatants. In northern Europe, things were similar: the Teutonic Knights exterminated whole tribes. But mass murder was not unique to Christians; the Mongols were also feared for
exterminating their enemies.

The Crusades were mostly directed outward; the inquisitions were
directed inward. The inquisition of the thirteenth century and the
Albigensian Crusade inflicted great slaughter on southern France.
The Spanish Inquisition, founded at the end of the fifteenth century

by Ferdinand and Isabella, was a powerful instrument of repression. The Roman Inquisition, reorganized in 1542, was charged with suppressing Protestantism. More Protestants fell victim to the inquisitions than Christians to the Romans. As intimated in connection with the inquisitions, conflicts between Christians were especially vicious. Protestants and Catholics cooperated in hunting Anabaptists. But this cooperation did not blunt the savagery of the wars between Protestants and Catholics that occupied the last half of the sixteenth century and the first half of the seventeenth. One-third of the population of Germany, the principal arena of these conflicts, perished in the Thirty Years' War. Disgust at this carnage issued in the principle of religious toleration.

It is questionable whether the slaughter of indigenous peoples by colonizing Europeans was a product of Christianity or of the technological advantage of the Europeans. In the case of the Americas, most of the victims of the Europeans were accidental: they died of European diseases. There were also efforts, by Catholic clergy in particular, to protect the Indians of the Americas. Father Bartolomé de Las Casas wrote the definitive exposé of the extermination of the natives of the Caribbean and persuaded Pope Paul III to declare that the Indians were free people and must not be converted by force. Between 1610 and 1768 in Paraguay and Brazil, the Portuguese Jesuits protected the natives from exploitation but did not prepare them for independence so that when the Jesuits were suppressed by the Spanish Catholics of Latin America, the Jesuit's Indian communities collapsed.

Slavery of Africans was justified by the theory that blacks were the cursed descendents of Ham (in Gen. 9:20–27 it is actually Ham's son Canaan who is cursed). On the other hand, in both the British Empire and the United States, Protestant Christians played a large role in the abolition of slavery. It was clearly the imperatives of Christianity that moved entire communities and eventually whole states and the United States as a nation toward that end in the nineteenth century.

The twentieth century was perhaps the bloodiest in history, and the role of Christianity must be assessed. World War I can be seen as a product of nationalism, which may owe something to the Israelite idea of the chosen people. But the Greeks and the Romans did not need the Bible to make their claim to being a superior breed or culture, and most peoples seem to see themselves as the best variety of humanity, so nationalism may also be traced to that. Starting as World War I was ending, Communism has perhaps more corpses on its account than any other system of thought. On the one hand, Marxism is a utopian vision which has roots in biblical prophecies of cataclysms that will usher into paradise. On the other hand, Communism has resolutely repressed religion in general and Christianity in particular. Although Communism has a greater total body count, Fascism can claim more victims per year for its fewer years in power. Japanese nationalism before and during World War II can be considered a species of Fascism and claimed millions of victims, especially in China, but it would be difficult to connect it to the biblical tradition. Nazism, however, with 12 million to 15 million intentional victims and millions more dead in the war that Hitler started, can be partly traced to Christianity. While Nazism was anti-Christian as well as anti-Jewish, Nazi hatred of Jews drew on the Christian tradition. For example, the Nazis republished Luther's two tracts against the Jews. Certainly Christian anti-Semitism made Nazi murder of Jews easier and its opposition the more delayed. On the other hand, anti-Semitism did not start with Christianity. Greek and Roman authors often expressed hostility toward Jews and tended to make "special arrangements" for them, sometimes constructive, often horrendously destructive.

Conclusion

So the biblical tradition has contributed to historical violence. The Hebrew Bible does not deal much with the problem of death. Not so the New Testament, which presupposes that Jesus entered immortality following his death. This seems to be good news, if it is true, but it has its less appealing side. Like the Jewish eschatology on which it drew, the Christian teaching asserted that while some would attain eternal bliss, others would receive eternal torment.

The Jewish eschatology took form in the struggle with foreign conquerors. For perhaps the first time, Jews died because they would not give up their religion. The belief arose not only that the nation would be restored by God but also that individuals who died in the conflict would be restored to life. In our study of Jewish martyrologies, we found five elements: belief that God wanted the martyr to die, desire of the martyr to die, fear of punishment motivating that desire, desire for revenge on the persecutor, and a certain sadomasochism. We found the same elements in Christian martyrology. We also found that Christian nonviolence was on the whole more prudential than pacifistic. Although some Christians condemned military service in principle because it was violent, others objected because it was idolatrous in practice. The New Testament uses military language and depicts Jesus and Christians, especially Paul, as friendly with Roman soldiers. Other ancient Christians attest that there were Christians in the imperial armies, speak of soldiers without censure, and even appeal to the government to use force against heretics. In sum, the early Christians were nonviolent because they knew they could not win an armed conflict against Rome.

Given the violent elements of Christian eschatology, the cult of martyrs, and the merely expedient nature of early Christian nonviolence, it should come as no surprise that when the Christians gained control of the Roman government, they used violence against their enemies and each other. From Constantine to the Spanish Inquisition, Christians have physically attacked their enemies. After the bloodbath of the early seventeenth century, the principle of religious toleration was adopted in Western Christianity, but it should not be forgotten that a large measure of religious toleration had been practiced a thousand years before in the Islamic world. Christianity has given much good to the world, and because of its focus on violence, this study has painted a rather dark picture of Christianity, but it is a picture that needs to be faced, examined, repented of, and transcended. It cannot be denied, ignored, justified, or glorified.

Notes

1. Theodore M. Ludwig, *The Sacred Paths of the West* (Upper Saddle River: Prentice Hall, 2001), 79–80.

2. S. A. Nigosian, *World Religions: A Historical Approach*, 3rd ed. (Boston/New York: Bedford/St. Martin's, 2000), 277.

3. Gizeh Papyrus.

4. Tacitus, *Annals*, 15.44.5 applied to Christians.

5. Alexander Roberts, James Donaldson, and A. Cleveland Coxe, eds., *Ante-Nicene Fathers* [hereafter *ANF*], vol. 7: *Lactantius, Venantius, Asterius, Victorinus, Dionnysius, Apostolic Teaching and Constitutions, 2 Clement, Early Liturgies* (Christian Literature Publishing, 1886; reprint, Peabody: Hendrickson Publishers, 1994), 309.

6. Jack Miles, *Christ: A Crisis in the Life of God* (New York: Alfred A. Knopf, 2001), 129.

7. J. Stevenson, ed., *A New Eusebius: Documents Illustrating the History of the Church to AD 337* [*sic*] [hereafter *NE*], rev. W. H. C. Frend (Cambridge: S.P.C.K., 1987), 1.

8. Ibid., 2; cf. 4 Maccabees 11:4.

9. Ibid., 13.

10. Ibid., 23–28.

11. Ibid., 34–43.

12. Lewis M. Hopfe, *Religions of the World*, 8th ed., rev. Mark W. Woodward (Upper Saddle River: Prentice Hall, 2001), 326–328.

13. Alexander Roberts and James Donaldson, eds., *Ante-Nicene Christian Library: Translations of the Writings of the Fathers down to A.D. 325* [hereafter *ANCL*], vol. 11: *The Writings of Tertullian* (Edinburgh: T. & T. Clark, 1869), 34–35.

14. *NE*, 249.

15. Ibid., 215.

16. Ibid., 216–217.

17. *ANF*, 7.305.

18. Ibid., 302.

19. Ibid.

20. Ibid.

21. Ibid., 303.

22. Ibid., 313.

23. Ibid., 314–315.

24. Ibid., 307.

25. Ibid., 317.

26. Ibid., 321.

27. Ibid.

28. Ibid., 321–322.

29. John Helgeland, Robert J. Daly, and J. Patout Burns, *Christians and the Military: The Early Experience* (Philadelphia: Fortress, 1985), say, "[Jesus'] preaching is an example of vivid teaching employing seemingly endless metaphors and parables, *yet none are drawn from military life*" (16; emphasis added).

30. Ibid., 46–47.

31. Peter Brock, *Varieties of Pacifism* (Syracuse: Syracuse University Press, 1998), 5.

32. Helgeland et al., *Christians and the Military*, 35.

33. Ibid., 35–36.

34. Ibid., 18.

35. Ibid.

36. *NE*, 36, 40.

37. *ANCL*, 11.118.

38. Ibid., 137–138.

39. Ibid., 110.

40. Ibid., 116.

41. Ibid., 125.

42. Ibid., 85.

43. Ibid., 170–171.

44. Ibid., 333.

45. Ibid., 333–334.

46. Ibid., 334.

47. Ibid.

48. Ernest Evans, *Tertullian's Treatise on the Resurrection* (London: S.P.C.K., 1960), 43.

49. *ANCL*, 11.347.

50. Ibid., 347–438.

51. Ibid., 350.

52. Ibid.

53. Ibid. 354–355.

54. Ibid., 334.

55. Helgeland et al., *Christians and the Military*, 51–53.

56. Ibid., 55.

57. *ANF*, 7.304–5.

58. Jean-Michel Hornus, *It Is Not Lawful for Me to Fight: Early Christian Attitudes toward War, Violence and the State*, rev. ed., trans. Alan Kreider and Oliver Coburn (Scottsdale: Herald Press, 1980), 129.

59. Ibid., 286 n. 73.

60. Helgeland et al., *Christians and the Military*, 33–34.

61. *ANF*, 7.305.

62. Helgeland et al., *Christians and the Military*, 19.

63. *NE*, 223.

64. Louis J. Swift, *The Early Fathers on War and Military Service*, vol. 19: *Message of the Fathers of the Church*, ed. Thomas Halton (Wilmington: Michael Glazier, 1983), 48.

65. Ibid.

66. Ibid., 49.

67. *NE*, 246.

68. Swift, *The Early Fathers*, 49.

69. Ibid.

70. Ibid., 35–36.

71. Ibid., 35.

72. Ibid., 50–51.

73. Ibid., 51.

74. Ibid., 52.

75. Ibid., 53.

76. Hornus, *It Is Not Lawful*, 83.

77. Helgeland et al., *Christians and the Military*, 39.

78. Ibid., 39–40.

79. Swift, *The Early Fathers*, 59.

80. Ibid., 54.

81. Hornus, *It Is Not Lawful*, 84.

82. Swift, *The Early Fathers*, 60.

83. Ibid., 61.

84. Adolf Harnack, *Militia Christi: The Christian Religion and the Military in the First Three Centuries*, trans. and intro. David McInnes Gracie (Philadelphia: Fortress, 1981), 31–32.

85. Ibid., 35.

86. Ibid., 63.

87. Helgeland et al., *Christians and the Military*, 57.

88. Ibid., 57–58.

89. Ibid., 58.

90. Ibid., 60.

91. Ibid., 60–61.

92. Swift, *The Early Fathers*, 74–75.

93. Helgeland et al., *Christians and the Military*, 62.

94. Ibid., 64.

95. Ibid.

96. Ibid.

97. Ibid., 65.

98. Henri Secrétan, "Le Christianisme des Premiers Siècles et le Service militaire," *Revue de Théologie et Philosophie* 2 (1914): 345–365; Roland Bainton, "The Early Church and War," *Harvard Theological Review* 39 (July 1946): 189–211; Hornus, *It Is Not Lawful*, 158; Stephen Gero, "Miles Gloriosus: The Christian and Military Service according to Tertullian," *Church History* 39 (September 1970): 285; Ramsay MacMullen, *Soldier and Civilian in the Later Roman Empire*, Historical Monographs Series, no. 52 (Cambridge: Harvard University Press, 1963), 1.

99. John Helgeland, "Christians and Military Service, A.D. 173–337," Ph.D. diss., University of Chicago, 1973, 133, cited in Harnack, *Militia Christi*, 14 n. 13.

100. *ANF*, 7.187.

101. Ibid., 169.

102. Ibid., 307.

103. Ibid., 322.

104. Ibid., 10.

105. Ibid., 318.

106. Ibid., 319–320.

107. Swift, *The Early Fathers*, 86.

108. Ibid., 87.

109. Ibid.

110. Hornus, *It Is Not Lawful*, 174–178.

111. Optatus, *On the Schism of the Donatists*, 1.22.

112. Augustine, *Contra Cresconium*, 3.82.

113. *Sermo de passione Donati*, 3.

114. Optatus, *Donatists*, app. 10.

115. Augustine, *Cresconium* 3.30; Optatus, *Donatists*, 1.19.

116. Optatus, *Donatists*, 3.4; Augustine, *Letter* 185.4.15.
117. Possidius, *S. Augustini Vita*, 9.
118. Letter of the Council of Cebarsussa.
119. *Codex Canonum Ecclesiae Africanae*, 93.
120. Augustine, *Against the Letters of Petilian*, 2.19.42, 92.202.
121. Helgeland et al., *Christians and the Military*, 80–83.
122. Ibid., 83–84.
123. Ibid., 84.
124. *Life of St. Martin*, 4.

CHAPTER 10

SECONDARY VIOLENCE:
ADDING INJURY TO INSULT

Dirk H. Odendaal

Three stories from my personal experience provide the setting for this chapter. While the stories differ widely, they are about the same thing—secondary violence and its nature, causes, and cures, particularly in the practice of the Christian religion. A very good friend still bears the scars of an experience that touched him indirectly. His family was large and dependent on the wages of his father, who was then a technician in a local industry. His mother was concerned about the future of one of her daughters, a bright, young girl who was at the point of completing high school. His mother went to see her local pastor for assistance despite being somewhat embarrassed by needing help. He replied to this black lady, "You know, you people should really learn to accept your position in life." It is not strange to say that they never went back to that church. My friend was not present for this pastoral abuse, but its secondary consequences violated his life and left scars and impairment from which he and his family were unable to recover completely.

My grandfather told me a story about his parents, members of a Reformed Church, who had attended revival meetings held by a charismatic group in their town around the beginning of the twentieth century. Their pastor subsequently called upon them and berated them for this inappropriate religious activity. Then they were disciplined by the church for attending these services. It is no surprise that they left that church for another.

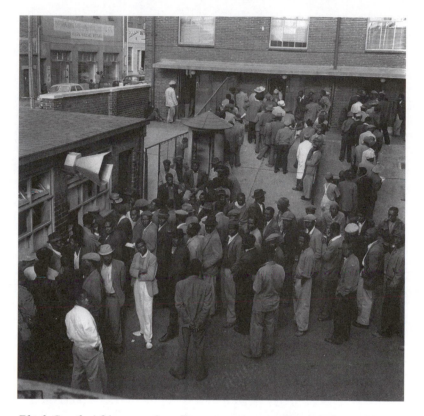

Black South African workers line up at a pass office in Johannesburg, South Africa, on April 8, 1960, to apply for new internal passbooks. The South African government enforced every black man to carry this document before he was allowed to move around the country and work. AP/Wide World Photos.

A pastor friend of mine was taken into custody by the South African police during a period in the apartheid years when emergency measures were in place. He was incarcerated in a prison near his pastorate, stripped naked, and held in solitary confinement. He felt humiliated and concerned about his family, as he was forbidden to contact them. They had no way of knowing that he was even alive. One of the most vivid memories he has of that period is being visited by a fellow minister of the Reformed Church who berated him for having turned against the apartheid government. He was reminded of biblical texts about obedience to the government, such as Romans 13, and urged to repent from his sinful ways. He was bitter about this for a long time. He remained in the church, but his mistrust of it also remains. The pain is still alive in his heart.

Secondary Violence

The point of these stories is that we inflict violence and abuse on people, often unwittingly, by the moral decisions that we make from positions of power, precisely when we may think we are trying to do the best good. The moral decisions can refer to religious, social, or moral beliefs that we try to impose on others or preserve in the society because we think them in the best interest of the community or the person. Sometimes, perhaps most of the time, our unconscious motivations are the preservation of a state of affairs that guarantees our privileged role or our position of power. This may result from the behavior of a pastor, therapist, counselor, judge, caseworker, or official of any kind. In the process of defending our position, we may inflict primary or secondary violence by words or deed. The violence is not our goal but rather a tool that we use consciously or unconsciously to achieve our goal. In some cases the goal is to protect vested interests, whether they be status, position, power, wealth, or privilege. Secondary violence can be caused with the best of intentions. This tragedy was transparent in many ways in the apartheid era of the Republic of South Africa, but it is present insidiously in every human community. The tragedy is compounded when religious communities or institutions are the perpetrators of this violation of persons, officially or incidentally.

The violence, on the one hand, can be very sophisticated and difficult to pinpoint. On the other hand, it may be extremely visible and crude. We often focus so completely on the official moral codes of the community that we lose sight of the more crucial immorality involved in the brutalization of interpersonal relations and society. The injury here is not experienced by the power people, but a closed hermeneutical circle is formed in which the belief leads to a principle, the principle leads to a code of action, and the action's regulatory outcome confirms the belief. The circle is closed because no new meanings are allowed to enter except those that are official doctrine or principle. Any information allowed into the circle must comply with the official understanding and is used to support the selected meanings and not to critique them. That is especially a characteristic of all forms of Fundamentalisms—Islamic, Judaic, Christian, or secular (Barr, 1984).

In my three stories, an official of some sort had to resolve an issue that was obviously of great importance to the people involved. There were several factors that had to be weighed in each situation, and the person of power had to come to a decision about what to do. He was in a position of power simply because he could make some good things happen for his people, and they trusted him to do so until he violated that trust. What was done in each case left damage that eventually affected the whole family or social constellation involved. The treatment of the perceived problem became the problem and led to more hurt; that is, the problem was "solved" for the power person by absorbing it into an ever increasingly larger problem. The tragedy was compounded in each of these cases by the fact that the injury was inflicted by persons who were identified as the agents of God in the lives of the suffering people.

When we speak of violence, images come to mind of people getting shot or physically mutilated, implying the possibility of death, images that are spectacular enough to be televised or printed in newspapers. Who can forget the images of the passenger planes flying into the World Trade Center in New York, the Twin Towers collapsing, or the aftermath of a bomb blast or combat. The daily television reports of the victims of conflict all around the world are graphically imprinted upon our minds. We are shocked by the violence that human beings have undergone. The past century is full of such images. In Africa we have no shortage of them, nor does the rest of the world.

Compared to such shocking experiences, can I still name as violence the kind of abuse that is the subject of my concern here? Is secondary violence really violence in any sense comparable to the physical horrors around the world? Are these secondary violations not just normal experiences of sensitive people? While secondary violence is usually subtle, the damage it inflicts is just as violating, devastating, pervasive, and wide reaching as the horrors created by a suicide bomber or a skilled and persistent sniper. My stories portray experiences that are not graphic and that happen out of the public eye. The secondary violence also is often committed by representatives of many of our most trusted institutions, the courts, the police, religious systems, and other institutions or social structures. Secondary violence is as common, insidious, and destructive as domestic violence.

Secondary Violence and Injury

Secondary violence is subtle and tacit and of course carries with it a form of respectability. Even when it is exposed, one tends to sympathize with the violator because of the reasonableness of the actions. He or she may have been in a difficult position not of his or her choice. At some stage all of us have been in a situation in which we became a violator or perpetrator of this form of violence. Violence always goes hand in hand with injury. We have to infer the violence from the injury we observe much of the time. Both the victim and the violator may actually be unaware of the extent of the violence in the encounter because of the sanction that such an event has from society. It may be cloaked as therapy, counseling, assistance, or the standard code. The injury is caused when members in need go to officials or authorities for support, and the official responds with some kind of guidance or action regarding the problem. The needs may be of a material nature or psychological or spiritual.

The injury that results from this type of violence is iatrogenic, induced by the action taken to solve the presenting problem (McLeod, 1985). When a physiotherapist has to treat a muscle injury, he or she may actually cause the injury to become chronic if it is treated inappropriately. To combat a life-threatening disorder, a surgeon may be so invasive as to irreparably damage healthy tissue, impairing the patient's function in other ways. Secondary violence is usually iatrogenic, induced by the erroneous treatment of the problem.

Secondary Violence in Therapy

O'Hanlon (1993) points out how clients can become injured in the process of a therapeutic encounter. The typical setting in which this violation takes place involves the use of "methods, techniques, assessment procedures, explanations and interventions that harm, discourage, invalidate, show disrespect, or close down the possibilities of change." This is not a positive approach that tries to minimize the real negative things that happen in the world and empower the constructive possibilities in the person or situation. In our therapeutic approaches, we can cause injury by focusing on the therapist's agenda rather than the patient's need. It may be that the therapist wants to give the client his or her insight, show up some inability in the client, or see the client as damaged goods. The patient may be blamed for his or her illness because of some bad or evil intention or characteristic. It may be that the client is seen as obstructing the work of the therapist and that these "barriers" have to broken down. In that sense the relationship becomes adversarial, and the therapist, as expert, is the power person in the relationship (O'Hanlon, 1993), hence dangerous, a potential violator.

Jenkins (1994) highlights the power issues involved when one becomes entangled in the criminal justice system. People from more privileged positions have more options to avoid welfare needs as well as police and justice intervention. People of less privilege are more likely to be apprehended. Thus, a myth is created that people who are financially disadvantaged are more likely to behave abusively. An economically "successful" businessman may be excused for his abusive behavior because of the important things he has on his mind. His high level of privilege gives him a high degree of credibility and frequently, even if temporarily, permits him to avoid accountability for his actions. Even the therapist working with people convicted of abusive behavior can continue this cycle of social injustice, taking a position of power in the interaction that assumes that the client is inherently inferior rather than simply troubled by a history of disapproved function. The recipe for the abusive encounter of the abuser in the first place and the relationship of the therapist and client have their inherent meaning against the background of an imbalance of power (Jenkins, 1994).

Structures of society give more privilege to people of approved status, position, race, and class. The violator is in a position of power as compared to the victim. Just the relationship of violator to victim highlights this power relationship. Because it is so subtle, the person in power is frequently insulated by accepted cultural practices from perceiving the violence involved. It would fall outside the norm to discontinue the standard social procedure. That does not mean that the violator is untouched by what happens. He or she might become aware of a sense of unease or feelings of guilt but have no other recourse, no other options for acting, except the standard practice unless he or she chose to heroically depart from what is generally conceived in that community as normal perspective and function.

In my three stories it would have been very difficult for the power persons operating in the official roles to have acted differently because it would have been expected of them that they would protect the established community attitudes, assumptions, styles, and procedures. Sometimes what is to be protected is the hard-earned financial resources of the community. In my friend's case, the third story, he was opposing the norms of society, and "he should have known better," especially because a policy such as apartheid had claimed some biblical support. The minister who visited him in prison would have assumed that the visit and the chastisement constituted a form of kindness for his well-being. He would have felt that he was doing his duty in service to his misguided colleague.

When we look closely at the example, there is no doubt as to who was in a position of power. This power was supplemented and certified with a good dose of moral sanction. In my friend's case, the minister who had come to see him had also received security clearance and acted with the sanction of the government of the day. Although both were ministers at that stage, my friend had less access to the "right" institutions and knowledge. By speaking out against an unjust society, he had also made enemies in places of power and restricted his ability to maneuver in that society in general. The minister who came to visit him would have operated with the assumption that he had developed a skill useful to his own advantage and that of his constituency or community.

How we act and the choices we make become second nature to us because of our embeddedness in society and society's embeddedness in us (Geertz, 1975). What this means for someone in a position of power is not only that he or she uses the power in a certain way but also that it is expected of him or her to act in this way. This power is maintained by the position, the formality of the language, the objectivity, and the impartiality in the position. When the person is cloaked or hidden in the position, he or she becomes culturally invisible as a person, in contrast to the visibility of the "offending other." Thus, the monopoly on power of the person of position is ensured. The position of power is compounded by a moral quality because he or she is not just an individual but also the representative of the society, of the cultural code, of the official institution, and of God in a certain way (White, 1995).

It is clear that there is no easy way out of this dilemma that we are in positions of power and are expected to use this power. It is similar to the dilemma of the surgeon who has to cause damage to healthy tissue in order to treat the infected or damaged tissue. I, from my position, find it difficult to understand the situation of the "victim," the person asking for help, because the neediness lies outside my realm of experiences and I am closed off from it. If I have positioned myself as an expert or official, it will become ever more difficult for me to change my approach because the insidious hermeneutical circle that is set up by the circumstances prevents me from getting any new information that might create new insight for me. The results of my actions will therefore start taking on the character of institutionalized and entrenched abuse and violence. In this position I will be protected from taking responsibility for the iatrogenic consequences of what I say and do because I in fact have become invisible to others and to myself, perhaps even to the victim, who will not know how to critique this standard procedure that violates him or her (White, 1995).

From this objective perspective, one can easily expect a victim of abuse to "accept his or her situation," "to get over it," to "do something about his or her situation." The official, in his or her involvement with the victim, loses sight of the fact that he or she has a position that gives access to resources and support that is not so readily available to the victim. The abuse and violence is even given different names, depending on where one stands in the violator-victim relationship. In the sanctioned position, the abuse will not be seen for what it is, secondary violence, a violation of the personhood and situation of the needy one. Other descriptions will be used to describe the act in which the position of the one in power is protected. "It was done with the best intentions!" (White, 1995). In the position of invisibility, the powerful will be unaware that he or she is being a violator. In being unaware, it becomes impossible to explore alternative possibilities of action. In the end, the loop of understanding remains closed and contributes to continuing a closed and unexamined loop of violence. It is clear that what I call secondary violence is difficult to define and involves our whole way of being as people in culture and society. People in power are especially susceptible to perpetrating acts of violence because they have become invisible in their positions and are cushioned from the effects of their actions.

Secondary Violence and Religion

Secondary violence as a phenomenon is not restricted to the secular world. The world of religion is an important part of society and therefore cannot expect to be exempt from the problems of society. Every human community is fraught with the violations addressed in this chapter. It would be expected that the situation described in this chapter would also be found in the world of religious practices regardless of the faith community.

Religious institutions and especially Christian institutions and practices place a very high premium on doctrine and moral codes; on how religious beliefs and faith shape ethical practices. Religious institutions have been entrusted by society as guardians of the moral code. Religions also place great emphasis on authority, leadership, and respect. Positions of leaders are also given additional sanction in that they are brought into relationship with the supernatural, with God and the authority and certification of God. Because people are seen as being called in a supernatural way to fill these roles and positions, they in fact easily become invisible as persons, and only God becomes visible in them. They become visible as god! This explains the great current tragedy of pedophilia in the Roman Catholic Church, a practice of violation and primary and secondary violence that depended for its pervasiveness and immunity directly upon the perception by the victims that the power person was not just a person but a god-person. However, directing a client on a course that proves to be destructive rather than healing is an equivalent violation for a therapist to perpetrate upon his or her victim. Although it is expected of officials, leaders, and practitioners to act sensitively and morally within their contexts, it is also easy to see how fraught with danger their roles can be, whether in a religious or secular position, in that they may be seduced by the standard system into failing to take responsibility for the roles that make their humanness and individuality invisible.

Iatrogenic abuse is such an insidious practice that the violators are not always even aware of what they are doing and of the devastating effect it has on the lives of other people. It is sometimes cloaked as rendering a service and as serving the interests of the community. In order for us to look at this problem from a religious context, it is useful to look at how this phenomenon is portrayed in texts in the Hebrew Bible and New Testament. Here we are confronted by texts that clearly show how an attempt to solve a problem may turn into a way of inflicting violence on the object of the action. The issue, in each text, is a combination of the function of power and of sanctioned position. This is also true in church history and present-day religious institutions.

Secondary Violence in the Old Testament

Violence is graphically portrayed in many of the narratives and sermons of the Bible, mostly in a very direct way as the result of some tragic confrontation. A Hebrew Bible example of an agent's action resulting in horrid secondary violence is the narrative of Jephthah's daughter who became the inadvertent victim of her fathers misguided piety (Judg. 11:29–40). A second example is the first

Philistine wife of Samson who was burned to death with her family as retribution for Samson's behavior in supposed defense of his community (Judg. 14:1 ff.). Another example that comes to mind is the narrative of Samuel rebuking Saul (1 Sam. 13:1–15) for not waiting as he was told to do by this divinely sanctioned authority, Samuel, the prophet.

An interesting example of secondary violence can be found in the book of Job in the Hebrew Bible. The text of Job presents us with a framework in prose (the prologue in chapters 1–2 and the epilogue in 42:7–17), straightforward narrative sections framing a much longer poetic core (chapters 3–42:6). Of interest to us are the relationships portrayed in the text: between Job and his wife and between Job and his four friends, Eliphaz, Bildad, Zophar, and Elihu. In a sense the course of the relationship of the four friends is already implied in the words that come from Job's wife at the beginning of the poetic section of the book.

After the poetic narrative describes the terrible catastrophes inflicted upon Job, the tragic loss of his property, his children, and his health, Job is shown sitting on the ash heap scraping himself with a piece of pottery (Job 2:7), symbols of abject grief, hopelessness, and degradation. His lethal skin disease would have ostracized him from his community in accordance with the social prescriptions of the day (Lev. 13:1 ff.). His position and status has changed drastically from being a wealthy and respected person to someone who was suddenly homeless and without any support. In Job 2:9 we infer from the words that his wife spoke that Job still remains faithful to God. She reviles him for "hanging on to his integrity." "Curse God and die," she spits at him.

Her reaction and her words about his position are shocking—instead of consolation, an urge to suicide. She suggests that he curse God and die. According to Pentateuchal law, blaspheming the Name of Lord was punishable by stoning to death (Lev. 24:10 ff.), a case of secondary violence. Job is helpless, terminally ill, without any support system. What his wife says can only add to his misery at best. In a sense one can try to understand her point. Because they are living in a patriarchal society, she is totally dependent on him for her social status and situation. Within a patriarchal society, the lot of the wife rests on the well-being and status of the husband.

What she says appears to be extremely callous and injurious, but look at the relationship. Her status and well-being depend upon Job's status and well-being. Her position of power is equivalent to his in that regard. Her only advantage of power is that she is well, and he is dying and alienated from the community, any support system, and resources of healing. She recognizes that he is still alive and still a man with integrity. In her discourse his life and death are juxtaposed. Both are acknowledged and raised as possibilities of choice. In saying this, she indicates that she thinks that Job still has *agency* in his life. Job's response then indicates that he does not see her words as being so terrible, and he responds by explaining to her why he has not done as she suggests. It might be that he can see her as part of his calamity and also sympathize with her in her frustration. He responds to her, "Shall we receive good from the hand of God, and not also receive the evil that comes?"

When his four friends, Eliphaz, Bildad, Zophar, and Elihu, visit Job, he comes close to following his wife's suggestion. It is not what they say that sets off his reaction but rather what they do. They are so distraught about what they see that they weep aloud, tear their robes, and throw dust in the air and on themselves. They also keep to the standard time for mourning for the dead, namely, seven days (Job 2:11–13). In other words, they actually start a mourning ritual at the sight of him and, without saying a word, pronounce him dead. Job is seen as a person who has now lost all possibilities for living and for choice.

It is in response to this "sign," this symbolic activity, that Job reacts. His first speech opens the discussion that takes place in the poetical section of the book. It is in how they keep quiet in his presence that he sees the desperateness of his own situation. Not only has he just lost his wealth, his health, and his place in community, but he sees himself through their eyes ("because they saw how great his suffering was"). It is when he looks at himself in this way that he appears to lose hope. He curses his birth date and all the elements that made his birth possible (Job 3:3 ff.), declaring that if God were just or merciful, he would have seen to it that Job was stillborn. Job is, in fact, indirectly cursing God the Creator.

From the poetical cycles that follow, for 38 chapters or so, we are informed about Job's contribution to his situation, his fault as seen through the eyes of his friends. With cause-and-effect argument, they challenge Job to reflect on what it is that he did that brought this calamity upon him. With circular moral arguments, designed to justify God in the face of the problem of pain, they point out what they claim is his guilt, as the sufferer, for causing the suffering. The innocent cannot suffer like this since God is just (Clines, 1989). Eliphaz argues that Job's suffering is temporary and purifying since his sin is unconscious and unknown to himself. Bildad adds to this argument that Job's children were punished for their wickedness, but the fact that Job is still living is proof that he is less guilty and is being chastised for being unrepentant of ordinary sins. Zophar, however, expresses the opinion that Job must be a terrible sinner and that his suffering is the result of his sin. God knows all, and he punishes people for their sin as he blesses those who are righteous; witness the providentially prospering status of the four friends, another good reason to listen to them. Elihu, a later entrant to the discussion (Job 32:1 ff.), is of the opinion that the suffering inflicted on people is a way in which God reveals himself to humans so that they can confess their sins and be restored by God into life and society (Clines, 1989). Even if they are not particularly sinful, confession is good for the soul, and we grow from our pain.

The relationships between Job, his wife, and his four friends are examples of secondary violence. The friends or companions are in a position of power; they also take a moral position, and what they say is done with the overt purpose of helping Job but in fact "puts him in his place" and contributes to the injury that he is already experiencing. Is it any wonder that Job finds no peace and health in the "corrections and consolations" of his companions or equals? If he finally finds some consolation and meaning, it is rather ambiguous, but it is found only in his relationship with God and the meaning issues that contemplating God raises in his spirit and sets before him (Job 40:6–34).

Secondary Violence in the New Testament

We can infer the occurrence of secondary violence in the New Testament texts from the Gospels particularly. The gospel of Luke, the physician, shows interest in how such injury was caused (Geldenhuys, 1962). Jesus frequently tried to prevent secondary injury as is portrayed in Luke 5:12–15. Jesus healed a man of leprosy and commanded him to tell no one, thus avoiding controversy that might be painful for both of them (Luke 5:14). Jesus did the same in stories of healing men of demon possession (Luke 4:35, 41). After Jesus' work became public knowledge and the Pharisees and Scribes began criticizing him and conspiring against him, Jesus encouraged his patients to tell everyone. However, in Luke 9:37–42 we have a story of Jesus curing a demon-possessed man who was violently thrown to the ground before the demon left him, a case of secondary violence if ever there was one (Sanders, 1987).

Moreover, in John 9, Jesus healed a blind man on the Sabbath. He could have done on any other day of the week. Because he chose the Sabbath, the religious leaders accosted the healed man and charged him and his healer of breaking the Sabbath law, casting the healed man out of the congregation and alienating him from his community and his family. One wonders whether his state of affairs may have been better blind than healed in this mode. Moreover, it appears that Jesus chose the Sabbath just to make a political and ethical point and call attention to himself as a revolutionary. He seems to have used the poor blind man, having no consideration for his well-being, which could have been ensured by healing him on Tuesday instead. In that case, everyone would have rejoiced, including the religious leaders. This is secondary violence consciously perpetrated by Jesus in exactly the way it is so often caused in our day by thoughtless or insensitive people in positions of authority.

Moreover, the authorities, in their intent on preserving the Deuteronomic law of the Sabbath, are willing to be very destructive to the healed man for the sake of enhancing the long-term well-being of the community and its religiosocial and ethical order. So the man is a victim of secondary violence from both sides of the fight between Jesus' claims for truth and the Pharisees' claims for law and order. In trying to protect the "moral quality" of their faith and religion, they harmed the formerly blind man and his family (Bultmann, 1971).

Secondary Violence in Church History

For a long time after the church came into being at Pentecost (Acts 2:1–13), it was a minority religion and was under suspicion as being subversive of the good order of both the Jews and the Romans. Christians were in a position of powerlessness and periodically were persecuted for their allegiance to Christianity. The Acts of the Apostles reports that in Jerusalem, communion and community were important aspects of the first congregation. In this position of powerlessness, through their lifestyle, the congregation attracted new adherents. They were "enjoying the favour of all people" (Acts 2:44–47, 4:32–36, 5:12–16). Differences that existed between the eastern and western branches of the early church, as well as between different sects, were tolerated. No bishop had any political authority that supported his theological viewpoints, and none could be "enforced" on any other. The only possibility that was available was to convince their opponents about their faith perspectives (Berkhof & De Jong, 1967).

This changed in 313 C.E., when Constantine and Theodosius certified the Christian Church as the official religious institution in the Empire. This put the church and its officials into a position of power and influence. Power became an issue for which the Church had not been prepared. People, Christian movements, and faith groups who had been fellow sufferers in the Roman persecutions, became the victims of the church's persecutions, namely, the Marcionites, Montanists, Donatists, Valentinians, Nestorians, and Noviates (Berkhof & De Jong, 1967).

Reactions against the power of the church produced such heroic figures as John Hus of Bohemia, who was burned at the stake on 6 July 1415 "for the preservation of the pure faith and its community, the church" (Berkhof & De Jong, 1967). Similarly, in 1616 a renowned Galileo Galilei was required to formally abandon the Copernican system and accept the Ptolemaic system under threat of death, "for the preservation of the true church and its holy gospel." Though he capitulated to the power of the church, Galileo was sentenced to life imprisonment under house arrest and died in 1642 in his villa; and although he was not put to death, he was isolated from the scientific community, and his writings were put on the Index of prohibited books until 1831 (Barrett, 2000). Only recently did Pope John Paul II announce that the church had erred in this case. For the sake of God's "truth," the truth was repressed and its champion abused.

In 1948 in South Africa, where I live, the National Party took power after the general elections. Much of the support for the National Party came from the white Afrikaans middle class and laborers. It also had the support of some of the ministers of the Reformed Churches. In 1955, after the publication of the Tomlinson Report about how the homelands policy should be implemented, the Dutch Reformed Church founded the black mission church in the Eastern Cape, the Transkei, and the Ciskei. My friend who was jailed was a minister who came out of this mission church. The colleague who came to see him was a white minister in the Dutch Reformed Church, and he came to see my friend because it was his duty as minister. He was member of the National Party, a white, and a minister of the influential Dutch Reformed Church. Embedded as he was in

that preferred position of power, I doubt if he could have acted differently than he did, but the secondary violence was blatant and
unfortunately typical in this bit of church history. Violator and
victim—permanent damage to both (Crafford, 1982).

Conclusion

Our examples from history point out how dangerous it is to align
ourselves in secular or religious modes, entrenched structures, and
institutions of power. It is when the agencies of religion align themselves with secular forces and institutions that they lose sight of their
roles in society, as witness to the claims of equality, unity, charity, and
peace. After the church became the official religion of the empire (the
Imperial Church), it became oppressive. Members of the church must
be constantly aware of the power issues that are involved in whatever
decisions have to be taken. When we take decisions for the sake of
institutional principle, we must be very careful and judicious. What is
being obscured? To what are we blinded by our power vision? What
place do the quiet and unempowered voices have in the power
process?

The early Christians were always questioned by society and sometimes vehemently opposed. Much of Jesus' ministry seems to have
been focused on exposing the hidden power agendas of institutionalized religion. In their discussions on iatrogenic injury and power,
Jenkins (1994), O'Hanlon (1993), and White (1995) give some point-
ers that could be useful for religious people on how to counter the
influences that lead to the subtleties of secondary violence. O'Hanlon
(1993) acknowledges that one can have secondary violence from an
abrasive encounter. Conversely, an encounter can instead promote
secondary healing. All these authors point to the necessity of being
reflective in any encounter about what is happening, especially about
how power is used, how it opens and closes possibilities for people.
The person in charge—judge, attorney, therapist, counselor, minister,
or any official and person of power—must take responsibility for
what happens and what his or her contribution is. He or she must be
careful not to hide behind the invisibility cloak of institutionalization
since it is he or she who has the power to create secondary harm or
healing, evil or good. The quiet voices must be allowed to be heard
and also to contribute to an open hermeneutic circle in which new
contributions of new insight may contribute to new meaning instead
of merely upholding traditional and institutionalized ways of think-

ing and acting. An approach that raises questions from a stance of curiosity and inquiry is more sensitive and allows people in situations of less power to contribute more. The Catholic Church's reaction to Galileo Galilei's theories led to a decline in scientific research in countries under Catholic influence. The thinking of the one in power is important. Thinking in an "I am right and he or she is wrong" manner tends to close the possibilities for curiosity and inquiring questions. Dogmatic interpretation of situations must not lead to the closing of the possibility for people to grow and change. It is better to try to interpret situations than people.

So we have seen that secondary violence is a subtle form of violence that occurs frequently in society and to which people in power unwittingly contribute. It often occurs specifically in situations in which sensitivity is of paramount importance, such as spiritual and therapeutic relationships. Unwitting abuse of power is an important aspect of this violence, especially because the power in the relationship is usually invisible. A person's power is enhanced by the role he or she has in society, a role that can be used to open or close possibilities for constructive action.

The church was more influential and successful when it had no power and was not aligned with any person or organization in power, that is, before the rise of the Imperial Church during the period 313–380 C.E. It was then able to hear and respond to the voice of the "widows" and "powerless," "fatherless" and "aliens" (Lev. 19:32, 33; Deut. 24:14, 17). Alignment with a power group closed off the possibilities for the church to make the voice of the powerless heard. The relationship of the church with the authority became a burden on the organization in its service to authentic spirituality. It became easier for the people in the church to confuse their opinions with ultimate or authoritative truth and the transcendent will of God. It is only when people involved in religion and faith reflectively acknowledge and expose their own positions and styles of using power that secondary violence can be prevented.

References

Barr, J. (1984). *Fundamentalism* (2nd ed.). London: SCM Press.

Barrett, P. (2000). *Science and theology since Copernicus: The search for understanding*. Pretoria: Unisa Press.

Berkhof, H. & De Jong, O. J. (1967). *Geschiedenis der Kerk* (Geheel Herziene Druk). Nijkerk: Uitgeverij G. F. Callenbach N.V.

Bultmann, R. (1971). *The Gospel of John.* Oxford: Basil Blackwell.

Crafford, D. (1982). *Aan God die dank: Geskiedenis van die sending van die Ned. Geref. Kerk binne die Republiek van Suid-Afrika en enkele aangrensende Buurstate* (Thanks be to God: A history of the mission of the Dutch Reformed Church within the Republic of South Africa and the various bordering territories). Pretoria: N. G. Kerkboekhandel Tvl.

Geertz, C. (1975). *The interpretation of cultures.* London: Hutchinson.

Geldenhuys, J. N. (1962). Luke the evangelist. In J. D. Douglas et al. (Eds.), *The new Bible dictionary* (755–56). London: Intervarsity Press.

Jenkins, A. (1994). Therapy for abuse or therapy as abuse. *Dulwich Centre Newsletter, 1,* 11–19.

McLeod, W. T. (1985). *The new Collins concise English dictionary.* London: Guild Publishing.

O'Hanlon, W. H. (1993). Possibility therapy: From iatrogenic injury to iatrogenic healing. In S. Gilligan & R. E. Price (Eds.), *Therapeutic Conversations* (3–17). New York: W. W. Norton.

Sanders, J. T. (1987). *The Jews in Luke-Acts.* Philadelphia: Fortress.

White, M. (1995). *Reauthoring lives: Interviews and essays.* Adelaide: Dulwich Centre Publications.

CHAPTER 11

THE MYTH OF REDEMPTIVE VIOLENCE

Walter Wink

Until modern times, virtually all warfare was explicitly religious. Even in modern secular societies, wars of national interest are given a patina of religious justification. No one, it seems, wishes to kill others and risk being killed themselves without justification by the highest authority in the universe. War is the ultimate appeal to religious sanctification, the offering up of human lives in a supreme sacrifice. Willingly or unwillingly, for millennia young men have marched off to slaughter in the name of their god. And that is as true today as it was at the dawn of civilization.

Our boys go marching off in no small part because they believe that violence is both necessary and right. It is what works. Violence seems to be the only solution, the last, and increasingly the first resort in conflicts, for example, President Bush's "preemptive strikes" or the U.S. Air Force's "anticipatory retaliation." Violence is the spirituality of our society. It has virtually been accorded the status of a religion, demanding from its devotees an absolute obedience unto death. Its followers are not aware, however, that the devotion they pay to violence is a form of religious piety. Violence is so successful as a religion precisely because it does not seem to be religious in the least. Violence simply appears to be the nature of things. It is embraced with equal alacrity by people on the left and on the right, by religious liberals as well as religious conservatives. The threat of violence, it is believed, is alone able to deter aggressors.

The roots of this devotion to violence are deep, and we will be well rewarded if we trace them to their source. When we do, we will discover that the religion of Babylon—one of the world's oldest religions—is thriving as never before in every sector of contemporary American life, even our synagogues and churches. It, and not Christianity, is the real religion of America. We can call it "the myth of redemptive violence" because it is the conviction that only violence can save us. Violence saves: this belief undergirds American popular culture, civil religion, nationalism, and foreign policy, and it lies coiled like an ancient serpent at the root of the system of domination that has characterized human existence since well before Babylon ruled supreme. In order to get our bearings, however, we have to go back to the mythic source.

The Origin of Redemptive Violence

Scholars differ sharply on the origin of war. Some archaeologists and anthropologists believe that the earliest societies were relatively egalitarian and nonviolent. Other insist that violence has been characteristic of human communities from the beginning of time. This much is clear: warfare, as opposed to random or small-scale violence, became chronic, widespread, and organized only around 4000 to 3000 B.C.E. It is then that mass graves begin to appear with regularity, with telltale signs of human violence, such as arrowheads embedded in human bones. Large-scale warfare coincided with the appearance of the conquest states, possibly the consequence, at least in part, of the domestication of animals. Without tame horses, conquest and pillage were unprofitable since all one seized had to be carried on one's back or in one's arms. But domesticated horses could carry large loads, made even larger by the invention of the wheel and thus the wagon. And the domestication of cattle, sheep, and goats meant that armies were free from carrying all their foodstuffs since herds could be driven alongside them.

When these herdsmen-become-cavalry poured into the Mesopotamian valley from the Russian steppes, they ran into ineffectual opposition. The city-states they encountered were not walled, and the weapons their defenders used were more suited for hunting than for warfare. As the invaders conquered one city after another, they found themselves having to invent bureaucracies, wall their cities, design new weapons, form standing armies, and create communication networks. In order to support the rulers, priesthood, army, and bureaucracy, none of whom produced anything, it was necessary to continually extend the empire. The plunder they seized flowed to the center, the great city-states of Sumeria, Babylon, and later Assyria, Persia, Greece, Rome, Parthia, and so on. Captive women became slaves, concubines, members of harems, and occasionally wives. The surplus of females cheapened the value of all women; even aristocratic women belonged to a tier inferior to their men. Women were compensated for their loss of power by being able to lord it over captive women and men. All hints of the previously more egalitarian society disappeared. The vast majority of people were consigned to serving the powerful, constructing city fortifications and buildings, and offering up their lives in the king's armies. In order to support those at the apex of the pyramid of power, taxes were levied with the intent of siphoning off all the food surplus peasants could produce. From that time until now, two-thirds of humanity have gone to bed hungry at night as they continue to grow crops most of which they will never eat. Thus began the history of the conquest state. Whether by military might, or political power, or economic exploitation, the conquest state has perdured until this very day.

One might think that the sheer human misery that such a system inflicted on the vast majority of people would lead to slave and peasant revolts. They did not. Herein lies the wisdom of extortionistic taxation: underfed people lack the calories to fight. But even more insidiously: people were made to believe that the world they inhabited was the only possible world. This could be accomplished by telling a certain kind of story and retelling it so often that people forgot it was a story at all but simply an account of the way things are as seen by the well-born and powerful. The particular story or myth told in Babylon was the *Enuma Elish*, or the Babylonian Creation Story. Here is the myth as it appeared around 1250 B.C.E. but based on traditions considerably older.

In the beginning, Apsu and Tiamat, the sweet and saltwater oceans, bear Mummu, the mist. From them also issue the younger gods, whose frolicking makes so much noise that the elder gods resolve to kill them so they can sleep. This plot of the elder gods is discovered. The younger gods kill Apsu. His wife Tiamat, the Dragon of Chaos, pledges revenge. The rebel gods in terror turn for salvation to their youngest, Marduk. He exacts a steep price: if he succeeds, he must be given chief and undisputed power in the assembly of the gods. Having extorted this promise, he catches Tiamat in a net, drives an evil wind down her throat, and shoots an arrow that bursts her distended belly and pierces her heart; he then splits her skull with a club and scatters her blood in out-of-the-way places. He stretches out her corpse full length, and from it creates the cosmos.[1]

We are indebted to the philosopher Paul Ricoeur for his perceptive analysis of this myth.[2] In it, he says, the creation of the world is an act of violence. Tiamat represents Chaos, the enemy of Order. Order prevails by a violent victory over an enemy older than creation. "Good" is whatever overcomes chaos. Evil is prior to good.

The biblical creation myth in Genesis 1 is diametrically opposed to all this. There, a good God creates a good world. Evil enters the picture only in Genesis 2–3, an older creation myth now given new meaning by its subordination to the newer myth in Genesis 1. The latter, we must note, was written *in* Babylon during Israel's captivity there. Since the Jews had been conquered by the Babylonians, it appeared that Israel's god, Yahweh, had been defeated by Babylon's god, Marduk. As a counter to the *Enuma Elish*, Jews developed a story in which chaos does not resist order; indeed, it scarcely makes a showing: it is merely the inert "stuff" that God would shape into matter. Nor does Yahweh have to struggle to subdue chaos; God simply speaks a word, and effortlessly, all things come to be. And after every act of creation, the refrain echoes, "And God saw that it was good." In the Babylonian creation story, as we saw, violence is no problem. It is simply the way things are. In the Genesis creation story, for the first time, violence is seen to be a problem for which the whole subsequent history of humanity is the search for an answer.

But there is more to the Babylonian myth. After the world has been created, the story continues, the gods imprisoned by Marduk for siding with Tiamat complain of the poor meal service in their jail. Marduk and Ea therefore execute one of the captive gods, and from his blood, Ea creates human beings to be servants to the gods.

If we are created from the blood of an assassinated god, if the very blood that courses through our veins has been drained from a deity, then there is little chance that we might ever become nonviolent. Killing is in our blood. We are not the cause of violence; on the contrary, we come into a world organized for violence, and we perpetuate it. Nor are we given dignity by exercising dominion over the world. Instead, we exist but to serve as slaves of the gods and of their earthly regents.

An added dimension of depth was given the myth when Marduk, represented by the king, was amalgamated with Tammuz, a vegetation god. Now the god/king is pictured as undergoing ritual humiliation at the New Year's Festival. The priest strikes the king's face and pulls his ears. This may have been associated with death and lamentation as the god descends into the underworld. The people, thrown into confusion, weep for him as for a suffering and dying god. Creation reverts to chaos (winter). With the aid of the ritual, the god is revived, liberated, and released (spring). His enthronement is reenacted, and the people celebrate the victory of order over chaos in a magnificent feast. Finally, a sacred marriage revives all the life-giving forces in nature and humanity. This motif of the "suffering of the hero" is central to our own contemporary depictions of the myth, as we shall see.

This myth is highly militaristic. Marduk's task is to subdue the nations round about his own domain and bring tranquillity through war. The whole cosmos is a state, and the god rules through the king. Salvation *is* politics: identifying with the god of order against the god of chaos and offering oneself up for the holy war required to impose order on others outside. And because chaos threatens repeatedly, in the form of barbarian attacks, an ever expanding imperial policy is the automatic correlate of Marduk's ascendancy over all the gods.

As Ricoeur concludes, this myth enshrines a theology of holy war founded on the identification of the enemy with the powers that the god has vanquished and continues to vanquish in the drama of creation. Every coherent theology of holy wars ultimately reverts to this basic mythological type.

This myth is the original religion of the status quo, the first articulation of "might makes right." It is the basic ideology of what I call the "domination system," which is characterized by oppressive political relations, unjust economic relations, biased racial relations, and hierarchical power relations, all of them held together by violence. The gods favor those who conquer. Conversely, whoever conquers must have the favor of the gods. This is a fail-safe theology! Religion exists to legitimate power and privilege. Life is combat. Any form of order is preferable to chaos, according to this myth. Ours is neither a perfect nor a perfectible world; it is, rather, a theater of perpetual conflict in which the prize goes to the strong. Peace through war; security through strength: these are the core convictions that arise from this ancient myth.

The Myth of Redemptive Violence in Popular Culture Today

The myth of redemptive violence inundates us on every side. We are awash in it yet seldom perceive it. It is perceptible in its impact on foreign policy, nationalism, the Cold War, militarism, the media, and televangelism. But first we must identify its simplest, most pervasive, and finally most influential form, where it captures the imaginations of each new generation: children's comics, cartoon shows, video games, computer games, and movies.

Here is how the myth of redemptive violence structures the standard comic strip or television cartoon sequence. An indestructible good guy is unalterably opposed to an irreformable and equally indestructible bad guy. Nothing can kill the good guy, though for the first three-quarters of the strip or show, he, rarely she, suffers grievously, appearing hopelessly trapped, until somehow the hero breaks free, vanquishes the villain, and restores order until the next installment. Nothing finally destroys the bad guy or prevents his reappearance, whether he is soundly trounced, jailed, drowned, or shot into outer space.

I am referring not to programs that do not feature violence but rather to what I call the "classic" type of cartoon, where the mythic pattern of redemptive violence is straightforward. Examples include Superman, Wonder Woman, Teenage Mutant Turtles, Mighty Morphin Power Rangers, Transformers, Rocky and Bullwinkle, Captain America, Lone Ranger and Tonto, Superfriends, Courageous Cat, Batman and Robin, Roadrunner and Wile E. Coyote, and, going way back, Tom and Jerry. A variation on the classic theme is provided by humorous antiheroes whose bumbling incompetence guarantees their victory despite themselves (Underdog, Super Chicken, the Banana Splits, Super Six, GoGo Gophers, Wackey Racers). Then there is a more recent twist where an evil or failed individual undergoes a transformation into a monstrous creature who—amazingly—does good (Spider Man, The Hulk, Iron Man, Shazzam, the Herculoids). It is almost as if people no longer believe that heroes of sterling character can arise in our society and that goodness can be produced only by a freak of technology (such as electrocution or chemicals). In all these cartoons, however, the mythic structure is rigidly adhered to no matter how cleverly or originally it is re-presented.

Few cartoon shows have run longer or been more influential than Popeye and Bluto. In a typical segment, Bluto abducts a screaming and kicking Olive Oyl, Popeye's girlfriend. When Popeye attempts to rescue her, the massive Bluto beats his diminutive opponent to a pulp while Olive Oil helplessly wrings her hands. At the last moment, as our hero oozes to the floor and Bluto is trying to all effects to rape Olive Oil, a can of spinach pops from Popeye's pocket and spills into his mouth. Transformed by this gracious infusion of power, he easily demolishes the villain and rescues his beloved. The format never varies. Neither party ever gains any insight or learns from these encounters. Violence does not teach Bluto to honor Olive Oyl's humanity, and repeated pummelings do not teach Popeye to swallow his spinach *before* the fight.

Only the names have changed. Marduk subdues Tiamat through violence, and though he kills Tiamat, chaos incessantly reasserts itself and is kept at bay only by repeated battles and by the repetition of the New Year's Festival, where the heavenly combat myth is ritually reenacted. The structure of the combat myth is thus faithfully repeated on television week after week: an aggressive attack by a superior force representing chaos; the champion fights back, defensively, only to be humiliated in apparent defeat; the evil power satisfies its lusts while the hero is incapacitated; and the hero escapes, defeats the evil power decisively, and reaffirms order over chaos. Willis Elliott's observation underscores the seriousness of this entertainment: "Cosmogony [the birth of the world] is egogony [the birth of the individual]: you are being birthed through how you see 'all things' as being birthed." Therefore, "*Whoever controls the cosmogony controls the children.*"[3]

The psychodynamics of the television cartoon or comic book are marvelously simple: children identify with the good guy so that they can think of themselves as good. This enables them to project out onto the bad guy their own repressed anger, violence, rebelliousness, or lust and then vicariously to enjoy their own evil by watching the bad guy initially prevail. (This segment of the show actually consumes all but the closing minutes, allowing ample time for indulging the dark side of the self.) When the good guy finally wins, viewers are then able to reassert control over their own inner tendencies, repress them, and reestablish a sense of goodness. *Salvation is guaranteed through identification with the hero.*

This structure cannot be altered. Bluto does not simply lose more often, he must *always* lose. Otherwise this entire view of reality would collapse. The good guys must always win. In order to suppress the fear of erupting chaos, the same mythic pattern must be endlessly repeated in a myriad of variations that *never in any way alter the basic structure.*[4]

Cartoon strips like Superman and Dick Tracy have been enormously successful in resolving the guilt feelings of the reader or viewer by providing totally evil, often deformed and inhuman scape-

goats on whom one can externalize the evil side of one's own personality and disown it without coming to any insight or awareness of
its presence within oneself. The villain's punishment provides catharsis; one forswears the villain's ways and heaps condemnation on him
in a guilt-free orgy of aggression.[5] No premium is put on reasoning,
persuasion, negotiation, or diplomacy. There can be no compromise
with an absolute evil. Evil must be totally annihilated or totally converted.

Cartoon and comic characters cast no shadows. They are immor-
tals; they cannot be killed. They are not beset by the ordinary temp-
tations, never take advantage of damsels in distress, accept no bribes,
receive no remuneration, and generally live above the realm of sin.
Repentance and confession are as alien to them as the love of enemies
and nonviolence. As Ariel Dorfman puts it, "The Lone Ranger himself contains not a single internal contradiction."[6]

Superman, for his part, merely beats the bad guys to a pulp. Villains
are relegated to outer darkness but not redeemed from their bondage
to evil or restored to true humanity.[7]

Batman, who lacks the superhuman qualities of Superman, com-
pensates with commitment. To avenge the murder of his parents, he
swears to spend "the rest of my life warring on all criminals." He will,
in short, be a vigilante. He communicates well with the police com-
missioner, to be sure, but "the Caped Crusader" is answerable to no
one in his role as a self-appointed crime stopper. His is rather a sacred
vow, binding him to holy war on all the vermin of evil. His motives
are not generous at all. He wants revenge.[8]

In this respect Batman parallels the classic gunfighters of the
"western," who settle old scores by shootouts, never by due process
of law. The law, in fact, is suspect, too weak to prevail in the conditions of near anarchy that fiction has misrepresented as the Wild
West. The gunfighter must take matters into his own hands, just as,
in the anarchic situation of the big city, a beleaguered citizen finally
rises up against the crooks and muggers and creates justice out of the
barrel of a gun, as in the movie *Dirty Harry* and, in real life, Bernard
Goetz.

As Robert Jewett points out, this vigilantism betrays a profound
distrust of democratic institutions and of the reliance on human
intelligence and civic responsibility that are basic to the democratic
hope. It regards the general public as passive and unwise, incapable
of discerning evil and making a rational response, as in the film *High
Noon*. Public resources are inadequate, so the message goes; we need

a messiah, an armed redeemer, someone who has the strength of character and conviction to transcend the legal restraints of democratic institutions and save us from an evil easily identifiable in villainous persons.

These vigilantes who deliver us by taking the law into their own hands will somehow do so without encouraging lawlessness. They will kill and leave town, thus ridding us of guilt. They will show selfless and surpassing concern for the health of our communities, but they will never have to practice citizenship or deal with the ambiguity of political decisions. They neither run for office nor vote. They will reignite in us a consuming love for impartial justice, but they will do so by means of a mission of personal vengeance that eliminates due process of law.[9]

The possibility that an innocent person is being executed by our violent redeemers is removed by having the outlaw draw first or shoot from ambush. The villain dresses in dark clothing and is swarthy, unshaven, and filthy, and his personality is stereotyped so as to eliminate any possibility of audience sympathy. The death of such evil beings is necessary in order to cleanse society of a stain. The viewer, far from feeling remorse at another human being's death, is actually made euphoric. Some movie audiences actually stand and cheer when the villain is blown away.[10] Such villains cannot be handled by democratic means; they are far too powerful, for they are archetypally endowed with the transcendent qualities of Tiamat. So great a threat requires a Marduk, an avenger, a man on a white horse.

Rather than shoring up democracy, the strongman methods of the superheroes of popular culture reflect nostalgia for simpler solutions. They bypass constitutional guarantees of legal procedure in arrest or the tenet that a person is to be regarded as innocent until proven guilty. What we see instead is a mounting impatience with the laborious processes of civilized life and a restless eagerness to embrace violent solutions. Better to mete out instant, summary justice than risk the red tape and delays and bumbling of the courts.[11] The yearning for a messianic redeemer who will set things right is thus, in its essence, a totalitarian fantasy.

The myth literally replays itself, without any awareness on the part of those who repeat it, under the guise of completely secular stories. Take the movie *Jaws*, for example. Recall that in the Babylonian myth, Marduk spread a net over Tiamat, and when she opened her jaws to devour him, he drives an evil wind down her throat and shoots an arrow that bursts her distended belly and pierces her heart.

A still from the 1975 film *Jaws.* © Photofest.

With her destruction, order is restored. The community is saved by an act of redemptive violence.

In the movie *Jaws,* Police Chief Brody encounters a shark larger by a third than any known shark, of which a preview says, "It is as if nature had concentrated all its forces of evil in a single being." Brody kicks an oxygen tank into the attacking shark's throat, then fires a bullet that explodes the tank, thus forcing into the shark's body a wind that bursts it open. Brody is transformed into a superhero, chaos is subdued, and the island is restored to a tourists' paradise.[12]

Or take the spy thriller. In the service of one's country, the spy is permitted to murder, seduce, lie, steal, commit illegal entry, tap phones without a court order, and otherwise do anything necessary to protect the values of Christian civilization, as in the James Bond movies, *Mission Impossible,* and the like. The basic attitude is summed up in an episode of that ultimate spoof on the spy thriller, *Get Smart.* As I recall the scene decades after viewing it, the show ends with the villain being blown off a cliff to his death on the rocks below, tricked by a loaded cigarette. His sidekick, Agent 99, watches in horror, then comments, "You know, Max, sometimes I think we're no better than they are, the way we murder and kill and destroy people." To which Smart retorts, "Why, 99, you know we have to murder and kill and destroy in order to preserve everything that's good in the world."

And who are 99 and Smart fighting week after week? An international conspiracy of evil intent called CHAOS. And for whom do they work? CONTROL.

The archetype is able to duplicate itself not only in the public media but also in actual history. In the mid-1970s, Congressman Les Aspin uncovered a secret CIA operation intended to disrupt domestic dissident groups in the 1960s. Though its work was expressly forbidden by law, this surveillance operation infiltrated fully legal antiwar groups and organizations that were attempting to rectify injustices and sought to undermine them, often by trying to provoke violence. The name of the program: OPERATION CHAOS. History itself becomes mythic.

How is it possible that this ancient archetypal structure still possesses such power in a modern, secular, scientific culture? Thanks to the American penchant for letting viewer interest determine programming, the story lines of cartoons, television shows, comics, and movies tend to gravitate to the lowest common denominator of mythic simplicity. The head of programming at a major network was asked to describe the thinking process that led to the network's selection of programs. He answered that there was no thinking process whatsoever. Television and film producers provide whatever fare the ratings and box offices tell them will generate the most immediate profit.[13] With important exceptions, such as Mr. Rogers, Captain Kangaroo, Sesame Street, and a few of the more benign cartoons, the entertainment industry does not create materials that will be good for children to watch, material that will inculcate high values, ethical standards, honesty, truthfulness, mutual care and consideration, responsibility, and nobility of character. Instead, what children themselves prefer determines what is produced. It is the gastronomical equivalent of allowing your child to eat chocolates all day. The myth of redemptive violence is the simplest, laziest, most exciting, uncomplicated, irrational, and primitive depiction of evil the world has ever known. Furthermore, its orientation toward evil is *one into which virtually all modern children, boys especially, are socialized in the process of maturation*. The myth that lay like a threshold across the path of burgeoning empires also lies across the path of each individual bred in such societies. Children select this mythic

structure because they have already been led, by culturally reinforced cues and role models, to resonate with its simplistic view of
reality. Its ubiquity is not the result of a conspiracy of Babylonian
priests secretly buying up the mass media with Iraqi oil money but
rather a function of inculcated values endlessly reinforced by the
international system of domination.[14]

Once children have been indoctrinated into the expectations of a
dominator society, they may never outgrow the need to locate all evil
outside themselves. Even as adults, they tend to scapegoat others—
the Commies, the Americans, gays or straights, blacks or whites—for
all that is wrong in the world. They continue to depend on group
identification and the upholding of social norms for a sense of well-
being. There is a ritual dimension to television violence involving the
public in a reaffirmation of group values through the ritualization of
collective ideas. It is tragic that the mass media, which could be so
effectively used, and occasionally are, to help people mature beyond
the infantilisms of scapegoating behavior, have been made the chief
exponent of the myth of redemptive violence.

In a period when Christian Sunday schools are dwindling, the myth
of redemptive violence has won children's voluntary acquiescence to
a regimen of religious indoctrination more exhaustive and effective
than any in the history of religions. Estimates vary widely, but the
average child is reported to log roughly 36,000 hours of television by
age 18, including some 15,000 murders.[15] In prime-time evening
shows, our children are served up about 16 entertaining acts of violence (two of them lethal) every night; on the weekend the number of
violent acts almost doubles (30). By age 16, the average child spends
as much time watching television as in school.[16] What church or synagogue can even remotely match the myth of redemptive violence in
hours spent with children or quality of presentation? Think of the
typical "children's sermon"—how bland by comparison!

No other religious system has ever remotely rivaled the myth of
redemptive violence in its ability to catechize its young so totally.
From the earliest age, children are awash in depictions of violence
as the ultimate solution in human conflicts. Nor does saturation in
the myth end with the close of adolescence. There is no rite of passage from adolescent to adult status in the national cult of violence
but rather years-long acclimatization to adult television and movie
fare. Not all shows for children or adults are based on violence, of
course. Reality is far more complex than the simplicities of this
myth, and more mature minds will demand more subtle, nuanced,

complex presentations. But the basic structure of the combat myth underlies the pap to which a great many adults turn in order to escape the harsher realities of their everyday lives: spy thrillers, westerns, cop shows, and combat programs. It is as if we must watch so much "redemptive" violence to reassure ourselves, against the deluge of facts to the contrary in our actual day-to-day lives, that reality really is that simple.

With the right kinds of support, children might outgrow the simplicities of the myth of redemptive violence. Our modern tragedy is that just when boys ought to be transcending it, they are hit by an even more sophisticated barrage of unmitigated violence—violence so explicit and sexually sadistic that it cannot even be shown on television. I refer to a new wave of ever more brutal comic books and home videos. Recently I spent an hour browsing through a mall comic shop, examining such fare as The Uncanny X-Men, Swamp Thing, War of the Worlds, The Warlock Five, The Avengers, The Spectre, Shattered Earth, Scout: War Shaman, The Punisher, Gun Fury, The Huntress, Dr. Fate, The Blood Sword, and so on: an entire store devoted to the promulgation of a paranoid view of reality where the initiation of violence is the only protection against those plotting our doom. And boys are almost the exclusive readership. "Over the last decade, comics have forsaken campy repartee and outlandishly byzantine plots for a steady diet of remorseless violence."[17]

Likewise, the "video nasties," such as *The Texas Chain Saw Massacre*, *The Evil Dead*, or *Zombie Flesh-Eaters*, have reached new levels of inventiveness in brutality. "Adult only" home videos such as these have been viewed by one-quarter of British children aged seven to eight; by age 10, half have seen them, if not at home, then at a friend's. Many have their first introduction to explicit sex in these films in the form of rape, decapitation, dismemberment, and cannibalism. With alarming frequency, crimes are being committed that are modeled after video violence.[18]

If such shows only provided a needed catharsis of violence, they might be defensible; but over 700 studies conclude that video violence increases substantially the degree to which adolescent boys engage in serious violence. Why, then, do we put up with this violence-producing myth? The answer is quite simple: the promise of salvation. The myth of redemptive violence offers salvation through identification with Marduk and his earthly regents. The modern individual, stripped of the values, rites, and customs that give a sense of belonging to traditional cultures, is the easy victim of the fads of style, opinion, and prejudice fostered by the communications media. At once isolated and yet absorbed into the masses, people live under the illusion that the views and feelings they have acquired by attending to the media are their own.[19] Overwhelmed by the gigantism of sports, corporations, bureaucracies, universities, the military, and celebrities, individuals sense that their only escape from utter insignificance lies in identifying with these giants and idolizing them as the true bearers of their own human identity.

The Canadian cartoon "For Better or for Worse" catches the irony of salvific identification. Hockey fans in a bar are rooting for their team on television. Their team is on the attack when suddenly, "Here's Roberts behind the net!—it's out to Jacquot . . . over to Williams from the point. . . . He scores! He scores! It's all over! What a blistering blast from the Sultan of Slap!" And everyone in the bar starts chanting, "We're number one! We're number one! We're number one! We're number . . ." at which one turns to his buddy and says, "Uh . . . Mike? WE didn't DO anything!!"

Salvation through identification: whether it be in cartoon shows or westerns or confrontation with a foreign power, one's personal well-being is tied inextricably to the fortunes of the hero-leader. Right and wrong scarcely enter the picture. Everything depends on victory, success, the thrill of belonging to a team, a school, or a nation capable of imposing its will on others.

But there is an even more significant aspect of the myth of redemptive violence that we have not developed: its contribution to the maintenance of international conflict.

Redemptive Violence and the National Security State

In every age, the myth of redemptive violence reappears in one form or another as a religion dedicated to the support of the powerful and privileged through violence. In the original Babylonian story, the price Marduk exacts for killing Tiamat is rulership over the pantheon of the gods. In that myth the council of the gods, and their mode of governing the universe, exactly reproduces the structure of the Babylonian kingdom.

In the past two centuries, scholars regarded this correspondence between heavenly and earthly powers as merely the projection onto the cosmos of the power arrangements of the state. The myth was thus seen as a mystification of actual power relations that provided divine legitimacy for oppressive earthly institutions.

This reductionistic reading misses the mark.[20] The gods are not a fictive masking of the power of the human state; *they are its actual spirituality.* The *Enuma Elish* depicts the ascendancy of Marduk, the youngest god, to supreme authority over the other gods in the heavenly council, simultaneous with the ascendancy of the king of Babylon over the surrounding region. That myth, far from mystifying power relations, shows by the precise correspondence between heavenly and earthly events that it has faithfully and accurately brought to expression the actual power relations at work. As above, so below: Babylon is explicitly said to be "a likeness on earth of what he [Marduk] has wrought in heaven" (*Enuma Elish* VI.113); so also VI.104: "Let his utterance be supreme above and below." This masks nothing. The myth plainly shows, for everyone to see, that Babylon has acquired hegemony over the other city-states in Mesopotamia. It states clearly that the king acts on behalf of Marduk to suppress chaos and impose order. The state is a mirror of cosmic order; therefore, resistance or rebellion is a crime against heaven.

We saw earlier that in the myth of redemptive violence, the survival and welfare of the nation is elevated as the highest earthly and heavenly good. There can be no other gods before the nation. This myth not only establishes a patriotic religion at the heart of the state but also gives that nation's imperialistic imperative divine sanction. As Georges Khodr notes, all war is metaphysical; one can go to war only religiously.[21] The myth of redemptive violence is thus the spirituality of militarism. By divine right, the state has the power to order its citizens to sacrifice their lives to maintain the privileges enjoyed by the few. By divine decree, it utilizes violence to cleanse the world of evil opponents who resist the nation's sway. Wealth and prosperity are the right of those who rule in such a state. And the name of God—any god, the Christian God included—can be invoked as having specially blessed and favored the supremacy of the chosen nation and its ruling caste.

On this view, all times are times of war. Peace is nothing more than the conventional name given to the continuation of war by other means. All politics is a politics of war. In Kosovo or South Africa or El Salvador or Guatemala, what this has meant in actual practice is that the army and its weapons are not used against outer geopolitical threats so much as against *their own people.* The national security ideology is thus nationalism raised to ultimacy. Though our contemporary idolaters never tire of speaking about the democracy and Christianity that they are defending with dictatorship and war (and the war never ends), the real faith of these "national securocrats" is redemptive violence.

Since such a nationalism cannot accept the existence of a higher power, it must destroy any forms of Christian faith that go beyond mere cultural inheritance. Nevertheless, national security ideologues saturate their language with religious platitudes. Their documents are drenched with phrases cribbed from the Bible and from papal encyclicals, and they may even be active attenders of church. But it is clear that what they mean by Christianity is merely the perpetuation of the privileges of a tiny capitalistic minority by whatever means necessary. It is new-old redemptive violence, the domination system pure and simple.

Zealous nationalism of this stripe cannot simply be dismissed as aberrant, however; it is, indeed, "biblical." The Bible is full of blood-thirsty deeds of Yahweh, and those who wish to "think God's thoughts after him" can easily multiply references: the "ban" requiring the total destruction of every living being at Ai and Jericho, the atrocities committed by Jehu in the name of the prophet Elisha, Phinehas' zeal in murdering a couple whose sin was racial intermarriage, the picture of sinners being tortured in fire and brimstone for all eternity that Matthew has added to his sources, the lust for vengeance in the book of Revelation—all these and many, many more examples attest to the success of the myth of redemptive violence in penetrating the Bible itself.[22]

The myth of redemptive violence thus uses the traditions, rites, customs, and symbols of Christianity in order to enhance the power of a wealthy elite and the goals of the nation narrowly defined. It has no interest in compassion for the poor, or for more equitable economic arrangements, or for the love of enemies. It merely uses the shell of religion—a shell that can be filled with the blasphemous doctrine of the national security state. Emptied of their prophetic vitality, these outer forms are then manipulated to legitimate a power system intent on the preservation of privilege at all costs.[23]

This longing to identify with a winner was glaringly evident after the first Persian Gulf War of 1991. The orgy of patriotism unleashed in the United States revealed how strongly people wanted to be able to think well of their nation again. Here at last was what seemed to many a truly "just" war, and its incomparably successful military prosecution led to a flood of self-congratulatory euphoria. Regardless of what we may decide about the justice of that war, for Christians, the death of 100,000 Iraqi soldiers created in the image of

God was an occasion not for celebration but for grief. But for our militarists, salvation comes not by insight, repentance, and truth but by identification with American military might: the Marduk solution.

The structure of the ancient combat myth is not, then, just the basis of comics and cartoons; it is the framework of much that passes as foreign policy. Subdue Tiamat, the argument runs, and a new world order will prevail. It is so simple, so unarguable, so irresistible. Before such a prospect, who would think of negotiating a peace that requires all parties involved to concede their own culpability for the crisis and to surrender advantages they have gained unjustly, especially if we are confronting the mightiest empire ever to rule the world?[24]

Redemptive Violence and the American Empire

Jay Bookman, writing in the *Atlanta-Journal Constitution* of September 29, 2002, wonders why the official story on Iraq never made sense. The connection that the Bush administration tried to draw between Iraq and al Qaeda always seemed contrived and artificial. Why would smart people in the Bush administration start a major war based on such flimsy evidence?

The pieces just did not fit, Bookman says. Something else had to be going on; something was missing. Those missing pieces have finally begun to fall into place. As it turns out, it was never really about Iraq. Nor was it about Osama bin Laden, or weapons of mass destruction, or terrorism, or Saddam Hussein, or UN resolutions:

> This war . . . is intended to mark the official emergence of the United States as a full-fledged global empire, seizing sole responsibility and authority as planetary policeman. It would be the culmination of a plan 10 years or more in the making, carried out by those who believe the United States must seize the opportunity for global domination, even if it means becoming the "American imperialists" that our enemies always claimed we were.
>
> Once that is understood, other mysteries solve themselves. For example, why does the administration seem unconcerned about an exit strategy from Iraq once Saddam is toppled? Because we won't be leaving. Having conquered Iraq, the United States will create permanent military bases in that country from which to dominate the Middle East, including neighboring Iran.

The blueprint for this "Pax Americana" is laid out in the "National Security Strategy of the United States of America," released by the administration on September 20, 2002. This official government policy statement marks a significant departure from previous approaches, a change that it attributes largely to the attacks on 9/11. In fact, however, this approach was already spelled out in a report issued in September 2000 by the Project for the New American Century, drafted by a group of conservative interventionists outraged by the thought that the United States might be forfeiting its chance at a global empire. By 2002, almost all the drafters of the project held the highest positions of U.S. government. Both the 2000 and the 2002 documents embrace the vision of American domination of every region on the globe, unfettered by international treaties or concerns. Thus, the revoking of the ABM and the Kyoto treaties and the refusal to sign a treaty to ban land mines were perfectly consistent with the desire to be free to act unilaterally, using persuasion where possible, coercion where necessary. The same logic calls for self-reliance and the virtual shelving of the United Nations.

Such a global hegemony is expensive. So the Bush administration increased the defense budget by 11 percent. War in Iraq would cost an additional $100 billion to $200 billion. But these are the costs of performing "constabulary duties," the United States acting as policeman of the world. American soldiers are already quartered in 130 countries!

An even earlier document from the Defense Department in 1992 envisioned the United States as a colossus astride the world, imposing its will and keeping world peace through military and economic power. When leaked in final draft form, however, the proposal drew so much criticism that it was hastily withdrawn and repudiated by the first President Bush. There has been no such uproar this time. By the way, Dick Cheney was one of the drafters of that document, as was Paul Wolfowitz, who at the time was Defense Undersecretary for Policy and who today is Deputy Secretary of Defense.

Many commentators have stressed the oil connection. Iraq sits on the second-largest oil reserve in the world. Iraq is already negotiating with other countries for sale of its oil. Conquest of Iraq would allow the United States to rewrite those agreements in favor of American oil interests and thus prevent disruptions in our oil supply. Likewise, a decisive war against Iraq will serve as an object lesson for nations such as Iran and Syria. Sensible conservation could have freed us completely from the need for Middle Eastern oil. But the administration would have nothing of it. There is no profit in conserving.

In conclusion, Bookman says,

> The lure of empire is ancient and powerful, and over the millennia it
> has driven men to commit terrible crimes on its behalf. But with the

end of the Cold War and the disappearance of the Soviet Union, a global empire was essentially laid at the feet of the United States. To the chagrin of some, we did not seize it at the time, in large part, because the American people have never been comfortable with themselves as a New Rome.

Bookman's essay makes a number of things suddenly intelligible. It explains why the administration is not serious about helping to rebuild Afghanistan. It has achieved its purpose, which is to clear the way for an oil pipeline and to build military bases. It explains Bush's fascination with "preemptive strikes," when the American ideal has been to wage defensive wars only after first being attacked. But "offensive warfare" is necessary for conquest. It explains the unevenness of treatment between North Korea and Iraq: the former has no oil. It explains why Bush is willing to occupy Iraq indefinitely, perhaps on the model of General MacArthur in Japan. American troops are still in Germany and Japan 58 years after World War II. Only such direct control can guarantee perpetual sovereignty over Iraq's oil.

It explains why the administration is willing to use violence against any and all who resist its designs. Why did Bush seem to want weapons inspections to fail, as if he were itching for a fight? *Because a diplomatic settlement would not give him access to Iraq's oilfields and land for bases.*

American pretensions to empire also explain why successive administrations of both parties have supported the Star Wars missile defense system, even though many of its weapons tests have failed. In addition to bringing lucrative contracts to congressional districts, this "weaponization of space" also meets the demands of empire. As Achin Vanaik, an Indian disarmament specialist put it, "Missile defenses" are "not geared to protecting the U.S. from potential enemies or to make the world safer." They are "aimed not only at institutionalizing current military-nuclear dominance for the next half century, but at greatly extending and strengthening this hegemony militarily, technologically and economically." The U.S. Joint Chiefs of Staff call this "full spectrum dominance" and "the ability to dominate space" ("Vision for 2020"). U.S. dominance of space means being able to destroy any target on earth, thus intimidating all potential enemies *and friends.*

Empires remain pretty much the same, going all the way back to the first conquest states. Domination is still the name of the game. The goal is to bring everything under control. To relax that demand will bring chaos. An ever expanding empire is global in its reach. It cannot be satiated. Nothing is ever enough. How curious that we are once again struggling over land in the same region where the domination system first arose some 5,000 years ago: the Mesopotamian river valley.

Redemption from Redemptive Violence?

Is there no escape from this myth of redemptive violence? Yes, there is, but it is difficult. To face the fear of enemies would finally require us to acknowledge our own inner evil, and that would cost us all our hard-earned self-esteem. *We* would have to change, laboriously, struggling daily to transform or redeem our shadow side. We would have to see ourselves as no different in kind from our enemy, however different we may be in degree. It would mean seeing God in the enemy as we learn to see God in ourselves, a God who loves and forgives and can transform even the most evil person or society in the world. Such insight would require conversion from the myth of redemptive violence to the God proclaimed by the prophets and by Jesus. Our leaders will have to abandon their fantasies of world domination and return to the values exemplified by the Marshall Plan. We will have to stop relying on dictatorships to do our bidding and instead foster real democracy, not only elsewhere but in our own land as well, owned as it is by gigantic corporate interests. We will have to be vigilant against those who undermine civil liberties. We will demand a return to authentic American values being hijacked by people whose only desire is power, power, and more power. We can no longer justify un-Christian means to preserve at all costs the hollow shell of a "Christian civilization" that has, in effect, been filled with the creed of redemptive violence.

The myth of redemptive violence is nationalism become absolute. This myth speaks *for* God; it does not listen for God to speak. It invokes the sovereignty of God as its own; it does not entertain the prophetic possibility of radical denunciation and negation by God. It misappropriates the language, symbols, and scriptures of Christianity. It does not seek God in order to change; it claims God in order to prevent change. Its God is not the impartial ruler of all nations but a biased and partial tribal god worshiped as an idol. Its metaphor is not the journey but a fortress. Its symbol is not the cross but a rod of iron. Its offer is not forgiveness but victory. Its good news is not the unconditional love of enemies but their final liquidation. Its salvation is not a new heart but a successful foreign policy. It usurps the revelation of God's purposes for humanity in Jesus. It is blasphemous. It is idolatrous. And it is immensely popular.

I love my country passionately; that is why I want to see it do right. There is a valid place for a sensible patriotism. But from a Christian point of view, true patriotism acknowledges God's sovereignty over all the nations and holds a healthy respect for God's judgments on the pretensions of any power that seeks to impose its will on others. There is a place for a sense of destiny as a nation.[25] But it can be authentically embraced and pursued only if we separate ourselves from the legacy of the myth of redemptive violence and "enter a long twilight struggle against what is dark within ourselves."[26] There is a divine vocation for the United States (and every other nation) to perform in human affairs. But it can perform that task, paradoxically, only by abandoning its lust for empire and accepting a more limited role within the family of nations.

Notes

This chapter is a modified version of "The Myth of the Domination System," chapter 1 of Walter Wink's *Engaging the Powers: Discernment and Resistance in a World of Domination* (Minneapolis: Fortress Press, 1992), 12–31. Used by permission of Fortress Press.

1. Text in James B. Prichard, *Ancient Near Eastern Texts Relating to the Old Testament*, 3rd ed. (Princeton: Princeton University Press, 1969), 60–72.

2. Paul Ricoeur, *The Symbolism of Evil* (New York: Harper and Row, 1967), 175–210.

3. Willis Elliott, "Thinksheet," no. 2196, November 8, 1987.

4. Conversation with my five-year-old grandson: "Do the good guys ever get killed?" I asked. "No! Never!" "Why?" "Because they're such good fighters." "Do the bad guys always lose?" "Yes." "Why?" "Because they're not such good fighters."

5. Arthur Asa Berger, *The Comic-Stripped American* (Baltimore: Penguin Books, 1973), 128.

6. Ariel Dorfman, *The Empire's Old Clothes* (New York: Pantheon Books, 1983), 97.

7. John T. Gallaway Jr., *The Gospel According to Superman* (Philadelphia: A. J. Holman, 1973), 93.

8. Berger, *The Comic-Stripped American*, 161.

9. Robert Jewett, *The Captain America Complex*, rev. ed. (Santa Fe: Bear and Co., 1984), 94–95; Robert Jewett with John Sheldon Lawrence, "The Fantasy Factor in Civil Religion," *Mission Journal* 17 (1983): 72–73, and *The American Monomyth* (Garden City: Doubleday, 1977), 196, 210–211, 215.

10. Ibid.

11. Berger, *The Comic-Stripped American*, 158.

12. Jewett and Lawrence, *The American Monomyth*, 157.

13. Michael N. Nagler, *America without Violence* (Covelo: Island Press, 1982), 27.

14. Andrew J. McKenna, "The Law's Delay: Cinema and Sacrifice," *Legal Studies Forum* 15, no. 3 (1991): 199–213.

15. *U.S. News and World Report*, October 27, 1986, 64. Senator Paul Simon reports even higher figures in *Parade* magazine, December 29, 1985. The National Coalition on Television Violence estimates 230,000 violent acts on television by age 18 (*NCTV News*, July–September 1990, 11).

16. William F. Fore, "Media Violence: Hazardous to Our Health," *Christian Century*, September 25, 1985, 836. Surveys indicate that the amount of violence on television continues to rise, up 50 percent since 1980 on weekends alone. Consider also that 99 percent of American homes have television and that the average viewer now watches over six hours daily, according to Kenneth Curtis, *Telecult: How the Television Culture Has Become Our Real Religion*, Valley Forge: Gateway Films, 1948.

17. Joe Queenan, "Drawing on the Dark Side," *New York Times Magazine*, April 30, 1989, 32–34, 79, 86.

18. Geoffrey Barlow and Alison Hill, eds., *Video Violence and Children* (New York: St. Martin's Press, 1985), 67. Note that the violent killing of a female and her dismemberment is a central feature of the Marduk myth.

19. See Jacques Ellul, *Propaganda: The Formation of Men's Attitudes* (New York: Vintage Books, 1973).

20. Walter Wink, *Naming the Powers* (Philadelphia: Fortress, 1984), 131–37.

21. Georges Khodr, "Violence and the Gospel," *Cross Currents* 37 (winter 1987–1988): 405; see also Nagler, *America without Violence*, 19.

22. In two passages of the Old Testament, Yahweh is actually depicted in language evocative of Marduk: Psalm 74:14 and Isaiah 27:1.

23. José Comblin, *The Church and the National Security State* (Maryknoll: Orbis Books, 1984), 64–98, 107.

24. Richard Slotkin speaks of the "myth of regenerative violence" as the structuring metaphor of the American experience in *Regeneration through Violence* (Middletown: Wesleyan University Press, 1973), 5.

25. On angels of nations, see my *Unmasking the Powers* (Philadelphia: Fortress, 1984), chap. 4.

26. Jewett, *The Captain America Complex*, 253.

AFTERWORD

Chris E. Stout

Series Editor
Contemporary Psychology

Religion and politics. Lightning rods and powder kegs. Such are the thoughts and images that may be conjured up reviewing this dynamic collection of works. Few topics can stir more opinion, bring more varied viewpoints, stimulate more debate and contention, or spark more potentially volatile reactions than discussions of religion as a motivator for murder, terrorism, and even war. Dr. Ellens has successfully assembled some of the best and the brightest contemporary scholars to expound on this most controversial, yet classically delicate, relationship.

So it is fitting that this set of volumes launches the new Praeger Series in Contemporary Psychology. In this series of books, experts from various disciplines will peer through the lens of psychology to examine human behavior as this new millennium dawns. Including modern behaviors rooted back through history, the topics will include positive subjects like creativity and resilience, as well as examinations of humanity's current psychological ills, with abuse, suicide, murder, and terrorism among those. At all times, the goal of the series remains constant—to offer innovative ideas, provocative considerations, and useful beginnings to better understand human behavior.

Developing a collection of the size, substance, and quality shown in *The Destructive Power of Religion* is no easy task. Indeed, I first met Dr. Ellens when he contributed to my earlier, similar four-volume set,

The Psychology of Terrorism (Westport: Praeger, 2002). The goal was
to organize well-researched content and weave it into a fabric appealing to readers of differing backgrounds and interests. Certainly, this
goal was achieved in Dr. Ellens' volumes.

While no editor of such a work wishes for homogenization of the
content, it becomes a fine balance between maintaining thematic con-
sistency among chapters with a healthy tension between differing
perspectives. Therein again, this collection succeeds.

The first time I had the honor and the pleasure of meeting Dr.
Ellens, he struck me as a virtual Roman candle of intellectual enthusiasm. Therefore, it comes as no surprise that he has been successful
in gathering some of the greatest thinkers on the topic from around
the world, including a Pulitzer Prize–winning author.

There is potential for these volumes to unleash a Niagara of discussion and debate.

Ideally, there is potential for these volumes to spark understanding
that will trigger solutions to the problem of destructive powers
unleashed in the name of religion.

This is to Dr. Ellens' credit, and it is to us readers' marked benefit.

INDEX

ABOUT THE SERIES

As this new millennium dawns, humankind has evolved—some would argue has devolved—exhibiting new and old behaviors that fascinate, infuriate, delight, or fully perplex those of us seeking answers to the question, "Why?" In this series, experts from various disciplines peer through the lens of psychology telling us answers they see for questions of human behavior. Their topics may range from humanity's psychological ills—addictions, abuse, suicide, murder, and terrorism among them—to works focused on positive subjects including intelligence, creativity, athleticism, and resilience. Regardless of the topic, the goal of this series remains constant—to offer innovative ideas, provocative considerations, and useful beginnings to better understand human behavior.

Chris E. Stout
Series Editor

About the Series Editor
and Advisory Board

CHRIS E. STOUT, Psy.D., MBA, holds a joint governmental and academic appointment in Northwestern University Medical School and serves as Illinois' first chief of psychological services. He served as an NGO special representative to the United Nations, was appointed by the U.S. Department of Commerce as a Baldridge examiner, and served as an adviser to the White House for both political parties. He was appointed to the World Economic Forum's Global Leaders of Tomorrow. He has published and presented more than 300 papers and 29 books. His works have been translated into six languages.

BRUCE E. BONECUTTER, Ph.D., is director of behavioral services at the Elgin Community Mental Health Center, the Illinois Department of Human Services state hospital, serving adults in greater Chicago. He is also a clinical assistant professor of psychology at the University of Illinois at Chicago. A clinical psychologist specializing in health, consulting, and forensic psychology, Bonecutter is also a longtime member of the American Psychological Association Taskforce on Children and the Family.

JOSEPH A. FLAHERTY, M.D., is chief of psychiatry at the University of Illinois Hospital, a professor of psychiatry at the University of Illinois College of Medicine, and a professor of community health science at the University of Illinois College of Public Health. He is a founding member of the Society for the Study of Culture and Psychiatry. Dr. Flaherty has been a consultant to the World Health Organization, to the National Institutes of Mental Health, and also to the Falk Institute in Jerusalem.

MICHAEL HOROWITZ, Ph.D., is president and professor of clinical psychology at the Chicago School of Professional Psychology, one of the nation's leading not-for-profit graduate schools of psychology. Earlier, he served as dean and professor of the Arizona School of Professional Psychology. A clinical psychologist practicing independently since 1987, his work has focused on psychoanalysis, intensive individual therapy, and couples therapy. He has provided disaster mental health services to the American Red Cross. Dr. Horowitz's special interests include the study of fatherhood.

SHELDON I. MILLER, M.D., is a professor of psychiatry at Northwestern University and director of the Stone Institute of Psychiatry at Northwestern Memorial Hospital. He is also director of the American Board of Psychiatry and Neurology, director of the American Board of Emergency Medicine, and director of the Accreditation Council for Graduate Medical Education. Dr. Miller is also an examiner for the American Board of Psychiatry and Neurology. He is founding editor of the *American Journal of Addictions* and founding chairman of the American Psychiatric Association's Committee on Alcoholism.

DENNIS P. MORRISON, Ph.D., is chief executive officer at the Center for Behavioral Health in Indiana, the first behavioral health company ever to win the JCAHO Codman Award for excellence in the use of outcomes management to achieve health care quality improvement. He is president of the board of directors for the Community Healthcare Foundation in Bloomington and has been a member of the board of directors for the American College of Sports Psychology. He has served as a consultant to agencies including the Ohio Department of Mental Health, Tennessee Association of Mental Health Organizations, Oklahoma Psychological Association, the North Carolina Council of Community Mental Health Centers, and the National Center for Health Promotion in Michigan.

WILLIAM H. REID, M.D., MPH, is a clinical and forensic psychiatrist and consultant to attorneys and courts throughout the United States. He is clinical professor of psychiatry at the University of Texas Health Science Center. Dr. Miller is also an adjunct professor of psychiatry at Texas A&M College of Medicine and Texas Tech

University School of Medicine, as well as a clinical faculty member at the Austin Psychiatry Residency Program. He is chairman of the Scientific Advisory Board and medical adviser to the Texas Depressive & Manic-Depressive Association, as well as an examiner for the American Board of Psychiatry and Neurology. He has served as president of the American Academy of Psychiatry and the Law, as chairman of the Research Section for an International Conference on the Psychiatric Aspects of Terrorism, and as medical director for the Texas Department of Mental Health and Mental Retardation.

About the Editor
and Advisers

J. HAROLD ELLENS is a Research Scholar at the University of Michigan, Department of Near Eastern Studies. He is a retired Presbyterian theologian and ordained minister, a retired U.S. Army Colonel, and a retired professor of philosophy, theology, and psychology. He has authored, coauthored, and/or edited 86 books and 165 professional journal articles. He served 15 years as Executive Director of the Christian Association for Psychological Studies and as founding editor and Editor-in-Chief of the *Journal of Psychology and Christianity*. He holds a Ph.D. from Wayne State University in the Psychology of Human Communication, a Ph.D.(Cand.) from the University of Michigan in biblical and Near Eastern studies, and master's degrees from Calvin Theological Seminary, Princeton Theological Seminary, and the University of Michigan. He was born in Michigan, grew up in a Dutch-German immigrant community, and determined at age seven to enter the Christian ministry as a means to help his people with the great amount of suffering he perceived all around him. His life's work has focused on the interface of psychology and religion. He is the founder and director of the New American Lyceum.

LeROY H. ADEN is Professor Emeritus of Pastoral Theology at the Lutheran Theological Seminary in Philadelphia, Pennsylvania. He taught full-time at the seminary from 1967 to 1994 and part-time from 1994 to 2001. He served as Visiting Lecturer at Princeton

Theological Seminary, Princeton, New Jersey on a regular basis. In 2002 he coauthored *Preaching God's Compassion: Comforting Those Who Suffer* with Robert G. Hughes. Previously, he edited four books in a Psychology and Christianity series with J. Harold Ellens and David G. Benner. He served on the Board of Directors of the Christian Association for Psychological Studies for six years.

ALFRED J. EPPENS was born and raised in Michigan. He attended Western Michigan University, studying history under Ernst A. Breisach, and receiving a B.A. (Summa cum Laude) and an M.A. He continued his studies at the University of Michigan, where he was awarded a J.D. in 1981. He is an Adjunct Professor at Oakland University and at Oakland Community College, as well as an active church musician and director. He is a director and officer of the Michigan Center for Early Christian Studies, as well as a founding member of the New American Lyceum.

EDMUND S. MELTZER was born in Brooklyn, New York. He attended the University of Chicago, where he received his B.A. in Near Eastern Languages and Civilizations. He pursued graduate studies at the University of Toronto, earning his M.A. and Ph.D. in Near Eastern Studies. He worked in Egypt as a member of the Akhenaten Temple Project/East Karnak Excavation and as a Fellow of the American Research Center. Returning to the United States, he taught at the University of North Carolina–Chapel Hill and at the Claremont Graduate School (now University), where he served as Associate Chair of the Department of Religion. Meltzer taught at Northeast Normal University in Changchun from 1990 to 1996. He has been teaching German and Spanish in the Wisconsin public school system and English as a Second Language in summer programs of the University of Wisconsin–Stevens Point. He has lectured extensively and published numerous articles and reviews in scholarly journals. He has contributed to and edited a number of books and has presented at many national and international conferences.

JACK MILES is the author of the 1995 Pulitzer Prize winner *God: A Biography*. After publishing *Christ: A Crisis in the Life of God* in 2001, Miles was named a MacArthur Fellow in 2002. Now Senior Adviser to the President at J. Paul Getty Trust, he earned a Ph.D. in Near Eastern languages from Harvard University in 1971 and has been a Regents Lecturer at the University of California, Director of the Humanities Center at Claremont Graduate University, and Visiting

Professor of Humanities at the California Institute of Technology. He has authored articles that have appeared in numerous national publications, including the *Atlantic Monthly*, the *New York Times*, the *Boston Globe*, the *Washington Post*, and the *Los Angeles Times*, where he served for 10 years as Literary Editor and as a member of the newspaper's editorial board.

WAYNE G. ROLLINS is Professor Emeritus of Biblical Studies at Assumption College, Worcester, Massachusetts, and Adjunct Professor of Scripture at Hartford Seminary, Hartford, Connecticut. His writings include *The Gospels: Portraits of Christ* (1964), *Jung and the Bible* (1983), and *Soul and Psyche: The Bible in Psychological Perspective* (1999). He received his Ph.D. in New Testament Studies from Yale University and is the founder and former chairman (1990–2000) of the Society of Biblical Literature Section on Psychology and Biblical Studies.

GRANT R. SHAFER was educated at Wayne State University, Harvard University, and the University of Michigan, where he received his doctorate in Early Christianity. A summary of his dissertation, "St. Stephen and the Samaritans," was published in the proceedings of the 1996 meeting of the *Societe d'Etudes Samaritaines*. He has taught at Washtenaw Community College, Siena Heights University, and Eastern Michigan University. He is presently a Visiting Scholar at the University of Michigan.

About the Contributors

LeROY H. ADEN is Professor Emeritus of Pastoral Theology at the Lutheran Theological Seminary in Philadelphia, Pennsylvania. He taught full-time at the seminary from 1967 to 1994 and part-time from 1994 to 2001. He served as Visiting Lecturer at Princeton Theological Seminary, Princeton, New Jersey, on a regular basis. In 2002 he coauthored *Preaching God's Compassion: Comforting Those Who Suffer* with Robert G. Hughes. Previously, he edited four books in a Psychology and Christianity series with J. Harold Ellens and David G. Benner. He served on the Board of Directors of the Christian Association for Psychological Studies for six years.

PAUL N. ANDERSON is Professor of Biblical and Quaker Studies and Chair of the Department of Religious Studies at George Fox University, where he has served since 1989 except for a year as a visiting professor at Yale Divinity School (1998–99). He is author of *The Christology of the Fourth Gospel: Its Unity and Disunity in the Light of John 6* and *Navigating the Living Waters of the Gospel of John: On Wading with Children and Swimming with Elephants*. In addition, he has written many essays on biblical and Quaker themes and is editor of *Quaker Religious Thought*. He serves on the steering committee of the Psychology and Biblical Studies Section of the Society of Biblical Literature and teaches the New Testament Interpretation course in the Psy.D. program of George Fox University. His Ph.D. in the New Testament is from Glasgow University (1989), his M.Div. is from the

Earlham School of Religion (1981), and his B.A. in psychology and B.A. in Christian ministries are from Malone College (1978).

DONALD CAPPS, Psychologist of Religion, is William Hart Felmeth Professor of Pastoral Theology at Princeton Theological Seminary. In 1989 he was awarded an honorary doctorate from the University of Uppsala, Sweden, in recognition of the importance of his publications. He served as president of the Society for the Scientific Study of Religion from 1990 to 1992. Among his many significant books are *Men, Religion, and Melancholia: James, Otto, Jung, Erikson and Freud; The Freudians on Religion: A Reader; Social Phobia: Alleviating Anxiety in an Age of Self-Promotion;* and *Jesus: A Psychological Biography.* He also authored *The Child's Song: The Religious Abuse of Children.*

RAFAEL CHODOS has been a practicing business litigation attorney in the Los Angeles area for nearly 25 years. He holds a B.A. in philosophy from UC–Berkeley (1964). He earned his way through college teaching Hebrew, Latin, and Greek, intending to become a rabbi. But after graduating from Berkeley he entered the then-fledgling computer software field, where he worked for 15 years. He founded his own software company, which developed expert systems and sold them to most of the Fortune 500 companies. He then returned to law school and received his J.D. from Boston University in 1977. He is the author of several articles on legal topics as well as topics relating to computers, software design, operations research, and artificial intelligence. He has authored two books: *The Jewish Attitude Toward Justice and Law* (1984) and *The Law of Fiduciary Duties* (2000).

JOHN J. COLLINS is Holmes Professor of Old Testament Criticism and Interpretation at Yale University. He previously taught at the University of Chicago and at Notre Dame. He received his Ph.D. from Harvard (1972). His more recent books include a commentary on *The Book of Daniel* (1993), *The Scepter and the Star: The Messiahs of the Dead Sea Scrolls* (1995), *Jewish Wisdom in the Hellenistic Age* (1997), *Apocalypticism in the Dead Sea Scrolls* (1997), *Seers, Sibyls, and Sages* (1997), *The Apocalyptic Imagination* (revised ed., 1998), and *Between Athens and Jerusalem: Jewish Identity in the Hellenistic Diaspora* (revised ed., 2000). He has served as editor of the *Journal of Biblical Literature,* as president of the Catholic Biblical Association (1997), and as president of the Society of Biblical Literature (2002).

CHARLES T. DAVIS III studied at Emory University with Dr. Norman Perrin, graduating with the B.D. and Ph.D. degrees after special study at the University of Heidelberg. Although specializing in New Testament Studies, he has also published articles and book reviews in the fields of American religion, computers and the humanities, philosophy, and Buddhist studies. He is the author of the book *Speaking of Jesus* and currently serves as Professor of Philosophy and Religion at Appalachian State University, where he teaches biblical literature, Islam, and seminars on symbols and healing.

SIMON JOHN DE VRIES, an ordained minister in the Presbyterian Church, was born in Denver. He served in the U.S. Marines during World War II as a First Lieutenant, pastored three churches, and received his Th.D. from Union Theological Seminary in New York in Old Testament Studies before beginning seminary teaching in 1962. He is the author of numerous scholarly articles and reviews in the field of Old Testament exegesis and theology in addition to nine books, the latest of which is *Shining White Knight, A Spiritual Memoir.*

J. HAROLD ELLENS is a Research Scholar at the University of Michigan, Department of Near Eastern Studies. He is a retired Presbyterian theologian and ordained minister, a retired U.S. Army Colonel, and a retired professor of philosophy, theology, and psychology. He has authored, coauthored, and/or edited 86 books and 165 professional journal articles. He served 15 years as Executive Director of the Christian Association for Psychological Studies and as founding editor and Editor-in-Chief of the *Journal of Psychology and Christianity.* He holds a Ph.D. from Wayne State University in the Psychology of Human Communication, a Ph.D.(Cand.) from the University of Michigan in biblical and Near Eastern studies, and master's degrees from Calvin Theological Seminary, Princeton Theological Seminary, and the University of Michigan. His publications include *God's Grace and Human Health* and *Psychotheology: Key Issues,* as well as chapters in *Moral Obligation and the Military, Baker Encyclopedia of Psychology, Abingdon Dictionary of Pastoral Care, Jesus as Son of Man, The Literary Character: A Progression of Images,* and *God's Word for Our World* (2 vols.).

MARK ADAM ELLIOTT holds M.Div. and Th.M. degrees from the University of Toronto and a Ph.D. in New Testament from the University of Aberdeen, U.K. His area of concentration is Christian origins in Judaism. His first major publication was *Survivors of Israel:*

A Reconsideration of the Theology of Pre-Christian Judaism (2000). He has served as pastor in both the United Church of Canada and Baptist Convention of Ontario and Quebec, and taught biblical studies in two Ontario universities. Presently, he is executive director of the *Institute for Restorationist and Revisionist Studies* (www.irrstudies.org) and carries out research at the University of Toronto.

ALFRED J. EPPENS was born and raised in Michigan. He attended Western Michigan University, studying history under Ernst A. Breisach, and receiving a B.A. (Summa cum Laude) and an M.A. He continued his studies at the University of Michigan, where he was awarded a J.D. in 1981. He is an Adjunct Professor at Oakland University and at Oakland Community College, as well as an active church musician and director. He is a director and officer of the Michigan Center for Early Christian Studies, as well as a founding member of the New American Lyceum.

JACK T. HANFORD is a Professor Emeritus of Biomedical Ethics at Ferris State University in Michigan. He is a member of the American Philosophical Association, the American Academy of Religion, the Christian Association for Psychological Studies, and the Association of Moral Education. He is also an associate of the Hastings Center, the foremost center for biomedical ethics, the American Society of Bioethics and Humanities, the Center for Bioethics and Human Dignity, and the Kennedy Institute of Ethics, as well as several other societies. He has published many professional articles, including those in *Religious Education*, the *Journal for the Scientific Study of Religion*, the *Journal of Psychology and Christianity*, and the *Journal of Pastoral Psychology, Ethics, and Medicine*. His highest degree is a Th.D.

RONALD B. JOHNSON has worked as a clinical psychologist in private practice for 30 years. His academic background includes a B.S. at the University of Wisconsin, M.Div. at Denver Seminary, and M.A. and Ph.D. in psychology from the University of Iowa. He is currently working on a Post-Doctorate in Neuropsychology. He holds licenses in several states and in Canada. His interests are in therapy with men and children, the psychology of men, psychological evaluations, and forensic psychology. He writes in the areas of "friendly diagnosis," which includes personality type, intelligences, gender differences, personal development, and theological-psychological integration.

D. ANDREW KILLE received his Ph.D. from the Graduate Theological Union in Berkeley in Psychological Biblical Criticism.

He is the author of *Psychological Biblical Criticism: Genesis 3 as a Test Case* (Fortress Press, 2001). A former pastor, Dr. Kille teaches psychology and spirituality in the San Francisco Bay area and is principal consultant for Revdak Consulting. He has served as cochair of the Psychology and Biblical Studies Section of the Society of Biblical Literature and on the steering committee of the Person, Culture, and Religion Group of the American Academy of Religion.

CASSANDRA M. KLYMAN is Assistant Clinical Professor at Wayne State University College of Medicine, where she teaches Ethics, and the Psychology of Women to residents in psychiatry and supervises their clinical cases. Klyman is also a lecturer at the Michigan Psychoanalytic Institute and chairperson of the Michigan Psychoanalytic Society's Committee on Psychoanalysis in Medicine. She is a Life-Fellow of the American Medical Association, the American Psychiatric Association, and the College of Forensic Examiners. She is also Past-President of the Michigan Psychiatric Society. She has published papers nationally and internationally in peer-reviewed journals. Most of her time is spent in the private practice of psychoanalysis and psychoanalytically informed psychotherapy. She earned her M.D. at Wayne State University.

EDSON T. LEWIS is an ordained minister (emeritus) of the Christian Reformed Church. During 47 years of active ministry, he served a suburban New York City congregation for 8 years, an inner-city parish in Hoboken, New Jersey, for 12 years, and the campus of the Ohio State University, Columbus, Ohio, for 17 years. He is a graduate of Calvin Theological Seminary (B.D.), New York Theological Seminary (STM), and Trinity Lutheran Seminary (D.Min). During the 1990s, he played a key role in the revitalization of the church's higher education ministries in the United States and Canada. His participation in antipoverty and peacemaking ministries has been extensive.

ZENON LOTUFO JR. is a Presbyterian minister (Independent Presbyterian Church of Brazil), a philosopher, and a psychotherapist, specializing in Transactional Analysis. He has lectured for undergraduate and graduate courses at universities in São Paulo, Brazil. He coordinates the course of specialization in Pastoral Psychology of the Christian Association of Psychologists and Psychiatrists of Brazil. He is the author of the books *Relações Humanas* (Human Relations) and *Disfunções no Comportamento Organizacional* (Dysfunctions in

Organizational Behavior), and coauthor of *O Potencial Humano* (Human Potential). He has also authored numerous journal articles.

CHARLES MABEE is Full Professor and Director of the Masters of Divinity Program at the Ecumenical Theological Seminary in Detroit, Michigan. He is also a Visiting Lecturer and United Ministries in Higher Education Ecumenical Campus Minister at Oakland University, where he founded two subsidiary institutions, the Institute for the Third Millennium and the Detroit Parliament for World Religions. He is a founding member of the Colloquium on Violence and Religion, chairman of the American Biblical Hermeneutics Section of the Society of Biblical Literature/American Academy of Religion, southeast region, and has been Chair of the Department of Religious Studies at Marshall University in West Virginia. Early in his career, he was a Research Associate for the Institute for Antiquity and Christianity at Claremont Graduate University.

J. CÁSSIO MARTINS is a Presbyterian minister (Presbyterian Church of Brazil) and a clinical psychologist. As a minister, he held pastorates in São Paulo and Rio de Janeiro. As a psychologist, he runs his own clinic in São Paulo. He holds a Master of Theology degree from Union Theological Seminary, Richmond, Virginia. He is one of the coordinators of the course of specialization in Pastoral Psychology of the Christian Association of Psychologists and Psychiatrists of Brazil. He has taught psychology at the Methodist University in São Paulo, as well as courses and seminars to pastors and psychologists throughout Brazil, leading the creation of and exercising the Office of Pastoral Support of his denomination until July 2002. He has written numerous articles on psychology and theology.

MARTIN E. MARTY is the Fairfax M. Cone Distinguished Professor Emeritus at the University of Chicago Divinity School, where he taught for 35 years and where the Martin Marty center has since been founded to promote "public religion" endeavors. An ordained minister in the Evangelical Lutheran Church of America, he is well known in the popular media and has been called the nation's "most influential interpretor of religion." He is the author of 50 books, including *The One and the Many: America's Search for a Common God*, as well as a 3-volume work entitled *Modern American Religion*. He has written more than 4,300 articles, essays, reviews and papers. Among his many honors and awards are the National Humanities Medal, the National Book Award, the Medal of the American

Academy of Arts and Sciences, and the Distinguished Service Medal of the Association of Theological Schools. He has served as president of the American Academy of Religion, the American Society of Church History and the American Catholic Historical Association. Marty has received 67 honorary doctorates.

CHERYL McGUIRE is a member of the Colloquium on Violence and Religion, and her work was presented at Purdue University during the colloquium in 2002. She is a graduate of the University of Michigan master's program in Ancient Civilizations and Biblical Studies and is now involved with postgraduate work at the University of Detroit.

EDMUND S. MELTZER was born in Brooklyn, New York, and attended Erasmus Hall High School. He developed a passion for the ancient world, especially Egypt, and attended the University of Chicago, where he received his B.A. in Near Eastern Languages and Civilizations. He pursued graduate studies at the University of Toronto, earning his M.A. and Ph.D. in Near Eastern Studies and working in Egypt as a member of the Akhenaten Temple Project/East Karnak Excavation. He also worked as a Fellow of the American Research Center in Egypt. After returning to the United States, he taught at the University of North Carolina–Chapel Hill and at the Claremont Graduate School (now University), where he served as Associate Chair of the Department of Religion. In 1990, Meltzer and his family traveled to China, where he taught at Northeast Normal University in Changchun for six years. Subsequently he has been teaching German and Spanish in the Wisconsin public school system and English as a Second Language in the summer programs of the University of Wisconsin–Stevens Point. He has lectured extensively and published numerous articles and reviews in scholarly journals. He has contributed to and edited a number of books and has presented at many national and international conferences.

JACK MILES is the author of the 1996 Pulitzer Prize winner, *God: A Biography.* After publishing *Christ: A Crisis in the Life of God* in 2001, Miles was named a MacArthur Fellow in 2002. Now Senior Adviser to the President at J. Paul Getty Trust, he earned a Ph.D. in Near Eastern languages from Harvard University in 1971 and has been a Regents Lecturer at the University of California, Director of the Humanities Center at Claremont Graduate University, and Visiting Professor of Humanities at the California Institute of Technology. He has authored articles that have appeared in numerous national publications, including the *Atlantic Monthly*, the *New York Times*, the *Boston Globe*, the *Washington Post*, and the *Los Angeles Times*, where he served for 10 years as Literary Editor and as a member of the newspaper's editorial board.

MICHAEL WILLETT NEWHEART is Associate Professor of New Testament Language and Literature at Howard University School of Divinity, where he has taught since 1991. He holds a Ph.D. from Southern Baptist Theological Seminary and is the author of *Wisdom Christology in the Fourth Gospel; Word and Soul: A Psychological, Literary, and Cultural Reading of the Fourth Gospel*, and numerous articles on the psychological and literary interpretation of the New Testament.

DIRK H. ODENDAAL is South African and was born in what is now called the Province of the Eastern Cape. He spent much of his youth in the Transkei in the town of Umtata, where his parents were teachers at a seminary. He trained as a minister at the Stellenbosch Seminary for the Dutch Reformed Church and was ordained in 1983 in the Dutch Reformed Church in Southern Africa. He transferred to East London in 1988 to minister to members of the United Reformed Church in Southern Africa in one of the huge suburbs for Xhosa-speaking people. He received his doctorate (D.Litt.) in 1992 at the University of Port Elizabeth in Semitic Languages. At present, he is enrolled in a Master's Degree course in Counseling Psychology at Rhodes University.

RICARDO J. QUINONES is Professor Emeritus of Comparative Literature at Claremont McKenna College. He is author of *Renaissance Discovery of Time* (1972), *Mapping Literary Modernism* (1985), *The Changes of Cain: Violence and the Lost Brother in Cain and Abel Literature* (1991), and several volumes on Dante, including *Foundation Sacrifice in Dante's Commedia* (1996). He is also Founding Director of the Gould Center for the Humanities.

ILONA N. RASHKOW is Professor of Judaic Studies, Women's Studies, and Comparative Literature at the State University of New York, Stony Brook. She has also been the visiting chair in Judaic Studies at the University of Alabama. Among her publications are *Upon the Dark Places: Sexism and Anti-Semitism in English Renaissance Bible Translation* (1990), *The Phallacy of Genesis* (1993), and *Taboo or Not Taboo?: Human Sexuality and the Hebrew Bible* (2000). Her areas of interest include psychoanalytic literary theory as applied to the Hebrew Bible and, more generally, as applied to Judaic studies, religious studies, feminist literary criticism, and women's studies.

WAYNE G. ROLLINS is Professor Emeritus of Biblical Studies at Assumption College, Worcester, Massachusetts, and Adjunct Professor of Scripture at Hartford Seminary, Hartford, Connecticut. His writings include *The Gospels: Portraits of Christ* (1964), *Jung and the Bible* (1983), and *Soul and Psyche: The Bible in Psychological Perspective* (1999). He received his Ph.D. in New Testament Studies from Yale University and is the founder and former chairman (1990–2000) of the Society of Biblical Literature Section on Psychology and Biblical Studies.

GRANT R. SHAFER was educated at Wayne State University, Harvard University, and the University of Michigan, where he received his doctorate in Early Christianity. A summary of his dissertation, "St. Stephen and the Samaritans," was published in the proceedings of the 1996 meeting of the *Societe d'Etudes Samaritaines*. He has taught at Washtenaw Community College, Siena Heights University, and Eastern Michigan University. He is presently a Visiting Scholar at the University of Michigan.

DONALD E. SLOAT, is licensed as a psychologist in Arizona, California, and Michigan. His training includes a B.A from Bethel College (Indiana), an M.A. from Michigan State University, and a Ph.D. from the University of Southern Mississippi. Since 1963, he has devoted his professional life to helping damaged people find healing for their pain. He has worked most often with people who have been trauma victims, including those with post-traumatic stress disorder (PTSD) and other effects of physical, emotional, verbal, sexual, and spiritual abuse. He has worked with Detroit's Youth for Christ, with outpatient drug-treatment programs, a community health center, psychiatric hospitals, and in his current private practice. He authored two books detailing spiritual abuse, *The Dangers of Growing Up in a Christian Home* and *Growing Up Holy and Wholly*. In addition, he has presented workshops on spiritual abuse and shame at national conferences. His professional affiliations include the American Psychological Association, American Association of Christian Counselors, Christian Association for Psychological Studies, and the International Society for the Study of Dissociation. He has served on the advisory board of the National Association for Christian Recovery. His private practice is in Michigan.

MACK C. STIRLING was born in 1952 in St. George, Utah. He was a Mormon missionary in Norway from 1971 to 1973 and graduated from Brigham Young University studies in chemistry in 1975. He received the M.D. degree from Johns Hopkins University in 1979 and thereafter underwent specialty training at the University of Michigan, where he was Assistant Professor of Thoracic Surgery from 1987 to 1990. Since 1990, he has been Director of Cardiothoracic Surgery at Munson Medical Center in Traverse City, Michigan.

ARCHBISHOP DESMOND TUTU is best known for his contribution to the cause of racial justice in South Africa, a contribution for which he was recognized with the Nobel Peace Prize in 1984. Archbishop Tutu has been an ordained priest since 1961. Among his many accomplishments are being named the first black General Secretary of the South African Council of Churches and serving as archbishop of Cape Town. Once a high school teacher in South Africa, he has also taught theology in college and holds honorary degrees from universities including Harvard, Oxford, Columbia, and Kent State. In addition to the Nobel Peace Prize, he has been awarded the Order for Meritorious Service presented by President Nelson Mandela, the Archbishop of Canterbury's Award for outstanding service to the Anglican community, the Family of Man Gold Medal Award, and the Martin Luther King Jr. Non-Violent Peace Award. The many publications Archbishop Tutu has authored, coauthored, or made contributions to include *No Future without Forgiveness* (2000), *Crying in the Wilderness* (1986), and *Rainbow People of God: The Making of a Peaceful Revolution* (1996).

JOHAN S. VOS is Associate Professor of New Testament, Faculty of Theology, Vrije Universiteit te Amsterdam, The Netherlands. He was born in Gouda, The Netherlands. He studied theology at the University of Utrecht, the University of Tübingen, and Union Theological Seminary in New York. He received his Th.D. from the University of Utrecht in 1973 and was Assistant Professor of New Testament Studies at the University of Leiden in 1974 and 1975. From 1975 to 1981, he worked as a social therapist at a psychiatric clinic for delinquents in Nijmegen. He has been Associate Professor at Vrije Universiteit since 1981 and has published many articles on New Testament subjects. He recently authored *Die Kunst der Argumentation bei Paulus* (The Art of Reasoning in the Letters of Paul), WUNT 149, 2002.

WALTER WINK is Professor of Biblical Interpretation at Auburn Theological Seminary in New York City. Previously, he was a parish minister and taught at Union Theological Seminary in New York City. In 1989 and 1990, he was a Peace Fellow at the United States Institute of Peace. His most recent book is *The Human Being: The Enigma of the Son of the Man* (2001). He is author of a trilogy, *The Powers: Naming the Powers: The Language of Power in the New Testament* (1984), *Unmasking the Powers: The Invisible Forces That Determine Human Existence* (1986), and *Engaging the Powers: Discernment and Resistance in a World of Domination* (1992). *Engaging the Powers* received three Religious Book of the Year awards for 1993, from Pax Christi, the Academy of Parish Clergy, and the Midwestern Independent Publishers Association. His other works include *Jesus and Nonviolence* (2003), *The Powers That Be* (1998), and *When the Powers Fall: Reconciliation in the Healing of Nations* (1998). He has published more than 250 journal articles.